Society: A Brief Introduction

Ian Robertson

Society

A Brief Introduction

WORTH PUBLISHERS, INC.

Society: A Brief Introduction

Copyright © 1989 by Worth Publishers, Inc.

All rights reserved

Library of Congress Catalog Card Number: 88-51380

ISBN: 0–87901–412–1

Printed in the United States of America

Printing: 3 4 5 6 7 8   Year: 0 1 2 3 4

Editors: Peter Deane, Toni Ann Scaramuzzo

Art director: George Touloumes

Layout design: Patricia Lawson, David Lopez

Design: Malcolm Grear Designers

Illustrator: Demetrios Zangos

Picture Editor: June Lundborg Whitworth

Typography: York Graphic Services, Inc.

Printing and Binding: R. R. Donnelley & Sons Company

Cover photograph: © Geoffrey Gove

Text and illustration credits appear on pages 441–443, which constitute an extension of the copyright page.

Worth Publishers, Inc.

33 Irving Place

New York, New York 10003

Preface

Well over a decade ago, I set out to write a comprehensive—and, if possible, definitive—textbook of the discipline of sociology. That book, *Sociology,* now in its third edition, has since been used at many hundreds of schools in more than twenty countries, and its warm reception by both teachers and students has delighted me. A comprehensive textbook, of course, is not suited for all courses, and over the years, a great many instructors have urged me to write a book for briefer courses, or one that would be more appropriate to their own teaching styles. Some of these instructors prefer to use a series of paperbacks rather than a single textbook, and some prefer to use a core text, amplifying the course with their own materials.

This book, then, is intended to meet the demand for a crisp, readable, and stimulating overview of the essentials of sociology. In preparing the book I have, of course, drawn freely on the most successful material in the third edition of *Sociology*. However, I have made extensive deletions, additions, and organizational changes in order to produce a concise and coherent book—one that can stand alone as a brief introduction to the discipline, or serve as a core text in conjunction with other readings. I might add that while this book has its own distinctive character, it is shaped by the same basic premise as the larger book. That premise is that sociology can and should be a profoundly liberating discipline. By providing an acute awareness of the human authorship—rather than the apparent inevitability—of the social environment, sociology offers the crucial sense of options and choice that is essential to human freedom.

Content

In selecting and organizing the material, I have attempted to provide a succinct, fifteen-chapter overview of the basic fields, issues, and findings of contemporary and classical sociology. The first chapter presents an introduction to the discipline, its theories, and its research methods. The next six chapters explore the relationship between the individual, culture, and society, showing how social and cultural forces influence personal experience and group behavior. These chapters cover culture, society, socialization, social groups, deviance, and sexuality. The next three chapters deal in a unified manner with various forms of social inequality, showing how political, economic, and ideological factors underlie social, racial and ethnic, and gender and age stratification. The following three chapters cover six major social institutions: family and religion; education and medicine; and the economic and political systems. The final two chapters deal with more global issues: human ecology and social change in the modern world.

Throughout the book, I have taken pains to integrate theory in a systematic and meaningful way. The three main theoretical approaches of the discipline—the functionalist, conflict, and interactionist perspectives—are applied where appropriate in a consistent manner. I have also tried, wherever possible, to illustrate sociological theories and concepts with practical and interesting examples—sometimes historical, sometimes contemporary, sometimes cross-cultural. Indeed, I have tried throughout to enliven the narrative with brief references to cultural practices in other societies, particularly preindustrial communities. This feature may help undermine students' ethnocentrism by highlighting, through comparison, distinctive features of American society that might otherwise be taken for granted.

Additionally, I have developed an important theme throughout the book: the emergence of postindustrial society. The United States in now such a society, in the sense that most of its workers are engaged in the provision of services and information rather than in industrial manufacturing. It seems to me that a relevant sociology text must look not only at the past and present, but must also address the kind of society we are so rapidly becoming. The change from preindustrial to industrial and now postindustrial society has been accompanied by a shift in loyalties away from the community and tradition, and I examine the implication of this trend toward self-fulfillment and individualism in various areas of social life.

Pedagogical Aids

Several features of the book are designed to aid the teaching and learning process. I have always believed in the importance of artwork and other illustrations to a textbook, and have taken great care in selecting photographs, paintings, cartoons, and other visual elements—many of them in color—that can significantly complement the narrative. I have also made liberal use of up-to-date tables, charts, and graphs to enhance students' understanding of sociological concepts and data.

In addition, each chapter begins with a brief outline of its major topics and ends with a numbered, point-by-point summary of key ideas. All important terms are printed in boldface and are immediately defined. (As an aid to reviewing, the important terms in each chapter are listed at the end of the chapter, along with the number of the page on which they are defined.) The book also contains an extensive glossary—virtually a mini-dictionary—of over three hundred important sociological terms. The glossary can be used both for ready reference and for reviewing purposes.

Supplementary Materials

A number of supplementary materials are available to complement the text.

The Social World, which I have edited, is an anthology of fifty-nine readings in sociology, drawn from both academic and popular sources. This reader has articles relating to all the chapters in the text, and should provide a useful, stimulating accompaniment to it.

A study guide, *Understanding Society,* by Carla B. Howery of the American Sociological Association, will help students understand, review, and test their mastery of the material in the textbook. The guide includes learning goals, exercises for identifying core concepts, chapter summaries, applications, and multiple-choice questions for self-testing.

A *Test Bank,* by Dale A. Lund of the University of Utah, and *Computest,* a computerized test-generation system, are available to instructors.

An *Instructor's Manual* suggests essay questions, discussions and demonstrations, projects, lecture topics, case studies, and application exercises that can enliven the course.

A set of computer simulations, *Dynamic Encounters,* has been prepared by John Stimson (William Paterson College), Ardyth Stimson (Kean College), Stephen Shalom (William Paterson College), and Robert C. Rosen (William Paterson College). The simulations consist of seven interesting and stimulating games that help students explore sociological concepts.

Thanks

I am grateful to many sociology instructors for offering suggestions concerning the topics that should be covered in this book, and to a number of colleagues who reviewed either parts of the present book or major sections of the third edition of *Sociology* that served as a foundation for it. The reviewers were Carolie Coffey, Cabrillo College; Tom Gervasi, Center for Military Research and Analysis; James Glasson, Community College of Rhode Island; Carla B. Howery, American Sociological Association; Donald P. Irish, Hamline University; Dale A. Lund, University of Utah; Patrick H. McNamara, University of New Mexico; Vincent N. Parrillo, William Paterson College; John Plott, Tallahassee Community College; David Raye, Hartnell College; James T. Richardson, University of Nevada. Of course, the responsibility for the final manuscript is entirely my own.

I am also grateful to June Lundborg Whitworth for her excellent work as picture editor.

Finally, I am fortunate to continue my association with Worth Publishers, a small and vigorous publishing house with an unparalleled commitment to quality at every stage of the publishing process. For their support and encouragement, I am grateful to the Worth staff, particularly to George Touloumes, Toni Ann Scaramuzzo, Demetrios Zangos, Pat Lawson, and David Lopez of the production staff, and to my uniquely skilled and valued editor, Peter Deane.

Ian Robertson

Contents

CHAPTER 3   **Society**   **51**

CHAPTER 4   **Socialization**   **69**

CHAPTER 5   **Social Groups**   **95**

CHAPTER 6   **Deviance**   **115**

not much

The Author

Ian Robertson spent most of his early years in South Africa, where he obtained a B.A. degree in political science at the University of Natal. As president of the multiracial National Union of South African Students, he organized several campaigns against that country's apartheid laws, until he was arbitrarily placed under restriction by Prime Minister Vorster. Among other prohibitions, he was forbidden to teach, write, belong to organizations, enter college premises, or be with more than one other person at any time. He was eventually allowed to leave South Africa, and thereafter he studied at Oxford, Cambridge, and Harvard universities, supporting himself through scholarships and his writings on a variety of social topics.

Ian Robertson trained as a teacher at Oxford, where he was awarded a Diploma in Education in English and Latin. At Cambridge he took a First-Class Honors degree and M.A. in sociology and was elected Senior Scholar in Sociology at King's College. At Harvard he was awarded both a master's degree and a doctorate in the sociology of education. Dr. Robertson has a wide teaching experience: he has taught basic curriculum to retarded children in England, social studies to high school students in Massachusetts, sociology of education to Harvard graduates, social sciences to Cambridge undergraduates, and introductory sociology at the University of California, Los Angeles, and the William Paterson College of New Jersey. He is currently devoting himself to his writing.

In addition to various articles, Dr. Robertson has published *Readings in Sociology: Contemporary Perspectives* (Harper & Row, 1976), *Race and Politics in South Africa* (Transaction Books, 1978), *Social Problems,* 2nd ed. (Random House, 1980), *Sociology,* 3rd ed. (Worth, 1987), and *The Social World,* 3rd ed. (Worth, 1987).

Society: A Brief Introduction

CHAPTER *1*

Sociology: A Perspective on the World

Society surrounds us and penetrates our being, almost as much as the air we breathe. We humans are social animals—not just from force of habit but because otherwise we could not survive. We are all born into human groups and derive our identities, hopes, fears, troubles, and satisfactions from them. We live out our brief lives, for better or worse, in a society that existed long before we were born and will presumably exist long after we are gone.

Over countless generations, our ancestors pondered human nature as it seemed to reveal itself in the social life of our species. Why do human beings form families, and why do they worship gods? Why is the way of life of one group so different from that of another? What makes some people break social rules while others obey them? Why are some people rich when others are poor? What makes one group go to war with another? What might a human being who had not been raised in the company of other people be like? What holds societies together, and why do all societies continually change over time?

Until quite recently the answers to these and similar questions came from intuition, from speculation, and from the dead weight of myth, superstition, and "folk wisdom" handed down from the past. Only in the course of the past century or so has a new method been applied to the study of human society and social behavior—the method of science, which provides answers drawn from facts collected by systematic research.

This new mode of inquiry has produced the lively discipline of sociology. **Sociology** is the scientific study of human society and social behavior. Its subject matter is huge, complex, and varied, and the knowledge produced by sociological research remains imperfect in many ways. Yet, in the brief time that the discipline has been in existence, it has taught us a great deal about ourselves that we could never have learned by relying on speculation alone. We have learned to conceive of human beings and social life in an entirely new way—a way you will find sometimes disconcerting, yet often fascinating.

The Sociological Perspective

The world does not consist of a reality that everyone sees in exactly the same way. A house may seem to be simply a house, but different people will look at it and interpret it quite differently. An architect, a real estate broker, a burglar, an artist, and a demolition expert, for instance, would each view the house from a distinctive perspective and would see quite different things as a result. In the same way, sociology offers a particular perspective on society and social behavior, a viewpoint quite unlike that of, say, the poet, the philosopher, the theologian, the lawyer, or the police officer.

The sociologist C. Wright Mills (1959) described the perspective of the discipline as "the sociological imagination"—a vivid awareness of the relationship between personal experience and the wider society. People usually see the world through their limited experience in a small orbit of family, relatives,

Figure 1.1 The "sociological imagination" enables us to trace the links between individual experience and social forces. The options and lifestyles of these people—from the upper class in Great Britain, and from a poor settlement in India—are very different. People's lives are shaped by historical and social forces over which they have little personal control.

friends, and fellow workers. This viewpoint places blinders on their view of the wider society. But it does more than that. Paradoxically, it also narrows their view of their own personal worlds, for those worlds are shaped by broader social forces that can easily pass unrecognized.

The sociological imagination allows us to escape from this cramped personal vision—to stand apart mentally from our own place in society and to see with a new clarity the link between personal and social events. When a society becomes industrialized, rural peasants become urban workers, whether they like it or not. When a nation goes to war, spouses are widowed and children grow up as orphans, for reasons that are beyond their personal power to control. When an economy sags, workers are thrown out of their jobs, no matter how efficiently they have performed them. The sociological imagination permits us to trace the intricate connection between the patterns and events of our own lives and the patterns and events of our society.

The basic insight of sociology is this: *Human behavior is largely shaped by the groups to which people belong and by the social interaction that takes place within those groups.* We are what we are and we behave the way we do because we happen to live in particular societies at particular points in space and time. If you had been born, say, a modern Chinese peasant, or an African Pygmy, or an ancient Greek, or a feudal aristocrat, your personality, your options in life, and your social experience would be utterly different. This fact seems obvious enough, but it is easily overlooked. People everywhere tend to take their social world for granted, accepting their society and its customs as unquestioningly as they do the physical world that also surrounds them. But the sociological perspective enables us to see society not as something to be taken for granted as "natural" but as a temporary social product, created by human beings and therefore capable of being changed by them as well.

The sociological perspective invites us to look at our familiar surroundings as if for the first time. It allows us to get a fresh view of a world we have always taken for granted, to examine our own social landscape with the same curiosity and fascination that we might bring to an exotic, alien culture. As Peter Berger (1963) has observed, sociology is nothing less than a special form of consciousness. It encourages us to focus on features of our social environment we have never noticed before and to interpret them in a new and richer light.

Sociology also gives us a window on the wider world that lies beyond our immediate experience, leading us into areas of society we might otherwise have ignored or misunderstood. Sociology can take us into the worlds of the rich and the powerful, the poor and the weak, the worlds of politicians, doctors, professional athletes, and of slum dwellers, addicts, cult members, and criminals. Because these people have different social experiences, they have quite different definitions of social reality. Sociology enables us to appreciate viewpoints other than our own, to understand how these viewpoints came into being, and in the process, to better understand our attitudes, ourselves, and our own lives.

Sociology as a Science

We have said that sociology is the *scientific* study of human society and social behavior. Before we explore sociology as a science, let's briefly look at the characteristics of science itself.

Science is a body of knowledge obtained by logical, systematic methods of research. All science assumes that there is some underlying order in the universe. Events, whether they involve molecules or human beings, are not haphazard. They follow a pattern that is sufficiently regular for us to be able to make **generalizations**—statements that apply not just to a specific case but to most cases of the same type. It is possible to generalize, for example, that hydrogen and oxygen will always form water if they are combined at an appropriate temperature. Similarly, it is possible to generalize that all human societies will create some system of marriage and family. Generalizations are crucial to science because they place isolated, seemingly meaningless events in patterns we can understand. It then becomes possible for scientists to analyze relationships of cause and effect and thus to *explain* why something happens and to *predict* that it will happen again under the same conditions in the future.

Science relies for its generalizations, explanations, and predictions on careful, systematic analysis of verifiable evidence—that is, evidence that can be checked by others and will always yield the same results. This does not mean that a nonscientific, "common-sense" approach cannot provide accurate explanations and predictions; it can, and often does. However, the problem is that without using the methods of science, there is no way to tell whether common sense is correct. After all, for centuries common sense told people that the world is the center of the universe and that the earth is flat. It took the methods of science to prove that the earth is a round object circling the sun.

Frequently, in fact, scientific findings contradict important social beliefs of the time. But such challenges tell us something else about science: there are no areas so sacred that science cannot explore them. Any question that can be answered by the scientific method is, in principle, an appropriate subject for scientific inquiry—even if the investigation and the findings outrage powerful interests or undermine cherished values. Yet science is not arrogant: it recognizes no ultimate, final truths, for it is always possible that new facts will come to light or that the available data will be reinterpreted in a new way, shattering the existing assumptions.

Figure 1.2 *In their work, scientists sometimes run afoul of the popular assumptions and the established authorities of their time. Galileo, who invented the telescope early in the seventeenth century, proved that the earth moves around the sun, and not vice versa. His finding contradicted Church teachings, and in 1633 he was placed on trial by the Inquisition. On pain of death, Galileo was forced to renounce his view—but legend has it that at the end of his disavowal, he muttered under his breath, "It moves nevertheless."*

The sciences are generally divided into two main branches: the **natural sciences**, the disciplines that study physical and biological phenomena; and the **social sciences,** the disciplines that study various aspects of human behavior. There are four major social sciences in addition to sociology. *Economics* is the study of the production, distribution, and consumption of goods and services. *Psychology* is the study of human mental processes, such as emotion, memory, perception, and intelligence. *Political science* is the study of the forms and processes of government. *Anthropology* is the study of human evolution and of small-scale, traditional communities. Of course, human behavior does not fit neatly into compartments, and in practice the boundaries between the social sciences are vague and constantly shifting. Each of the disciplines has different historical origins, and the distinctions among them have been preserved largely as a matter of convenience. But social scientists realize how much the concerns of the various disciplines overlap, and they freely invade each other's territory whenever it seems useful.

In this book we will make use of findings from the other social sciences whenever this is helpful for the understanding of human behavior. For our purposes, we will emphasize two particular subfields that sociology shares with two of its sister disciplines. One subfield is **social psychology,** the study of how personality and behavior are influenced by the social context. The other is **cultural anthropology,** the study of the ways of life of other peoples, particularly in small-scale, traditional societies. The research of social psychologists often throws light on the ways in which the social environment influences behavior, and the reports of cultural anthropologists enable us to highlight aspects of our own society by comparing our practices with those of other peoples.

"I'm a social scientist, Michael. That means I can't explain electricity or anything like that, but if you want to know about people I'm your man."

Drawing by Handelsman; © 1986
The New Yorker Magazine, Inc.

The Scientific Status of Sociology

On the whole, social life does not consist of a series of random events: under most conditions, society and its processes are ordered and patterned. Most Americans or most Russians, for example, will continue to act in much the same way tomorrow as they did yesterday. Consequently, sociology is able to employ the same general methods of investigation that all sciences do, and to use its findings to make reasonably reliable generalizations. Like natural scientists, sociologists construct theories, collect and analyze data, conduct experiments and make observations, keep careful records, and try to arrive at precise and accurate conclusions.

Like the other social sciences, however, sociology is relatively less advanced as a discipline than most of the natural sciences. The main reason is that the study of human behavior presents many problems that natural scientists do not have to confront. Sociologists are dealing with people—in other words, with subjects who are self-aware and capable of changing their behavior when they choose to. Unlike rocks or microbes, people may be deliberately uncooperative. They may behave in unforeseen ways for private reasons of their own. They may radically change their behavior when they know they are being studied. They cannot in good conscience be made the subject of research that affronts their dignity or infringes on their basic human rights. And the origins of social behavior are almost always extremely complex, involving many social, psychological, historical, and other factors. After all, it is relatively easy to establish why water boils or what effect pressure has on the volume of a gas. It is much more difficult to establish why fashions change, why civilizations decay, why new religions emerge, or why people fall in love with the people that they do.

Sociology, then, is not less "scientific" than biochemistry or astronomy: it simply faces greater problems of generalization, explanation, and prediction. Yet the suspicion persists in some quarters that sociology is not "really" a science. In part this is because the popular image of the scientist is often that of someone working in a laboratory in a white coat, something sociologists rarely do. But the origin of the suspicion probably lies deeper. Few people are experts in molecular biology or planetary motions, but all of us can consider ourselves experts on society, because we have had years of experience in social living. Sociologists, it is sometimes suggested, merely state the obvious in complicated language, telling us virtually nothing that our common sense has not told us already.

It is true that the language of sociology is sometimes a little strange to the beginner. The sociologist uses a specialized vocabulary and often employs everyday words, such as "status," "role," and "culture," in precise but unfamiliar ways. Sociologists use this vocabulary for the same reason that all scientists must: unless terms have an agreed-upon, definite meaning, communication will be ambiguous and confusing, and findings will be difficult to verify. We do not expect a chemist to say, "I took some white crystals, mixed in a bit of black powder and some yellow stuff, threw in a match, and blew the place up." Unless the chemist tells us he or she was using potassium chlorate, carbon, and sulfur in specific quantities under particular conditions, the information is useless.

Similarly, it is not enough for a sociologist to say, "I showed this violent movie to some kids, and afterward they started acting much rougher than before." We need to know what is meant by "violent": what sort of violence, in what context, involving what kind of people? We need to know about the "kids": how old, which sex, what background? We need to know what is meant by "rougher than before": what is "roughness," how is it measured, how rough were they, in what ways, under what circumstances, for how long afterward, and toward whom? Only when the experiment is described with precision does it have any value as science, for it can then be repeated by other scientists to check the original findings. The need for precision means that, as a general rule, sociological writing will not have you chewing your fingernails in suspense or guffawing out of your armchair at an author's wit and humor. Some sociological writing, in fact, is quite deadly. But you will find many sociological articles and books that are absorbing to read because they expand our understanding of the human animal.

Sociology and Common Sense

But does sociology merely state the obvious by reporting what common sense tells us anyway? Here are some widely held common-sense views about society and social behavior. As you read through them, you might like to check them off as true or false.

1. Human beings have a natural instinct to mate with the opposite sex. (T/F)

2. Lower-class people are more likely to commit crimes than upper-class people. (T/F)

3. Revolutions are more likely to occur when conditions remain very bad than when bad conditions are rapidly improving. (T/F)

4. It makes sense to choose a college major in the same field as one's intended career, because most graduates are employed in the general field of their college major. (T/F)

5. The amount of money spent on a school's facilities has a strong effect on the academic success of its pupils. (T/F)

6. A substantial proportion of the people on welfare could work if they really wanted to. (T/F)

7. One thing found in every society is romantic love. (T/F)

8. The income gap between American blacks and whites has narrowed significantly in recent years. (T/F)

9. The income gap between American male and female workers has narrowed significantly in recent years. (T/F)

10. Husbands are more likely to kill their wives in family fights than wives are to kill their husbands. (T/F)

11. Every society forbids sexual relations between parent and child and between brother and sister. (T/F)

12. The population explosion in the less developed countries of the world is caused by high birth rates in those regions. (T/F)

13. The better you do in college, the more successful you are likely to be in your career. (T/F)

14. Physicians can correctly diagnose the medical problems of most patients who bring complaints to them. (T/F)

All the above assumptions may seem to be in accord with common sense, but sociological research has shown that every single one of them is false.

1. Human sexual preferences are learned, not instinctive (Chapter 7); in fact, if instinct is defined as an inherited complex behavior pattern, human beings do not have any instincts at all (Chapters 2 and 4).

2. There is no evidence whatever that poor people are more likely to commit crimes than rich ones, although the poor do commit different kinds of crime (for example, petty theft rather than expense-account fraud) (Chapter 6).

3. Revolutions are actually more likely to occur when conditions have been bad but are rapidly improving. When conditions are bad and stay bad, people take their misfortune for granted, but when conditions suddenly improve, people develop higher aspirations and become easily frustrated (Chapter 15).

4. About half of all college graduates are not employed in the field of their college major. The percentage who are is likely to decrease even further in the years ahead, since people are increasingly likely to change jobs several times in their careers (Chapter 12).

5. The amount of money spent on a school's facilities seems to have little influence on pupils' achievement. Performance is related primarily to pupils' social-class backgrounds (Chapter 12).

6. Less than 2 percent of the people on welfare are adult males who have been out of work for several months. Nearly all are children, old people, handicapped people, and poor mothers of dependent children (Chapter 8).

7. Romantic love may seem part of "human nature" to us, but in many societies it is unknown, and in many others it is regarded as ridiculous or tragic (Chapter 11).

8. Despite civil rights and other legislation, the income gap between blacks and whites has stayed much the same in recent years; black workers still hold lower-paying jobs than whites and have a much higher unemployment rate (Chapter 9).

9. The income gap between male and female workers has narrowed very little: few women hold high-level positions; most are in low-paying jobs (Chapter 10).

10. Husbands and wives are equally likely to kill one another in marital disputes. Although husbands are usually stronger, wives are more likely to resort to lethal weapons, such as kitchen knives (Chapter 11).

11. Different societies define incest in very different ways, and a few have permitted parent-child or brother-sister incest in certain circumstances (Chapters 7 and 11).

12. The population explosion in the less developed countries is caused not by

high birth rates but by a decrease in death rates. Birth rates have actually declined, but people are living much longer, causing overall population size to swell (Chapter 14).

13. There is no consistent relationship between people's performance in college and their later career achievements. The talents required for academic success in college and practical success in the world beyond are not the same (Chapter 12).

14. Physicians are unable to find anything wrong with more than half the patients who come to them—although the physicians may not tell that to the patients (Chapter 12).

Of course, common-sense views are not always so relentlessly contradicted by sociological research. Indeed, intuition and common sense in sociology are a rich source of insights. But they can provide only hunches. The hunch must be tested by the methods of science.

The Development of Sociology

Before the mid-1800s the study of society was the domain of social philosophers, thinkers who were often less concerned about what society actually *is* like than what they thought it *ought* to be like. Yet in a relatively short period this entire emphasis was reversed.

The Origins

The new discipline of sociology began to emerge in the middle of the nineteenth century, in the context of the sweeping changes the Industrial Revolution brought to Europe. No social changes in history had been as widespread or as far-reaching, and this transformation—which is still taking place in the less developed nations of the world—cried out for analysis and explanation.

Industrialization threw into turmoil societies that had been rural and relatively stable for centuries. Rapid social change became the norm rather than an abnormal state of affairs, and people could no longer expect that their children's lives would be much the same as their own. New industries and technologies changed the face of the social and physical environment. Social problems became rampant in the teeming cities that arose in the wake of industrialization. A rising middle class clamored for democracy, and aristocracies and monarchies

Figure 1.3 *Sociology emerged as a separate discipline during the early stages of the Industrial Revolution, when traditional societies were suddenly thrust into an era of rapid social change and unprecedented social problems. Sociology was born out of the attempt to understand the transformations that seemed to threaten the stability of European society.*

crumbled and fell. Religion began to lose its force as an unquestioned source of moral authority. The ancient view that the social order was preordained by God began to collapse. The stability of society seemed in jeopardy, and the direction of the changes that were occurring was unclear. An understanding of what was happening was urgently needed.

Two other factors besides industrialization encouraged the development of sociology. One was the example of the natural sciences—if their methods could make so much sense of the physical world, could they not be applied successfully to the social world as well? The second factor was a flood of new anthropological information about radically different societies in Africa, Asia, and the Americas, which raised fresh questions about society in general. Why, for instance, were some societies apparently more advanced than others, and what lessons could the European countries learn from comparisons of various societies?

Early Sociologists

Given the social conditions that provoked their inquiry, the early sociologists focused their attention on the forces that hold society together and on the forces that fragment it.

Figure 1.4 *Auguste Comte*

Auguste Comte The title "founder of sociology" usually goes to the French philosopher Auguste Comte (1798–1857). Comte was a somewhat eccentric person (he claimed to practice "mental hygiene," meaning that he refused to read anyone else's books), but was one of the most original thinkers of his time. It was he who coined the term "sociology" and who argued, in 1838, that the methods of science should be applied to the study of society. Comte established two specific problems for sociological investigation. The first was the problem of order and stability—how and why do societies hold together and endure? The second was the problem of social change—what makes societies change and what shapes the nature and direction of the changes? Comte was so confident that the scientific method would unlock the secrets of society that he came to regard sociologists as a "priesthood of humanity," experts who would not only explain social events but would also guide society in the direction of greater progress. Although later sociologists have generally had more modest ambitions, they have continued to wrestle with the problems of social order and social change.

Figure 1.5 *Herbert Spencer*

Herbert Spencer Another important nineteenth-century figure was Herbert Spencer (1820–1903), who devised a theory to explain the problems of social order and change. Spencer compared human societies to living organisms. The parts of an animal, such as the lungs and the heart, are interdependent and contribute to the survival of the total organism. Similarly, Spencer argued, the various parts of society, such as the state and the economy, are also interdependent and work to ensure the stability and survival of the entire system. This theory took care of the problem of order. To explain change, Spencer pushed his analogy even further. Applying Darwin's theory of evolution to human societies, he argued that they gradually evolve from the forms found in the "primitive" societies of the world to the more complex forms found in the industrializing societies of his own time. Spencer believed that evolution means progress, and he strongly opposed attempts at social reform on the grounds that they might interfere with a natural evolutionary process. His ideas seem rather strange today, but they remain influential in a very modified form. Many sociologists still see society as a more or less harmonious system whose various parts contribute to overall stability. Many also believe there has been a general tendency for societies to move from the simple to the complex, although they do not necessarily regard this evolution as "progress" toward something better.

Figure 1.6 *Karl Marx*

Karl Marx The third and most important of the nineteenth-century social thinkers was Karl Marx (1818–1883). Marx was born in Germany, but after being expelled from various countries for his revolutionary activities, he eventually settled in England. An erratic genius, he wrote brilliantly on subjects as broad and diverse as philosophy, economics, political science, and history. He did not think of himself as a sociologist, but his work is so rich in sociological insights that he is now regarded as one of the most profound and original sociological thinkers. His influence has been immense. Millions of people accept his theories with almost religious fervor, and modern socialist and communist movements owe their inspiration directly to him. It is important to realize, however, that Marxism is not the same as communism. Marx would probably be dismayed at many of the practices of communist movements, and he cannot be held responsible for policies pursued in his name a century after his death. Even in his own lifetime, he was so appalled at the various interpretations of his ideas by competing factions that he declared, "I am not a Marxist."

To Marx, the task of the social scientist was not merely to describe the world: it was to change it. Whereas Spencer saw social harmony and the inevitability of progress, Marx saw social conflict and the inevitability of revolution. The key to history, he believed, is class conflict—the bitter struggle between those who own the means of producing wealth and those who do not. This contest, Marx claimed, would end only with the overthrow of the ruling exploiters and the establishment of a free, humane, classless society. Marx placed special emphasis on the economic base of society. He argued that the character of virtually all other social arrangements is shaped by the way goods are produced and by the relationships that exist between those who work to produce them and those who live off the production of others. Modern sociologists, including many who reject other aspects of Marx's theories, generally recognize the fundamental influence of the economy on other areas of society.

Figure 1.7 *Emile Durkheim*

Emile Durkheim The French sociologist Emile Durkheim (1858–1917) has strongly influenced the discipline. He argued that the subject matter of sociology should be what he called "social facts"—that is, "things" that are social in nature and exist independently of any individual, such as family systems, religions, legal rules, and the like. Although these socially created facts have no physical existence, people are confronted by them and affected by them almost as though they were solid objects, like mountains or snowdrifts.

Durkheim also dealt with the problem of social order; he argued that societies are held together by the shared beliefs and values of their members, especially as these are expressed in religious doctrine and ritual. Like Spencer, he wanted to discover how the various parts of society contribute to the maintenance of the whole. His method was to ask what function, or positive consequence for the social system, a given element has—an approach that has been highly influential in modern American sociology. Durkheim also made the first real breakthrough in sociological research with his painstaking statistical study of a particular social fact—suicide in various population groups. He was able to show that suicide rates vary consistently from one group to another, proving that the act of suicide is influenced by social forces and is not simply the individual matter that it might appear to be.

Figure 1.8 *Max Weber*

Max Weber The German sociologist Max Weber (1864–1920), a contemporary of Durkheim, has perhaps had a stronger influence on Western sociology than any other single individual. He was a man of prodigious learning whose sociological investigations covered such diverse fields as politics, law, economics, music, cities, and the major world religions. Weber remains an enigmatic and somewhat melancholy figure in sociological history. He viewed the direction of social change in industrial societies with distaste, feeling that the world was being "disenchanted" by bureaucracy, by the cold rationality of petty experts who knew no value other than efficiency. Humanity, he believed, was becoming trapped in an "iron cage."

Much of Weber's work can be seen as "a debate with the ghost of Karl Marx." Although he deeply admired much of Marx's writing, Weber took issue with him on several points. He regarded trends toward greater social equality as inevitable, but he did not particularly welcome them, because he foresaw that such moves would involve an increase in the power of the state over the individual. Weber did not believe that social change could always be directly traced to changes in the economy, as Marx had implied. He suggested that other factors, such as religious ideas, could also play an independent role. Perhaps most important, Weber believed that sociologists should aim at the goal of **value-freedom**— the absence of personal values or biases—in their professional work. His stance in this respect was quite unlike that of Marx, who had no qualms about using a **value judgment**—an opinion based on personal values or biases—whenever he felt so inclined.

Modern Developments

The major development of sociology in this century has taken place in the United States, where the discipline has sunk roots far deeper than in any other country. Lester Ward (1841–1913) repeated Comte's call for social progress guided by sociological knowledge, and under his influence the discipline rapidly became committed to social reform. William Graham Sumner (1840–1910) studied the minute aspects of daily life found in the ordinary customs of the people. Under the influence of these men, American sociologists lost most of their interest in the larger problems of social order and social change and began to concentrate instead on the study of smaller and more specific social problems.

Until about 1940 the University of Chicago's sociology department dominated the discipline in the United States. Sociologists such as George Herbert Mead developed the new discipline of social psychology, and others such as Robert E. Park and Ernest Burgess turned their attention to social problems and the lives of criminals, drug addicts, prostitutes, and juvenile delinquents. Many of the "Chicago School" sociologists were Protestant ministers or the sons of Protestant ministers, and under their leadership sociology became strongly identified with the concerns of social reform.

From the 1940s to the early 1960s, the center of attention shifted from Chicago to such universities as Harvard, Columbia, Michigan, and Wisconsin, and from reform to the much more neutral field of developing theories. Talcott Parsons (1902–1979) influenced a generation of American sociologists, notably Robert Merton, with his abstract models of society as a fairly stable, harmonious system of parts with interrelated functions. Other sociologists concentrated on perfecting research methods and statistical techniques, and the earlier activist strain in the discipline was almost lost. C. Wright Mills, a vociferous critic of this trend, seemed to be crying in the wilderness. During the 1960s, however, the social turmoil caused by the Vietnam war and the civil rights movement encouraged a revival of the activist tradition in American sociology. During that decade, too, female and minority-group sociologists began to play a significant part in a discipline that had previously been almost wholly dominated by white males.

The sociology of the 1970s and 1980s has not been dominated by any one viewpoint or concern; and today, sociologists' interests are more varied than ever, ranging from such old problems as inequality to such new ones as the impact of modern industrial society on the natural environment. Sociologists, too, are found in ever more diverse professional positions. Twenty years ago, nearly all sociologists were engaged in teaching and research. Today, many soci-

Figure 1.9 *Talcott Parsons*

Figure 1.10 *Robert Merton*

Figure 1.11 *C. Wright Mills*

ologists are employed in such fields as criminology, epidemiology, city planning, personnel management, social work, demography, or policy-making at every level of government. Others, although not employed specifically as sociologists, put their training to use in politics, journalism, business, and other professions.

Still, the question of whether the sociologist should be detached and value-free or activist and committed remains controversial. Some sociologists take the view that the science should attempt only to understand social processes and add to the sum of scientific knowledge. Others argue that sociological knowledge should be used to criticize and reform existing social arrangements.

Theoretical Perspectives

A crucial element in sociology, as in all science, is theory. A **theory** is a statement that organizes a set of concepts in a meaningful way by explaining the relationship among them. If the theory is valid, it will correctly predict that identical relationships will occur in the future if the conditions are identical. Although it is sometimes thought that "the facts speak for themselves," they do nothing of the kind. Facts are silent. They have no meaning until we give meaning to them, and that meaning is provided by theory.

We are often prone to poke fun at "theorists" and to regard more highly the "practical" person. But theory and practice cannot be separated; virtually every practical decision you make and every practical opinion you hold has some theory behind it. A person may reject the views of prison reformers as being "theory" and prefer the "practical" approach that criminals should be severely punished in order to discourage crime. But in actuality this practical approach implies several theories—the theory that people always rationally choose whether or not to commit crimes, the theory that people try to avoid punishment, the theory that the most severe punishments make the best deterrents to crime. Even the most practical gadgets of everyday life, from can openers to automobiles, could not be constructed or used without some theory of how they operate. Theory is not an intellectual luxury practiced only by academics in their ivory towers.

Theory makes the facts of social life comprehensible. It places seemingly meaningless events in a general framework that enables us to determine cause and effect, to explain, and to predict. Sociological theories vary greatly in their scope and sophistication. Some are sweeping explanations of major issues such as social change, but most theories attempt to explain only a small aspect of reality, such as why some people become cocaine addicts, or switch their political allegiance.

Despite this preference for more limited theories, most sociologists are guided in their work by a major **theoretical perspective**—a broad assumption about society and social behavior that provides a point of view for the study of specific problems. There are three of these general perspectives in modern sociology, and you will meet them repeatedly throughout this book. They are the functionalist, the conflict, and the interactionist perspectives. We shall now look briefly at each in turn.

The Functionalist Perspective

The **functionalist perspective** is a view of society that focuses on the way various parts of society have functions, or positive effects, that maintain the stability of the whole. The perspective draws its original inspiration from the work of Herbert Spencer and Emile Durkheim. As we have seen, Spencer compared societies to living organisms. Any organism has a **structure**—that is, a set of interrelated components, such as a head, limbs, a heart, and so on. Each of these parts has a **function**—that is, a positive consequence for the whole system, in this case a living organism. In the same way, Spencer argued, a society has a structure. Its

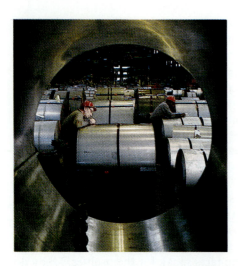

Figure 1.12 *The functionalist perspective focuses on the functions, or consequences, that a given element has in society. Economic activity, for example, functions to provide the goods and services on which society depends for its existence. It also gives people roles in life, enabling them to earn a living and to draw a sense of identity from the work they do. These functions contribute to the stability of the social system as a whole.*

interrelated parts are the family, religion, the military, and so on. Ideally, each of these components also has a function that contributes to the overall stability of the social system. Modern structural-functionalism (usually called functionalism) does not press the analogy between a society and an organism. But it does retain the same general idea of society as a system of interrelated parts.

The Social System   Functionalist theory implies that under normal conditions, all the elements in the social system—such as the schools, the family, and the state—tend to "fit together," with each element helping to maintain overall stability. The family, for example, functions to regulate sexual behavior, to transmit social values to children, and to take care of young and aged people who could not otherwise survive. Functionalist theory also implies that the members of a society share a basic consensus on values.

In the functionalist view, a society has an underlying tendency to be stable, or in balance. Social change is therefore likely to be disruptive unless it takes place relatively slowly, because changes in one part of the system usually provoke changes elsewhere in the system. If the economy, for example, requires an increasing number of highly trained workers, the government will pour more money into education, and the schools and colleges will produce more graduates. But if the economy expands (or contracts) so rapidly that the other elements in the social system cannot "catch up," imbalance will result. In times of very rapid economic growth, the educational system may be unable to provide qualified personnel quickly enough to fill the new jobs; during a recession, on the other hand, the system may continue to produce graduates even though there are not enough jobs for them.

Functions and Dysfunctions   How does one determine what the functions of a given component in the social system are? Essentially, sociologists ask what its *consequences* are—not what its *purposes* are believed to be. They do this because a component can have functions other than those that were intended. Robert Merton (1968) distinguishes between a **manifest function**—a consequence that is obvious and intended—and a **latent function**—a consequence that is unrecognized and unintended. The schools, for example, have the manifest function of teaching literacy and other skills that are essential in a modern industrial society. But they also have latent functions that are not intended or generally recognized. For example, they keep children in an industrial society off the streets and occupied until they are old enough to work. In the same way, the welfare system has the manifest function of preventing the poor from starving, but it also has the latent function of averting the civil disorder that might result if millions of people had no source of income.

Merton also points out that not all features of the social system are functional at all times: on occasion some element can have a **dysfunction,** a negative consequence that may disrupt the social system. Population growth in the less developed countries of the world, for example, is dysfunctional for societies whose economies cannot support ever increasing numbers of people. Sometimes a component of the social system can be functional in one respect and dysfunctional in another. American industry, for example, is functional in that it provides the goods on which the society's way of life depends, but it is also dysfunctional in that it seriously pollutes the environment. The full implications of any element in the social system therefore have to be carefully explored.

The functionalist perspective, then, is obviously useful in explaining why some elements in a society exist and persist, but it also has some disadvantages. An important criticism of the functionalist view is that it tends in practice to be inherently conservative. Because their main emphasis is on social order and stability, functionalists risk the temptation of dismissing disruptive changes as dysfunctional, even if those changes are necessary, inevitable, and beneficial in the long run.

The Conflict Perspective

The **conflict perspective** is a view of society that focuses on social processes of tension, competition, and change. The perspective derives its inspiration from the work of Karl Marx, who saw the struggle between social classes as the "engine" of history and the main source of change. However, modern conflict theory does not simply focus, as Marx did, on class conflict; it sees conflict among many groups and interests as a fact of life in any society. These conflicts may involve, for example, the old versus the young, producers versus consumers, urbanites versus suburbanites, or one racial or ethnic group versus another.

Figure 1.13 *The conflict perspective focuses on tensions, disagreements, and competition in society. Conflict is assumed to be a permanent and inevitable aspect of social life and an important source of change. Conflict over nuclear energy, for example, may lead to significant changes in American energy policies in the future.*

Conflict and Change Conflict theorists assume that societies are in a constant state of change, in which conflict is a permanent feature. "Conflict" does not necessarily mean outright violence; it includes tension, hostility, competition, and disagreement over goals and values. This conflict is not an occasional event that disrupts the generally smooth workings of society: it is a continuing and inevitable part of social life. The things that people desire—such as power, wealth, and prestige—are always scarce, and the demand for them exceeds the supply. Those who gain control of these resources are able to protect their own interests at other people's expense. Conflict theorists regard the functionalists' vision of a general consensus on values as pure fiction: what actually happens, they argue, is that the powerful influence or even coerce the rest of the population into compliance and conformity. In other words, social order is maintained not by popular agreement but rather by the direct or indirect exercise of power.

Conflict theorists do not see social conflict as necessarily destructive, although they admit that it may sometimes have that effect. They argue that conflict binds groups together as they pursue their own interests, focuses attention on social problems, and leads to beneficial changes that might otherwise not have occurred. In this way, social movements—such as those for women's rights or against nuclear power—become an important source of change. The changes caused by social conflict prevent society from stagnating.

Who Benefits? The conflict perspective, then, leads the sociologist to inquire, Who benefits or suffers from existing arrangements? In analyzing social inequality, for example, conflict theorists argue that it exists not because it is functional for society as a whole but because some people have been able to achieve political and economic power and have managed to pass on these advantages to their descendants. In the same way, conflict theorists would not see environmental pollution as a "dysfunction" of industrialism. Instead, they would point to the fact that powerful corporate interests make their profits from manufacturing processes that they fully realize pollute the environment.

To conflict theorists, social order and social change are influenced by the shifting relationships and interests of groups competing for their own advantage. A modern society contains a wide spectrum of opinions, occupations, lifestyles, and social groups. On any social issue there are some people who stand to gain and some who stand to lose. Social processes cannot be fully understood without referring to this conflict of interest, a conflict whose outcome always favors the stronger party. Thus, to understand many features of American society, we must pay particular attention to the values and interests of those who exercise power—primarily people who are white, middle-aged, Protestant, wealthy, male, and of Anglo-Saxon background.

The conflict perspective has the advantage of highlighting features of society that the functionalist perspective, with its emphasis on consensus and stability, tends to ignore. But this fact also suggests an important criticism of the conflict perspective. By focusing so narrowly on issues of competition and change, it fails to come to grips with the more orderly, stable, and less controversial aspects of social reality.

The Interactionist Perspective

The **interactionist perspective** is a view of society that focuses on the way in which people act toward, respond to, and influence one another. The perspective drew much of its original inspiration from Max Weber, who emphasized the importance of understanding the social world from the viewpoint of the individuals who act within it. Later developments in interactionist theory have been strongly influenced by social psychology and by the work of early leaders in the Chicago School, particularly George Herbert Mead. The important difference between this perspective and the two we have already considered is that it does not focus on such large structures as the state, the economy, or social classes. Instead, it is concerned primarily with the everyday social interaction that takes place as people go about their lives.

Figure 1.14 *The interactionist perspective focuses on social behavior in everyday life. It tries to understand how people create and interpret the situations they experience, and it emphasizes how countless instances of social interaction produce the larger structures of society—government, the economy, and other institutions.*

Interaction: The Basis of Social Life
The main reason interactionist theorists are wary of the emphasis other sociologists place on the major components of society is that concepts such as "the economy" or "the state" are, after all, abstractions; they cannot exist or act by themselves. It is people that exist and act, and it is only through their social behavior that society can come into being at all. Society is ultimately created, maintained, and changed by the social interaction of its members.

Some interactionist theorists focus on people's actual behavior—on the way people play their different roles and shape one another's actions, and on the little rules and niceties of social life. Others focus on how, through their interaction, people impose shared meanings on the world. Half a century ago, the American sociologist W. I. Thomas observed that "if people define situations as real, they are real in their consequences." Thus, if members of a society believe that the earth is flat, that witches exist, or that there are such things as X-rays, then these things will become as much a part of their reality as any other feature of their world. They will act in terms of that reality—by not sailing to the edge of the earth, by burning witches, by avoiding or making use of radiation. Although the interactionist perspective includes a number of loosely linked approaches, the most widely used one is that of symbolic interaction.

Symbolic Interaction   A **symbol** is anything that can meaningfully represent something else. Signs, gestures, shared rules, and, most important, written and spoken language are examples of symbols. **Symbolic interaction** is the interaction that takes place between people through symbols. Much of this interaction takes place on a face-to-face basis, but it can also occur in other forms: for example, symbolic interaction is taking place between you and the author as you read this sentence, and it occurs whenever you obey (or disobey) a traffic signal. The essential point is that people do not respond to the world directly: they place a social meaning on it and respond to that meaning. The words of this book, the red light of a traffic signal, a wolf whistle in the street, have no meaning in themselves. Rather, people learn to attach symbolic meaning to these things, and they order their lives on the basis of these meanings. We live in a symbolic as well as in a physical world, and our social life involves a constant process of interpreting the meanings of our own acts and those of others.

The interactionist perspective, then, leads the sociologist to inquire into people's interpretations of, and responses to, their interaction with others. Sociologists using this perspective usually focus on the specific, detailed aspects of personal everyday life. By what process, for example, does someone become a prostitute? Why is it that strangers in elevators so scrupulously avoid eye contact with each other, staring anywhere—at their shoes, at the ceiling, at the nearest wall—rather than directly into another passenger's face? How does someone learn to experience marijuana smoking as pleasurable? What unspoken tactics are used by a male doctor and a female patient to minimize embarrassment during a vaginal examination? What processes are involved in group decision making? What happens if you stand "too" close to someone during a conversation, and why?

The interactionist perspective provides a fascinating insight into the mechanics of everyday life, and it has the advantage of revealing fundamental social processes that other perspectives easily overlook. But the perspective is open to the important criticism that it neglects larger social institutions and societal processes of stability and change—institutions and processes which, after all, become social facts, with powerful effects on our social interaction and personal experience.

An Evaluation

Since each of these perspectives starts from different assumptions, and each leads the investigator to ask different questions, each viewpoint is likely to produce different types of conclusions. In many respects the approaches seem quite contradictory. But this does not mean that one of them is "better" than the others, or even that they are always incompatible. The reason is that each perspective focuses on a different aspect of reality: functionalism focuses primarily on social cohesion and order; conflict theory, primarily on social tension and change; and interactionism, primarily on the ordinary experiences and understandings of everyday life. Each perspective has a part to play in the analysis of society. In fact, there is nothing unusual in a scientist's using apparently incompatible theories to study the same subject. Physicists find it useful to regard light sometimes as a continuous wave and sometimes as streams of particles, depending on the situation, and they gain a better understanding of the nature of light as a result.

Thus all three perspectives could be applied, for example, to the study of education. A functionalist approach would emphasize the functions that the schools play in maintaining the social system as a whole. It would point out how education provides the young with skills they need in later life, how it sorts and selects people for different kinds of jobs, how it transmits cultural values from one generation to the next, and even how it keeps millions of adolescents off the streets. A conflict approach would emphasize that while education is an important avenue to social and financial success in life, this avenue is obstructed for certain groups. It would point out, for example, how social-class background affects a pupil's academic achievement, how school districts tend to be segregated along class and racial lines, and how educational credentials are used by different individuals and groups jockeying for competitive advantage. An interactionist approach would emphasize the daily activities that take place within the school. It would point to the forms of interaction between teachers and pupils, the types of influence the student peer group has over its individual members, or the ways in which the school rules are broken or followed. None of these approaches gives answers that are any more "true" than the others, and taken together they provide a broader and deeper understanding of the entire institution of education.

In this book, then, you will regularly encounter all three perspectives. The interactionist perspective will be used particularly in the discussion of "micro" (small-scale) processes; the functionalist and conflict perspectives, in the discussion of "macro" (large-scale) processes. Sometimes the perspectives will contradict each other. When this happens, we shall evaluate their respective merits. At other times they will complement each other, giving a fuller and richer understanding of the subject.

Principles of Sociological Research

Sociological research offers the challenge of going as a "stranger" into the familiar world, often to find one's assumptions shattered by the facts that one discovers. Research in sociology is really a form of detective work—it poses the same early puzzles and suspicions, the same moments of routine sifting through the evidence and inspired guessing, the same disappointments over false leads and facts that do not fit, and, perhaps, the same triumph when the pieces finally fall into place and an answer emerges. Research in sociology is where the real action takes place. It is in the field, far more than in the lecture room, that sociologists come to grips with their subject matter.

Both theory and research are essential to the sociological enterprise, and each thrives on the other. Facts without theory are utterly meaningless, for they lack a framework in which they can be understood. Theories without facts are unproved speculations of little practical use, because there is no way to tell whether they are correct. Theory and research are thus parts of a constant cycle. A theory inspires research that can be used to verify or disprove it, and the findings of research are used to confirm, reject, or modify the theory, or even to provide the basis of new theories. The process recurs endlessly, and the accumulation of sociological knowledge is the result.

To explain any aspect of society or social behavior, the sociologist must understand relationships of cause and effect. One basic assumption of science is that all events have causes—whether the event is a ball rolling down a hill, a nuclear bomb exploding, an economy improving, a political party losing support, or a student passing an examination. A second basic assumption is that under the identical circumstances, the same cause will repeatedly produce the same effect. If we did not make these assumptions, the world would be utterly unpredictable and therefore unintelligible to us. The problem facing the sociologist is to sort out cause from effect in the complexities of social life, and to determine which of several possible causes, or which combination of causes, is producing a particular effect.

Variables

Like all scientists, the sociologist analyzes cause and effect in terms of the influence of variables on one another. A **variable** is any characteristic that can change or differ—for example, from time to time, from place to place, or from one individual or group to another. Differences in age, sex, race, and social class are variables. So are the rates of homicide, divorce, and narcotics addiction. So are differences in intelligence, nationality, income, and sense of humor. Causation occurs when one variable, such as the quantity of alcohol a driver consumes, influences another variable, such as the likelihood of the driver's being involved in a traffic accident. A theory simply attempts to generalize about the influence of one variable on another: "Drunken driving contributes to traffic accidents." Such a statement serves to link variables in a cause-and-effect relationship.

An **independent variable** is one that influences another variable—in other words, it acts as a cause. A **dependent variable** is one that is influenced by another variable—in other words, it is affected. Thus, degree of drunkenness is one independent variable (though not necessarily the only one) that can produce the dependent variable of a traffic accident.

Correlations

Determining cause and effect, then, involves tracing the effect of variables upon one another. But how does the sociologist do this?

The basic method is to establish whether there is a **correlation**—that is, a relationship between variables that occurs regularly. By analyzing the statistics, the sociologist can easily establish whether there is a correlation between drunk driving and traffic accidents. The evidence shows that the correlation is very high. In fact, not only are drunk driving and traffic accidents closely associated, but the more alcohol drivers consume, the more likely they are to have traffic accidents. This seems to prove the case. But does it?

Logically, no. The fact that two variables are highly correlated does not prove that one caused the other, or even that they are related in any way at all. In North America, for example, there is a high correlation between the sale of ice cream and the incidence of rape, but, obviously, eating ice cream does not cause rape, nor does rape cause people to eat ice cream. Rather, the correlation is explained by a third variable that influences the other two: the heat of summer.

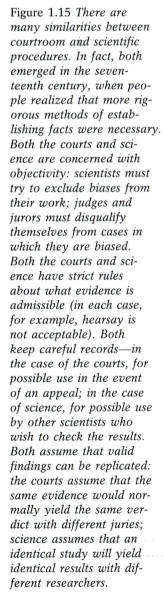

Figure 1.15 *There are many similarities between courtroom and scientific procedures. In fact, both emerged in the seventeenth century, when people realized that more rigorous methods of establishing facts were necessary. Both the courts and science are concerned with objectivity: scientists must try to exclude biases from their work; judges and jurors must disqualify themselves from cases in which they are biased. Both the courts and science have strict rules about what evidence is admissible (in each case, for example, hearsay is not acceptable). Both keep careful records—in the case of the courts, for possible use in the event of an appeal; in the case of science, for possible use by other scientists who wish to check the results. Both assume that valid findings can be replicated: the courts assume that the same evidence would normally yield the same verdict with different juries; science assumes that an identical study will yield identical results with different researchers.*

Basic Statistical Terms

Although some sociological research uses sophisticated mathematics, introductory students will be able to find their way through most sociological writing by relying on a few basic statistical concepts. The concepts you will encounter most frequently are those of averages and correlations.

Averages. The word "average" is often used loosely in ordinary conversation. There are actually three ways of calculating averages, or *central tendencies,* and each method can produce a different figure from the same data.

Suppose a researcher has studied nine individuals and finds that their annual incomes are:

$3000	$3800	$ 9000
$3000	$6500	$ 9000
$3500	$9000	$150,000

For some purposes it may be sufficient to present all this information in the form given above, but it is often more useful to provide a single figure that reveals the central tendency of all the numbers involved.

The *mode* is the number that appears most often in the data. In our example the mode is $9000. The mode is useful for the researcher to show which figure recurs most frequently. It has the disadvantage, however, of not giving any idea of the range of the data as a whole.

The *mean* is the figure obtained by dividing the total of all the figures by the number of individual cases involved. In this case the total is $196,800; divided by nine, it gives a mean figure of $21,866.66. The mean has the advantage of taking account of all the data, but it can give misleading results. In our example, the central tendency is distorted by the presence of one extreme figure, $150,000, which hides the fact that all the other individuals earn $9000 a year or less. (The mean is the measure of central tendency that we usually call the "average" in ordinary speech.)

The *median* is the number that falls midway in a range of numbers; in our example, it would be $6500. If the number of cases were an even rather than an odd number—say, ten instead of nine—the median would be the mean ("average") of the two numbers in the middle, namely the fifth and sixth items. The median is sometimes useful because it does not allow extreme cases, such as the income of $150,000, to distort the central tendency. Sociologists often present an average in more than one form, particularly when a single measure might give a misleading impression.

Correlations. A correlation is a regular relationship between two variables. The strength of that relationship is usually expressed as a number called a *correlation coefficient.* When two variables have absolutely no consistent relationship to one another (as in the case of volcanic eruptions in Japan and the birth rate in Dallas), the correlation coefficient is zero. When one variable is always associated with the other (as in the case of the moon's gravitational pull and the oceans' tides), there is a perfect *positive* correlation, expressed as a correlation coefficient of 1.0. Weak positive correlations of around 0.2 or 0.3 are not very significant (the variables in these cases being related only two or three times out of ten), but stronger correlations of around 0.6 and above indicate an increasingly significant relationship between the variables. When the presence of one variable is always associated with the absence of the other (as in the case of snowstorms and sunbathers), there is a perfect *negative* correlation, and the correlation coefficient is −1.0.

A high correlation coefficient may suggest a causal relationship between the variables involved, but it is always possible that the correlation is coincidental or is produced by a third variable that influences the other two. Correlations therefore must be interpreted with great care.

People eat more ice cream when it is hot than when it is cold, and rapes are far more likely to occur in the summer than in the winter. The rape–ice cream association exists, but it is a **spurious correlation**—one that is merely coincidental and does not imply any causal relationship whatever. Spurious correlations, which are often not as obvious as this one, present a constant trap for the careless researcher.

Controls

How, then, can we determine whether a correlation is a causal one? To find out, sociologists must apply **controls**—ways of excluding the possibility that some other factors might be influencing the relationship between two variables. It might be, for example, that most people who drive when they are drunk do their drunken driving when bars close, after dark, and that poor visibility, not alcohol consumption, is the prime cause of the accidents. The sociologist has to control for this variable by comparing the accident rates of both drunken and sober drivers during daylight and at night. If the drunken drivers are still proportionately more likely to become involved in traffic accidents under both driving conditions, the possibility that visibility is the independent variable is eliminated.

Only when the sociologist has controlled for the other possibilities—often a difficult task, because some possibilities are not immediately obvious and may be overlooked—can it be said with confidence that a causal connection exists between the variables. In the cases of our drunken drivers, a high correlation still exists when other possible independent variables have been eliminated. Have we now proved conclusively that drunken driving causes traffic accidents?

Not necessarily. The fact that a causal relationship exists between two variables does not tell us which is the independent and which is the dependent variable. To find out which is the cause and which is the effect, we must ask which came first, for a cause always precedes an effect. Since the drinking occurs before the traffic accidents rather than the other way around, we can conclude that it is the drunken driving that causes the accidents.

In summary, then, there are three criteria for a causal relationship: a correlation, or a regular association, between variables; the elimination, through controls, of other possible causes; and a logical analysis of the time sequence of the relationship in question. These criteria do not apply just to science; they apply to our everyday experience, where misinterpretation of cause-and-effect relationships is a major source of sloppy thinking. You will continually hear, in public statements and in private conversations, unproved assertions based on mere statistical association—for example, that an increase in sex education has caused an increase in teenage pregnancy; that an increase in executions has slowed an increase in homicides; that an increase in divorce has led to an increase in juvenile delinquency; and so on. Any of these statements might be true, reflecting a cause-and-effect relationship, but they might just as easily be false, reflecting a spurious correlation. A hallmark of an educated mind is the realization that such statements are merely hunches, requiring more evidence and analysis before final conclusions can be drawn.

Basic Research Methods

Reliable research results require reliable research methods. Sociologists can use one or more of four basic methods: the experiment, the survey, the observational study, and the use of existing sources of information. Each of these has its advantages and its drawbacks, and the success of a research project depends largely on the researcher's choice of an appropriate method.

Experiments

Social life is a complex business, in which so many variables may be operating at once that it is difficult to sort them out, or to determine which causes are having what effects. So the sociologist may use an **experiment,** a method for studying the relationship between two variables under carefully controlled conditions. In the typical experiment, an independent variable is introduced into a carefully designed situation and its influence on a dependent variable is recorded. Let's

How to Read a Table

Sociologists frequently use statistical tables, both as a source of data and as a way of presenting the results of their own research. You will be able to grasp the information in a table quickly if you follow a systematic procedure. Here are the main steps you should follow (using the accompanying table as a model).

1. *Read the title.* The title should tell you exactly what information the table contains. Our table tells about the willingness of Americans to vote for a female president.

2. *Look for headnotes.* Immediately below the title you will sometimes find a headnote. The headnote may give information about how the data were collected, how they are presented, or why they are presented in a particular way. In this case, the headnote tells us the exact form of the question that was asked.

3. *Examine the source.* At the bottom of a table you will find a statement of the source of the data. The source helps you to judge the reliability of the information and tells you where to find the original data if you want to check the statistics further. In the example the source is a reliable one, the Gallup poll.

4. *Read the labels.* There are two kinds of labels in a table, the column headings at the top and the headings along the left-hand side. You must make sure that you understand the labels, and you will have to keep both column and side headings in mind as you read the table. In our table the column headings represent national, female, and male opinions, while the side headings indicate the years in which the surveys were made.

5. *Find out what units are used.* The statistics in a table may be presented in hundreds, thousands, percentages, rates per 1000, rates per 100,000, and so on. Sometimes this information is not contained in the headnote but appears instead in the column or side headings. In our table, the overall column head indicates that figures are presented as percentages.

6. *Make comparisons.* Compare the data in the table, both horizontally and vertically, and notice any differences, similarities, or trends in the statistics. If you read our table horizontally, you will be able to compare the percentage of the nation willing to vote for a female president with the percentages of women and men willing to do so. If you read the table vertically, you will be able to compare opinions in any category from one year to another.

7. *Draw conclusions.* Finally, draw conclusions about the data and consider any questions that the statistics raise. You will notice, for example, that willingness to vote for a woman president has increased dramatically between 1937, when a minority of both men and women were favorable, and 1987, when an overwhelming majority of both sexes would vote for a woman. You will also note that in earlier years the idea of a woman president drew comparatively more support from women, but that in later years both sexes favored it equally, and you may want to investigate this further.

Willingness of Americans to Vote for a Woman President

Question: If your party nominated a woman for president, would you vote for her if she were qualified for the job?

	Would Vote for Woman President (in percent)		
	National	Women	Men
1937	34	41	27
1949	50	53	47
1955	54	59	49
1963	57	53	61
1978	80	81	80
1984	78	78	78
1987	82	83	81

Source: Gallup poll.

The most common form of observational study is the **case study**—a complete and detailed record of an event, group, or social process. Some case studies deal with events that have already taken place. The sociologist reconstructs these events through extensive interviews with the participants and by referring to other sources of data, ranging from police records to newspaper files. This method is often used for the analysis of infrequent, temporary events such as riots. Other case studies are conducted at the time the action is taking place. These "eyewitness" studies are a rich source of sociological information.

The sociologist in a case study may choose to be either a detached observer or a participant observer. **Detached observation** is a method in which the researcher remains as aloof as possible, and the subjects may not even know they are being studied. Observing from a distance may obscure the view, however. Many sociologists therefore prefer **participant observation,** a method in which the researcher becomes directly involved in the social behavior under study. Sometimes the participant observer makes it clear to the subjects at the outset that he or she is a sociologist; at other times the sociologist pretends to be an ordinary member of the group. The latter approach has the advantage that people will behave in more typical ways if they do not know they are being observed, and it also enables the sociologist to gain access to groups—such as some religious sects—that would not normally allow themselves to be studied. Concealing one's identity can raise serious ethical problems, however, because the sociologist is using deceit to observe the details of people's lives.

Observational studies place a heavy obligation on the sociologist, for the method relies on the skills and subjective interpretations of the observer. Gaining access to the group and winning the trust of its members can be difficult, especially if the backgrounds of the sociologist and the subjects are dissimilar. Systematic notes must be kept each day while memory is fresh. The observer must be careful not to influence the behavior he or she is studying. Observational studies have the advantage that they come to grips with real-life situations, thereby offering insights that years of experimenting and surveying might overlook. They have the disadvantage, however, of sacrificing scientific precision to some extent. The observer may misinterpret events, may unwittingly ignore things that are relevant and focus on things that are trivial, and may become so emotionally involved with the lives of the subjects that objectivity suffers. Another disadvantage is that the case studied may have been exceptional in unknown but important ways, so the findings of a single observational study cannot be generalized to all apparently similar cases.

Existing Sources

Sometimes the sociologist does not have to generate new information through experiments, surveys, or observational studies. The relevant data may already exist and may merely have to be collected and analyzed. A great deal of useful information is available in published or unpublished form, whether it consists of the statistics issued by government agencies, newsreels, diaries, letters, court records, song lyrics, works of art and literature, historical records, or the research findings of sociologists and other social scientists.

Emile Durkheim's classic study of suicide, first published in 1897, remains an outstanding example of the use of existing sources. Durkheim wanted to find out why people commit suicide, and he suspected that explanations focusing on the psychology of the individual were inadequate. Experiments on suicide were obviously out of the question. Case studies of past suicides would be of little use, because they could not provide reliable generalizations about all suicides. Survey methods were hardly appropriate, because one cannot survey dead people. But statistics on suicide were readily available, and Durkheim chose to analyze them.

Figure 1.17 *Suicide seems a highly individual act, yet the motives for a suicide can be fully understood only by reference to the social context in which it occurs. On the left, an Indian woman throws herself on her husband's funeral pyre—an act that was once considered a moral duty in parts of India. Her behavior is approved and encouraged by her community, and she kills herself in response to social pressure. The young American leaping to his death on the right probably has very different reasons, stemming from loneliness, despair, and a lack of meaningful bonds with other people. His behavior is disapproved by the community—in fact, police officers try unsuccessfully to prevent it—but social pressure is inadequate to keep him from killing himself.*

Durkheim was able to dismiss some theories of suicide—such as the possibility that suicidal tendencies are inherited—by applying statistical controls to the data and eliminating those variables. He was left with an interesting and suggestive pattern: suicide rates varied from one social group to another and did so in a consistent manner over the years. Protestants were more likely to commit suicide than Catholics; people in large cities were more likely to commit suicide than people in small communities; people living alone were more likely to commit suicide than people living in families. Durkheim isolated one independent variable that lay behind these differences: the extent to which the individual was integrated into a social bond with others. People with fragile ties to their community are more likely to take their own lives than people who have stronger ties.

Durkheim then compared suicide in such circumstances with a form of suicide that is more typical of traditional societies: the suicide that takes place because it is expected by the community. In ancient Rome or traditional Japan, for example, a suicide was regarded as a highly honorable act under some circumstances. In traditional Indian society, a widow was sometimes expected to burn herself to death on her husband's funeral pyre and was considered a dutiful wife if she did so. In these cases it is not the *weakness* but the *strength* of the individual's ties to the community that accounts for the suicide. People in these societies may actually take their own lives in response to social expectations they themselves share, whereas in our society people may take their lives because they do not share social expectations with anybody.

Durkheim was thus able to use existing sources to show that suicide—surely the most individual act anyone is capable of—can be fully understood only in its social context, particularly in terms of the presence or absence of shared social expectations that influence individual behavior. To understand why a specific person commits suicide, of course, we must look at that person's personality and the pressures to which he or she has been subjected. To understand why suicide rates are higher for some groups than for others, however, we have to look at the larger social forces that predispose individuals to suicide. Durkheim's insight—that individual behavior can be fully understood only in its social environment—has become the basis of the modern sociological perspective.

A Research Model

Suppose you wanted to conduct some sociological research. Exactly how might you go about it? Most research in sociology—and indeed in all science— follows the same basic, step-by-step procedure. The one outlined here is merely an ideal model, and not all sociologists stick to it in every detail, but it does provide the guidelines for most research projects.

1. *Select the problem.* The first step is to choose a suitable topic for a research project. The general area selected will usually be one in which the sociologist takes a personal interest—and probably one for which research funds are available.

2. *Review the literature.* The existing sociological research bearing on the problem must be tracked down and reviewed. Knowledge of this literature provides background information and saves the sociologist the labor and embarrassment of unwittingly duplicating research that has already been done.

3. *Formulate a hypothesis.* The research problem must be stated in such a way that it can actually be tested. This is achieved by formulating a **hypothesis,** a tentative statement that predicts a relationship between variables. The hypothesis might be "AIDS education reduces promiscuous behavior." However, ideas like "AIDS education" and "promiscuous behavior" are too vague to operate with effectively, for they can mean different things to different people. For each idea in the hypothesis, therefore, the researcher has to create an **operational definition**—one that states a variable, for the purposes of research, in terms that can be measured. Thus, "AIDS education" might be exposure to a particular film; "promiscuous behavior" might be measured by numbers of partners during a specific period. Different researchers may produce different operational definitions of the same terms, which is one reason why investigations of what seems to be the same subject may produce varying conclusions.

4. *Choose a research design.* The sociologist must now select one or more means of gathering data—a survey, an experiment, an observational study, the use of existing sources, or a combination of these. The **research design**—the actual plan for the collection and analysis of the data—is the crux of the research process.

5. *Collect the data.* The conclusions will be no better than the data on which they are based, so the researcher must take great care in collecting and recording information in accordance with the requirements of the research design.

6. *Analyze the results.* When all the data are in, the sociologist can begin to classify the facts, clarifying trends and relationships and tabulating the information in such a way that it can be accurately analyzed and interpreted. The theory, as expressed in the hypothesis, can now be confirmed, rejected, or modified.

7. *Draw a conclusion.* Assuming that all has gone as planned, the sociologist can now draw up a succinct report of the project, tracing the steps already mentioned and concluding with a discussion of the findings. If the research makes a significant contribution to sociological knowledge, it may be published, probably in the form of an article in a scholarly journal. It then becomes the common property of the scientific community, whose members can attempt to "replicate" the study—that is, repeat it to verify the findings—if they wish to do so.

Throughout the research process, the sociologist is expected to aim at **objectivity**—an interpretation that eliminates the influence of personal values. This is no easy matter. After all, if the world consisted of some self-evident reality that everyone perceived in exactly the same way, there might be no disagreement among observers. But the truth of the matter is that what we see in the world is not determined by what is "out there." It is shaped by what our past experience has prepared us to see and by what we consciously or unconsciously

A Research Model

Define the Problem
Choose a topic for research.

Review the Literature
Become familiar
with existing theory and
research on the subject.

Formulate a Hypothesis
State the problem as
a testable hypothesis
and construct operational
definitions of variables.

Choose a Research Design
Select one or more
research methods:
experiment, survey,
observational study, or
use of existing sources.

Collect the Data
Collect and record
information in accordance
with the research design.

Analyze the Results
Arrange the information
in orderly form
and interpret the findings.
Confirm, reject, or
modify the hypothesis.

Draw a Conclusion
Discuss the significance of
the findings, relating them to
existing theory and research
and defining problems
for future research.

Figure 1.18 *This chart shows the seven basic steps that a researcher might follow in any sociological research project.*

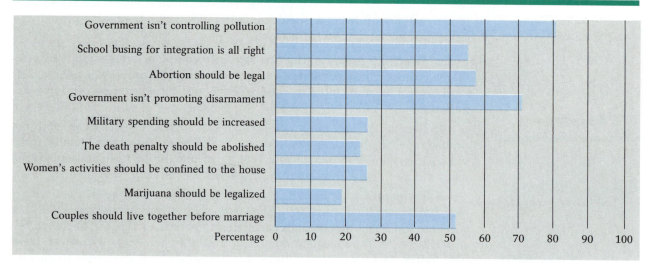

First-Year Students' Attitudes on Political and Social Issues

Percentage of those who agree somewhat or strongly with the statements below

Source: Alexander Astin et al., *The American Freshman: National Norms for Fall* (American Council of Education and University of California at Los Angeles, 1987).

Figure 1.19 *This graph shows some attitudes of a recent national sample of first-year college students. Essentially, the findings reveal biases on one side or another of public issues. Do any of the findings surprise you? How do your own attitudes compare? If your attitudes differ in some respects, what social factors—such as religion, age, sex, class, place of residence, race, or peer-group influences—might explain these differences? How "biased" or "unbiased" do you think you are?*

want to see. So sociologists, like anyone else, will inevitably bring to their work some measure of **bias**—the tendency, often unconscious, to interpret facts according to one's own values. How can this problem be resolved?

The sociological community has developed an ethical code requiring that researchers be intellectually honest—that they attempt to be aware of their own values and not allow these values to distort their work; that they relentlessly hunt down the relevant facts and not ignore those that are inconvenient for their pet theories; that they not manipulate data to prove a point; and that they not use research to suppress or misuse knowledge. Moreover, the sociological community does not have to rely entirely on the integrity of the individual to ensure that objectivity is strived for. When research is published, other sociologists can assess the findings and attempt to verify them by repeating the research to see if it yields the same result. This procedure provides an extremely effective check against bias and other distortions.

The pursuit of objectivity does not necessarily mean that sociologists should not express personal opinions, or value judgments. It means that these judgments should be clearly labeled as such and that they should not intrude into the actual process of research and interpretation. It would be perfectly legitimate, therefore, for a sociologist to give as objective an account as possible of a social problem, and then to add a subjective judgment—provided that the judgment was presented as a matter of personal opinion.

Summary

1. Sociology is the scientific study of human society; it provides a unique perspective on society, enabling us to see the intimate relationships between social forces and individual experience.

2. Science is a body of knowledge obtained by logical, systematic methods of research. Science assumes order in the universe, and it attempts to establish generalizations that can be used for the purposes of explanation and prediction. Sociology is one of the social sciences.

3. The subject matter of sociology poses many problems the natural sciences do not face, but sociology nonetheless has the same commitment to the scientific method. Sociological explanations are therefore more reliable than those based only on common sense.

4. Sociology emerged in the middle of the nineteenth century, in the context of the changes caused by the Industrial Revolution. Early sociologists, such as Comte, Spencer, Marx, Weber, and Durkheim, concentrated on problems of social order and social change. The subsequent development of sociology, which has taken place largely in the United States, has focused primarily on more restricted theories and studies and on the refinement of research techniques. There has been controversy over whether sociologists should be value-free or socially committed.

5. There are three major theoretical perspectives in modern sociology. The functionalist perspective focuses primarily on processes of order and stability; the conflict perspective, on processes of competition and change; the interactionist perspective, on processes of everyday social behavior. These three perspectives are not necessarily incompatible.

6. All events have causes, and the task of science is to trace these causes in the form of the influence of variables upon one another. Cause and effect can be traced by establishing correlations between independent and dependent variables, applying controls to exclude the possibility that some other variable is influencing the relationship. Logical analysis is also necessary to establish that a relationship is causal, not spurious.

7. There are four basic methods of sociological research. The experiment permits careful study of the effect of independent upon dependent variables, but requires the use of experimental and control groups for valid conclusions to be drawn. The survey is useful for obtaining information about a population, but must be based on a random sample if it is to be representative. Observational studies, particularly case studies using detached or participant observation, are useful for in-depth analyses of social processes but rely heavily on the skills of the researcher. Existing sources of various kinds can often be used to generate new information, as in the case of Durkheim's pioneering study of suicide.

8. An ideal research model consists of the following basic steps: selecting the problem, reviewing the literature, formulating a hypothesis, choosing a research design, collecting the necessary data, analyzing the results, and drawing a conclusion. Scientists are expected to strive for objectivity.

Important Terms

sociology (1)

science (3)

generalization (3)

natural sciences (4)

social sciences (4)

social psychology (4)

cultural anthropology (4)

value-freedom (10)

value judgment (10)

theory (11)

theoretical perspective (11)

functionalist perspective (11)

structure (11)

function (11)

manifest function (12)

latent function (12)

dysfunction (13)

conflict perspective (13)

interactionist perspective (14)

symbol (15)

symbolic interaction (15)

variable (17)

independent variable (17)

dependent variable (17)

correlation (17)

spurious correlation (18)

controls (19)

experiment (19)

experimental group (20)

control group (20)

survey (20)

sample (20)

respondents (20)

random sample (21)

case study (23)

detached observation (23)

participant observation (23)

hypothesis (25)

operational definition (25)

research design (25)

objectivity (25)

bias (26)

CHAPTER 2

Culture

Unlike other animals, we human beings are not born with rigid, complex, behavior patterns that enable us to survive in specific habitats. Instead, we must learn and invent means of adapting to different physical and social environments, ranging from arctic snows to desert wastelands and teeming cities. In short, the members of each society must develop and share a **culture**—an entire way of life.

In ordinary speech, the word "culture" is often used to refer to sophisticated tastes in art, literature, or music. But the sociological use of the term is much wider, and implies that anyone who participates in society is "cultured." To the sociologist, culture includes everything that a human society produces and shares. These products are of two basic kinds—material and nonmaterial. **Material culture** consists of all the artifacts, or physical objects, human beings create and give meaning to—wheels, clothing, schools, factories, cities, books, spacecraft, totem poles. **Nonmaterial culture** consists of abstract human creations—languages, ideas, beliefs, rules, customs, myths, skills, family patterns, political systems.

It is possible, at least conceptually, to distinguish "culture" from "society." Culture consists of the *way of life* of society; society consists of the interacting *people* who share a culture. But the two are closely interrelated. A culture cannot exist without a society to maintain it, and without culture, neither individual human beings nor human society could survive. The reason lies in the unique characteristics of our own species.

The Significance of Culture

The planet earth is about 4.7 billion years old. The first living organisms emerged in the oceans approximately 3 billion years ago. The earliest land animals, amphibian creatures, appeared about 400 million years ago and eventually evolved into reptiles. Mammals, which evolved from reptiles about 180 million years ago, are a recent but very successful evolutionary development, primarily because they are more intelligent and adaptable than other life forms. They have an exceptional capacity to learn from experience, and in the higher mammals, particularly the primates, learning becomes progressively more important in shaping behavior. This development reaches its climax in human beings. Our almost total reliance on learned behavior is the single most important characteristic distinguishing us from other creatures.

Our species, *homo sapiens*, is the most creative in the planet's history. It has spread to every continent, frequently driving other animal species to extinction in the process. It has become the most widely dispersed species on the planet, able to occupy mountains and valleys, deserts and jungles, shorelines and tundra, because it has always found some specialized means of living in these widely differing environments.

Figure 2.1 *The significance of culture is that it enables us to invent and learn ways of adapting to our environments and to changing conditions. All other animals must rely on the slow and accidental process of biological evolution to adapt them to their environments, but we can use cultural knowledge and artifacts to adapt quickly to radically different conditions.*

What accounts for the unprecedented success that our species has enjoyed thus far? The answer, in a word, is culture. We create culture, but culture in turn creates us. We make our own social environment, inventing and sharing the rules and patterns of behavior that shape our lives, and we use our learned knowledge to modify the natural environment. Our shared culture is what makes social life possible. Without a culture transmitted from the past, each new generation would have to solve the most elementary problems of human existence over again. It would be obliged to devise a family system, to invent a language, to discover fire, to create the wheel, and so on.

Clearly, the contents of culture cannot be genetically transmitted. There is no gene that tells us to believe in a particular god, to get married, to drive on the right, to build houses, or to write computer programs. Everything in culture is learned. Culture is thus a substitute for "instinct" as a means of responding to the environment, and it provides a vastly superior way of doing so. Culture frees us from reliance on the slow, random, accidental process of physical evolution by offering us a flexible and efficient means of adapting to changing conditions. If we waited for the process of evolution to enable us to live at the North Pole, to fly, or to live under the sea, we would wait forever. But cultural inventions enable us to be insulated from the cold of the arctic, to travel through air, and to live in submarines. The emergence of a species that depends for its survival on a learned culture is perhaps the greatest breakthrough in evolutionary history.

"Human Nature"

There are many divergent—and often inaccurate—conceptions of "human nature." For example, a substantial majority of Americans agree with the statement "Human nature being what it is, there will always be wars and conflict." The problem with such ideas about "human nature" is that they are deeply colored by the cultural beliefs of the societies in which they are found. In the industrialized countries of the world, particularly in the West, we tend to think of people as being "naturally" self-seeking, selfish, competitive, and even aggressive. But this kind of behavior is virtually unknown among many of the "primitive" peoples of the world, such as the Arapesh of New Guinea, the Pygmies of the Ituri forest in central Africa, the Shoshone of the western United States, or the Lepcha of the Himalayas. These and many other societies never fight wars at all, and their inhabitants obviously have a very different conception of "human nature" (Montagu, 1978).

In fact, "human nature," if there is such a thing at all, is highly flexible. Our behavior is a product of an interaction between our basic biological heritage and the learning experiences of the particular culture in which we happen to live. For example, we have the biological capacity to speak, but which language we use and how we use it depend on our environment. We have the biological capacity to laugh, to cry, to blush, to become angry, but the circumstances under which we might do any of these things are learned. Nature provides us with legs, but we are not obliged to use them only for walking. We can use them to kick a ball, or to kick other people, or to ride a bicycle, or to do a war dance, or to cover with pants, or to sit cross-legged while contemplating.

Most modern psychologists agree that human beings do not have any "instincts." An *instinct* is a behavior pattern with three essential features: it is complex, it is unlearned, and it appears in all normal members of the species under identical conditions. For example, all members of some bird or insect species will, as soon as the nesting season begins, build complex nests of exactly the same type, even if they have never seen such nests built before. Any instincts we once had, however, have been lost in the course of our evolution. The idea that we do not have instincts is difficult for some people to accept, because it seems to run counter to "common sense." One reason for the difficulty is that the word "instinct" is often used very loosely in ordinary speech. People talk about "instinctively" stepping on the brake or "instinctively" mistrusting someone, when these actions and attitudes are, in fact, culturally learned. Another reason is that much of our learned behavior is so taken for granted that it becomes "second nature" to us. The behavior seems so "natural" that we lose the awareness that it is learned, not inherited. But if you think about it, you will see that there is no human behavior that fits the definition of instinct above.

We do have some genetically determined types of behavior, of course, but these are *simple reflexes*—involuntary muscular responses, such as starting at an unexpected loud noise, throwing out our arms when we lose our balance, pulling back our hand when it touches a hot surface. We also have a few inborn, basic *drives*—organic urges, such as our desires for self-preservation, for food and drink, for sex, and perhaps for the company of other people. But we are not programmed to satisfy these drives in any particular way, for if we were, we would all fulfill them in a rigid, identical manner. Rather, we satisfy these drives in a great variety of ways, all learned through cultural experience. In fact, unlike all other species, we can even learn to override our drives completely. We can ignore the drive for self-preservation by committing suicide or by risking our lives for others. Protesters can ignore the drive for food and go on hunger strikes, even if it means starvation. Priests and others can suppress the sex drive and live out their lives in celibacy. Hermits can override the drive for human company and live in isolation.

Within very broad limits, "human nature" is what we make of it, and what we make of it depends largely on the culture in which we happen to live. One of the most liberating aspects of the sociological perspective is that it strips away myths about our social behavior, showing that what seems "natural" or "instinctive" is usually nothing more than a cultural product of a specific human society at a particular moment in history.

Norms

When the explorer Captain Cook asked the chiefs in Tahiti why they always ate apart and alone, they replied, "Because it is right" (Linton, 1945). If we ask Americans why they eat with knives and forks, or why their men wear pants instead of skirts, or why they may be married to only one person at a time, we are likely to get similar and very uninformative answers: "Because it's right." "Because that's the way it's done." "Because it's the custom." Or even "I don't know."

The reason for these and countless other patterns of social behavior is that they are controlled by social **norms**—shared rules or guidelines that prescribe the behavior appropriate in a given situation. Norms define how people "ought" to behave under particular circumstances in a particular society. We conform to norms so readily that we are hardly aware they exist. In fact, we are much more likely to notice departures from norms than conformity to them. You would not be surprised if a stranger tried to shake hands when you were introduced, but you might be a little startled if he or she bowed, curtsied, started to stroke you, or kissed you on both cheeks. Yet each of these other forms of greeting is appropriate in other parts of the world. When we visit another society whose norms are different, we quickly become aware that we do things *this* way, they do them *that* way.

Some norms apply to every member of society. In the United States, for example, nobody is permitted to marry more than one person at the same time. Other norms apply to some people but not to others. There is a very strong norm in American society against the taking of human life, but this norm generally does not apply to police officers in shootouts, soldiers in combat, or people acting in self-defense against armed attackers. Other norms are even more specific and prescribe the appropriate behavior for people in particular situations, such as college students in lecture rooms, waiters in restaurants, or presidential candidates on the campaign trail.

Folkways and Mores

Norms ensure that social life proceeds smoothly, for they give us guidelines for our own behavior and reliable expectations for the behavior of others. This function of norms is so important that there is always strong social pressure on people to conform. But although most of us conform to most norms most of the time, all of us tend to violate some norms occasionally. In the case of certain norms, the folkways, a fair amount of nonconformity may be tolerated, but in the case of certain other norms, the mores, very little leeway is permitted (Sumner, 1906).

Folkways are the ordinary conventions of everyday life. Conformity to folkways is expected but not absolutely insisted upon. We expect people to keep their lawns mowed, to refrain from picking their noses in public, to show up on time for appointments, and to wear a matching pair of shoes. Those who do not conform to these and similar folkways are considered peculiar and eccentric, particularly if they consistently violate a number of folkways. But they are not considered immoral or depraved, nor are they treated as criminals.

Mores (pronounced "mor-ays") are strong norms that are regarded as morally significant, and violations of them are considered a serious matter. (The word "mores" was the ancient Romans' term for their most respected and even sacred customs.) Theft, drug abuse, murder, rape, desecration of the national flag, and contemptuous use of religious symbols all bring a strong social reaction. People believe that their mores are crucial for the maintenance of a decent and orderly society, and the offender may be strongly criticized, physically attacked, imprisoned, committed to a mental asylum, or even executed. Some violations of mores are made almost unthinkable by a **taboo**—a powerful social belief that some specific act is utterly loathsome. In the United States, for example, there is a strong taboo against eating human flesh, a taboo so effective that most of the states do not even have laws prohibiting the practice.

Not all norms can be neatly categorized as either folkways or mores. In practice, norms fall at various points on a continuum, depending on how seriously they are taken by society. There is also a constant shift in the importance attached to some norms. Throughout most of the history of the Western world, for example, there have been changes in the norms concerning the length of men's hair. Thus, in the early United States, national heroes such as Washington, Jefferson, and Franklin wore very long hair, even if it was in the form of wigs. But during the first half of the twentieth century, it was fashionable for men to wear their hair short. At first a folkway, this fashion gradually developed into one of American society's mores. In the 1960s, when young males once more began to grow their hair long, they found that much of adult society considered the practice morally offensive—outrageous, in fact. By the early 1970s, however, long hair on males had become almost a folkway, and today the society's norms allow males a much wider personal choice in the matter—although shorter hair is presently more fashionable. But in time, no doubt, the norms will change again, and people will be scandalized at long hair, short hair, dyed hair, hats, helmets, wigs, ribbons, or even bald heads on the young men, or young women, or both, of the future. (How will you react in the years ahead if *your* children shave their heads or wear long green hair or sport powdered wigs?)

Some norms, particularly mores, are encoded in law. A **law** is a rule that has been formally enacted by a political authority and is backed by the power of the state. The law usually codifies important norms that already exist, but sometimes political authorities attempt to introduce new norms by enacting appropriate laws. Such attempts are not always successful. As the prohibition of liquor in the United States in the 1920s clearly demonstrated, laws that run counter to cultural norms, particularly in the area of personal morality, are often ineffectual and eventually tend to fall into disuse.

Social Control

Every society must have some system of **social control,** a set of means of ensuring that people generally behave in expected and approved ways. Some of this social control over the individual can be exercised by others—either formally through such agencies as the police and government inspectors, or informally through the reactions of other people in the course of everyday life. All norms, whether they are codified in law or not, are supported by **sanctions,** rewards for conformity and punishments for nonconformity. The positive sanctions may range from an approving nod to a ceremony of public acclaim; the negative sanctions may range from mild disapproval to imprisonment or even execution.

Figure 2.2 Every society has both formal and informal means of ensuring that social norms are generally followed. If informal means fail, then social control can be applied formally. This picture shows police action against members of a Los Angeles gang.

Only a tiny fraction of social behavior can be policed by formal agencies of control, and most sanctions are applied informally by such people as neighbors, family members, coworkers, and friends.

Most social control, however, does not have to be exercised through the direct influence of other people. We exercise it ourselves, internally. Indeed, we usually follow social expectations automatically, without question. Growing up in society involves the **internalization of norms**—the unconscious process of making conformity to cultural norms a part of one's personality. Like the chiefs on Tahiti and like people all over the world, we think and act in ways that are to a great extent shaped by the society we live in, though we are seldom aware of this fact. For the most part, we behave as we do because "That's the way it's done."

Values

The norms of a society are ultimately an expression of its **values**—socially shared ideas about what is good, right, and desirable. The difference between values and norms is that values are abstract, general concepts, whereas norms are specific guidelines for people in particular kinds of situations.

The Importance of Values

The values of a society are important because they influence the content of its norms. If a society values education highly, its norms will make provision for mass schooling. If it values a large population, its norms will encourage big families. In principle at least, all norms can be traced to a basic social value. For example, the norms that require a student to be more polite and formal to a professor than to fellow students express the value that society places on respect for authority and learning. The mid-century norms that insisted on short hair for men reflected the high value placed on men's "masculinity" in American culture—a value that was threatened by long hair because it was regarded as "effeminate."

Although all norms express social values, many norms persist long after the conditions that gave rise to them have been forgotten. The folkway that requires us to shake hands, especially when greeting a stranger, seems to have originated long ago in the practice of showing that no weapon was concealed in the right hand. The folkway of throwing rice or confetti over a bride and groom may seem rather meaningless, but it actually stems from an ancient practice of showering newlyweds with nuts, fruits, and seeds as symbols of fertility.

American Values

Unlike norms, whose existence can easily be observed in everyday behavior, values are often more difficult to identify. The values of a society have to be inferred from its norms, so any analysis of social values relies heavily on the interpretations of the observer. The United States presents a particular problem, for it has a heterogeneous culture drawn from many different racial, ethnic, religious, and regional traditions, and so lacks the unquestioned consensus on values that smaller, traditional communities tend to display. Sociologists have therefore concentrated on detecting "core" values that appear to be shared by the majority of Americans. The most influential of these attempts is that of Robin Williams (1970), who found a number of basic value orientations in the United States. These include achievement and success, activity and work, humanitarianism, efficiency and practicality, progress, material comfort, equality, freedom, conformity, science and rationality, nationalism and patriotism, democracy, individualism, and the belief in the superiority of some racial or ethnic groups over others.

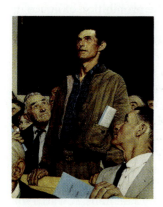

Figure 2.3 *Freedom is one of the most strongly held of all American values. This 1943 painting,* Freedom of Speech, *by the American artist Norman Rockwell, captures an important aspect of this ideal. Yet the reality often falls short of the ideal: opinion polls show that most Americans would not want to allow a speech in their community by an atheist, a racist, a homosexual, a communist, or an advocate of military government.*

Printed by permission of the Estate of Norman Rockwell. Copyright © 1943 Estate of Norman Rockwell.

Figure 2.4 *Military recruitment posters reveal a long-term shift from values emphasizing responsibility to values emphasizing self-fulfillment. The famous "Uncle Sam" poster of World War I appealed to a sense of duty to country; recent posters appeal to the wish for adventure, job training, or personal development.*

It is obvious that some of these values are not entirely consistent with one another. Many of them, too, are accepted by some Americans but rejected by others. Also, Williams's listing does not exhaust all the possibilities, and other writers have identified rather different values. James Henslin (1975), for example, includes several values cited by Williams but adds others such as education, religiosity, male supremacy, romantic love, monogamy, and heterosexuality. Moreover, values change over time, and some of those cited by Williams may be eroding. Questions have been raised, for example, about the meaning of "progress," and about new problems posed by science and technology, such as pollution of the environment. There is perhaps less insistence now on the value of conformity, and certainly less emphasis on racial- or ethnic-group superiority, than there was a few decades ago. But are any new values emerging?

Several observers have suggested that, at least among relatively young, middle-class people, an important new value has, in fact, been gaining ground in the United States over the past decade or so—**self-fulfillment,** the commitment to achieving the development of one's individual personality, talents, and potential. This preoccupation with the self as "number one" is distinctive and unusual: it would be quite foreign to many cultures, where individualism is less valued—even discouraged—and where obligations to kin, work, and community are assigned more priority.

The evidence for the spread of the new value is still fragmentary. One strong indication is opinion polls that show young people to be much more concerned about material success, and less concerned about social reform, than were the young of the 1960s and 1970s (Astin et al., 1987). Another indication is the profusion of "self-help" or "personal development" books that now fill whole sections in bookstores and are recurrently on the best-seller lists—books with titles like *Power and How to Use It, How to Be Your Own Best Friend, Looking Out for Number 1, Living Alone and Liking It, How to Get What You Really Want, The Art of Selfishness, Eat to Win, Having It All, Rich Is Better, How to Find Another Husband, Psychocybernetics and Self-Fulfillment,* and so on. And, of course, much has been written in the popular press about the "me generation" and the self-centered ambitions of the "yuppies."

Most social critics have reacted unfavorably to the new value, primarily because it seems to undermine other values, particularly those relating to social responsibility. It does seem that this new value has already affected several aspects of American social and cultural life, and in later chapters we will trace its impact on such areas as the family, religion, gender roles, and the economy.

Variation Among Cultures

The culture of every society is unique, containing combinations of norms and values that are found nowhere else. Americans eat oysters but not snails. The French eat snails but not locusts. The Zulus eat locusts but not fish. The Jews eat fish but not pork. The Hindus eat pork but not beef. The Russians eat beef but not snakes. The Chinese eat snakes but not people. The Jalé of New Guinea find people delicious. We spend our lives accumulating possessions for our private use; the BaMbuti of the Congo forests spend their lives sharing their goods; the Kwakiutl of the Pacific Northwest periodically gave their possessions away or even destroyed them at great ceremonies. Women in traditional Arab societies must cover the entire body and even the face; American women may expose their faces but must keep their breasts and the entire pelvic region concealed; women in many parts of Africa may expose their breasts and buttocks but not the genital region; women in Tierra del Fuego may not expose their backs; and the Mundurcú of Brazil proceed about their daily lives stark naked. The range of cultural variation is so immense that probably no specific norm appears in every human society. How can we account for this variation?

The Ecological Context

People create culture as a means of adapting to the environment, and so their cultural practices are necessarily affected by the particular pressures and opportunities of the surroundings in which they live. Many social scientists therefore study cultural variations through an **ecological approach**—one that analyzes cultural elements in the context of the total environment in which a society exists.

The culture of the desert Bedouin Arabs offers an obvious illustration for this approach, because the Bedouins' harsh desert environment sets severe limits on their cultural options. These people live in a region so arid that farming is impossible: accordingly, they cannot form permanent settlements or live in houses. Instead, they are nomads, spending a large part of the year wandering from one oasis to another, always moving on when the water dries up. Their shelter necessarily consists of tents, the only form of housing that can be easily transported. They have herds of camels, not pigs or moose, because camels are the only suitable animals living in the region that can withstand long periods without water. Their material possessions are neither many nor large, for they must be regularly packed, moved for tens or hundreds of miles, and then unpacked again. The Bedouins have evolved norms about the conservation of water, and unlike North Americans, they are not offended if people do not wash for days or weeks on end. They place a high value on the ability to navigate the almost featureless desert. Their religion does not include gods of the sea or spirits of the jungle; instead, like many pastoral peoples, they conceive of a god who is like a shepherd to his human flock. When they think of paradise, they imagine a place of cool shade, pleasing fountains, and an abundance of fresh fruits—the things that they lack in this world. In short, many important elements of their culture can be traced to the influence of the environment in which they live (Vidal, 1976).

The relationship of other cultural practices to the total environment is not always as obvious, but the ecological approach has been applied to several otherwise puzzling practices. Marvin Harris (1974, 1986), for example, uses it to explain a striking cultural feature of India: the apparently irrational veneration Indians have for cows. Although only one Indian in fifty has an adequate diet,

Figure 2.5 *Many of the variations among cultures can be explained in ecological terms. The way of life of the Eskimos differs radically from that of these Asians, for each people faces very different environmental pressures and opportunities.*

Figure 2.6 *Cows are highly valued in India—so much so that they roam the streets unmolested, even though many Indians are malnourished. This veneration of the cow seems inexplicable—yet it is a fundamental assumption of sociology that all human behavior, no matter how puzzling it may seem at first, can be rationally explained.*

the Hindu religion has a taboo against the slaughter of cows. As a result, over 100 million cows roam freely through the countryside and cities of India, snarling traffic and defecating in public places. Western observers are apt to regard most of these cows as "useless." They are scrawny animals, yielding little milk and apparently contributing nothing of value to Indian social or economic life.

Harris points out, however, that the cows are vital to the Indian economy. A large part of the population lives on small farms that require at least one pair of oxen for plowing. These farm families live on the brink of starvation and cannot afford tractors. They must use oxen, and their oxen can be produced only by cows. Widespread cow slaughter would worsen the already critical shortage of draft animals, making the existing farms too unproductive and driving tens of millions of people into the severely crowded cities. Moreover, the cows provide India annually with hundreds of millions of tons of manure. About half is used as fertilizer by farmers who could not possibly afford chemical substitutes. The remainder serves as cooking fuel, a vital resource in a country that has little oil or coal and an acute shortage of wood. And when the cows finally die, they are eaten, not by Hindus, but by impoverished outcastes who are not bound by the Hindu religion. The hides of the animals are then used in India's huge leather-working industry. The cows themselves do not compete with human beings for food, such as grain, but scavenge what they can from roadsides and other unproductive land. In short, the sacred cow is not such a cultural mystery after all, for it is an important element in the entire Indian ecology.

Different societies, of course, may adopt different solutions to similar ecological problems. Many societies, for instance, face the problem that their environment does not offer enough resources to maintain a growing population. The Eskimos solved the problem by deliberately leaving many aged, unproductive people out in the snow to die. The Yanamamö of Brazil control their population by killing or deliberately starving female infants and by practicing incessant and bloody fighting among males. The Keraki of New Guinea limit population increase by requiring males to engage in exclusively homosexual relations for several years after puberty. The Chinese restrict population growth by penalizing parents of large families, by encouraging abortion, and by using such cultural artifacts as contraceptives. But whatever their specific solutions to problems posed by the ecological context, all cultures must ultimately adapt to the constraints of their environment—a fact that we are often inclined to overlook in the more industrialized nations of the world.

Figure 2.7 *Functionalists analyze social and cultural phenomena in terms of their social effects. Religion, for example, helps to maintain social values and social cohesion among believers.*

Culture: A Functionalist View

The environment provides the general context in which culture develops. One way of analyzing specific components of culture more closely is to look for the *functions* they perform, or the effects they have, in maintaining the social order as a whole. Functionalist theorists regard society and culture as a system of interdependent parts. To explain a particular cultural trait, therefore, one has to establish its functions in making the entire system "work."

An important value in traditional Eskimo society was that of hospitality to travelers, including complete strangers. A male host was obliged to do everything possible to make travelers comfortable, even if he found them personally offensive. (There was even a norm requiring him to offer his wife to a male guest for the night.) As strange as this culture trait of obligatory hospitality might seem to us, it was highly functional in Eskimo culture. Travel through snows and arctic blizzards would be utterly impossible unless the traveler could rely on the certainty of food, warmth, and rest at the next settlement, and the host in turn could expect the same hospitality when he traveled. Without this norm, communication and trade among various groups might have been too hazardous. A similar norm does not exist in modern societies, where it would make no sense. These societies have created other cultural arrangements, such as restaurants and motels, to serve the same function.

The Cheyenne Indians periodically gathered for a sun-dance ceremony. Why? The activity brought no obvious rewards and seemed only to distract the various bands from the more mundane activities of making a living in their own areas. A functionalist analysis again suggests the reason. The sun dance gave the entire tribe an opportunity to gather together for a common purpose, to reestablish social bonds, and to confirm their sense that they were not simply a scattering of isolated bands but rather a tribe united by similar cultural practices. In the same way, an American ritual such as Thanksgiving can be explained in terms of its function in drawing families together to reaffirm faith in the American way of life.

By showing that certain cultural elements serve to meet specific needs, functionalist theory can help us to understand why a particular trait may be present in one society but not in others. The approach sometimes has the disadvantage, however, of focusing on how things "fit together" at a particular moment in cultural history and thus neglecting cultural change. It must be remembered that changes—the introduction of snowmobiles to the Eskimo, or of Christianity to the Cheyenne, for example—may throw other parts of the cultural system into some disorder, creating new problems that require fresh cultural solutions.

Culture: A Conflict View

Another way to analyze some components of culture is to see them as the product of social tension. Conflict theorists regard society and culture as being in a constant state of change, much of it caused by tension and competition among different groups. In any society, they argue, various groups will create cultural arrangements that serve their own interests, and the strongest groups may be able to impose their own cultural preferences on the society as a whole. To explain aspects of culture—or to explain the direction of cultural change—it may therefore be useful to ask, Who benefits?

A good illustration for the conflict approach is the political culture of the Republic of South Africa, where a small white minority enforces racial segregation and inequality on a large nonwhite majority. The country has a total population of 33 million, classified at birth into one of four groups: whites (15 percent); Asians (3 percent); "coloreds," or people of mixed race (9 percent); and blacks (73 percent). There are over 300 racial laws that require members of each

**South Africa:
Racial Contrasts**

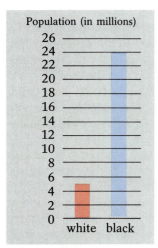

Population (in millions)

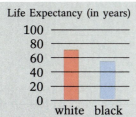

Life Expectancy (in years)

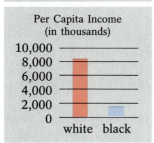

Per Capita Income
(in thousands)

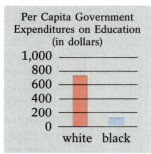

Per Capita Government
Expenditures on Education
(in dollars)

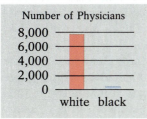

Number of Physicians

Source: Time, August 25,
1985, p. 29.

Figure 2.8 *As this chart shows, South Africa's resources are unequally distributed between the ruling white minority and the large black majority. A conflict analysis suggests that many aspects of South African culture, such as racial segregation and lack of democratic rights, are the outcome of a competition for control of these resources. Conflict theorists argue that many other cultural phenomena reflect underlying social tensions.*

group to live in their own areas and to use separate facilities such as hospitals and schools. Asians and coloreds have limited political rights, but the blacks have no vote or direct representation in the government, even though they constitute nearly three-quarters of the population.

Instead of giving blacks democratic political rights, South Africa has created ten black reservations, or "homelands." These territories, which consist of a mostly barren 13 percent of the country's area, are gradually being granted "independence." In theory, blacks are expected to become citizens of the "homelands" and to exercise political rights there—even though they mostly live and work in South Africa itself. Already, four "homelands" have been granted independence, enabling the government to deprive 5 million blacks of some citizenship rights on the grounds that they are now foreigners. None of these independent states has been recognized by the rest of the world, and it is fairly easy to see why. Consider KwaNdebele, which will be the next "homeland" to be given independence. This "country" consists of 380 square miles of prairie, with a capital of tin huts and enough jobs for 2 percent of its population. It has no resident doctor and only one paved road, which is used primarily to transport its citizens back to their jobs in South Africa.

How can we make sense of the cultural phenomenon of South Africa's political system? Conflict theorists suggest that it arises from competition among racially defined groups for control of South Africa's wealth and other resources. Most of those resources are presently enjoyed mostly by the whites (see Figure 2.8). If we ask who benefits from this disparity, the answer, obviously, is the ruling minority. To conflict theorists, the elaborate but meaningless political "rights" granted to the other groups are simply a way to divide the majority, deflect their power, and make it easier to control them. Moreover, a conflict analysis also predicts that tension will produce social and cultural change in South Africa in the future. Since the mid-1980s, in fact, riots, shootings, and interracial disturbances have become so commonplace that a revolution may already be under way.

Conflict theory cannot explain all aspects of culture: it does not help us understand, for example, why the Eskimo sometimes built igloos or why Americans are so fond of hamburgers. But wherever different groups are in competition—whether they are white settlers and Indians on the American frontier in the nineteenth century, or different industries lobbying Congress for preferential treatment today—the cultural outcomes can be analyzed in terms of the shifting power relationships of the contenders.

Cultural Universals

In the midst of this variety, are there any **cultural universals**—practices found in every culture? The answer is that there are a fairly large number of general cultural universals, but there do not seem to be any specific ones. Every culture, for example, has norms prohibiting murder, but different cultures have different ideas about which homicides constitute murder and which do not. We would consider human sacrifice murder, but the Aztecs did not. Vietnamese peasants no doubt considered the American bombing of their communities as murder, but many Americans did not. We would consider the slaughter of an inoffensive stranger as murder, but there are still some small, isolated societies—such as the Kreen Akrore of the Amazon jungle—in which the norms permit any outsider to be killed on the spot, as a potential threat to the group.

Cultural universals derive from the common problems the natural and social environments pose for our species. The weather is often too hot or too cold for comfort, so clothing and housing must be made to adapt us to the climate. Children need care and attention, and some cultural provision must be made for this requirement. People become sick, and attempts must be made to cure them. Individuals must be distinguished from one another, and so they are given names. Life is often hard and death awaits us all, and people everywhere maintain religious beliefs to explain the human predicament.

The anthropologist George Murdock (1945) compiled a lengthy list of cultural universals, including the following: athletic sports, bodily adornment, cooking, cooperative labor, courtship, dancing, dream interpretation, family, feasting, folklore, food taboos, funeral ceremonies, games, gift-giving, incest taboos, laws, medicine, music, myths, numerals, personal names, property rights, religion, sexual restrictions, toilet training, tool-making, and weather-making efforts. But these are only general traits; their specific content varies from one culture to another.

Ethnocentrism

Cultures may vary, but most human beings spend their entire lives within the culture in which they were born. Knowing little about other ways of life, they see their own norms and values as inevitable rather than optional. As Ralph Linton (1936) observed:

> It has been said that the last thing which a dweller in the deep sea would discover would be water. He would become conscious of its existence only if some accident brought him to the surface and introduced him to air. . . . The ability to see the culture of one's own society as a whole . . . calls for a degree of objectivity which is rarely if ever achieved.

For this reason, people in every society are bound to have some measure of **ethnocentrism**—the tendency to judge other cultures by the standards of one's own. People everywhere are apt to take it for granted that their morality, their marriage forms, their clothing styles, or their conceptions of beauty are right, proper, and the best of all possible choices. Here are some examples of ethnocentric thinking. Our women put rings through their ears and cosmetics on their faces because it enhances their beauty; their women put bones through their noses and scars on their faces because, in their pitiful ignorance, they don't realize how ugly it makes them. We won't eat cats or worms because that would be cruel or disgusting; they won't eat beef or drink milk because of some silly food taboo. We cover our private parts because we are decorous and civilized; they walk around naked because they are primitive and shameless. Our brave troops achieve glorious victories over them; their fanatical hordes perpetrate bloody massacres on us. Our religion is divinely inspired truth; theirs is heathen superstition.

Ethnocentrism is particularly strong in isolated, traditional societies that have had little contact with other cultures. But even in the modern world, where citizens have such advantages as formal education, mass communication, and international travel, such attitudes still prevail. Ethnocentrism can have many undesirable effects. It can encourage racism, it can cause hostility and conflict between groups, and it can make a people unwilling to see the need for changes in their own culture.

Figure 2.9 *The norms and values of a culture cannot be arbitrarily judged by those of another culture. From the perspective of American culture, the traditional Middle Eastern practice of hiding the entire female body from view seems silly: from the perspective of these Arab women, the American practice of exposing so much of the female body would be shameful and obscene. Neither viewpoint is objectively "right," for each practice can be fully understood only in its own cultural context. In fact, before we smile too quickly at how easily other people are shocked by matters of public attire, we might consider the reaction that would be likely to be provoked if the American women wore their bikinis to a church, a corporate office, or a college lecture hall.*

Ethnocentrism also poses a severe problem for social scientists analyzing other cultures, because it may lead them to make unconscious and often unfounded assumptions about other people and their practices. Even trained observers experience "culture shock" when confronted with cultures radically unlike their own. Napoleon Chagnon, an anthropologist who studied the Yanamamö of Brazil, was aghast when he first met his subjects. They stank to him (though not, of course, to themselves), the heads of the men were covered with scars from their incessant fighting, and they were under the influence of a local psychedelic drug—one of whose effects was to produce thick strings of green mucus that seemed to hang constantly from their noses. Chagnon (1967) recalls:

> I am not ashamed to admit . . . that had there been a diplomatic way out, I would have ended my fieldwork there and then. I did not look forward to the next day when I would be left alone with the Indians: I did not speak a word of their language, and they were decidedly different from what I had imagined them to be. The whole situation was depressing, and I wondered why I had ever decided to switch from civil engineering to anthropology in the first place.

Yet Chagnon was eventually able, after living among the Yanamamö for many months, to adjust to their culture and to develop a sympathetic understanding of their way of life.

Cultural Relativism

The ability to fully understand another culture depends largely on one's willingness to adopt the position of **cultural relativism,** the recognition that one culture cannot be arbitrarily judged by the standards of another. We are quick to complain when foreign critics—the Russians, for example—judge us in terms of their own values, for we feel that such a judgment distorts the reality of our culture and society. We have to be equally on guard against arbitrarily using our own standards to judge other cultures.

It is probably never possible to be entirely free of bias in favor of the cultural world we know. Opinion polls consistently show, for example, that Americans in every state of the Union are overwhelmingly convinced that their state is the very best place in the world to live—even though most of them have visited only a few other states, let alone other countries! Thus, no matter how hard we try, the sneaking feeling is likely to persist that our standards *are* better. Yet we must recognize that judgments about good and bad, moral and immoral, depend very much on who is doing the judging; there is no universally accepted standard to appeal to. An inability to adopt the position of cultural relativism is simply another example of ethnocentrism, and the problem with ethnocentrism is that it works both ways. We are shocked at the traditional Eskimo practice of leaving the aged to perish in the snow, or the Yanamamö practice of killing unwanted female children; but the Japanese are appalled at our practice of leaving aged parents to die in nursing homes, and the San ("Bushmen") of the Kalahari could not begin to comprehend how Americans can permit poverty to exist in the United States in the midst of so much wealth.

Cultural relativism does *not* mean moral relativism—the position that one morality is as good as another. That view could quickly lead us to an "anything goes" position, in which wife-beating, scalping, cannibalism, and gas chambers are all equally acceptable. What cultural relativism does mean is that the practices of another society can be fully understood only in terms of its own norms and values. Thus, if we inquire why the Eskimo sometimes left old people to die in the cold, we find that they did so only in times when dwindling food supplies threatened the group with starvation. Under such conditions, those most likely to die were the weakest—the very young and the very old. The Eskimo chose to sacrifice the old, who represented a growing burden, in favor of the young, who represented the group's future. The aged went to their deaths willingly, for they had been taught since childhood that this was a sacrifice they might one day have to make—just as, years before, others might have made the same sacrifice for them. Once we have learned all this, we can better *understand* the Eskimo practice, even though we still may not *approve* of it. For the practical purposes of studying human behavior it is vital that we try, as far as possible, to remove the blinders of our own culture when we are looking at another. In the process, we may lose a certain self-righteousness about our own assumptions, and may even learn something more about our own culture, too.

Variation Within Cultures

There is variation not only among different cultures but also within any specific culture. As a general rule, there is less variation in traditional, preindustrial societies than in modern, industrialized ones. In traditional societies, which tend to be smaller, people live similar lives and share similar values, and cultural change takes place relatively slowly. Modern societies tend to be larger, to contain more diverse populations, and to experience more rapid and uneven cultural change.

No matter how much diversity there is within a culture, however, no culture is simply a random collection of elements. There has to be some degree of **cultural integration**—the tendency for norms, values, beliefs, practices, and other characteristics to complement one another. The reason is that a culture must "fit together" to a considerable extent if it is to survive at all. Thus, rapid and massive cultural change—occurring, for example, when one society is invaded, conquered, and colonized by another—can jeopardize a culture's very existence.

Real Culture and Ideal Culture

One common source of variation within a culture is the discrepancy that some-times exists between **ideal culture**—the norms and values a society adheres to in principle—and **real culture**—the norms and values a society adheres to in prac-tice. Americans, for example, claim to believe in the value of human equality, yet the United States contains people who are millionaires and people who are impoverished. Similarly, Americans are especially proud of their democratic rights, yet almost half the adults cannot be bothered to go to the polls in presi-dential elections. Americans also have a traditional norm that sex should take place only in the context of marriage, but the statistics on premarital and extra-marital intercourse show that this norm is violated by the great majority of Americans at one time or another.

A society is often able to overlook the contradictions between its real and ideal culture. As devout Buddhists, fishermen in Burma are forbidden to kill anything, including fish. Yet they must fish to live. How do they overcome the contradiction? What happens is that the fish are first caught and then "are merely put on the bank to dry after their long soaking in the river, and if they are foolish or ill-judged enough to die while undergoing the process, it is their own fault" (Lowie, 1940). Sometimes, however, the discrepancy between real culture and ideal culture creates serious social problems. For example, strain in the United States between the value of equality and the reality of slavery and then continuing racial discrimination led to a civil war and decades of tension before the society was brought into a condition of greater, but by no means complete, cultural integration. Other common practices that contradict the norms and values in ideal culture, such as crime and drug abuse, also pose severe problems—a topic we will discuss in detail in Chapter 6 ("Deviance").

Subcultures and Countercultures

Another source of variation and often strain within a culture arises from the existence of groups that do not participate fully in the dominant culture of the society.

Subcultures A **subculture** is a group that shares in the overall culture of the society but also has its own distinctive values, norms, and lifestyle. In North America, for example, there are subcultures of the young, of the rich and the poor, of different racial and ethnic groups, and of different regions. Smaller

Drawing by D. Reilly; © 1987 The New Yorker Magazine, Inc.

"On the Coast, you sit on the desk. In New York, you don't sit on the desk."

subcultures exist in the military, in prisons, on college campuses, among drug addicts, or among street-corner gangs. People in each of these subcultures tend to be ethnocentric in relation to other subcultures, for membership in a subculture colors one's view of reality. A member of a wealthy subculture of Wall Street stockbrokers doubtless has a different perspective on American social reality than someone from, say, a subculture of Hell's Angels. If the differences between subcultures are sufficiently great, the results may be social tension and conflict.

Countercultures   A **counterculture** is a subculture whose values, norms, and lifestyle are fundamentally at odds with the dominant culture. Such a group consciously rejects some of the most important norms of the wider society, and is usually proud of it. In North America, the Hare Krishna religious sect is one such counterculture: in religion, dress, values, behavior, and general lifestyle, its members challenge basic assumptions of the surrounding society. The movement has few adherents, however, and so has little cultural impact. In contrast, the youth movement of the 1960s attracted millions of participants and supporters. It challenged a whole range of treasured American norms and values, including those centered on conformity, avoidance of drugs, "proper" attire, hard work, materialism, wartime patriotism, white superiority, and sexual restrictiveness. A large counterculture inevitably generates strain in society, and indeed the 1960s were a time of great social turmoil.

Language

One of the most important of all human characteristics is our capacity to communicate with one another through language. Although apes can be taught to construct "sentences" by using hand signs or by manipulating physical objects, only human beings have spoken language. Language is a form of communication that differs radically from the kinds used by other species. Other animals can communicate with sounds, gestures, touch, and smell, but the meanings of these signals are fixed, and their use is limited to the immediate situation. With the exception of the artificial "languages" that gorillas and chimpanzees have been taught to use, the signals in animal communication are genetically predetermined responses to given conditions. These signals can be used to warn of danger, to indicate the presence of food, to claim territory, or to express fear, contentment, aggression, and sexual arousal—but little else. They cannot be combined in new ways to produce different or more complex information. A monkey can signal "food!" but not "bananas, tomorrow!"

Language, on the other hand, does not consist of fixed signals: it consists of learned symbols. A **symbol** is anything that can meaningfully represent something else. Gestures, facial expressions, drawings, and numbers are all symbols, but the most useful and flexible symbols are spoken or written words. Words are symbols for objects and concepts, and every human language consists of hundreds of thousands of words whose meaning is socially agreed upon. These words can be combined according to grammatical rules to express any idea of which the human mind is capable.

The Importance of Language

Language is the keystone of culture. Without it, culture could not exist, for without the medium of words, complex patterns of thought, emotion, knowledge, and belief could not be passed from individual to individual or generation to generation. When an animal dies, everything it has learned from experience perishes with it. But language gives human beings a history—it provides access to the social experience and accumulated knowledge of the generations that have gone before.

*"Damn it, Negelson, I like
the way you keep using
'awesome.'"*

Drawing by W. Miller; © 1985
The New Yorker Magazine, Inc.

Equally important, language enables us to give meaning to our existence. Without language, all but the most rudimentary forms of thought are impossible. With language, we can apply reason to the world. We can think logically from premises to conclusions: we can categorize; we can order our experience; we can contemplate the past and the future, the abstract and the hypothetical; we can formulate and utter ideas that are entirely new. Nearly all that we learn in human culture is learned through language in social interaction with others. It is through language that we become cultured and thus fully human.

Linguistic Relativity

Shortly after World War II, George Orwell published his futuristic novel *1984*, which depicted a totalitarian dictatorship where every aspect of social behavior was strictly controlled. The rulers of the state had even deliberately constructed a new language, Newspeak, whose vocabulary and grammar made it impossible for people to think certain thoughts:

> The word *free* still existed in Newspeak, but it could only be used in such statements as "This dog is free from lice" or "This field is free from weeds." It could not be used in the old sense of "politically free," or "intellectually free," since political and intellectual freedom no longer existed as concepts, and were therefore of necessity nameless. . . . Countless other words such as *honor, justice, morality, internationalism, democracy, science,* and *religion* had simply ceased to exist. A few blanket words covered them, and, in covering them, abolished them. All words grouping themselves around the concepts of liberty and equality, for instance, were contained in the single word *crimethink,* while all words grouping themselves around the concepts of objectivity and rationalism were contained in the single word *oldthink*. [Orwell, 1949]

Is it possible for the language we speak to structure our reality in this way? For centuries people assumed that all languages reflect reality in the same basic way and that words and concepts can be freely and accurately translated from one language to another. But in the course of this century some social scientists have raised the intriguing possibility that this assumption is unfounded. Studies of many of the thousands of languages in the world have revealed that they often interpret the same phenomenon quite differently, and several writers have suggested that languages do not so much mirror reality as structure it.

The Linguistic-Relativity Hypothesis

The **linguistic-relativity hypothesis** holds that speakers of a particular language must necessarily interpret the world through that language's unique vocabulary and grammar. This hypothesis was strongly propounded by two American linguists, Edward Sapir and his student Benjamin Whorf, and is sometimes known as the Sapir-Whorf hypothesis. Sapir (1929) argued forcefully that "the worlds in which different societies live are distinct worlds, not merely the same world with different labels attached."

In what ways do languages "slice up" and organize the world differently? The most common differences are in vocabulary: some languages have words for objects and concepts for which other languages have no words at all. The Aztecs, for example, used a single word for snow, frost, ice, and cold, and presumably tended to see these as essentially the same phenomenon. We have only one word for snow; the Eskimo have no general word for snow at all, but have over twenty words for different kinds of snow—snow on the ground, snow falling, snow drifting, and so on. Their language forces them to perceive these distinctions, while our language predisposes us to ignore them. The Koya of South India do not distinguish among snow, fog, and dew, but their language forces them to make distinctions among seven types of bamboo—distinctions that are important to them but that we would be unlikely to notice.

Even the color spectrum is dissected in different ways by different languages. The human eye can make between 7 million and 10 million different color discriminations, but all languages recognize only a handful of different colors. Most European languages recognize black, white, and at least six basic colors—red, orange, yellow, green, blue, and purple. Many languages, however, recognize only two colors: the Jalé of New Guinea, for example, divide the spectrum into the colors *hui* and *ziza*, representing the warm and cold colors of the spectrum, respectively. Other cultures, such as the Arawak of Surinam, the Toda of India, and the Baganda of Uganda, recognize only three colors. All these peoples see the same color spectrum, but they divide it up in their own ways (Berlin and Kay, 1969).

Other distinctions exist in the grammatical usages of different languages. For example, the language of the Hopi Indians does not recognize the categories of time and space that we do. The Hopi language lacks the equivalent of past, present, and future tenses, and organizes the universe instead into categories of "manifest" (everything that is or has been accessible to the physical senses) and "manifesting" (everything that is not physically accessible to the senses). If this concept is difficult to understand, it is because our language is poorly equipped to express it, just as the Hopi language has difficulty expressing our concepts of time and space.

The linguistic-relativity hypothesis does not imply that speakers of different languages are *incapable* of expressing the same ideas or seeing the world in the same way. What the hypothesis does suggest is that the language we speak *predisposes* us to make particular interpretations of reality. We need only consider the likely attitudes of a white child who is taught to call blacks "niggers" or of a black child who is taught to call whites "honkies" to see the truth of this statement. A different kind of example is the widespread use of euphemism and jargon to conceal rather than to reveal meaning. Advertisements tell of a car that is "affordable" and "previously owned," meaning expensive and used. Politicians speak of the need for "revenue enhancement," meaning a tax increase. Hospitals record a "negative patient-care outcome," meaning that the patient died. Corporations report a "negative contribution to profits," which means a loss. Military statements tell of "air support," which is bombing, and "pacification," which is making war. We have learned of an "energetic disassembly and rapid oxidation" at a nuclear power plant, which turned out to be an explosion and a fire. And the event in which hundreds of millions of living human beings might be annihilated is called a "nuclear exchange"—as if it involved no more than some sort of technological swap. All these linguistic usages are calculated to, and do, predispose us to see things in a less concerned way. Language and culture, then, are in constant interaction: culture influences the structure and use of language, and language can influence cultural interpretations of reality.

The Arts

Among the most striking of human endeavors are the **arts**—unique, skilled, and creative cultural products intended to inspire or entertain. Depending on the culture or subculture in which they are produced, the arts can take innumerable forms, ranging from jazz and tribal dance to vampire movies or disco light shows. Some art is high culture—classical music, ballet, sculpture, "masterpiece" paintings, and so on. Other art is part of popular culture—country music, breakdancing, romance paperbacks, TV "sitcoms," and the like.

The fundamental insight of the sociology of art is this: artistic expression tends to reflect the social and cultural concerns of the society in which it is produced. Religious societies produce predominantly religious art; traditionalist societies produce mainly traditional art; conformist societies produce mostly conformist art; diverse societies produce diverse art. The creation of art thus requires much more than a talented individual. Artistic production is a social process, for the form that art takes, and the amount of acceptance it wins, are deeply influenced by the surrounding cultural environment. The social process of artistic production can be illustrated by two examples: rock music and the abstract painting known as "modern art."

Rock Music

Rock music provides a good illustration of the interplay of social, cultural, and technological factors in the creation and acceptance of art. This form of popular culture emerged in a particular context—the United States and Britain in the prosperous years of the late 1950s, the era when the word "teenager" came into common usage for the first time, reflecting the emergence of a vast and unprecedented market of young people with money to spend on their own cultural interests. The new art form drew heavily on the existing tradition of popular music (especially rhythm and blues), and its subsequent growth and spread has been greatly influenced by available technologies: the amplified guitar, FM radio, techniques for creating and recording synthetic and layered sounds, and, more recently, cable TV and rock video.

Figure 2.10 *Rock music has always been most successful when it has had an aura of innovation and even rebellion. The career of an artist such as Billy Idol depends in large measure on the continuing ability to appear provocative.*

The cultural appeal of rock depends not only on its intrinsic musical qualities but also on an energy that derives from rock's aura of rebellion. Yet rock always risks becoming stale, and so, to maintain excitement, rock artists have continually replenished the music by using it to challenge social conventions. Sometimes they have done this through their lyrics, which spread messages (often inaudible or incomprehensible to an older generation) about sex, drugs, politics, materialism, or whatever issues are of current concern to the young. Sometimes the artists create excitement through behavior that is deliberately calculated to outrage the establishment. The history of rock is thus filled with such phenomena as Elvis Presley's pelvis; the Rolling Stones' surly arrogance; the Beatles' long hair; Jimi Hendrix's drug lyrics; Janis Joplin's raucous lifestyle; Alice Cooper's live python; Kiss's elaborate makeup; the Sex Pistols' profanities; Donna Summer's erotic innuendos; Boy George's ambiguous gender; Madonna's brash public persona; the Dead Kennedys' bad taste. In time, of course, all their art may eventually seem tame, to be relegated to the status of "golden oldies." But the irreverent, iconoclastic nature of rock tells us why this music, despite its huge international popularity, is created and performed primarily in the Western democracies. Rock flourishes only in a cultural atmosphere that can tolerate diversity of opinions and lifestyles. Authoritarian governments, ranging from communist regimes to right-wing dictatorships, loathe rock, which they uniformly brand as immoral and depraved—for they fear that it will introduce their young to subversive cultural influences. Thus, like any art form, rock's emergence, development, and spread can be fully understood only in its social context.

Modern Art

If, five centuries ago, Michelangelo had completely covered his surfaces with black paint and declared them art, his contemporaries would surely have considered him a lunatic; but when the American artist Frank Stella painted all-black pictures a few decades ago, he was hailed as a genius. The most striking aspect of contemporary high-culture painting—or "modern art," as it is usually known—is its heavy reliance on abstract forms. Paintings of this kind often command huge prices, even though most people in most cultures might not recognize them as works of art at all. How can this possibly be the case?

Figure 2.11 *The subject matter of art always reflects the characteristics and concerns of the society in which it is produced, and the most highly prized art is always that which the affluent are willing to support. Currently, the American elite places a high value on innovative abstract works—a trend that reflects the culture's emphasis on change, individualism, and diversity. A work such as* Door to the River, *by Willem de Kooning, is presently worth hundreds of thousands of dollars— although in time, of course, cultural tastes may change.*

Throughout the history of Western culture, a primary goal of painting was to depict the world as realistically as possible—to use techniques of color and perspective to reproduce three-dimensional reality on a flat surface. But in the nineteenth century, the invention of photography allowed anyone to reproduce the world more accurately than any artist ever could. So some Western artists began to redefine their purpose: it was now to express, rather than merely depict, reality. By the early twentieth century, artists such as Picasso were using ''unrealistic'' colors and distorted forms to reveal mood and other aspects of reality that might escape the camera lens. Eventually, some artists abandoned the attempt to paint reality altogether, and instead explored geometric and other abstractions. This trend reached a climax in the United States in the 1950s, when artists, primarily in New York, created the genre of ''abstract expressionism,'' which is characterized by huge canvases bearing mostly amorphous forms.

But why is abstraction the most prized form of art in the United States? By definition, the most prized art is the art people will pay the most for, and those who can pay the most are the elite. Indeed, the possession of unique and expensive works enhances the prestige of the owners, providing conspicuous proof of their elite position. In earlier centuries, artists were commissioned by the aristocratic or religious elite to paint specific subjects that decorated, and celebrated, their way of life. Modern art, by contrast, is much more democratic and capitalistic: painters paint whatever they wish to and the wealthy elite of today either do or do not buy it. Currently, what the elite value most in painting is novelty, a situation that reflects the culture's emphasis on diversity and innovation. Therefore, the most prized art is that which seems to achieve something new. The first artist to drip paint rather than apply it with a brush, or to adorn a canvas with household objects, or to slash it, or to paint it all one color, or to make it trapezoid rather than rectangular, or to scribble on it, or to paint on fur instead of canvas, is hailed as a major talent; the second artist to do so is ignored. (That is why a black canvas by Stella is worth tens of thousands of dollars and the identical canvas by you would be worth nothing.)

Prisoners of Culture?

Through its profound effects on our behavior, values, attitudes, and personalities, the culture into which we are born influences our sense of who we are and what our goals in life should be. But where does this leave human freedom? Are we simply the prisoners of our cultures?

The answer is no. Culture makes us, but we also make culture. Culture sets certain limitations on our options and behavior, but it cannot control us completely. If it did, there would be no cultural change, for we would all conform rigidly to existing norms and values. Culture provides general guidelines for behavior, but there are times when human beings must be creative, imaginative, and ready to improvise. The broad limits within which we do these things are determined by culture, but our specific acts often break with tradition and generate change. As individuals, few of us have the opportunity to modify culture; collectively, we do it all the time. Culture is created, sustained, and changed by the acts of human beings, and that is the measure of our freedom.

Summary

1. Culture consists of the entire way of life of a society, including both material and nonmaterial products. Culture and society are closely related and cannot exist independent of one another.

2. Our species has exceptional capacity for learning. Compared with reliance on instinct, culture provides a superior mode of adaptation to the environment. It enables us to adapt quickly to changed conditions, or even to change the environment to meet our needs.

3. Social scientists generally accept that human nature is extremely flexible, and is the product of an interaction between biological potentials and cultural learning.

4. Norms are shared rules or guidelines that prescribe appropriate behavior. Violations of folkways are more readily tolerated than violations of mores. Some acts are prohibited by taboos and some by laws. Norms are an important element in the system of social control through which a society ensures that its members behave in approved ways. Norms are formally or informally enforced through positive or negative sanctions.

5. Values are shared ideas about what is good or desirable. Norms express social values. The United States has a unique set of important values, some of them contradictory or changing. Self-fulfillment is emerging as an important new value.

6. Cultures vary widely and each is unique. Ecological factors provide environmental influences on every culture. Some cultural variation can be explained in terms of the functions that particular elements (such as Eskimo hospitality) serve in maintaining the social system. Some cultural variation (such as the South African political system) can be explained as the product of conflict over scarce resources.

7. There are a number of general cultural universals, but no specific practices are found in every society. We tend to be ethnocentric toward other cultures, judging them in terms of our own standards. It is important that a social scientist adopt a position of cultural relativism and attempt to understand other cultures and subcultures in their own terms.

8. The norms, values, beliefs, and practices of a culture tend to be integrated, so changes in one area of culture often provoke changes in other areas. One source of cultural strain is the gap between real and ideal culture. Strain can also arise from differences between the dominant culture and subcultures or countercultures.

9. Language is fundamental to society and culture; it permits the transmission of culture and the interpretation of reality. The linguistic-relativity hypothesis holds that different languages predispose speakers to interpret reality in different ways.

10. The creation and acceptance of art is a social process that reflects features of the surrounding society, as the cases of rock music and modern art illustrate.

11. We are not the prisoners of culture. Culture shapes us, but collectively we, in turn, shape and change the culture we pass on from generation to generation.

Important Terms

culture (29)

material culture (29)

nonmaterial culture (29)

norms (32)

folkways (32)

mores (32)

taboo (32)

law (33)

social control (33)

sanctions (33)

internalization of norms (34)

values (34)

self-fulfillment (35)

ecological approach (36)

cultural universals (39)

ethnocentrism (40)

cultural relativism (41)

cultural integration (42)

ideal culture (43)

real culture (43)

subculture (43)

counterculture (44)

symbol (44)

linguistic-relativity hypothesis (45)

arts (46)

CHAPTER **3**

Society

We are the ultimate social animals. The quality we call "humanity" can be achieved only through social living, for there is no such thing as a person whose personality and behavior have not developed within some human society. We take social living so much for granted that we sometimes overlook the immense influence society has on us. But in the complex interaction between the individual and society, the latter is usually dominant. Society precedes us and survives us. Our society gives content, direction, and meaning to our lives, and we, in turn, in countless ways, reshape the society that we leave to the next generation.

We are not social animals just because we happen to find social living convenient. Without society we could not exist. No infant could reach maturity without the care and protection of other people, and no adult could remain alive without using the vast store of information about the world that has been learned and passed on through society. Almost everything that we do is social in some sense—learned from others, done with others, directed toward others. Some very rare individuals try to escape from society, yet even they carry with them into their isolation the techniques, the ideas, and the identities they have learned from others. Hermits in their caves live with society in their memories.

What exactly is a society? Several conditions must be met before people can be said to be living in one. First, they must occupy a common territory. Second, they must share the same government or other political authority. Third, they must to some extent have a common culture and a sense of membership in, and commitment to, the same group. We may say, then, that a **society** is a population that occupies the same territory, is subject to the same political authority, and participates in a common culture. In the modern world, most societies are nation-states—that is, countries like Canada or China. Societies and nation-states are not necessarily identical, however, as many nation-states include smaller societies within their borders. Several Latin American countries, for example, contain tribal societies of indigenous Indian peoples who have not been integrated into the larger society.

Many other animals are also social—such as ants, herrings, geese, and elephants. But these species depend for their survival primarily on unlearned ("instinctive") patterns of behavior. As a result, different societies of any one species, be they termites or zebras, are virtually identical, with little difference in the social behavior of the members from one society to another. When you have seen one nest of a particular termite species, you have for most purposes seen all the nests of that species. Human societies, on the other hand, are astonishingly diverse, because they are created by human beings themselves and are learned and modified by each new generation. Consequently, every human society is different—so different that a person suddenly transplanted from, say, the United States to a jungle tribe of Brazil (or vice versa) would be mystified by the new social environment and unable to behave appropriately. Each society thus presents a unique and exciting challenge to the sociologist's understanding.

In this chapter we shall look at two main topics. First, we shall examine the social structure that underlies all human societies. Second, we shall consider some basic types of societies, showing how and why they differ from one another. In particular, we shall examine the radical differences between modern industrialized societies and the traditional, preindustrial societies that they are rapidly replacing all over the world.

Social Structure

All complex things, from bacteria to planets, have a structure—that is, they consist of a set of interrelated parts. The structure of a building, for example, consists of a floor, walls, a roof, an entrance, and probably such fittings as windows and utility lines. All buildings have much the same basic structure, although the character of any particular building—such as a cottage, a warehouse, a shack, or a high-rise office tower—depends on the precise nature of its parts and their relationship to one another.

Sociologists sometimes find it helpful to use the metaphor of "structure" when they analyze human societies. A society is not just a chaotic collection of randomly interacting people: there is an underlying regularity, or pattern, to social behavior in any society. To sociologists, therefore, **social structure** is the pattern of relationships among the basic components in a social system. These components provide the framework for all human societies, although the precise character of the components and the relationships among them vary from one society to another. The most important components of social structure are statuses, roles, groups, and institutions. These concepts are of fundamental importance in sociology, and you will encounter them throughout this book.

Statuses

Figure 3.1 *There are two kinds of social status— those that are* ascribed *to people on grounds over which they have no control, and those that are* achieved *by individuals through personal effort. The status of the queen of Great Britain is an ascribed one: Elizabeth II has the status because she was next in line of succession to her father, the late king. The status of prime minister of Great Britain is an achieved one: Margaret Thatcher has the status because she won the leadership of her party and a national election. Of course, both the queen and the prime minister have other statuses as well—for example, each has the ascribed status of middle-aged woman, and each has the achieved status of wife.*

In ordinary speech, "status" usually refers to prestige, but the sociological use of the word is different. To the sociologist, a **status** is a position in society. Everybody occupies a number of statuses—positions such as student, carpenter, son, old person, senator, and so on. A person's status indicates where that individual "fits" in society and how he or she should relate to other people. The status of daughter, for example, determines the occupant's basic relationships with other family members; the status of corporation president determines the occupant's basic relationships with employees, shareholders, or presidents of other corporations.

Naturally, a person can have several statuses simultaneously, but one of them, usually an occupational status, tends to be the most significant. This becomes a **master status,** the position most important in establishing an individual's social identity. Generally, a person's various statuses fit together fairly smoothly, but some people experience **status inconsistency,** a situation in which aspects of an individual's status or statuses appear contradictory. For example, black professionals find that they sometimes receive honor for their occupational status but at other times suffer prejudice because of their racial status. Successful blacks who move to affluent suburbs sometimes find that visiting white salespeople assume they are household servants (Williams, 1985).

In fact, there is a crucial distinction between statuses that society arbitrarily attaches to us and those that we can earn (or lose) by our own actions. An **ascribed status** is one that is attached to people on grounds over which they have no control. Whether you are young or old, male or female, or black or white, for example, there is not much you can do about it. On the other hand, an **achieved status** is one that depends to some extent on characteristics over which the individual has some control. At least partly through your own efforts you can become a spouse, a college graduate, a convict, or a member of a different religion. Sometimes an ascribed status can make it difficult for the individual to earn an achieved status. For example, if you are Hispanic and female (ascribed statuses), you will find it more difficult to become president of the United States (an achieved status) than if you were an "Anglo" male.

In most societies there is considerable inequality among different statuses. The person who has the status of Supreme Court justice, for example, enjoys more wealth, power, and prestige than the person who has the status of janitor. A **social class** is a category of people of roughly equivalent status in an unequal society. The members of any particular social class enjoy greater access to the society's wealth and other resources than do people with lower statuses, but have less access than people with higher statuses. The fact that statuses may be ranked unequally has profound consequences for both the individual and society, as we shall see in later chapters.

Roles

An actor plays many different parts, or roles, whose content depends on the demands of the particular character being portrayed. The sociological concept of "role" is derived directly from the theater, and refers to the part or parts a person plays in society. Specifically, a **role** is a set of expected behavior patterns, obligations, and privileges attached to a particular social status. The distinction between status and role is a simple one: you *occupy* a status, but you *play* a role (Linton, 1936). Status and role are thus two sides of the same coin.

College professor, for example, is a social status. Attached to this status is a professorial role, defined by social norms prescribing how the occupier of the status should behave. The status of professor is a fixed position in society, but the role is more flexible, for different occupants of the status actually play their roles in somewhat different ways. In practice, a single status may involve a number of roles. The status of college professor includes one role as teacher, one role as colleague to other professors, one role as researcher, and perhaps other roles, such as student adviser or writer of scholarly articles.

The roles we play in life thus depend on the statuses we happen to occupy at a given time. If you are talking to your professor as a student, you will behave differently than you might if, years later, you return to visit the campus as a wealthy benefactor. Similarly, we respond to people according to the roles they play for us. If someone playing the role of physician asks you to undress, you will comply, but if the same person asks you to undress when playing the role of host at dinner, you will probably respond quite differently.

Figure 3.2 *Any status carries with it a number of different roles. Your status of student, for example, requires that you adopt somewhat different roles in your interaction with people who have other statuses and roles. Although student is only one of your statuses, it is probably your most important status, or master status, at present.*

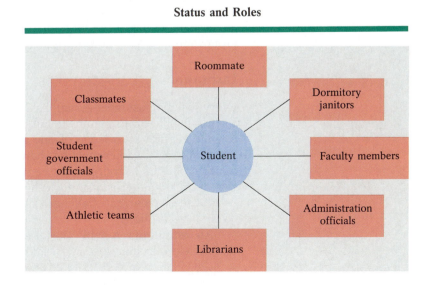

Status and Roles

The fact that a person may have several different statuses, each with a number of roles attached, can often cause difficulty and confusion in social relationships. One such problem is **role conflict,** a situation in which two or more of a person's roles have contradictory requirements. For example, police officers sometimes find themselves in a position where they ought to arrest their own children; in such circumstances, the role expectations of parent and police officer can be at odds with one another. But for the most part our role-playing ensures the smooth and predictable course of social interaction. Roles enable us to structure our own behavior along socially expected lines. We can anticipate the behavior of others in most situations, and we can fashion our own actions accordingly.

Groups

Most social behavior takes place within and among groups that are constantly being formed and re-formed. A **group** is a collection of people interacting together in an orderly way on the basis of shared expectations about each other's behavior. Put another way, a group is a number of persons whose statuses and roles are interrelated. A group therefore differs from a mere aggregate of people who just happen to be in the same place at the same time, such as pedestrians in a busy street. Because human beings are essentially cooperative social animals, groups are a vital part of social structure.

The distinctive characteristics of any society depend largely on the nature and activities of the groups that it contains. Groups can be classified into two main types, primary and secondary. A **primary group** consists of a small number of people who interact over a relatively long period on a direct, intimate basis. The members know one another personally and interact in a manner that is informal and has at least some emotional depth. Examples of this kind of group are families, cliques of friends and peers, and close neighbors. These groups are important building blocks of social structure; in fact, some small-scale, traditional societies are organized almost entirely around family or kinship groups.

In contrast, a **secondary group** consists of a number of people who interact on a relatively temporary, anonymous, and impersonal basis. The members either do not know one another personally, or, at best, know one another only in terms of particular formal roles (such as mail carrier or math teacher) rather than as whole people. Secondary groups are usually established to serve specific purposes, and people are generally less emotionally committed to them than they are to their primary groups. Examples of secondary groups are formal organizations such as corporations, political parties, or government bureaucracies. These large organizations are not found in the simplest of human societies, but they are increasingly important in large modern societies. (Both primary and secondary groups are discussed in more detail in Chapter 5, "Social Groups.")

Institutions

Every society must meet certain basic social needs if it is to survive and provide a satisfying life for its members. For example, children must be raised and cared for; the cultural knowledge of one generation must be passed on to the next; important social values must be shared and upheld; social order must be maintained; goods and services must be produced. Over time, the members of each society create patterns of thought and action that provide an appropriate solution for these recurrent challenges. These patterns of behavior are what sociologists call institutions.

An **institution** is a stable cluster of values, norms, statuses, roles, and groups that develops around a basic social need. (Figure 3.3 lists major institutions of modern societies, with examples of each of these elements.) Thus, the family institution provides for the care of children. The educational institution transmits cultural knowledge to the young. The religious institution provides a set of shared values and the rituals that reaffirm them. The political institution allocates power and maintains order. The economic institution provides goods and services. These major institutions, too, contain smaller units within themselves: for example, baseball is an activity within the overarching institution of sport; the hospital is part of the overall medical institution; the prison is an aspect of the legal institution; and so on.

Characteristics of Institutions   Institutions such as the family, science, religion, and medicine may seem very different, but in fact the institutions of any society usually share certain common features.

1. *Institutions tend to be resistant to change.* Patterns of social behavior become "institutionalized," or securely established, only when they have been reinforced by custom and tradition to the point where they are accepted almost without question. People tend to resent and resist any attack on the institutions they know. Imagine, for example, the likely response in North America to a serious attempt to abolish the family, to end compulsory schooling, to replace existing churches with new cults, or to apply the principles of communism to the economy.

Figure 3.3 *Institutions arise over time as people develop social responses to the particular needs of their society. Each institution is a stable cluster of values, norms, statuses, roles, and groups; and each provides an established pattern of thought and action that offers a solution to recurrent demands of social living. This table lists the major institutions that have been created to serve the needs of modern society, with examples of each of the elements involved.*

Major Social Institutions

Institution	Some Social Needs	Some Values	Some Norms	Some Statuses/Roles	Some Groups
Family	Regulate sexual behavior; provide care for children.	Marital fidelity.	Have only one spouse.	Husband; grandmother.	Kinship group.
Education	Transmit cultural knowledge to the young.	Intellectual curiosity.	Attend school.	Teacher; student.	High school clique; college seminar.
Religion	Share and reaffirm community values and solidarity.	Belief in God.	Attend regular worship.	Rabbi; cardinal.	Synod; congregation.
Medical system	Take care of the sick.	Good health.	Save life if possible.	Physician; patient.	Hospital staff; ward of patients.
Economic system	Produce and distribute goods and services.	Free enterprise.	Maximize profits.	Accountant; vendor.	Corporate board; labor union.
Political system	Distribute power; maintain order.	Freedom.	Vote by secret ballot.	Senator; lobbyist.	Legislature; political party.
Science	Investigate social and natural world.	Unbiased search for truth.	Conduct research.	Physicist; anthropologist.	Research team; science society.
Military	Aggress or defend against enemies of the state.	Discipline.	Follow orders.	General; marine.	Platoon; army division.
Legal system	Maintain social control.	Fair trial.	Inform suspects of their rights.	Judge; lawyer.	Jury; cell mates.
Sport	Provide for recreation and exercise.	Winning.	Play by the rules.	Umpire; coach.	Baseball team; fan club.

2. *Institutions tend to be interdependent.* A society's major institutions tend to uphold similar values and norms, to reflect compatible goals and priorities, and to benefit or penalize the same groups or interests. Thus a society with a capitalist economy is likely to have a political system that supports capitalism, a major religion or other belief system that endorses free enterprise, an educational system that encourages competition and teaches the superiority of capitalism, and so on. Conversely, a society with a socialist economy will tend to have institutions that mesh with that particular system.

3. *Institutions tend to change together.* When institutions do change, they rarely do so in isolation. Because institutions are so interdependent, significant modifications in one must usually be accompanied by changes in others if cultural integration is to be maintained. This is especially true of changes in the economy, for the way a society makes its living has multiple effects on almost everything else. For example, the Industrial Revolution of the eighteenth and nineteenth centuries resulted in sweeping changes in every other institution—families became smaller, government expanded, people stayed in school longer, traditional religion lost influence, science developed rapidly, and so on.

4. *Institutions tend to be the site of major social problems.* Because institutions are centered on basic social needs, any significant institutional failure is likely to be regarded as a serious social problem. For example, unemployment is a social problem of the economy; marital breakdown is a problem of the family; high crime rates are a problem of the legal institution. Social problems that are located in social institutions are not easily solved: there are some groups that benefit and some that suffer under any institutional arrangement, so there is always controversy over the need for change, as well as over the rate and direction it should take.

Functionalist and Conflict Approaches   We have seen in earlier chapters that functionalist and conflict theories provide two rather different ways of examining large-scale aspects of society. This is especially true when it comes to their approaches to institutions.

Functionalist theorists are apt to ask what functions, or effects, a given institution has in maintaining the social system. They recognize that stability is essential if a society is to survive, and see institutions as regulating and channeling human behavior into predictable patterns that help the social system work smoothly. Functionalists are inclined to regard any failings of institutional arrangements as dysfunctions—negative effects that must be corrected to bring the system into balance once more. Conflict theorists, on the other hand, are inclined to ask who benefits from existing institutional arrangements. They are generally more critical of institutions, arguing that if they maintain order, they thereby support the status quo and the "haves" against the "have nots"; if they channel behavior, they thereby inhibit freedom. Conflict theorists are likely to see failings in institutions as the result of power struggles among various interests—struggles that may bring about needed changes in the long run.

As we shall see in later chapters when we examine specific institutions in detail, there is often validity to both the functionalist and conflict approaches, for each addresses a different aspect of society. Institutions do, indeed, make life stable and predictable by providing for central human needs; but they also tend to favor one group over another and to restrict choice—and thereby individual liberty. This dual nature of society—as something that makes human life possible, stable, and worthwhile, but that at the same time channels human behavior and imposes limits on our freedom—is an enduring sociological paradox.

Types of Societies

If we compressed the entire history of life on the planet into a single year, the first modern human being would not appear until December 31 at about 11:53 P.M., and the first civilizations would emerge only about a minute before the end of the year. Yet our cultural achievements in the brief time that we have occupied the planet have been remarkable. Some 15,000 years ago our ancestors were practicing religious rituals and painting superb pictures on the walls of their caves. Around 11,000 years ago, some human groups began to domesticate animals and plants, thereby freeing themselves from total dependence on the food that they could hunt and gather. About 6,000 years ago people began to live in cities, to specialize in different forms of labor, to divide into social classes, and to create distinct political and economic institutions. Within a few thousand years empires were created, linking previously isolated groups and bringing millions of people under centralized rule. Advanced agricultural technologies improved the productivity of the land, resulting in growing populations and the emergence of large nation-states. A mere 250 years ago the Industrial Revolution began, thrusting us into the modern world of factories and computers, jet aircraft and nuclear reactors, instant global communications and terrifying military technologies.

These historical developments are part of a general trend of **sociocultural evolution,** the tendency for societies' social structures and cultures to grow more complex over time. This process has some similarities with biological evolution. Like a living organism, a society has to subsist by adapting to its environment in order to exploit food and other resources. Various societies have used different subsistence strategies, and those societies that have found more productive strategies have tended to grow larger and more complex, often enjoying their success at the expense of societies using more primitive technologies. This process of sociocultural evolution is not in any sense a "law" applicable to all societies. Some societies have evolved further and faster than others; some have become "stuck" at a particular level; some have disintegrated and disappeared; and all have changed in ways that are unique to themselves. Sociocultural evolution represents only a widespread pattern that has been observed in the historical and archaeological evidence (Parsons, 1966; Lenski and Lenski, 1987).

As we indicated in the previous chapter, the **ecological approach** is one that analyzes social and cultural elements in the context of the total environment in which a society exists. By applying this approach to different societies that have existed in the course of sociocultural evolution, we can explain much of the variation in their social structure and culture. In fact, although thousands of often dissimilar societies have existed since the beginning of human history, they can be broadly classified into five basic types according to the subsistence strategies they have used to exploit the environment—hunting and gathering, pastoralism, horticulture, agriculture, or industrialism. Additionally, a new, sixth type of society is beginning to emerge in the most technologically advanced parts of the world: the postindustrial society.

At each stage in this evolutionary process, social structure and culture grow more complex. The reason is that a more efficient subsistence strategy allows a society to create a greater amount of **surplus wealth,** that is, more goods and services than are necessary to meet their producers' basic needs. As a result, an increasing proportion of the population is freed from the job of food production and can play a whole range of other social roles instead. The result is a significant increase in the **division of labor,** the specialization by individuals or groups in particular economic activities. In the most technologically simple societies, virtually the entire able-bodied population is engaged in food production. But in the most technologically advanced societies, less than 5 percent of the work force can feed the rest, enabling them to pursue a variety of occupational, social, and cultural opportunities (Lenski, 1966; M. Harris, 1979, 1980).

Figure 3.4 *The San people of the Namibian desert are one of the few hunting and gathering peoples that have survived into the modern world. They live in small nomadic groups based mainly on kinship. While we might regard their life as a hard one, the San feel very few "needs," and are able to satisfy them with only a few hours' work each day. Their way of life is doomed, however, for their society is being influenced and absorbed by the industrializing societies of southern Africa.*

Hunting and Gathering Societies

As the name implies, a **hunting and gathering society** is one relying for its subsistence on such wild animals and vegetation as its members can hunt or gather. All societies used this subsistence strategy from the dawn of human existence until only a few thousand years ago, and even today there are still a handful of isolated peoples, such as the Aranda aborigines of the central Australian desert, who retain this way of life.

An immediate consequence of this strategy is that hunting and gathering societies usually consist of very small, scattered groups. The reason is simple: the environment cannot support a large concentration of people who rely on whatever food they can find or catch from one day to the next. Hunting and gathering peoples therefore live in small primary groups that rarely exceed forty members. Even so, each group may require several hundred square miles of territory to support itself, so contact between groups is brief and infrequent. The groups are based on kinship, with most members being related by ancestry or marriage. In fact, the family is almost the only distinct institution in these societies. Religious institutions are rudimentary. The religions of these peoples almost never include a belief in a powerful god or gods who are active in human affairs; instead, they tend to see the world as populated by unseen spirits that must be taken account of, but not necessarily worshiped. Political institutions are absent: statuses in these societies are essentially equal, and although there is sometimes a part-time headman with very limited authority, most decisions are arrived at through group discussion.

Actually, there are very few statuses in these societies except for those based on sex, age, or kinship. The roles performed by men and women, by the young and the old, and by various kin are somewhat different, but there are no other specialized roles. Most members of the group do much the same things most of the time, and as a result of their common life experiences, they share almost identical values and beliefs.

Hunting and gathering peoples are constantly on the move, and since possessions would be a hindrance to them, they own very few goods. Thus no one can acquire wealth because there is no wealth to be acquired. Individuals who find food, the only significant resource in these societies, are expected to share it with the whole community. Intergroup fighting is extremely uncommon among hunters and gatherers, partly because they have so little in the way of material goods to fight about. Yet, contrary to popular belief, the life of these groups is not usually one of constant hardship on the brink of starvation. Their needs are simple and easily satisfied, and they spend less time working for their living than the average inhabitants of any other type of society. They are among the most leisured people on earth.

The use of hunting and gathering as a subsistence strategy thus has a very strong influence on social structure and culture. The social structure of these societies is necessarily very simple, and their cultures cannot become elaborate and diversified.

Pastoral Societies

A **pastoral society** is one relying for its subsistence primarily on domesticated herd animals. The first pastoral societies emerged between 10,000 and 12,000 years ago, when some hunting and gathering groups began to capture, breed, and tend species of wild animals they had previously hunted. This strategy has since been adopted by many peoples living in deserts or other regions that are not suited to the cultivation of plants, but which contain animals—such as goats or sheep—that can be readily tamed and used as a food source. Many pastoral societies still exist in the modern world, particularly in Africa and in the Middle East.

Pastoralism is a much more reliable and productive strategy than hunting and gathering. It assures a steady food supply, and the size of the herds can be increased over time through careful animal husbandry. An important result is that societies can grow much larger, perhaps to include hundreds or even thousands of people. Equally significant, the greater productivity of this strategy allows pastoralists to accumulate a surplus of livestock and food. Through such means as trade, this surplus can be converted into other forms of wealth, such as wine, weapons, or gold—which can be used, in turn, to acquire power. For the first time, some individuals can become more powerful than others and can even pass on their status to their descendants. Patterns of hereditary chieftainship begin to appear, as powerful and wealthy families are able to secure their positions in the society.

Pastoralists are usually nomadic because they must constantly take their herds to new grazing grounds. As a result, their material possessions are few in number, but are more elaborate than those of hunting and gathering peoples because they can be carried by animals. Cultural artifacts in these societies therefore consist of items that are easily transportable—tents, woven carpets, simple utensils, jewelry, and so on. Their nomadic way of life often brings pastoralists into contact with other groups. One consequence is the development of systematic trading; a second is that disputes over grazing rights frequently lead to intergroup fighting. Slavery, unknown in hunting and gathering societies, makes its appearance as captives in battle are put to work for their conquerors.

Figure 3.5 *Pastoralists in Kenya rest their goat herd. Typically, pastoralists take their herds from one place to another in search of grazing and water, using some of their animals for meat and milk. Surplus animals are sold or traded for other needed items. Not all pastoralists, however, are nomadic; those that live in areas that can support continuous grazing are able to form small, settled communities.*

Pastoral peoples tend to develop a belief that is found in very few religions: they commonly believe in a god or gods who take an active interest in human affairs and look after the people who worship them. This belief seems to have been suggested by the pastoralists' experience of the relationship between themselves and their flocks. The few modern religions based on this view of the relationship between human beings and a god—Judaism and its offshoots, Christianity and Islam—originated among pastoral peoples. (In fact, the word "pastor" originally meant shepherd.)

The subsistence strategy of pastoral societies thus provides distinctive social and cultural opportunities and limitations. Populations become larger, political and economic institutions begin to develop, and both social structure and culture become more complex.

Horticultural Societies

A **horticultural society** is one relying for its subsistence primarily on the hoe cultivation of domesticated plants. These societies also first appeared between 10,000 and 12,000 years ago, when some hunters and gatherers began to deliberately sow, tend, and harvest edible vegetation. Horticulturalists are essentially gardeners, working small plots by hand with hoes or digging sticks. Unlike pastoralists, they live a relatively settled life, although they must periodically move their gardens or villages short distances. Their subsistence strategy is typically based on a "slash and burn" technology, in which they clear areas of land, burn the vegetation they have cut down for use as fertilizer, raise crops for two or three years until the soil is exhausted, and then repeat the process elsewhere. Horticulture is really an alternative to pastoralism, and is much more likely to be adopted if the soil and climate favor crop cultivation. Many horticultural societies still exist in Africa, Asia, South America, and Australasia.

Like pastoralism, horticulture is much more efficient than hunting and gathering because it provides an assured, expandable food supply and the possibility of a surplus. Again, this surplus allows some wealthy individuals and families to become more powerful than others, and in advanced horticultural societies, political institutions emerge in the form of hereditary chieftainships. A food surplus also means that some people can do work other than cultivation, so specialized new statuses and roles appear, such as those of shaman, trader, or craft worker. Because they live in relatively permanent settlements, horticulturalists can create more elaborate cultural artifacts than can hunters and gatherers or pastoralists. They can produce, for example, houses, thrones, or large stone sculptures.

Figure 3.6 *Lacking draft animals, horticulturalists tend their gardens by hand, a process that limits the productivity of the land. Because the soil may quickly become exhausted, many horticultural peoples must either leave some of their gardens fallow every two or three years or find new areas for cultivation. Horticulturalists in the Amazon use a "slash and burn" technology: they cut down the vegetation, burn it, grow crops until the land is exhausted, and then repeat the process elsewhere. Horticulture permits relatively settled communities, and it can also provide enough food to support fairly large populations in the same area.*

In the more advanced horticultural societies, political and economic institutions become well developed as conquest and trade link various villages together, and populations can run to several thousand people.

The emergence of some of humanity's grimmer endeavors is also closely associated with horticulture. Intertribal fighting and blood feuds, for example, are fairly common in horticultural societies, and the rare practices of cannibalism, headhunting, and human sacrifice are found almost exclusively in a few of the more aggressive societies of this type. The emergence of human sacrifice coincides with the tendency of advanced horticultural peoples to believe in capricious gods who must be worshiped and appeased, a development that is probably associated with their own experience of chieftainship and social inequality.

The use of the horticultural strategy thus produces a set of distinctive consequences. It permits a settled way of life with relatively large populations, a situation that in turn encourages more complex social structures and cultures that are richer in material artifacts.

Agricultural Societies

An **agricultural society** is one relying for its subsistence primarily on the cultivation of crops through the use of plows and draft animals. The use of the plow, which was invented about 6,000 years ago, greatly improves the productivity of the land; it brings to the surface nutrients that have sunk out of reach of the roots of plants, and it returns weeds to the soil to act as fertilizers. The same land can be cultivated almost continuously, and fully permanent settlements become possible. The use of animal power to pull the plow makes one agriculturalist far more productive than several horticulturalists. As a result, large fields replace small gardens, food output is greatly increased, and a substantial surplus can be produced.

The potential size of agricultural societies is much greater than that of horticultural or pastoral communities; it can run to several million people. A substantial minority of this population does not have to work the land and can engage instead in highly specialized, full-time roles (such as those of blacksmith, barber, artisan), most of which are conveniently performed among concentrations of other people. Agricultural subsistence thus allows for the establishment of cities, consisting essentially of people who directly or indirectly trade their specialized skills for the agricultural products of those who still work the land. The society itself often consists of several such cities and their hinterlands, loosely welded together through periodic shows of force by those in central authority.

Figure 3.7 *Agriculture can be a fairly productive strategy. Agriculturalists, like this Asian peasant, cultivate the soil with plows instead of hoes and digging sticks. Nutrients are thus returned to the soil, and the land can be continuously cultivated year after year. The relatively high productivity of agriculture frees a large part of the population from the need to toil on the land, permitting them to engage in other specialized roles.*

As political institutions grow much more elaborate, power becomes concentrated in the hands of a single individual, and a hereditary monarchy tends to develop. The power of the monarch is usually absolute, literally involving the power of life and death over his or her subjects. In the more advanced agricultural societies the state emerges for the first time as a separate social institution with an elaborate court and government bureaucracy. Distinct social classes also make their appearance in virtually all agricultural societies. The wealth of these societies is almost always very unequally shared, with a small landowning minority of nobles enjoying the surplus produced by a working majority of peasants; one example of this pattern was the old feudal system of Europe. Religion also becomes a separate social institution, with full-time officials, temples, and considerable political influence. The religions of agricultural societies often include a belief in a "family" of gods, one of whom, the "high god," is regarded as more powerful than other, lesser gods. This belief probably stems from people's experience of different levels of political authority, ranging from local rulers to the absolute monarch. A distinct economic institution also develops; trade becomes more elaborate, and money comes into use. The need for accurate records of crop harvests, taxation, and government transactions encourages the invention of some system of writing, which appears in virtually all advanced agricultural societies.

Agricultural societies tend to be almost constantly at war and sometimes engage in systematic empire-building. These conditions demand an effective military organization, and permanent armies appear for the first time. The need for efficient transport and communications in these large societies leads to the development of roads and navies, and previously isolated communities are brought into contact with one another. The relative wealth of agricultural societies and their settled way of life permit surplus resources to be invested in new cultural artifacts—paintings and statues, public buildings and monuments, palaces and stadiums.

A society relying on agriculture as a subsistence strategy thus has a far more complex social structure and culture than any of the less evolved types of societies. The number of statuses and roles multiplies, population size increases, cities appear, new institutions emerge, social classes arise, political and economic inequality becomes built into the social structure, and culture becomes much more diversified.

Industrial Societies

An **industrial society** is one relying for its subsistence primarily on mechanized production. Originating in England in the Industrial Revolution about 250 years ago, this mode of production proved so immensely successful that it has since spread all over the world, absorbing, transforming, or destroying other types of society in the process.

Industrialism is based on the application of scientific knowledge to the technology of production, enabling new energy sources to be harnessed and permitting machines to do the work that was previously done by people or animals. Because inventions and discoveries build upon one another, the rate of technological innovation in industrial societies is swift. New technologies—such as the steam engine, the internal combustion engine, electrical power, or atomic energy—tend to stimulate changes in the economy and other institutions. Unlike preindustrial societies, therefore, industrial societies are in a continual state of rapid social change.

Industrialism is a highly efficient subsistence strategy, for it allows a small minority to feed the rest of the people. Industrial societies can thus become very large, with populations running into tens or even hundreds of millions. In fact, populations grow very rapidly in the early stages of industrialization because

Figure 3.8 *Industrial societies rely on advanced technology and mechanized production for their subsistence. This strategy is so efficient and produces so much wealth that industrialism is rapidly becoming the dominant mode of production all over the world. Despite its many advantages, however, industrialism poses a host of new problems to human society, ranging from pollution to overpopulation.*

people live longer as a result of better health and living standards. (In more advanced industrial societies population size tends to stabilize as birth control becomes popular.) Industrial societies are also highly urbanized, with the bulk of the population living in or around cities, where most jobs are located. In this mass environment, organizations such as corporations and government bureaucracies flourish, and more and more social life takes place in secondary groups rather than primary groups.

Industrialism has a dramatic effect on institutions. The economy, of course, becomes vast, complex, and pervasive in its effects on the whole society. The family loses many of its earlier functions; it is no longer a unit of economic production, nor does it have the main responsibility for the education of the young. The influence of traditional religion also shrinks, for people no longer share similar life experiences and consequently hold many different and competing values and beliefs. Science, however, emerges as a new and important social institution, because technological innovation depends on scientific knowledge. Similarly, education becomes a major institution, for an industrial society requires mass literacy. Other institutions, such as law, sport, medicine, and the military, grow more elaborate.

Another effect of industrialism is, on the whole, to eventually reduce social inequality. In the early stages of industrialism there is usually a yawning gap between the incomes of the rich and the poor as the rural peasantry is transformed into an urban work force, often under the most wretched conditions; but thereafter there is usually a steady reduction in inequalities of social class. Government becomes more representative as hereditary monarchies pass away, generally to be replaced by more representative political institutions.

Industrial societies have frequently used their superior military technology to invade and even colonize preindustrial societies. But they are not as inclined to fight one another: although preparedness for war may reach new heights of intensity, actual outbreaks of warfare among industrial societies are relatively infrequent. The reason may lie more in self-interest than in pacifism: warfare can be ruinous for an advanced industrial society, largely because it involves such devastating weaponry and such severe economic dislocation. Indeed, were there to be a nuclear war, it is doubtful if the major industrial societies would survive at all.

Industrial society is rapidly becoming the dominant form in the modern world. Its huge surplus wealth makes possible extraordinary material conveniences and a far more heterogeneous culture than any found in preindustrial societies. But this success has caused a variety of new problems. Industrial societies have to contend with the ravaging of the environment through pollution, resource depletion, and species extinction; the destruction of traditional values and communities; the disruption of kinship systems; mass anonymity in mushrooming cities; the threat of nuclear war; and a breakneck rate of social change that constantly threatens to disorganize the existing social structure.

Postindustrial Societies

There is no reason to suppose that sociocultural evolution has come to an end with the development of industrial societies. But what lies beyond? Predicting the future is always a risky exercise, but many sociologists are convinced that the most advanced industrial nations, such as the United States, Canada, Japan, Sweden, Switzerland, and West Germany, are in transition to a new societal type. This is the **postindustrial society,** one relying for its subsistence primarily on the production of services and information. The United States is regarded as the pioneer in this trend because, in the latter half of the twentieth century, it has become the first society in history whose population does not work mostly at food production or industrial manufacturing. Instead, a majority of the workers provide services, ranging from auto repairs to teaching to investment banking. Many of these service jobs involve the production or manipulation of information by people in such roles as scientist, news reporter, government clerk, computer programmer, travel agent, consultant, lawyer, and the like (Touraine, 1971; D. Bell, 1973; Lipset, 1979; Toffler, 1980).

Postindustrial society produces knowledge—particularly technological knowledge—that can be leased, sold, or used to produce goods, services, or still more knowledge. Agriculture and manufacturing do not disappear in a postindustrial society; they are simply made more efficient through automation and other technological innovations that allow fewer workers to produce an ever greater surplus. However, certain industries that still rely heavily on manual labor, like clothes making or shipbuilding, go into decline: they can operate more cheaply in less technologically advanced societies where wages are far lower. Indeed, a postindustrial society can exist only in an environment of global interdependence, where labor, capital, raw materials, and technological expertise can be combined and utilized with little regard for national boundaries. In turn, the postindustrial society thrives by supplying itself and other societies with advanced theoretical knowledge and with products based on this knowledge, such as computers, telecommunications, defense systems, genetic engineering, medical equipment, or aerospace vehicles.

In a society that values theoretical knowledge and technical efficiency, two institutions become crucial: education and science. Education becomes a key to knowledge and thus to high statuses, for the most successful people are typically those who can control information and decision making—and not necessarily, as in other societal types, just those who own property. The average educational level in a postindustrial society is far higher than in any industrial or preindustrial society. Science grows more important because technological innovation depends on continued scientific research, which is supported by massive infusions of public and corporate funds. Indeed, a feature of the emerging postindustrial society is its supreme faith in technology—including a conviction that technology can be used to solve the problems that earlier technologies have created, such as the threats of pollution or modern weapons.

The postindustrial subsistence strategy has profound effects on the economy, for its huge surplus wealth permits an unprecedented standard of living

Figure 3.9 *A striking feature of the emerging postindustrial societies is that the bulk of their workers do not produce food or other goods. Instead, most people make their living by providing services or information. Postindustrial societies rely heavily on scientific innovation and international communications and trade. These exceptionally affluent societies are highly complex and diversified, with an extraordinary number of statuses, roles, and subcultural lifestyles.*

and more diverse statuses and roles than ever. In fact, the postindustrial society offers so many different jobs that workers can anticipate changing their occupational statuses several times during their careers. Most people are "white collar" workers, doing jobs that require mental rather than physical effort. As a result of the size, mobility, educational level, and widely differing life experiences of their populations, postindustrial societies have relatively varied, tolerant, and heterogeneous cultures. Subcultures and "lifestyles" proliferate, and people become deeply concerned with individual self-fulfillment. The emerging postindustrial societies show an unusual concern for the equality of the sexes and for the rights of individuals and minorities, and it is no accident that they are all highly democratic societies in which governments can be periodically chosen or dismissed by the voters.

Inhabitants of the emerging postindustrial societies face many problems, some of them a legacy from industrialism: the search for self-fulfillment in a mass society; economic imbalances caused by rapid change; unprecedented shortages of water, energy, land, and living space; and dilemmas of global interdependence in an overpopulated world where, despite the affluence of a handful of technologically advanced societies, billions of people are desperately poor. And lurking in the background is another problem, potentially devastating but easy to overlook. Despite their appearance of supreme mastery of the environment, postindustrial societies are ultimately dependent on two delicate systems: the biological life-supports of the earth's ecology, and the network of international political and economic cooperation. In any serious global disruption—caused, say, by natural disasters, nuclear war, or economic collapse—the hunters and gatherers of the world might continue to feed themselves, and be unaffected. But what would become of societies where most people are trained to produce neither food nor goods, nor little else besides that ultimate inedible, knowledge? This inherent danger does not imply that all postindustrial societies are necessarily doomed; it does mean that they are more fragile than they might appear.

Because the United States is a society in transition from one societal type to another, it displays shared characteristics of both industrial and postindustrial societies. On the one hand, the country remains the most powerful and productive industrial society in the world; on the other, most workers are now employed outside manufacturing in service and information jobs. But if the American present is still ambiguous, the future is surely postindustrial. We cannot know what form the society will take in the decades ahead, for there are no precedents to guide us, and the future will be influenced in any case by technological and other developments we cannot yet foresee. But therein lies part of the challenge and fascination of American life. In many other parts of the world, people wait for the future to arrive, as it were, second hand—as the latest fads and fashions, trends and techniques, goods and gadgets, arrive from the distant lands where they have already been tried out. But Americans inhabit a society that is (among other things) a veritable sociological laboratory, a place where experiments are being made—here, now, and by the people themselves—that may shape the human future.

Preindustrial and Industrialized Societies: A Comparison

The story of sociocultural evolution gives us a powerful reminder that, no matter what we make of our lives, we do it in the context provided by our society and the subsistence strategy it offers. Most readers of this book will spend their working lives sitting at a desk. Yet, in an earlier societal type, you might have spent your days on an assembly line; plowing fields for your feudal lord; hoeing your turnip patch or tending your yaks; or poking under a likely rock for some chewy bug.

Figure 3.10 *The most significant change in the history of sociocultural evolution is that between traditional, preindustrial societies and modern, industrialized ones. This table lists some of the typical differences that exist between each type of society.*

The Great Transformation

	Preindustrial Society	Industrialized Society
Subsistence strategy	Hunting and gathering, pastorialism, horticulture, agricultural.	Industrialism, postindustrialism.
Social structure	Relatively simple: few statuses and roles; few developed institutions other than the family.	Complex: many statuses and roles; many highly developed institutions, such as education, science, etc.
Statuses	Mostly ascribed.	Some ascribed, but many achieved.
Social groups	Mostly primary (personal, intimate).	Mostly secondary (impersonal, anonymous).
Community size	Typically small (villages).	Typically large (cities).
Division of labor	Relatively little, except on grounds of age and sex.	A great deal: occupations are highly specialized.
Social control	Mostly informal, relying on spontaneous community reaction.	Often formal, relying on laws, police, and courts.
Values	Tradition-oriented, religious.	Future-oriented, secular.
Culture	Homogeneous: most people share similar norms and values; few subcultures.	Heterogeneous: many subcultures holding different norms and values.
Technology	Primitive, based mainly on human and animal muscle power.	Advanced, based mainly on machines and energy in the form of electricity, etc.
Social change	Slow.	Rapid.

In the course of sociocultural evolution thus far, however, the sharpest break occurs between what in this book we shall call "traditional," or "preindustrial," societies, on the one hand, and "modern," or "industrialized," societies on the other. Essentially, preindustrial societies are characterized by intimate, face-to-face contact, strong feelings of community solidarity, and commitment to tradition; industrialized societies are marked by impersonal contacts, individualism rather than group loyalty, and rapid social change. Some of the basic differences between preindustrial and industrialized societies are summarized in Figure 3.10 on the preceding page. The changes wrought by this great transformation are entirely new in the history of the human species, and modern societies are still in the difficult process of adjusting to them.

Summary

1. Human beings are social animals, by habit and by necessity. A society is a population occupying the same territory, subject to the same political authority, and sharing a common culture.

2. Social processes are generally patterned and predictable. The basic components of a social system tend to be linked in an organized relationship, called social structure. Important components of social structure are statuses, roles, groups, and institutions.

3. A status is a socially defined position in society. Ascribed statuses are arbitrarily assigned by society; achieved statuses are earned. Some statuses rank higher or lower than others; people of roughly equivalent status form a class.

4. A role is the set of behavior patterns, obligations, and privileges attached to a particular status. Social norms prescribe how particular roles should be played. Role conflict occurs when two or more of a person's roles impose conflicting demands.

5. A group consists of a number of people interacting on the basis of shared expectations. A primary group is small and intimate; a secondary group is more anonymous. Groups are important building blocks of social structure.

6. Institutions are stable clusters of norms, values, statuses, roles, and groups that develop around basic needs of society. They tend to resist change, to be closely interrelated within the social structure, to adjust to significant changes in other institutions, and to be the site of major social problems. Functionalist and conflict analyses emphasize different aspects of institutions.

7. There has been a general trend of sociocultural evolution from small and simple societies to large and complex ones. This involves a progressively greater division of labor (resulting in more statuses and roles) within the population. Societies can be classified according to their basic subsistence strategies. The main types of societies are hunting and gathering societies, pastoral societies, horticultural societies, agricultural societies, and industrial societies. A new type, the postindustrial society, is emerging. Culture and social structure grow more complex at each stage, for more productive strategies produce greater surplus wealth, which can support larger and more diverse populations.

8. Modern industrialized societies are radically unlike traditional, preindustrial societies. They experience a rapid rate of social change, and virtually all aspects of culture and social structure are transformed by the modernization process that accompanies industrialization. Sociologists are still attempting to grasp the full significance of these changes.

Important Terms

society (51)

social structure (52)

status (52)

master status (52)

status inconsistency (52)

ascribed status (52)

achieved status (52)

social class (53)

role (53)

role conflict (54)

group (54)

primary group (54)

secondary group (54)

institution (54)

sociocultural evolution (57)

ecological approach (57)

surplus wealth (57)

division of labor (57)

hunting and gathering society (58)

pastoral society (59)

horticultural society (60)

agricultural society (61)

industrial society (62)

postindustrial society (64)

CHAPTER *4*

Socialization

At birth the human infant is a helpless organism. The newborn knows nothing, and cannot survive for more than a few hours without the help of other people. Unlike other animals, the infant will have to learn virtually all its later patterns of behavior. Somehow this biological being must be transformed into a fully human being, a person able to participate effectively in society. That transformation is achieved through the complex process of socialization.

Socialization is the process of social interaction through which people acquire personality and learn the way of life of their society. It is the essential link between the individual and society—a link so vital that neither individual nor society could survive without it. Socialization enables the individual to learn the norms, values, languages, skills, beliefs, and other patterns of thought and action that are essential for social living. And socialization enables the society to reproduce itself socially as well as biologically, thus ensuring its continuity from generation to generation.

One of the most important outcomes of socialization is the development of individual **personality,** the fairly stable patterns of thought, feeling, and action that are typical of an individual. Personality thus includes three main elements: the *cognitive* component of thought, belief, perception, memory, and other intellectual capacities; the *emotional* component of love, hate, envy, sympathy, anger, pride, and other feelings; and the *behavioral* component of skills, aptitudes, competence, and other abilities. Nobody is born a great mathematician, the life of the party, or a skillful carpenter. People may be born with the potential to become any of these, but what they actually become is primarily the product of their unique experiences.

Social interaction takes place according to the norms and values of the culture in question. The content of socialization and the personality types that are most admired therefore vary from one society to another. As a result, there are characteristic personality traits in every society—patterns that result from a common experience of socialization in a unique culture. Within every society, however, each person is different, and these differences are also largely the product of socialization. We are born and live not only in a society but also in a specific part of it, and we are therefore influenced by particular subcultures of class, race, religion, and region, as well as by specific groups such as family and friends. Distinctive new experiences in these contexts are continually blended with old ones, so every person's biography and personality are unique. The socialization process thus helps to explain both the general *similarities* in personality and social behavior within a society and the many *differences* that exist between one person and another.

Socialization continues throughout the **life course**—the biological and social sequence of birth, childhood, maturity, old age, and death. At each stage in this lifelong process, we continually encounter new or changing conditions, both personal and social, and must learn to adjust to them. The most important social-

The second child, Isabelle, was about six. Her grandfather had kept her and her mother—a deaf-mute—in a dark room most of the time. When Isabelle was discovered, her behavior toward other people, especially men, was "almost that of a wild animal." At first it was thought that she was deaf, for she did not appear to hear the sounds around her, and her only speech was a strange croaking sound. The specialists who worked with her pronounced her feebleminded and did not expect that she could ever be taught to speak.

Unlike Anna, however, Isabelle was trained by a skilled team of doctors and psychologists. After a slow start, she suddenly spurted through the stages of learning that are usually characteristic of the first six years of childhood, taking every stage in the usual order but at much greater speed than normal. By the time she was about eight years old she had reached an apparently normal level of intellectual development and was able to attend school with other children. Her greater success seems to have been related to the fact that her mother was present during her isolation.

Since these early cases, there have been several subsequent reports of children raised in isolation. The effects on all these children are similar: without socialization, they lack normal social, psychological, and even physical development. (See the box on "Genie," p. 73.)

Institutionalized Children

The socialization of children who are raised in orphanages and similar institutions differs in one important respect from that of children who are raised in families. Institutionalized children rarely have the chance to develop close emotional ties with specific adults, for although the children may interact with a large number of staff members, the attendants simply do not have the time to devote much personal attention to any one child. The standard of nutrition and other physical care in institutions is sometimes good and comparable to that in private homes, but relationships between child and adult are usually minimal.

In 1945, the psychologist René Spitz published an influential article on the effects that these conditions have on children's personalities. Spitz compared some infants who were being raised by their own mothers with infants of the same age who had been placed in the care of an orphanage. The infants living with their mothers had plenty of opportunity for close social interaction, but those in the institution received only routine care at mealtimes and when their clothing or bedding was changed. Spitz found that the infants in the orphanage were physically, socially, and emotionally retarded compared with the other infants—a difference that increased steadily as the children grew older.

Spitz's report was followed by a large number of studies on the effects of institutionalization on infants and children, most of which have arrived at similar conclusions. William Goldfarb (1945), for example, compared forty children who had been placed in foster homes soon after birth with forty children who had spent the first two years of life in institutions before being transferred to foster homes. He found that the institutionalized children suffered a number of personality defects that persisted even after they had left the institutions. They had lower IQ scores, seemed more aggressive and distractible, showed less initiative, and were more emotionally cold. Many other studies have reported similar depressing effects on physical, cognitive, emotional, and social development, and have confirmed that such disabilities suffered in early childhood tend to persist or even worsen in later years (Bowlby, 1969, 1988; Rutter, 1974).

Monkeys Raised in Isolation

Harry Harlow (1965) has conducted a series of important experiments on the effects of isolation on rhesus monkeys. Harlow's work has shown that even in

Genie: A Case of Childhood Isolation

Cases of childhood isolation reveal a great deal about "human nature," for they give us a harrowing glimpse of what a virtually unsocialized person can be like. The following case concerns Genie, a California girl who was kept locked in a small, nearly barren room by her father from the time she was twenty months old until the age of thirteen and a half. During most of every day she was left naked and unattended, harnessed to an infant's potty seat or caged in a crib. She had virtually no contact with the world outside her room. The only language she heard was her father's swearing when he was in a rage. The description that follows was written by Susan Curtiss, a psycholinguist who worked with Genie for several years after she was discovered in 1970. It outlines Genie's typical behavior during her first year of treatment. (After six years of being cared for, first in a hospital and then in a foster home, Genie could speak in sentences, attend a special school, and form emotional attachments.)

Source: Susan Curtiss, *Genie* (New York: Academic Press, 1977).

Genie was pitiful. Hardly ever having worn clothing, she did not react to temperature, heat or cold. Never having eaten solid food, Genie did not know how to chew, and had great difficulty in swallowing. Having been strapped down and left sitting on a potty chair, she could not stand erect, could not straighten her arms or legs, could not run, hop, jump, or climb; in fact, she could only walk with difficulty, shuffling her feet, swaying from side to side. Hardly ever having seen more than a space of 10 feet in front of her (the distance from her potty chair to the door), she had become nearsighted exactly to that distance. Having been beaten for making noise, she had learned to suppress almost all vocalization save a whimper. . . . She was incontinent of feces and urine. Her hair was sparse and stringy. She salivated copiously, spitting onto anything at hand. Genie was unsocialized, primitive, hardly human.

Surprisingly, however, Genie was alert and curious. She maintained good eye contact and avidly explored her new surroundings. She was intensely eager for human contact and attention. In the face of her hunger for contact with her new world, her almost total silence had an eerie quality. Except for a high-pitched whimpering and a few words she is reported to have imitated when she was first admitted to the hospital, she was a silent child who did not vocalize in any way, who did not even sob when she cried. Her silence was complete even in the face of frenzied emotion. Sometimes, frightened and frustrated by both her former life and her new surroundings, Genie would erupt and have a raging tantrum, flailing about, scratching, spitting, blowing her nose, and frantically rubbing her face and hair with her own mucus, all the time trying to gouge or otherwise inflict pain on herself—all in silence. Unable to vocalize, Genie would use objects and parts of her body to make noise and help express her frenzy: a chair scratching against the floor, her fingers scratching against a balloon, furniture falling, objects thrown or slammed against other objects, her feet shuffling. These were Genie's noises during her sobless silent tantrum. At long last, physically exhausted, her rage would subside, and Genie would silently return to her undemonstrative self. . . .

Genie had a habit of walking around during mealtime, stopping at other children's places at the table, sometimes attempting to take their portions of foods she especially liked (applesauce, milk, ice cream, etc.). She often walked around with her mouth stuffed with food, and . . . would sometimes spit it out onto the nearest plate.

Genie had other personal habits that were not socially acceptable. She blew her nose onto anything or nothing, often making a mess of her clothing. At times, when excited or agitated, she would urinate in inappropriate places—leaving her companion to deal with the results. But it was her lack of socialization that was most difficult to deal with, especially in public. If anyone she encountered in the street or in a store or other public place had something she liked, she was uncontrollably drawn to him or her, and without obeying any rules of psychological distance or social mores, she would go right up to the person and put her hands on the desired item. It was bad enough when she went up to someone else's shopping cart to reach in to take something out; but when the object of attention was an article of clothing, and Genie would simply attach herself to the person wearing that clothing and refuse to let go, the situations were extremely trying. . . .

Genie masturbated excessively, which proved to be the most serious antisocial behavior problem of all. Despite admonishments, she continued to masturbate as often as possible, anywhere and everywhere. . . . Many of the items she coveted were objects with which to masturbate, and she would attempt to do so, regardless of where she was. She was drawn to chair backs, chair arms, counter edges, door knobs, door edges, table corners, car handles, car mirrors, and so forth; in essence, indoors and outdoors she was continually attempting to masturbate. . . . The first month, when I saw Genie almost daily, I spent the time trying to get to know her and to establish a relationship with her that would help her develop trust in me and enable me to work with her effectively. At that time she was still not testable, and was so bizarre in her behavior that had I attempted to gain information formally from her, I would not have known how to interpret her performance.

Figure 4.2 *In his experiments with monkeys raised in isolation, Harry Harlow has found that the animals prefer a soft, cuddly "mother" substitute to a "mother" that feeds them but is made of wire. The young monkeys clung to this cuddly "mother" for much of the time, especially if they were frightened. The wire "mother" was used only as a source of food. Harlow's study shows that the young monkeys placed great priority on intimate contact.*

monkeys, social behavior is learned, not inherited. The monkeys raised in isolation in his labs behave in some ways like human psychotics. They are fearful of, or hostile to, other monkeys, make no attempt to interact with them, and are generally withdrawn and apathetic. Monkeys reared in isolation do not know how to mate with other monkeys and usually cannot be taught how to do so. If female monkeys who have been isolated since birth are artificially impregnated, they become unloving and abusive mothers, making little or no attempt to take care of their offspring. In one experiment, Harlow provided isolated monkey infants with two substitute mothers—one made of wire and containing a feeding bottle and one covered with soft cloth but without a bottle. The infant monkeys preferred the soft, cuddly "mother" to the one that fed them. This wretched substitute for affection became the most important focus in their lives.

Like all animal studies, Harlow's experiments must be treated with caution when inferences are made for human behavior. After all, we are not monkeys. His studies show, however, that without socialization, monkeys cannot develop normal social, sexual, emotional, or maternal behavior. Since we know that human beings rely much more heavily on learning than monkeys do, it seems fair to conclude that the same would be true of us.

The evidence from these varied sources, then, points overwhelmingly in the same direction: without socialization, we are almost devoid of personality and are utterly unable to face even the simplest challenges of life. Lacking the "instincts" that guide the behavior of other animals, we can become social and thus fully human only by learning through interaction with other people.

The Emergence of the Self

At the core of personality lies the **self**—the individual's conscious experience of a distinct, personal identity that is separate from all other people and things. Unlike other animals, we are fully self-conscious, capable of thinking as subjects about ourselves as objects. You can be "proud of yourself" or "ashamed of yourself"; you can "love yourself," "change yourself," or "lose control of yourself"; and you can even "talk to yourself."

The concept of "self" is perhaps a rather vague one. But we certainly experience it as real, for all of us have some fairly definite notion of who and what we are. A standard sociological method of investigating this sense of self is a test in which subjects (usually college students) are asked to complete twenty statements that begin "I am . . . ." The answers to this test consistently show that our sense of self seems to derive primarily from the various social roles we play and the various personality traits we believe we possess.

But how does our sense of self develop? The answer is that it is a social product, created and modified throughout life by interaction with other people. At the time of birth we have no sense of self, no awareness of having a separate identity. The infant shows no recognition of other people as distinct beings until around six months of age and does not begin to use words such as "I," "me," and "mine" until at least the age of two. Only in the ensuing years do young children gradually come to realize that other people also have distinct selves, with needs and outlooks different from their own. And only then can they begin to appreciate that their own self is an identity separate from all others. Two related theories explain how social interaction leads to the emergence of the self.

Cooley: The Looking-Glass Self

Charles Horton Cooley (1864–1929) was an American economist turned social psychologist. He held that self-concepts are formed early in childhood and then reevaluated throughout life whenever a person enters a new social situation.

The central concept in Cooley's theory is the **looking-glass self**—a self-concept derived from a social "mirror" in which we can observe how others react to us. Our concept of ourselves is derived from this reflection, for we learn from other people's responses to us whether we are attractive or ugly, popular or unpopular, respectable or disreputable. According to Cooley (1902), the process of developing the self involves three steps.

1. *Imagining our own appearance.* First, we imagine what appearance and personality we present to others. We may imagine ourselves as witty, intelligent, slim, helpful, or perhaps as something quite the opposite.

2. *Interpreting others' reactions.* Second, we imagine how others judge the appearance and personality that we think we present. Do they really see us the way we imagine we appear, or are they receiving a different impression?

3. *Developing self-concept.* Third, we use our interpretation of others' judgments to develop feelings about ourselves. If the image we find in the social mirror is favorable, our self-concept is enhanced; if the image is unfavorable, our self-concept is diminished.

Of course, people may misjudge the way others see them. All of us make misinterpretations at times, and some people habitually misjudge the opinion of others and have unrealistically high or low self-concepts as a result. But whether our reading of the image in the "looking glass" is accurate or not, it is through this interpretation that we learn our identity. There can be no self without society, no "I" without a corresponding "they" to provide our self-image.

Figure 4.3 *According to Charles Horton Cooley, we learn our concept of self through the "looking glass" provided by society. Just as we learn what we look like by examining our reflection, so we learn our sense of self through the reflection provided by the "mirror" of other people's reactions to us.*

Mead: Role-Taking

George Herbert Mead (1863–1931) is one of the most important figures in American social science. A philosopher and social psychologist, Mead was a fascinating lecturer, yet he never wrote a book—his attempts to commit his ideas to paper led him to agonies of frustration. His students and colleagues, however, compiled and published his work from lecture notes and other sources.

Mead (1934) pointed out that a vital outcome of socialization is the ability to anticipate what others expect of us and to shape our own behavior accordingly. This capacity, he argued, is achieved by **role-taking**—pretending to take or actually taking the roles of other people, so that one can see the world and one's self from their viewpoints. In childhood we are able to internalize the expectations only of the **particular other**—specific other people such as parents. But as we grow older, we gradually learn to internalize the expectations of the **generalized other,** the attitudes and viewpoint of society as a whole. This internalized general concept of social expectations provides the basis for self-evaluation and hence for self-concept.

Mead showed how, as children progress through three stages of increasingly sophisticated role-taking, they gain a better understanding of themselves and of social life.

1. *Imitation.* Children under the age of about three lack a developed sense of self and so have difficulty distinguishing their roles from those of others. They merely mimic or imitate people in the immediate environment, such as family members, and they do so only occasionally and spontaneously—a gesture here, a word there. This is not really role-taking, but serves as preparation for it.

2. *Play.* After the age of about three, children begin to play at taking the roles of specific other people: they walk around in their parent's shoes; pretend

Figure 4.4 *George Herbert Mead pointed out that the development of the self requires that we learn to take the role of other people, if only in our imagination. Once we can do this, we realize that others also have selves, and we can see our own self from their viewpoint. Children's games of pretending to be someone else are one of the first steps in this direction.*

to be an adult and scold a doll; or play "house," "doctors and nurses," and so on. By pretending to assume the roles of specific other people in this kind of play, children are taking the first steps in learning to see the world from a perspective that is not their own.

3. *Games*. By the early school years, children are ready to take part in organized games—preludes to the "game" of life—in which their roles are real and in which they must simultaneously take account of the roles and expectations of all the participants. A baseball pitcher, for example, must be aware not only of his or her own role requirements but also of the roles and likely responses of every other player. Very young children cannot play organized games: because they are still limited to their own perspective, they cannot grasp the role of other players, and thus cannot anticipate how others will respond to their actions.

Mead pointed out that socialization is never perfect or complete. He distinguished between what he called the "I" (the spontaneous, self-interested, impulsive, unsocialized self) and the "me" (the socialized self that is conscious of social norms, values, and expectations). The "I," he insisted, is never completely under the control of the "me." The socialized self is usually dominant, but we all have the capacity to break social rules and violate the expectations of others.

Learning to Think

One of the most important achievements of socialization is the development of cognitive abilities—intellectual capacities such as perceiving, remembering, reasoning, calculating, believing. Our knowledge of this process is based largely on the work of Jean Piaget (1896–1980), who emphasized that "social life is necessary for the individual to become conscious of his own mind."

Piaget's many experiments with children suggest that human beings gradually pass through four basic stages of cognitive development, with the attainment of new skills at each stage requiring successful completion of the previous stage. Each stage is characterized by the particular kinds of "operations," or intellectual processes, that a person at that stage can perform (1950, 1954).

1. *The Sensorimotor Stage.* In this stage, which lasts from birth until about the age of two, children's thinking is limited to their immediate sensory and physical experience with the environment. Infants cannot "think" about the world unless they are acting on it directly. In fact, until the age of four months or so, infants cannot even differentiate themselves from their environment. They are thus unaware of the results of their actions; they do not realize, for example, that their own movements cause a rattle to make a sound. Similarly, children under the age of eight months do not understand that objects have a permanent existence: if a toy is removed from their sight, or if a parent leaves the room, they react as though the toy or parent has ceased to exist. By the end of the sensorimotor stage, however, the child realizes that objects exist even when they are not in view. Indeed, the child is able to create mental images of things and events that he or she has experienced in the past.

2. *The Preoperational Stage.* This stage lasts from around the age of two to seven. Piaget called the stage "preoperational" because during this period children are unable to do many simple mental operations, largely because they have no real understanding of such concepts as speed, weight, number, quantity, or causality. Particularly during the early years of this stage, for example, children invariably assume that the larger of two objects must be the heavier. (They will typically state that a pound of feathers weighs more than a pound of lead.) They

Figure 4.5 *Children at the preoperational stage have great difficulty in understanding the concept of number, even though they may be able to count. Children at this stage typically assert that a long row of items contains more items than a shorter, more densely packed row with a similar or greater number of items.*

likewise assume that the taller of two containers holds more, even if the taller container is much narrower than the shorter one. They have a limited understanding of cause and effect—often believing, for example, that trees waving in the wind are actually making the wind. And they often attribute life to inanimate objects, such as the sun and moon, and may believe that a table is "hurt" when it is bumped.

3. *The Concrete Operational Stage.* In this stage, which lasts from about seven to twelve, children can reason about concrete situations, but not about abstract or purely hypothetical ones. If children of this age are asked to talk about abstract concepts, such as death or justice, they have great difficulty in doing so without referring to actual events or images, such as the death of a pet or the physical appearance of police officers. Children at this stage, however, are able to handle the concrete world with much the same cognitive skill as an adult. They can perform the various mental operations related to weight, speed, number, quantity, or causality that were not possible in the previous stage. They can also see other people's viewpoint and can thus take the roles of others. This new ability enables them to participate effectively in games and other organized social relationships.

4. *The Formal Operational Stage.* In this stage, which usually begins at the onset of adolescence, people are able to achieve formal, abstract thought. They can think in terms of theories and hypotheses and can manipulate complex mathematical, moral, and other concepts that are not tied to the immediate environment. They are able to use general rules to solve whole classes of problems, and they can reason logically from premises to conclusions with a sophistication that would not be possible in earlier stages. They can think about abstract personal goals and even utopian social conditions. Philosophic brooding may appear, on perennially favored topics of youth. (If sex is pleasant, why is it wrong? If God is good and all-powerful, why is there evil in the world and suffering among the innocent? If parents know best, why do they often make mistakes?)

It seems that the *process* of cognitive socialization is universal: in all societies, people advance through the same sequence of development. But the *content* is culturally variable: what and how much we learn depend on our social environment. If our culture believes the earth is flat, or that cause and effect are related to magic, then it is through these concepts that we will interpret the world. Moreover, not everyone reaches the final stage of formal operations; many adults have great difficulty in understanding abstract concepts, particularly if they have little exposure to formal thinking in their own socialization. In fact, more than half the people in the world today cannot read or write, for they live in societies that lacked the resources to make formal education available to them. Even within a given society, too, social and cultural factors encourage different categories of the population to think in different ways about different subjects: American men, for example, are socialized to be more likely than women to think in mathematical or engineering terms.

Learning to Feel

Another vital achievement of socialization is the development of emotional capacities—feelings such as love, hate, empathy, confidence, envy. One of the founders of modern psychology, Sigmund Freud (1856–1939), emphasized the importance of emotions in human personality, and showed that a good deal of emotional life is unconscious—that is, we are often unaware of the real reasons for our feelings and the actions that spring from them. Although Freud developed an elaborate theory of emotions, later psychologists found his ideas too speculative to be satisfactory. In fact, emotions seemed so vague and inaccessible that social scientists were generally reluctant to study the subject systematically until fairly recently.

Within the past decade, however, psychologists and sociologists have begun to study emotions in detail. They have learned, perhaps not too surprisingly, that emotional socialization parallels cognitive socialization in important respects. First, the *process* of learning emotions seems to be the same in all normal human beings: the various feelings develop in an orderly sequence, with each new emotion being built on those already attained. Second, the *content* of emotions is culturally variable: social factors strongly influence what, when, and how emotions are expressed (Hochschild, 1975; Kemper, 1978, 1987; Shott, 1979; Kagan, 1984; Dunn, 1988).

Preliminary studies by Jerome Kagan and his colleagues indicate that emotional development takes the following course. Initially, during the first few days and weeks of life, the emotions of the child consist of little more than reflexive reactions to the environment: pleasure, surprise, disgust, distress, and curiosity. Then, in the first few months, new emotions begin to appear as a result of accumulating experience: joy, anger, sadness, and fear. By the middle of the second year, the child shows signs of tenderness and affection toward others, but without any recognition that these others have separate selves and identities of their own. But by the time they are five or six years old, children are developing a clear sense of self, an ability to compare themselves to others, and a sense of how others judge them. The "looking glass" provided by this new social awareness then makes possible, for the first time, emotions that require a consideration of other people's judgments: confidence, insecurity, pride, humility, jealousy, envy. Being able to take the role of others, children can now understand other people's emotions too, and so develop feelings of sympathy and empathy. By the teenage years, the growing cognitive capacity for abstract thought allows the young person to extend empathy to whole categories of people, such as the poor or the oppressed. Around this time, too, the deepening awareness of self and others opens the possibility of romantic passion. Although the various emotions seem always to emerge in the same order, the process—as with the development of cognitive abilities—can be speeded up or slowed down by social factors. For example, infants do not normally show signs of fear and sadness until about seven or eight months, but infants who have been abused show these emotions as early on as three months.

Social life is clearly pervaded by emotions—after all, love, hate, pride, jealousy, and the like provide the motives for a great deal of social behavior. What is perhaps not so obvious is that emotions, in turn, are pervaded by social life. In other words, social conditions influence how we interpret our emotions and whether, and in what form, we express them. Even the physical sensations that accompany some emotions have to be interpreted: What does this tightening of the chest, that quickening of the pulse, actually mean? Fear, lust, hope, anxiety, or something else? And even when we have learned to interpret our emotions, we must learn also under what social conditions, if any, they may be expressed. It may be appropriate to vent feelings of romantic passion toward one's date in private, but not toward one's employer's spouse in public, even if the feeling is as strong and sincere in both cases. Indeed, each culture has its own "feeling rules," norms that encourage or discourage certain emotions like anger or envy and specify how we shall express them, if we do so at all (Hochschild, 1979).

Figure 4.6 *Different cultures permit or discourage the display of particular emotions in different contexts. In some Peruvian communities, for example, there are regular "feasts of the dead" in cemeteries. Such celebrations would be totally inappropriate in North America.*

Emotions do more than enrich social life; they help make it possible, too. As we noted in Chapter 2 ("Culture"), every society, if it is to survive, must have some form of social control—a set of means of ensuring that people generally behave in socially approved ways. Some of this control, we saw, is exercised externally, through such agencies as the police; but most of it is applied internally, through our self-control over our own behavior. Emotions play an important part in this process, for the experience of such learned feelings as pride, shame, guilt, and embarrassment enables us, consciously or unconsciously, to guide our own thoughts and actions along paths that are generally socially acceptable (Shott, 1979).

Agents of Socialization

The socialization process involves many different influences that affect the individual throughout life. The most important of these influences are **agents of socialization**—significant individuals, groups, or institutions that provide structured situations in which socialization takes place. Four of these agents—the family, the school, the peer group, and the mass media—are especially important in modern societies, for they affect almost everyone in a powerful and lasting way.

The Family

The family is without doubt the most significant single agent of socialization in all societies. One reason for the importance of the family is that it has the main responsibility for socializing children in the crucial early years of life. The family is where children establish their first close emotional ties, learn language, and begin to internalize cultural norms and values. To young children the family is all-encompassing. They have little social experience beyond its boundaries and therefore lack any basis for comparing and evaluating what is learned from family members. Each family therefore offers a unique experience to the children within it. In fact, different children within the same family have differing experiences, for they have a different set of older or younger brothers and sisters. There is considerable evidence that first-born children get more attention and discipline than children born subsequently, and that this may affect their later personalities: first-borns tend to do better in school and to be higher achievers later in life, while younger brothers and sisters tend to be more sociable and relaxed (Forer, 1976; Dunn and Kendrick, 1983).

A great deal of the socialization that takes place in the family is deliberate, but much of it is quite unconscious. The patterns of social interaction within the family may provide unintended models for the later behavior and personality traits of the children when they grow to adulthood. For example, parents who abuse their children were often abused by their own parents—and their own children, in turn, are more likely to become aggressive and abusive adults themselves. In this way, personality traits may be passed down over one or more generations.

Another reason for the importance of the family is that it has a specific location in the social structure. From the moment of birth, therefore, children have an ascribed status in a subculture of race, class, ethnicity, religion, and region—all of which may strongly influence the nature of later social interaction and socialization. For example, the values and expectations that children learn depend very much on the social class of their parents. Studies by Melvin Kohn (1963, 1976, 1977) show that working-class and middle-class parents raise their children in different ways. Working-class parents place greater value on conformity to traditional standards of behavior: they teach their children to obey the rules and stay out of trouble. Middle-class parents, on the other hand, place

Drawing by Weber; © 1984 The New Yorker Magazine, Inc.

"I find there's a lot of pressure to be good."

greater value on curiosity and initiative: they teach their children to rely more on self-control in deciding how to behave. As Kohn points out, these styles of parenting are related to the occupational experiences of the parents. Blue-collar jobs generally require that the worker follow exactly the instructions of the supervisor; white-collar jobs require more independence and initiative. Parents thus socialize their children for that part of the social world that they know best—and in doing so, they help to reproduce the class system in the next generation. In part because of such influences, the social-class background of a child's family is an excellent predictor of that child's later IQ, educational achievement, and ultimate social-class status.

The School

The school is an agent formally charged by society with the task of socializing the young in particular skills and values. In this setting, the young come for the first time under the direct supervision of people who are not relatives. The individual child is no longer considered somebody special; he or she is now one of a crowd, subject to the same regulations and expectations that everyone else is subject to. Personal behavior and academic achievements or failures become part of a permanent official record, and the schoolchildren learn to evaluate themselves by the same standards that others apply to them. Participation in the life of the school also lessens the children's dependence on the family and creates new links to the wider society beyond.

Drawing by Weber; © 1988
The New Yorker Magazine, Inc.

"The first one to fall asleep gets today's competitive-edge award."

The immediate task of the schools is to socialize the young in cognitive skills such as reading or mathematics and to provide knowledge about a variety of subjects, such as history or chemistry, that may not be available in the home. But the schools in every society also engage in outright indoctrination in values. We may find this fact more apparent in societies other than our own—until we consider the content of civics classes or the daily ritual of the Pledge of Allegiance. A schoolteacher who attended church and espoused capitalism would pass unnoticed in an American school; one who professed atheism and praised communism would soon be out of a job, for these views are inconsistent with

American values. At a more subtle level, the school socializes through the "hidden curriculum" implicit in the content of school activities, ranging from regimented classroom schedules to organized sports. Children learn that they must be neat and punctual. They learn to sit still, keep quiet, wait their turn, and not be distracted from their work. They learn that individuals who can outdo their classmates are rewarded, while those who cannot compete successfully are regarded as failures. They learn that they should respect and obey without question the commands of those who have social authority over them. In teaching these attitudes and behaviors, the school is subtly socializing children for their later roles in the work force, where punctuality and deferrence to superiors are highly valued.

The Peer Group

As children grow older, they spend more and more time in the company of their **peers**—people of roughly equivalent age and other social characteristics. As the influence of the peer group increases, that of the parents diminishes—especially in modern industrialized societies, where most parents work away from the home and where there has been a long-term erosion of the authority of elders. Young Americans of school-going age spend, on average, twice as much time with peers as with parents, and most of them prefer it that way. The influence of the peer group climaxes in adolescence, when young people are apt to form a distinctive subculture with its own tastes, leisure activities, dress, jargon, symbols, values, and heroes.

Membership in a peer group places children for the first time in a context where most socialization occurs without any deliberate design. Unlike the family or the school, the peer group is entirely centered on its own concerns and interests, and indeed its members can explore topics (like sex, drugs, and rock-and-roll) that other agents of socialization may wish to avoid. Within the peer group, the young are able for the first time to choose their own companions and to interact with others on a basis of equality. However, they cannot expect the

Figure 4.7 *The peer group is an important agent of socialization from childhood on, but it is particularly influential during late childhood and adolescence. Young people at this stage are exploring their identities, a process that may involve a reaction against earlier behavior patterns learned in the family and school. The peer group provides new norms and values for its members and the opportunity to interact with others as equals.*

automatic acceptance from peers that they can from family members, and so have to learn to present the self in ways that win the approval of the group. By rewarding members for conformity to group norms and criticizing or ostracizing them for nonconformity, the peer group helps shape their social behavior and personality. But although young people often seem to give their primary loyalty to their peers, appearances can be deceptive. Peers do have greater influence over matters of immediate lifestyle, such as musical tastes or leisure activities, but values learned in the family regarding religion, politics, education, and career goals tend to have greater long-term impact (Troll and Bengston, 1982; Davies and Kandel, 1981).

The Mass Media

The **mass media** are the various forms of communication that reach a large audience without any personal contact between the senders and the receivers of the messages: newspapers, magazines, books, television, radio, movies, videos, and records. This agent of socialization introduces the individual to an extraordinarily diverse array of people who are ''known'' only indirectly: sports figures, historic personages, politicians, authors, columnists, announcers, disk jockeys, talk-show hosts, newscasters, musicians, and even ordinary people interviewed in eyewitness news reports. We take this barrage of media socialization so much for granted that it is easy to forget that, until a few generations ago, most people's social exposure was limited to face-to-face contact with a handful of neighbors who were, in most respects, very similar to one another.

The media provide instant coverage of social events and social changes, ranging from news and opinions to fads and fashions. They offer role models, viewpoints, and glimpses of lifestyles that people might otherwise never have access to. Through the media, children can learn about courtroom lawyers, cowboys, police detectives, or even such improbable characters as Batman, E.T., and Rambo. Through media advertising, too, the young learn about their future roles as consumers in the marketplace, and about the high value the society places on youth, success, beauty, and materialism. Changing social norms and values are quickly reflected in the media and may be readily adopted by people who might not otherwise be exposed to them. The rapid spread of new trends in youth culture, for example, depends heavily on such media as popular records, television, FM radio, youth-oriented magazines, and movies.

The most influential medium is probably television. There is a TV set in 98 percent of American homes, and the average American between the ages of three and sixteen spends more time in front of the TV set than in school. Yet the influence of television, like that of the other media, is difficult to trace with any certainty, because it is inevitably entangled in a multitude of influences on personality. One major point of controversy has been the impact of television violence: by the time the average American reaches the age of sixteen, he or she has witnessed over 18,000 fictional murders, not to mention innumerable other acts of violence—but what effects does this have? After surveying over 2,500 studies on the relationship of television violence to actual behavior, the National Institute of Mental Health (1982) found overwhelming evidence that these portrayals do, in fact, encourage aggressive conduct among children and teenagers. Also, although television does bring a flood of information into the home, much of it is highly selective or distorted. News programs, for example, tend to feature the visually exciting or emotionally moving stories that draw large viewing audiences—even if this means omitting issues that are more sober but perhaps more significant also. Fictional portrayals, too, often overrepresent some categories of the population, such as the wealthy or physicians, and underrepresent others, such as the aged or minorities (Gerbner, 1981; Wright, 1986).

Other Agents

People may be influenced by many other agents of socialization—religious groups, youth organizations, and later in life, such agents as corporations, clubs, political movements, and retirement homes.

In extreme cases, the individual may experience **resocialization,** learning that involves a sharp break with the past and socialization into radically different norms and values. This frequently takes place in a context where people have been partly or wholly isolated from their previous background and experience. Resocialization occurs, for example, in conversion to a religious cult, in the experience of an anthropologist who lives among an alien people, or in "brainwashing" situations in which the individual's personality is systematically stripped away and rebuilt. It also occurs within a **total institution**—a place of residence where the inmates are confined for a set period of their lives, under the almost absolute control of a hierarchy of officials (Goffman, 1961). Examples of a total institution include an army boot camp, a naval vessel, a prison, a mental asylum, and a traditional boarding school. In each of these cases, the inmates experience an abrupt break from their former existence; they surrender control over much of their lives to an administrative staff; they are to some extent depersonalized by having to wear uniforms and obey rigid rules; and they are under great pressure to conform to the values and regulations of their new environment.

Figure 4.8 *Military trainees are subjected to systematic resocialization, a form of socialization that involves an abrupt break with earlier experiences. Resocialization takes place in the context of "total institutions," such as boot camps, mental hospitals, and prisons, where the inmates are segregated from the rest of society, placed in uniforms and treated alike, and made subject to rigid rules and the authority of officials.*

It is obvious that the influences of the various agents are not always complementary and can often be in outright conflict with each other. The family, for example, may hold quite different values from those of the military; the peer group, quite different values from those of the school. It is also obvious that people do not always learn what they are supposed to learn. The socialization process may fail in certain respects, and people may come to behave in ways that were never anticipated or intended. Personality and behavior are never entirely stable; they change under the influence of socialization experiences throughout the life course.

The Life Course

The human life course seems at first sight to be purely a matter of biology. But the sequence of birth, childhood, maturity, old age, and death is also a social one, for its length, stages, challenges, and opportunities depend very much on the society in which one lives. How long we live, for example, is strongly influenced by social as well as biological factors. In North America, people are not considered old until they are in their sixties or seventies; among the malnourished Ik of Uganda, old age sets in by the late twenties. In modern industrialized societies, we associate the idea of death with the aged, but in traditional, preindustrial societies more people died in childhood than in old age. Thanks to such social factors as modern medicine, improved nutrition, and higher standards of sanitation, infectious diseases such as smallpox, diphtheria, and cholera no longer kill more than half of all children before the age of ten. For the first time in history, most people can now expect to grow old.

Every society imposes its own conception of a life course upon the physical process of growing up and growing old. Consequently, the period from birth to death is arbitrarily sliced up into a series of stages, each offering distinctive rights and responsibilities to the relevant age group. The number, length, and content of these stages vary from one society to another. But each society must socialize its members into accepting and effectively performing their changing roles at each stage in the sequence from early childhood until death.

The Life Course

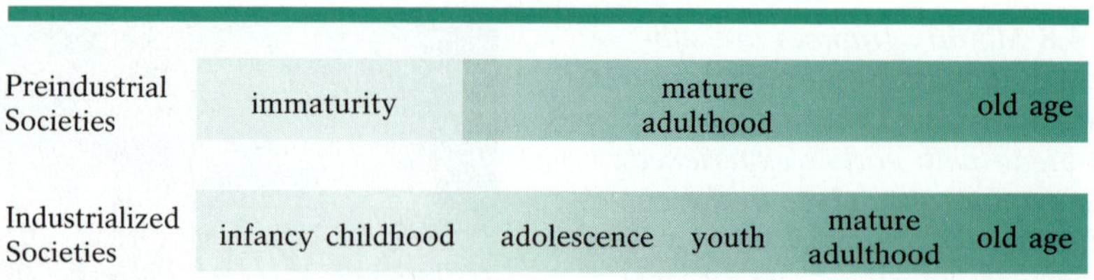

Figure 4.9 *The stages of the life course are influenced by social as well as biological factors. Preindustrial societies generally did not recognize separate stages of infancy, childhood, and adolescence. Childhood was not recognized in Europe until after the Middle Ages, and adolescence has been recognized in industrial societies only in this century. More recently, an additional, optional stage, that of youth, has appeared in the life course in the emerging postindustrial societies.*

Childhood

Childhood seems a "natural" part of the life course to us, yet the very concept of childhood is a comparatively recent one: preindustrial societies typically did not recognize it as a separate stage of life. Instead, the young passed directly from a prolonged immaturity into their adult roles. There was no separate way of life reserved for childhood, with the distinctive songs, toys, privileges, and activities that we take for granted today (Ariès, 1962; Gilles, 1974; de Mause, 1974). People began to play adult economic and social roles as soon as they were physically able to do so, and children of five or six would work in the fields as long as any adult. Child labor was not considered a scandal; there can be no concept of children's rights without a concept of childhood. Even in early industrial societies, children worked alongside adults: in the United States in 1900, a quarter of the boys aged ten to fourteen were in the labor force. And today, in such countries as Morocco, India, and Colombia, tens of millions of children between the ages of five and thirteen work full time, even in factories and coal mines.

The Nightmare of Childhood in Ages Past

In the modern world we tend to think of childhood as a period of special innocence in which the developing person needs and deserves care, kindness, and comfort. But as these excerpts from Lloyd DeMause's account of historical research reveal, childhood in earlier ages was often a nightmare of neglect, misery, and pain.

Source: Lloyd DeMause, "Our Forebears Made Childhood a Nightmare," *Psychology Today,* April 1975.

Virtually every child-rearing tract from antiquity to the 18th century recommended the beating of children. We found no examples from this period in which a child wasn't beaten, and hundreds of instances of not only beating, but battering, beginning in infancy.

. . .

One 19th-century German schoolmaster who kept score reported administering 911,527 strokes with a stick, 124,000 lashes with a whip, 136,715 slaps with his hand and 1,115,800 boxes on the ear. The beatings described in most historical sources began at an early age, continued regularly throughout childhood, and were severe enough to cause bruising and bloodying.

. . .

The baby was tied up tightly in swaddling bands for its first year, supposedly to prevent it from tearing off its ears, breaking its legs, touching its genitals or crawling around like an animal. Traditional swaddling, as one American doctor described it, "consists in entirely depriving the child of the use of its limbs by enveloping them in an endless bandage, so as to not unaptly resemble billets of wood, and by which the skin is sometimes excoriated, the flesh compressed, almost to gangrene . . ."

Swaddled infants were not only more convenient to care for, since they withdrew into themselves in sleep most of the day, but they were also more easily laid for hours behind hot ovens, hung on pegs on the wall, and, wrote one doctor, "left, like a parcel, in every convenient corner." In addition, they were often thrown around like a ball for amusement. In 16th-century France, a brother of Henri IV, while being tossed from one window to another, was dropped and killed.

. . .

Although there were many exceptions to the general pattern, the average child of parents with some wealth spent his earliest years in the home of a wet nurse, returned home at age three or four to the care of other servants, and was sent out to service, apprenticeship, or school by age seven, so that the amount of time parents of means actually spent raising their children was minimal. . . . Of 21,000 children born in Paris in 1780,

17,000 were sent into the country to be wet-nursed, 3,000 were placed in nursery homes, 700 were wet-nursed at home and only 700 were nursed by their own mothers. Even those mothers who kept their infants at home often did not breastfeed them, giving them pap (water and grain) instead.

. . .

Children were always felt to be on the verge of turning into actual demons, or at least to be easily susceptible to "the power of the Devil." To keep their small devils cowed, adults regularly terrorized them with a vast army of ghostlike figures, from the Lamia and Striga of the ancients, who ate children raw, to the witches of Medieval times, who would steal bad children away and suck their blood. One 19th-century tract described in simplified language the tortures God had in store for children in Hell: "The little child is in this red-hot oven. Hear how it screams to come out . . ."

. . .

Another method that parents used to terrorize their children employed corpses. A common moral lesson involved taking children to visit the gibbet, where they were forced to inspect rotting corpses hanging there as an example of what happens to bad children when they grow up. Whole classes were taken out of school to witness hangings, and parents would often whip their children afterwards to make them remember what they had seen.

. . .

In antiquity infanticide was so common that every river, dung-heap and cesspool used to be littered with dead infants. Polybius blamed the depopulation of Greece on the killing of legitimate children, even by wealthy parents. Ratios of boys to girls in census figures ran four to one, since it was rare for more than one girl in a family to be spared. Christians were considered odd for their opposition to infanticide, although even that opposition was mild, with few penalties. Large-scale infanticide of legitimate babies continued well into Medieval times, with boy-girl ratios in rich as well as poor families often still running two to one. As late as 1527, one priest admitted that "the latrines resound with the cries of children who have been plunged into them."

Figure 4.10 *Most traditional, preindustrial societies lacked a clear concept of childhood as a separate stage of life, and there was no distinct sphere of childhood games and other activities. Preindustrial Western art reflects this attitude: even as late as 1751, when this family portrait was painted, children were portrayed as "little adults" with serious, mature faces and none of the innocence or "cuteness" that we might look for in children today.*

Advanced industrialized societies, on the other hand, tend to be very child-centered. Children are socialized quite differently from adults: they have distinctive forms of dress and their own separate spheres of activity, ranging from children's TV and games to kindergartens and elementary schools. Adults tend to romanticize childhood as a period of carefree innocence, and they take pains to protect children from premature knowledge of such taboo subjects as death and sex. Children are exempted from playing full economic roles—in fact, the law forbids it—and have minimal social responsibilities.

Adolescence

In simple, preindustrial societies there were, in effect, only two main stages of life, immaturity and adulthood. In such societies the change from one status to another was usually a clear and abrupt one, often marked, in the case of males, by initiation ceremonies involving great pain or feats of endurance. As soon as these rituals were completed, the young person became an adult, with the same rights and responsibilities as other mature members of the community.

In the process of their development, modern industrial societies have added a new stage to the life course: instead of passing directly from childhood to adulthood, young people go through adolescence, a period roughly coinciding with the teenage years. Like childhood, adolescence is a social invention; in fact, the word came into use only at the beginning of this century. This new stage was introduced into the life course as a consequence of extended education.

In preindustrial and early industrial societies, most teenagers were full-time workers, and many were married, often in their early teens. But industrial societies required a work force whose members could at least read and write, and they needed a substantial number of professionals with highly sophisticated skills. Prolonged education therefore became necessary, but this inevitably entailed changes in the statuses and roles of those who now remained in school. The result was a large and unprecedented category of people who were physically and sexually mature, yet denied such adult responsibilities as full-time employment and marriage. At the turn of the century less than 7 percent of Americans completed high school, compared with over 80 percent today—a

Figure 4.11 *In many preindustrial societies the transition from childhood to adulthood is very abrupt. This transition usually takes place at puberty and is often marked by a social ceremony of initiation. These aboriginal boys in Australia are being held down by their elders while they undergo a painful circumcision ceremony, after which they will be able to take their place as adult members of the society. Traces of initiation ceremonies that mark changes in a young person's status are still found in modern societies—for example, the Jewish bar mitzvah, the "sweet sixteen" birthday party, the high school graduation ceremony, and the "hazing" that college freshmen sometimes face.*

significant and rapid change which, not surprisingly, has disrupted the traditional life course.

Because it is a relatively new stage of the life course in a rapidly changing society, adolescence is an ambiguous and often confusing period, marked by vaguely defined rights and responsibilities. The American socialization process equips people poorly for the challenges of adolescence, for teenagers are continually faced with contradictory demands and pressures. Having more freedom than children but less than adults, adolescents are constantly tempted to question or test the authority of parents and teachers. Segregated from other age groups in high schools, they tend to form their own subculture, with norms, values, and attitudes that may differ significantly from those of the society that surrounds them.

In emerging postindustrial societies, a large proportion of high school graduates continue on to college and even graduate school, further delaying their acceptance of full adult responsibilities. Kenneth Keniston (1970) suggests that yet another stage is now being introduced into the life course, that of "youth." This stage is an optional one that runs from about eighteen to thirty and contains students and other young people who for one reason or another do not immediately "settle down" into the usual defining characteristics of mature adulthood—a steady job, a permanent home, marriage, and a family.

Mature Adulthood

Sometime around the mid-twenties the individual enters mature adulthood. At this stage primary socialization is virtually completed, and the individual has developed a core identity that is henceforth unlikely to be radically modified (except under such extreme conditions as resocialization in a prison, mental hospital, or religious cult). For the most part, socialization now builds on the fairly stable foundations of prior experience.

Most people marry in their twenties or early thirties, establishing a home and a family. Their task becomes that of developing a fulfilling lifestyle and maintaining a warm relationship with their spouse and their offspring. In a rapidly changing modern society this task is harder, perhaps, than it would have been in a traditional society, for the future is more uncertain. The only real certainty, in fact, is that social change will render a good deal of prior socialization irrelevant. Only a few decades ago, for example, the roles of husband and wife were fairly rigid: the husband worked and was the economic mainstay of the family; the wife stayed home and raised the children. This pattern is now the exception rather than the rule, yet many adults have not been socialized for this change in traditional roles.

The forties and fifties are a period of consolidation. There is no more time now for illusion: root changes in personal, social, and economic life grow more unlikely, and what people have become is what, more or less, they will continue to be. Men and women both face the inevitable physical and psychological signs of aging: physical prowess and beauty fade, and an awareness grows that one's life is more than half over. It is now recognized that this period can sometimes include a "mid-life crisis," marked by increased rates of depression, alcoholism, divorce, and suicide. Men in particular may be vulnerable to the idea that if they have not "made it" in their chosen field by now, they probably never will. Yet a "crisis" is by no means inevitable, and, even if it occurs, it can usually be overcome. For the many people who have successfully negotiated the life course up to this point, these years are among the most comfortable and satisfying of their lives (Levinson, 1978; Gould, 1978; Pearlin, 1980).

Drawing by Richter; © 1985
The New Yorker Magazine, Inc.

"Are you sure this doesn't have mid-life crisis
written all over it?"

Old Age

Perhaps the greatest failure of the American socialization process is that it poorly prepares people to face old age (and later, death). Preindustrial societies were generally oriented toward the old rather than the young: the aged were respected for their wisdom and held an honored place in the family and the community. They had many roles to fill—familial, social, religious, and even economic, for they typically worked until advanced old age. In modern industrialized societies the situation is quite different. The knowledge of the elderly may seem obsolete, their authority may be negligible, and they may even be unwanted by their children: often, the best they can do is attempt not to be a "burden." There are few useful roles for the aged: they generally retire around age sixty-five, and are left with little or no part to play in economic life. On the whole, however, the situation of the elderly in the United States is much brighter than it was a decade or two ago. The average age of Americans is now higher than at any time in the nation's history, and the aged have used their numbers and influence to gain many benefits that have improved the quality of their lives.

Figure 4.12 *The elderly had an honored and respected role in traditional societies, and typically spent their last years living with their children and grandchildren. In the modern United States, however, the old are relatively segregated from the rest of society, sometimes being placed in old-age homes or nursing homes. More than two-thirds of all deaths now take place in hospitals and geriatric institutions.*

In time, too, the burden of the years affects everyone: signs such as baldness, wrinkling, and stiffness in the limbs all announce the gradual degeneration of the body that comes with advanced age. Of course, different people age physically at very different rates; but ill health becomes steadily more common until more than three-quarters of those aged sixty-five or over suffer from some chronic health condition. Yet the infirmity of some of the aged can have social as well as physical causes: if we offer the very old the role of an infirm person who has outlived any real usefulness to society, we must not be surprised that some of the elderly live up to these social expectations. Most of the aged, of course, are able to enjoy their retirement and to review a life with its share of satisfaction and fulfillment. But in a society that worships youth and gives power, wealth, and prestige to the middle-aged, old age can easily become a difficult and dismaying period (Foner, 1986). (The problems of the aged are discussed in more detail in Chapter 10, "Gender and Age Stratification.")

Death

Socialization for death is almost nonexistent in the United States. In preindustrial societies, deaths usually took place at home in the context of the family, and young people grew up with a close understanding of the experience. In modern America, however, death is very much a taboo subject; we speak of it in hushed tones and use such euphemisms as "passed away." As children we fear the subject; as adults we avoid it—even, and sometimes especially, when we are in the presence of someone who is dying.

The reason for this distinctively modern taboo seems to be that death, almost alone of natural processes, remains beyond the control of our advanced technology. Modern medicine, nutrition, and sanitation have all helped to extend our **life expectancy**—the number of years the average newborn in a given population can be expected to live. But they have had little, if any, effect on our **life span**—the maximum length of life possible in the species. The final point of the life course—the annihilation of the self, the ultimate confrontation with the unknown—mocks our claim to human mastery of the world, and we therefore try to deny the mystery and power of death by excluding it from our discussions and thoughts.

We also effectively exclude the dying from the ongoing life of the community. We have sanitized death and removed it as far as possible from everyday experience by ensuring that most people die in nursing homes, hospitals, and similar formal organizations that care for the sick and aged. Typically, therefore, the dying face their end in a bureaucratic environment, surrounded by other sick people and a professional staff, rather than in the intimacy of their homes with their loved ones. Sometimes, in fact, there is a conspiracy between professionals and relatives to hide the fact of death from the dying person. Research into the sociology of death and dying, however, has produced an impressive body of evidence to suggest that people die far more happily—even contentedly—if death is openly discussed with them beforehand (DeSpelder and Strickland, 1983). As the findings of sociological research into death and dying become more widely known, socialization for death is likely to become more effective: in recent years, for example, courses on the subject have appeared at high schools and colleges and have attracted large enrollments.

Socialization and Free Will

If our behavior and personalities depend so much on the content of our individual socialization, what becomes of human free will? Do we have any choice over our personal behavior, or is it all shaped for us by our past experiences?

Dennis Wrong (1961) has drawn attention to what he calls the "oversocialized conception" of human beings—the view that we are little more than the predictable products of a harmonious socialization into the social order. Wrong points out that people often feel coerced by society into doing things they do not want to do, a clear indication that socialization is less than perfect.

The experiences of past socialization are blended in unique ways by each person. Everyone faces the problem that different socializing influences contradict one another. The individual is pushed this way and that and constantly has to make personal judgments and decisions in unanticipated situations. Our personal histories may strongly influence our choices of action, of course. That is why courts are often willing to take an offender's past background into account before passing sentence, particularly when dealing with juveniles. But in practice the courts, like the rest of society, always insist at some point that people (unless they are mentally disordered) are capable of choosing courses of action and of "reforming" their personalities. We hold people responsible for their behavior precisely because they *can* exercise choice—particularly moral choice—over what they do.

For whatever reasons, everyone violates social norms at some time or another, often in novel and sometimes socially disapproved ways. Hearing a "different drummer," we do not keep pace with our companions—or, in George Herbert Mead's more sociological terms, the unsocialized "I" is never completely subservient to the socialized "me." Within the very broad limits provided by our place in history and society, we are free to fabricate our selves and our behavior as we wish—particularly if we understand the social process through which we became what we are.

Summary

1. Socialization is the lifelong process of social interaction through which people acquire personality and learn the way of life of their society. The process is essential for the survival of both the individual and society. People in the same culture tend to be similar in some general respects, but their unique experiences make them different.

2. The "nature versus nurture" debate is now recognized as a pointless one. Human personality and social behavior are the outcome of an interaction between biological potentials and cultural learning.

3. Evidence concerning children reared in isolation, children reared in institutions, and monkeys reared in isolation indicates that intimate social interaction is essential if later personal development is not to be severely impaired.

4. The emergence of the self is crucial for the development of personality. Cooley argued that the self emerges through experience of the "looking glass" supplied by the reactions of other people. Mead emphasized the development of the ability to take the role of others.

5. Cognitive or intellectual abilities develop through four basic stages: the sensori-motor stage, the preoperational stage, the concrete operational stage, and the formal operational stage. The content of thought, however, depends on the cultural environment.

6. Emotional development also seems to proceed in a definite sequence, although social factors affect how and whether emotions are expressed.

7. In the United States and most industrialized societies, there are four main agents of socialization: the family, the school, the peer group, and the mass media. Other agents also socialize the individual throughout life. In "total institutions," such as the military, resocialization may occur.

8. The content and stages of the life course are influenced by social as well as biological factors. American socialization often fails to equip people adequately for certain stages of the life course, particularly adolescence, old age, and dying. In modern industrialized societies, the life course now includes infancy and childhood, adolescence, youth (optionally), mature adulthood, old age, and death.

9. There is a danger of accepting an "oversocialized conception" of human beings. Socialization is never fully successful. We still retain a measure of free will and are responsible for our acts.

Important Terms

socialization (69)

personality (69)

life course (69)

self (74)

looking-glass self (75)

role-taking (76)

particular other (76)

generalized other (76)

agents of socialization (80)

peers (83)

mass media (84)

resocialization (85)

total institution (85)

life expectancy (91)

life span (91)

CHAPTER 5

Social Groups

"No man is an island," wrote the poet John Donne several centuries ago. He was acknowledging one of our most distinctive characteristics: the fact that we are social animals whose behavior and personalities are shaped by the groups to which we belong. Throughout life, most of our daily activities are performed in the company of others. Whether our purpose is working, playing, raising a family, learning, worshiping, or simply relaxing, we usually pursue it in groups, even if the group is as small as two or three people.

In its strictest sense, a **group** is a collection of people interacting together on the basis of shared expectations about one another's behavior. As a result of this interaction, members feel a common sense of "belonging." They distinguish members from nonmembers and expect certain kinds of behavior from one another that they would not necessarily expect from outsiders.

Every group has its own boundaries, norms, values, and interrelated statuses and roles, such as those of leader, follower, joker, or scapegoat. In some groups this structure is rigid and explicit: members may hold official positions, and values and norms may be embodied in written objectives and rules. In other groups the structure may be much more flexible: values and norms may be vague and shifting, and statuses and roles may be subject to negotiation and change.

People form groups for a purpose, generally one that the members cannot achieve satisfactorily through individual effort. The purpose of a group may be an explicit one, such as raising money for charity or waging war against an enemy, or it may be less clearly defined, such as having a good time. The fact that the members of a group share common goals means that they tend to be generally similar to one another in ways that are relevant to the group's purpose. If the goals of the group are political, the members tend to share similar political opinions. If the goals are leisure activities, the members tend to be of similar age and social class and to have common leisure interests. The more the members interact within the group, the more they are influenced by its norms and values and the more similar they are likely to become.

Primary and Secondary Groups

As we saw in Chapter 3 ("Society"), there are two basic types of social groups: primary and secondary.

A **primary group** consists of a small number of people who interact over a relatively long period on a direct, intimate basis. The relationships among the members have emotional depth, and the group tends to endure over time. Primary groups are always small because large numbers of people cannot interact in a highly personal, face-to-face manner. Large groups therefore tend to break down into smaller, more intimate cliques. Typical primary groups include the family, a gang, or a college peer group.

Figure 5.1 *A primary group consists of a small number of people who interact in direct and intimate ways, usually over a long period of time. In traditional societies virtually all social life took place in the context of primary groups. These Balinese, participating in a system of cooperative rice harvesting, form a primary group. They know one another well and interact together as full persons, not in terms of specific roles. Although in modern societies we still spend a good deal of time in primary groups, much of our social life takes place in less intimate settings.*

A **secondary group** consists of a number of people who interact on a relatively temporary, anonymous, and impersonal basis. The members come together for some specific, practical purpose, such as making a committee decision or attending a convention. There is limited face-to-face contact, and members relate to one another only in terms of specific roles, such as division manager, supervisor, and employee. Secondary groups can be either small or large.

Any newly formed small group is a secondary group at first, although it may become a primary group if its members eventually come to know one another well and begin to interact on a more intimate basis. A college seminar group, for example, may start out as a secondary group, but after a while it may become a primary group, or smaller primary groups may develop within it. All large groups, however, are secondary groups. These groups include organizations such as business corporations, large factories, government departments, political parties, and religious movements. Large secondary groups always contain smaller primary groups within them. Colleges and army camps, for example, are secondary groups, but they may contain hundreds of primary groups.

In traditional, preindustrial societies almost all social life took place in the context of primary groups, such as the kinship network or the small village. In modern industrialized societies, dense urban populations and the spread of large organizations have made social life much more anonymous. Many of our daily interactions involve secondary relationships with people we encounter in limited and specific roles and may never meet again.

Figure 5.2 *A secondary group contains a number of people who have few emotional ties to one another. The members usually meet together for some practical purpose, and they interact with one another in terms of specific roles rather than as full persons. Secondary groups, such as this athletic organization, are characteristic of modern societies.*

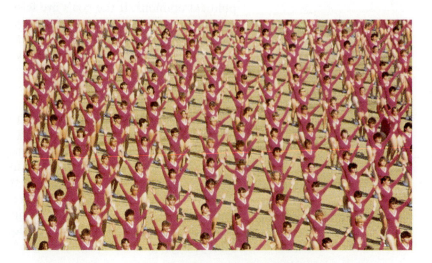

Small Groups

A **small group** is one that contains few enough members for the participants to relate to one another as individuals. Whether a small group is primary or secondary depends on the nature of the relationships among its members. A gathering of old friends is a primary group; a number of previously unacquainted people trapped in an elevator for half an hour is a small secondary group.

The Effects of Size

The single most important feature of small groups is probably their size, for this characteristic determines the kinds of interaction that can take place among the members. The smaller the group is, the more personal and intense the interaction can become.

The smallest possible group is a **dyad,** a group containing two people. A dyad differs from all other groups in that its members have to take account of each other. If one member ignores the conversation of the other or begins daydreaming, the interaction is disrupted, and if one member withdraws from the group, it simply ceases to exist. If another member is added, forming a **triad,** a group containing three people, the situation alters significantly. Any one member can ignore the conversation of the others without destroying the interaction in the group. Two members can form a coalition against one, so any individual can become subject to group pressure.

As more members are added, the nature of the interaction continues to change. People can take sides in discussions, and more than one coalition can be formed. In a group of up to about seven people, all the members can take part in the same conversation, but beyond that point it becomes progressively more likely that smaller groups will form, with several conversations taking place at the same time. If the group becomes larger than about ten or twelve people, it is virtually impossible for them to take part in a common interaction unless one member takes the role of leader and regulates the group's behavior so that everyone has a chance to contribute.

Leadership

In fact, leadership is one element that is always present in groups. A **leader** is someone who, largely by virtue of certain personality characteristics, is consistently able to influence the behavior of others. Groups have leaders even if the leaders do not hold formal positions of authority (and even if the group is determined *not* to have a leader).

Research has indicated that there are two distinct types of leadership in small groups. **Instrumental leadership** is the kind necessary to organize a group in pursuit of its goals. An instrumental leader proposes courses of action and influences the members to follow them. **Expressive leadership** is the kind necessary to create harmony and solidarity among group members. An expressive leader is concerned about keeping morale high and minimizing conflicts. The expressive leader is well liked by the group. When a newly formed group is asked to choose a leader, it usually gives both roles to the same person, because individuals who are well liked also tend to dominate group activities. Leaders generally do not fill both roles for long, however, because people who direct group activities tend to lose popularity. In such cases, the original leader may retain the instrumental role, but another group member emerges to assume the expressive role (Bales, 1953; Slater, 1955).

Do leaders have distinctive characteristics that are not shared by their followers? While there are certainly no hard and fast rules, it seems that leaders are likely to be taller than the average group member, to be judged better-looking than other members, to have a higher IQ, and to be more sociable, talkative, determined, and self-confident. In addition, leaders also tend to be more liberal in outlook, even in conservative groups (Crosbie, 1975). But personality characteristics alone cannot tell us who is likely to be a good leader, because different conditions require different leadership qualities. The kind of leadership required in a military battle or the aftermath of an earthquake may call for different qualities, and different people, than the kind of leadership required at a corporation board meeting or a political convention.

Style of leadership may be one of three basic kinds: *authoritarian,* in which the leader simply gives orders; *democratic,* in which the leader attempts to win a consensus on a course of action; and *laissez-faire,* in which the leader is easygoing and makes little attempt to direct or organize the group. In the United States, at least, the leaders who seem to be most effective in holding small groups together and seeing that they accomplish their tasks tend to be democratic. Authoritarian leaders are much less effective, because the work of the group becomes bogged down in internal conflicts. Laissez-faire leaders are usually ineffectual, for the group lacks directives and tackles problems in a haphazard way (White and Lippitt, 1960). This does not mean, however, that democratic leadership is the most effective in all situations. An authoritarian leader, for example, is more effective in emergency situations, where speed and efficiency outweigh other considerations. For this reason, leadership in armies, police forces, and hospital emergency rooms is typically authoritarian. Democratic leaders are more effective in situations where group members are concerned about individual rights or where there is disagreement over goals. However, research on American subjects, who have been socialized to react negatively to authoritarian leaders, cannot be automatically generalized to cultures where people expect authoritarian leadership and have virtually no experience of democratic decision making.

Group Decision Making

People often assume that when it comes to making decisions, two heads, or preferably several heads, are better than one. How valid is this belief? The answer depends to some extent on the problem that has to be solved. In "determinate tasks"—problems that have only one correct solution, such as a crossword puzzle—group effort increases the chances of finding the answer. As a matter of simple probability, a group is more likely to come up with the correct solution than a single person is. The situation is rather different for "indeterminate tasks"—problems that have no necessarily correct solution, such as selecting one of several applicants for a job or deciding on how to handle an aircraft hijacking. In such cases different groups may arrive at very different decisions, probably because each group is influenced by the opinions of particular dominant members. Sometimes group decisions for solving indeterminate problems seem better than those of individuals, but sometimes they seem worse.

When groups do make decisions, they usually do so through consensus and only rarely by the majority imposing its view on a reluctant minority. No matter what the views of the members are at the outset, the general tendency is for discussion to bring about greater agreement. For example, jury members often begin their discussions in disagreement or uncertainty, but they tend to move toward a common opinion and usually render a unanimous verdict. The only consistent exceptions occur in groups whose participants are representing the fixed opinions of others outside the group, and thus cannot easily budge—for example, in groups involving party politics or labor-management disputes.

However, unanimous decisions can cause a great deal of trouble if they also happen to be wrong. Irving Janis (1972; Janis and Mann, 1977) suggests one source of such poor judgment in groups: loyalty to the group may prevent individual members from raising controversial and uncomfortable questions. The members become so concerned with maintaining group harmony and consensus,

Drawing by C. Barsotti; © 1985
The New Yorker Magazine, Inc.

*"Then, gentlemen, it is the consensus of this meeting that we say
nothing, do nothing, and hope it all blows over before our next meeting."*

particularly when a difficult moral problem is involved, that they withhold their
reservations and criticisms. This "don't rock the boat" attitude results in what
Janis calls "groupthink," a decision-making process in which members ignore
information and alternatives that do not fit with the group's original assumptions. As an example of groupthink Janis cites the 1961 decision of President
Kennedy and his top advisers to sponsor the Bay of Pigs invasion of Cuba by
Cuban exiles dedicated to overthrowing Castro. This decision, which produced a
military and diplomatic fiasco, was based on strategic assumptions that were
almost ludicrous. Several members of the decision-making group had strong
private objections to the plan, yet the decision to launch the invasion was a
unanimous one.

Most group decision making, however, does involve debate among the participants. The process of decision making in small groups generally proceeds
through a sequence of stages. The first stage is that of collecting information; the
members orient themselves to the problem by establishing the facts. The second
stage is that of analyzing and evaluating the information; at this point members
express opinions and react to the opinions of others. The third stage is that of
reaching a decision. Emotional tensions may rise at this stage, particularly if
coalitions form and disagreements persist. The fourth stage occurs once the decision is made; it involves a general effort to restore harmony in the group. The
members react more positively to one another, and there may be a certain
amount of joking and frivolity. In this way the continuing solidarity of the group
is assured (Bales and Strodtbeck, 1951).

Group Conformity

The pressure to conform to social expectations is strong in every aspect of life,
but it seems to be particularly powerful in the intense atmosphere of a small
group. One of the most dramatic examples of this tendency comes from some
experiments by Solomon Asch (1955), who found that people seem willing to
disavow the evidence of their own senses if it is contradicted by the judgment of
the rest of the group.

Asch assembled groups consisting of between seven and nine college students in what was described as a test of visual discrimination. However, in each
group only one of the students was actually a subject in the experiment: the
others were secret accomplices of the experimenter. In a series of eighteen trials
Asch displayed pairs of cards like those shown in Figure 5.3. One card contained
a single line, which was to serve as a standard. The other card contained three
lines, one the same length as the standard, and the other two of significantly
different lengths from the standard and from each other. The members of the
group were asked one by one to state aloud which of the lines matched the
standard.

When the first pair of cards was presented, the group unanimously picked
the correct line. The same thing happened on the second trial. In twelve of the
remaining sixteen trials, however, all Asch's secret accomplices agreed on what

**Standard and Comparison
Lines in the Asch
Experiment**

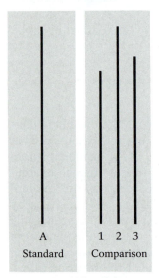

A
Standard

1   2   3
Comparison

Source: Adapted from Solomon Asch, "Effects of Group Pressure upon the Modification and Distortion of Judgments," in H. Proshansky and B. Seidenbert (eds.), *Basic Studies in Social Psychology* (New York: Holt, Rinehart and Winston, 1965), pp. 393–401.

Figure 5.3 *These are the lines presented to subjects in one trial in Asch's experiments. Asch asked the subjects to state which of the comparison lines appeared to be the same length as the standard line. Control subjects (who made the judgment without any group pressure) chose the correct line over 99 percent of the time; but experimental subjects who were under group pressure to choose the wrong line did so in nearly a third of the cases.*

was clearly an incorrect answer. How did the real subject of the experiment react to this uncomfortable situation? In about a third of the cases, the subject yielded to the majority and conformed to its decision. Subsequent interviews with these yielders revealed that only a few of them had, in fact, perceived the majority choice as correct: most of the yielders had judged the length of the lines correctly but did not want to be the "odd one out" by giving the right answer. The experiment vividly shows a group's power to induce conformity, although, like all laboratory experiments, it leaves open the question of whether people would react exactly the same way in "real life."

One type of conformity that does occur quite often is **bystander apathy**— the reluctance of people to "get involved" in an apparent emergency affecting a stranger in public. A particularly notorious case took place in 1964, when a woman named Kitty Genovese was murdered outside her home in New York in the early morning. Her assailant took half an hour to kill her, and her screams were heard by at least thirty-eight of her neighbors. These people watched the entire scene from their windows, but not one of them came to her aid or even bothered to call the police. Not all instances of bystander apathy are this extreme, of course, yet even people who will readily help friends or acquaintances in private often become mere onlookers in a public crisis. Why? The case of Kitty Genovese stimulated hundreds of research studies on bystander apathy, and this apparently callous behavior is now well understood.

Two factors seem central in bystander apathy. The first is that many possible emergencies are ambiguous. A person lying in a city street might be ill or dying, or might merely be asleep or drunk. What appears to be smoke pouring from a window might actually be steam from a radiator. People will not act in these situations until they have interpreted them, and this is where the second factor comes into play. In order to interpret the situation, people look for cues from other bystanders. If other people in the group appear unconcerned, the individual is unlikely to define the situation as an emergency. Each person is hesitant about "overreacting," because he or she will "lose face" and appear foolish if the wrong interpretation is made. In many situations, of course, the bystanders

Figure 5.4 *Bystander apathy, or the unwillingness of bystanders to "get involved" in the problems of others, is especially common in cities and other crowded environments. People are re-* *luctant to interpret a situation as an emergency unless "someone else" does so first, with the result that they all tend to ignore the problem.*

collectively mislead one another. Just as an entire group can panic when some of its members define a situation as dangerous, so it can maintain a collective unconcern when none of its members makes such a definition. Only when someone takes the responsibility to act do others tend to follow suit. But the larger the group, the less likely it is that anyone will assume this responsibility. If you encounter an emergency on your own, there is no way of escaping the moral responsibility to do something about it. But if a number of people are present, the moral responsibility to act is much more diffused; everyone tends to wait for "someone else" to take the initiative (Darley and Latané, 1968).

Spacing in Groups

People in groups can communicate with one another not only by speech and gesture, but also by manipulating the space between them. People have a very strong sense of some personal space that surrounds them and are greatly discomforted when it is invaded. Crowded subway cars, for example, are experienced as psychologically stressful even if they are not actually physically uncomfortable, and outbreaks of aggression are more likely in crowded situations than in less crowded situations that are otherwise similar.

Edward T. Hall (1959, 1966) suggests that there are four distinct zones of private space:

1. *Intimate distance.* This zone extends up to 18 inches from the body. It is reserved for people with whom one may have such intimate physical contact as lying together with bodies touching.

2. *Personal distance.* This zone extends from 18 inches to 4 feet. It is reserved for friends and acquaintances. Some physical intimacy is permitted within this zone, such as putting one's arm around another's shoulder or greeting someone with a hug, but there are limits.

3. *Social distance.* This zone extends from 4 to 12 feet. It is maintained in relatively formal group situations, such as job interviews. There is no actual physical contact within this zone.

4. *Public distance.* This zone extends for 12 feet and beyond, and is maintained by people wishing to distinguish themselves from the other people present. Speakers addressing an audience, for example, maintain this distance from the rest of the group.

Research has shown that the physical environment has some influence over the standing and seating arrangements in groups. The larger the area in which the interaction takes place, the closer the participants will approach one another. Living-room seating is generally arranged within an arc of 8 feet, since this is the maximum distance for comfortable conversation. Within such physical constraints, people's proximity is influenced by their precise relationship to one another. People generally approach closer to a friend than to an acquaintance or stranger, and maintain greater distance between themselves and others who are of a different age, race, or other social status. Pairs of females sit closer than pairs of males: the average distance between male pairs is as much as a foot greater than between female pairs. The distance between opposite-sexed pairs is more variable, for it depends on how intimate the partners are. Seating arrangements in groups are affected by the kind of interaction that is taking place. When the relationship is a friendly or cooperative one, the partners usually choose adjacent or corner seating; when it is competitive or formal, they tend to sit opposite one another (Sommer, 1979). All these manipulations of physical space convey subtle symbolic messages, for they reflect and maintain the social intimacy or distance that exists among the group members.

Figure 5.5 *People have a strong sense of personal space, and in the absence of other constraints will tend to arrange themselves more or less evenly over the available territory.*

Ingroups and Outgroups

Every group must have some boundaries, for there would otherwise be no way of distinguishing between members and nonmembers. In fact, all groups tend to develop a strong sense of the distinction between the "we" of the group and the "they" who are outside it. People tend to regard the **ingroup**—any group one belongs to and identifies with—as being somehow special. Correspondingly, they tend to regard the **outgroup**—any alternative group that one does not belong to or identify with— as less worthy, and may even view it with hostility. A common way of maintaining boundaries between groups, in fact, is through some form of conflict between them. The presence of a common enemy (real or imaginary) draws members together and increases the solidarity and cohesion of the group (Coser, 1956).

An experiment by Muzafer Sherif (1956) illustrates how ingroup loyalties can help to maintain group boundaries and solidarity. Sherif's subjects were eleven-year-old boys who did not know each other before the experiment began. Sherif took the boys for an extended stay at a summer camp, where they soon began to form friendship cliques. Once these groups had been formed, Sherif randomly divided the boys into two main groups and lodged them in separate cabins some distance apart. In doing so, he disrupted the cliques that had already formed, but the boys soon began to develop strong loyalties to their new groups. Next, Sherif pitted the two groups against each other in various competitive activities. The result was increasingly intense antagonism and hostility between the groups, including between those members on either side who had earlier been in the same friendship cliques. Finally, Sherif created some emergency situations, such as an interruption of the water supply, that required both groups to cooperate as a team. Within a short period, members of the two groups began to interact as a single group, their old hostilities forgotten. Sherif's experiment shows clearly how loyalty contributes to the maintenance of group boundaries, how conflict between groups heightens these loyalties, and how ingroup feelings lessen and disappear once the members of different groups unite in pursuit of common goals.

Networks

People and groups continually interact with other people and groups. These multiple contacts are organized into **social networks**—webs of relationships that link the individual directly and indirectly to other people. Your own network, for example, consists of all your primary ties (like relatives and close friends) and all your secondary ties (like your classmates or your dentist); additionally, it potentially includes all the ties of the members of your own network. A person's network is not exactly a group, because its members do not all interact together, but networks do contain groups and do provide indirect access to still other groups.

In principle, your social network can be depicted diagrammatically on a piece of paper, with a point to represent each acquaintance and a line between the points to represent a relationship. In practice, such a diagram would soon blunt your pencil in an illegible chaos of dots and crossing lines. The average person in a modern society has a pool of between 500 and 2,500 acquaintances, many of whom are in turn acquainted with one another (Milgram, 1967). If we tried adding the full networks of these other individuals to our diagram, it would soon include millions of people. That is why we sometimes find, on meeting a stranger, that we share a mutual acquaintance—a "coincidence" that leaves us musing, "It's a small world."

Networks form a vital part of social life. People's sense of "community," for example, depends to a great extent on the density of their local network—on the presence of many familiar faces. Similarly, people use their networks to get advice when they face unexpected problems or events: friends and acquaintances are asked to recommend a lawyer, a psychiatrist, a building contractor.

"It's not what you know, it's who you know, And who do I know? You!"

Drawing by Dana Fradon; © 1974 The New Yorker Magazine, Inc.

Research has also shown that networks are important for getting jobs and for career advancement. In fact, some people engage in what they actually call "networking"—going to parties, joining clubs, and attending specific functions in order to meet people who might prove influential or helpful later, on the general principle of "It isn't what you know, it's who you know." Part of the difficulty women have had in achieving high-status jobs is that their networks generally contain smaller, fewer, and lower-status groups than those of men, who are better able to utilize what is, literally, an "old-boy network." In general, people who join many groups, or who join large groups, greatly increase the size of their social networks—a fact that has long been appreciated by insurance agents, political candidates, and others who want ready access to many "contacts" (Lin, Ensler, and Vaughn, 1981; McPherson and Smith-Lovin, 1981).

Reference Groups

There is one kind of group to which people may feel they "belong" even if they are not actually members. This is the **reference group,** a group to which people refer when making evaluations of themselves and their behavior.

We constantly evaluate ourselves—our actions, our appearance, our values, our ambitions, our lifestyles, and so on. In making these evaluations, we always refer to the standards of some group. The group may be one of which we are a member, such as the family or the peer group. But it may also be one we do not actually belong to. People may judge themselves, for example, by the standards of a community they previously lived in or of a community they hope to join in the future. A sociology student who plans eventually to take a graduate degree may evaluate his or her progress in terms of the standards of graduate students rather than those of an undergraduate peer group. A medical student may refer to the standards of physicians rather than to those of fellow students.

Our evaluations of ourselves are strongly influenced by the reference groups we choose: if you get a B in an examination and compare yourself with A students, your self-evaluation will be very different than it would be if you were to compare yourself with C students. Reference groups are therefore an important element in the socialization process, for they can shape individual behavior and personality just as powerfully as any other group to which a person feels loyalty.

Drawing by M. Stevens; © 1987 The New Yorker Magazine, Inc.

"Here's a picture of some people doing the exact same thing we're doing, but they seem to be having a lot more fun."

Formal Organizations

Until a century or so ago, nearly all social life took place within the context of small primary groups—the family, the church congregation, the schoolhouse, the farm or shop, and the village community. Today the social landscape is dominated by large, impersonal organizations, such as corporations, colleges, or government departments, that influence our lives from the moment of birth.

Organizational Chart of a Publishing Company

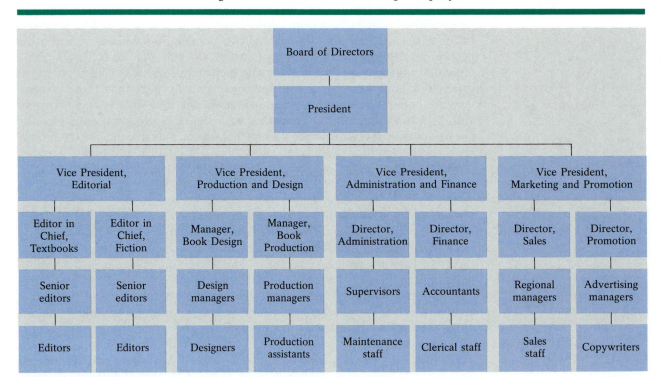

Figure 5.6 *This diagram is a typical organizational chart, setting out the formal chains of command and communication within a formal organization, a hypothetical publishing company. Similar charts, some of them extremely complex, can be drawn for any formal organization.*

Associations of this type are generally **formal organizations,** large secondary groups that are deliberately and rationally designed to achieve specific objectives. Unlike primary groups, which are informal, these organizations have a carefully designed structure that coordinates the activities of the members in the interests of the organization's goals. For example, formal organizations typically include a number of official statuses, such as those of president, secretary, and treasurer. Rights and responsibilities within the organization are attached primarily to the office a person occupies, not to the person as an individual. It is possible to draw a chart of any formal organization, showing the relationship of the various official positions to one another, without any reference to the actual individuals involved.

Most people seem to have an ambivalent attitude toward formal organizations. On the one hand, our affluence and our very way of life are clearly dependent on the existence of these organizations. On the other hand, the size, impersonality, and power of formal organizations are often seen as dehumanizing and threatening, and they have been held responsible for much of the feeling of alienation that is said to characterize modern industrialized societies.

Bureaucracy

The larger and more complex a formal organization becomes, the greater is the need for a chain of command to coordinate the activities of its members. This need is fulfilled by a **bureaucracy,** a hierarchical authority structure that operates under explicit rules and procedures. Understanding bureaucracy is the key to the analysis of formal organizations.

The word "bureaucracy" usually carries negative connotations in everyday speech. It brings to mind images of "red tape," forms in triplicate, lost files, incorrect bills, unanswered letters, clerks and officials blinded by petty regulations, "runarounds," and "buck-passing." Yet although "bureaucracy" often seems synonymous with "inefficiency" from the point of view of the individual, the bureaucratic form has thrived for the simple reason that it is, for most purposes, highly efficient. It is the most effective means ever devised for making a large organization work. Sociologists therefore use the word in a neutral sense, without the overtones it generally has in ordinary usage.

Weber's Analysis

The foundations for our understanding of bureaucracy were laid by Max Weber (1922). He analyzed the phenomenon in terms of what he called an ideal type. An **ideal type** is an abstract description, constructed from a number of real cases in order to reveal their essential features. (For example, an ideal type of an American college might refer to such features as the roles of college administrators, professors, and students; to such activities as teaching, learning, and research; and to other characteristics such as social organizations, honor societies, sports, and so on. The result would be an abstract description of a "typical" American college. For some purposes—explaining American education to a foreigner, for instance—this ideal type might be more useful than a description of a particular college.) Weber's ideal type of bureaucracy therefore shows us the essential characteristics of the bureaucratic form, although any individual bureaucracy will not necessarily conform to this description in every way.

According to Weber, a bureaucracy has the following typical features:

1. *Division of labor.* There is a clear-cut division of labor among the various officials. Each member of the organization has a specialized job to do and concentrates on this specific task.

2. *Hierarchy.* There is a hierarchy of authority within the organization. This hierarchy takes the shape of a pyramid, with greater authority for the few at the top and less for the many at the bottom. Each official takes orders from the officials immediately above and takes responsibility for those immediately below.

3. *Regulations.* An elaborate system of rules and regulations (mostly in written form) governs the day-to-day functioning of the bureaucracy. Decisions are based on these rules and on established precedents.

4. *Impersonality.* Officials remain impersonal in their contacts with the public, who they treat as "cases," not as individuals. They also adopt a detached attitude to other members of the organization, interacting with them in terms of their official roles. Personal feelings are thus excluded from official business.

5. *Record-keeping.* Complete written records—"the files"—are kept of all the organization's activities, and where possible, information is kept in a standardized format.

6. *Administrative staff.* There is a specialized administrative staff of managers, secretaries, record-keepers, and others. Their sole function is to keep the organization as a whole running smoothly.

7. *Career structure.* Employees are assumed to anticipate a career with the organization. Candidates for positions in the hierarchy are appointed on the basis of seniority or merit, or some combination of the two—not on the grounds of favoritism, family connections, or other criteria that are irrelevant to organizational efficiency.

Weber argued that such an organization would be highly efficient at coordinating the activities of its members and achieving specific objectives. As an ideal type, his analysis has stood the test of time. Later researchers have found it necessary to make one major modification, however, to take account of the informal, primary relationships that exist in all bureaucracies.

Figure 5.7 *A characteristic feature of bureaucracies is the anonymous, impersonal nature of the relationships between officials and outsiders. This* *painting,* Government Bureau, *by the modern American artist George Tooker, captures that impersonality.*

The Informal Structure of Bureaucracy

The formal structure of a bureaucracy is easily determined by a glance at its organizational chart, which will show the lines of authority from one official to another. In practice, however, no bureaucracy ever works strictly by the book (Blau and Meyer, 1973; Lehman and Etzioni, 1980; R. Hall, 1982; Perrow, 1986).

The formal structure of a bureaucracy always breeds informal relationships and practices, for people get to know one another as individuals, not simply as officials. Employees establish their own norms about how long a "lunch hour" should be. They swap tasks to make their work more varied and take over one another's duties when someone wants unofficial time off. They develop norms about the type and amount of company property that they can "take home" for private use. Because information travels slowly through official channels and because some decisions at the executive level are deliberately concealed from subordinates, an informal social network—"the grapevine"—develops to disseminate rumors. People who, in terms of the organizational chart, ought not to be in possession of important information often gain access to it.

Members of a bureaucracy are never treated entirely in terms of the offices they hold. One person, despite his or her high office, may be known as an incompetent whose advice should never be taken; another as an "old-timer," with valuable knowledge of rules and precedents and how to bend them; another as a "rising star" marked out for future promotion and worth cultivating in the meanwhile. Following the tortuous route of the official channels is no less irritating to members of a bureaucracy than it is to outsiders, and they quickly learn shortcuts through the system by way of informal networks of friendly officials. Bureaucrats may bend the rules to help someone who has gained their sympathy, or they may subtly obstruct a case involving a member of the public who has been rude or offensive.

Dysfunctions of Bureaucracy

Weber did not elaborate on the dysfunctions, or negative effects, of bureaucracy, although he was certainly aware of them. Other sociologists have subsequently identified a number of dysfunctions that are built into the bureaucratic form and that may well hinder its workings.

1. *Inefficiency in unusual cases.* Bureaucracies are efficient because their rules are designed for *typical* cases and problems. Officials can handle these cases quickly and effectively by applying uniform rules and procedures. Yet this means that the bureaucracy is ill equipped to handle *unusual* cases. When an unprecedented case arises that does not fit the rules, the bureaucracy is stumped. The problem may then circulate from desk to desk for weeks, months, or even years, before it finally reaches someone who is authorized and willing to make a decision on the problem.

2. *"Trained incapacity."* Blind adherence to existing rules and procedures may result in what Thorstein Veblen (1922) caustically termed "trained incapacity"— the inability to make any new, imaginative response because of previous bureaucratic training. Relying on their predictable routines, bureaucracies tend to respond to new, unfamiliar problems with old, familiar—and sometimes inappropriate—procedures.

3. *Goal displacement.* There is always a risk that, over time, officials will tend to forget the supposed goals of their organization and focus their energies elsewhere. Frequently, the task of running a large organization generates its own budgetary, personnel, and other administrative problems, and day-to-day bureaucratic behavior may concentrate on the "office politics" of these internal issues, displacing attention from the original goals. Another form of goal displacement occurs when an organization's objective has been achieved. The bureaucrats do not simply resign and look for other jobs: on the contrary, they tend either to claim that there is still work to do, or to look for other goals to keep the organization going.

4. *Bureaucratic enlargement.* A related problem is the general tendency of all bureaucracies to grow. C. Northcote Parkinson (1957) has suggested, only half satirically, that "work expands to fill the time available for its completion" (see box on page 108). It is almost unknown for a bureaucracy to voluntarily spend less than its budget, or to hire fewer officials than it is authorized to employ. Officials tend to believe that their organization's work is so important that more resources should be devoted to it, and that more resources would lead to greater effectiveness. United States government agencies, for example, invariably seek annual budget increases—and sometimes go on a spending spree at the end of the fiscal year, fearing that if they underspend, Congress will cut their budgets the following year.

Drawing by Leo Cullum; © 1986 The New Yorker Magazine, Inc.

"I was just going to say 'Well, I don't make the rules.'
But of course, I do make the rules."

nant group gets too far out of line with rank-and-file opinion, it risks being displaced by another group. Successful challenges to the power of the oligarchy have been recorded in a variety of bureaucratic organizations, ranging from labor unions to political parties to the military (Lipset et al., 1956; Zald and Berger, 1978). Michels also overlooked another vital aspect of organizations: whether they are oligarchic or not, they are often the best means of achieving a given goal. Many of the democratic advances of the past century have resulted, directly or indirectly, from the efforts of large-scale organizations.

Our democratic theories have their roots in the small-scale world of the eighteenth century. The thinkers and revolutionaries who created those theories could not anticipate the growth and spread of vast, formal organizations that separate us from control over major social, political, and economic decisions. In this respect, as in many others, the radical changes that have taken place in the group basis of social life present a range of new problems.

Other Forms of Organization

Most formal organizations today may conform closely to Weber's ideal type, but this is not the only conceivable type. Like any other aspect of culture, organizations are shaped by their social environment, and so vary from one time and place to another. There are significant differences, for example, among the Japanese corporation of the post-World War II years, the collectivist organization that has emerged in Western industrialized nations in recent years, and the modified formal organizations that may be emerging today.

The Japanese Corporation   The organizational model followed by the largest Japanese corporations draws on a long cultural tradition that emphasizes the importance of the group over the individual. When people join a major Japanese corporation, they are making a lifetime commitment, which the corporation reciprocates. Unless the employee commits a crime, he or she will not be fired or laid off. All promotions are made from inside the organization; outsiders are not even considered. Most promotions are based on seniority, so people of the same age move more or less together through the organizational hierarchy, with little competition among them. Workers are organized into small teams, and it is the teams—not the individual workers—whose performance is evaluated. Decision making is collective: rather than issue new policies, the top officials merely ratify them after they have been discussed and approved at every level of the organization (the Japanese word for this process literally means "bottom-up" decision making).

Unlike Western corporations, which usually limit the relationship between organization and employee to matters that are "strictly business," Japanese corporations take responsibility for their workers' welfare. They provide a whole range of services, sometimes including housing, recreation, health care, and continuing education. The workers, in turn, show great loyalty to the company—perhaps by wearing company uniforms, singing the company song, working exceptionally long hours, or taking part in company-organized sporting and other activities. This relationship between organization and worker reflects a deep difference between Japanese and Western cultures: to the Japanese, it indicates a bond of commitment that ensures security and solidarity; to Americans, it would seem like suffocating paternalism that prevents individual achievement and overlooks "whiz kid" potential (Vogel, 1980; Rohlen, 1979; Pascale and Athos, 1981; Reischauer, 1981; Ouchi, 1981).

Figure 5.9 *In many large Japanese corporations, the workers are required to exhibit company loyalty through such group activities as singing company songs and performing calisthenics before starting the day's duties. Americans, who value individualism, would probably resent these rules as an intrusion into their privacy, but the Japanese, who are more community-oriented, seem to appreciate them as a means of cementing the bonds between worker and organization.*

The Collective The period since the late 1960s has seen the spread in Western industrialized societies of a nonbureaucratic kind of organization, the collective. Typically, collectivist groups consist largely of volunteers or part-time workers who administer community projects such as free schools, alternative newspapers, medical or legal-aid clinics, or art centers. Those who choose this work often view the "establishment," as represented by large, formal organizations, with distaste.

As Joyce Rothschild-Whitt (1979) points out, the collectivist form differs sharply from the bureaucratic one in several respects. First, there is little division of labor, and individual members are encouraged to contribute a variety of talents to different jobs. Second, authority arises from the consensus of the collective as a whole, not from a hierarchy of officials. Third, individual initiative is more highly valued than rigid adherence to a set of rules. Fourth, members of the collective treat the public as individual people, not as a set of "cases." Fifth, the status of group members depends more on their personal qualities than on any official titles they might have.

Essentially, then, members of collectives are deliberately trying to create a setting that is the polar opposite of bureaucracy. But this effort is not without its own costs. Democracy is time-consuming, for long periods must be spent on staff discussions and consensus-seeking. The unconventional nature of collectives can cause them problems in dealing with more conventional organizations—for example, in trying to get bank loans. Most important, perhaps, collectives are suited only for small-scale enterprises in which virtually all relationships are primary; if collectives grew large, their informality would breed inefficiency. Although many thousands of collectives now exist in Western industrialized societies, there is little prospect of them replacing or even seriously competing with bureaucracies.

Organizational Reform   There is increasing pressure for reform of formal organizations. One source of this pressure is the new value of "self-fulfillment" discussed in Chapter 2 ("Culture"). The rigid requirements of bureaucracy are inconsistent with a value that emphasizes the personal growth of the individual. Rosabeth Kanter (1977) suggests various changes that might make formal organizations a more satisfying work environment. These include job rotation, periodic sabbaticals, the elimination of some levels of management so as to spread authority more evenly, and rewards for length of service as well as for position in the hierarchy.

Pressure for reform also comes from the professional advisers who are increasingly employed in formal organizations, such as economists, physicists, computer scientists, sociologists, and other highly trained experts. These professionals do not readily fit into the hierarchical structure of the bureaucracy. Their knowledge and expertise are individual properties, attaching to them as people rather than to their offices. Professionals require the freedom to innovate, experiment, and take risks, and they expect their work to be judged by others in their own reference group—not by a bureaucrat who has no knowledge of their field of expertise. As formal organizations come to rely more and more on advanced technologies and expert advice, there is likely to be some change in traditional hierarchical relationships (Blankenship, 1977).

Some writers have suggested that, in the future, bureaucracies will tend to become less centralized, perhaps through being reorganized into self-contained, more temporary units. For example, Alvin Toffler (1970, 1980) argues that rapidly changing modern conditions demand a more fluid type of organization, containing special-purpose units that are dissolved when their tasks are done. Other critics claim that bureaucracies will have to become more flexible and less hierarchical, and that in time, organizational charts might consist of a series of project groups, often making decisions through consensus, instead of the traditional hierarchies (Weiss and Barton, 1979; Kochen and Deutch, 1980). But this prospect is perhaps more tempting than persuasive. Although organizations may have to be modified to deal with new problems, many of their traditional concerns will remain, and their traditional structures are likely to remain as well. The real challenge of reform will be to develop better means of social control over bureaucracy and thus to ensure that we shall not be dominated by the organizations that were first established, after all, for our own efficiency and convenience.

Summary

1. Human beings are social animals who spend much of their time in groups. Primary groups consist of a small number of people who interact on an intimate basis. Secondary groups may be large or small, but their members interact without any emotional commitment to one another.

2. Extensive research has been devoted to small-group interaction. The size of groups influences the kind of interaction that can take place. Leadership in groups may be instrumental or expressive. Research suggests that, at least in America, democratic leaders are more effective than authoritarian or laissez-faire leaders. Groups are more effective than individuals at solving determinate problems, but group performance on indeterminate problems varies. Groups tend to arrive at decisions by consensus. There is sometimes a tendency toward "groupthink." Most group decisions proceed through a regular sequence of stages. There is strong pressure for conformity in groups, as suggested by Asch's experiments and the phenomenon of bystander apathy. Group members can communicate by manipulating the space between them.

3. Members of groups tend to regard their group as an "ingroup" and other groups as "outgroups." Conflict and tension between groups heighten feelings of group solidarity and loyalty, as Sherif's experiment shows.

4. Networks are webs of direct and indirect relationships. Networks are a vital part of social life.

5. Reference groups are those to which an individual refers when making self-evaluations. One need not be a member of a reference group in order to identify with it.

6. Large secondary groups generally take the form of formal organizations. These social groups dominate modern life.

7. Formal organizations are coordinated through bureaucracies. Weber saw bureaucracy as a form of rationalization, and by constructing an ideal type, analyzed the way bureaucracies operate. His analysis has since been modified to take account of the informal structure that exists in all bureaucracies. Although bureaucracies are highly efficient, they have many dysfunctions as well, particularly when faced with unprecedented or unfamiliar situations.

8. Bureaucracies tend to be oligarchic, a feature that Michels argued was incompatible with democracy.

9. Some alternative forms of organization are the Japanese corporation, the collective, and emerging types of reformed organization.

Important Terms

group (95)

primary group (95)

secondary group (96)

small group (97)

dyad (97)

triad (97)

leader (97)

instrumental leadership (97)

expressive leadership (97)

bystander apathy (100)

ingroup (102)

outgroup (102)

social network (102)

reference group (103)

formal organization (104)

bureaucracy (104)

ideal type (105)

oligarchy (109)

CHAPTER 6

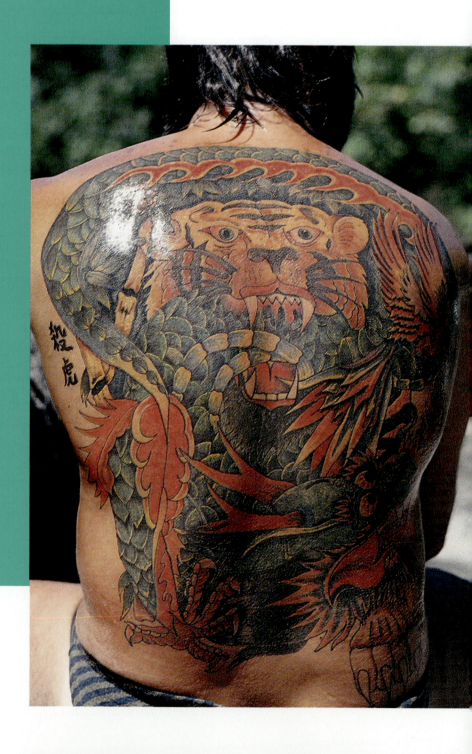

Deviance

Under most conditions, social behavior is remarkably orderly and predictable. You can generally rely on your sociology professor to show up for class, and you can expect that he or she will talk mostly about sociology and not something else. You can take it on faith that banks will be open during working hours, not closed because the tellers became bored and decided to throw a private party. And you can be almost certain that your neighbors will dress in much the same way tomorrow as they did yesterday, and will not appear on the streets half naked or painted with blue dye. In short, people generally fulfill their roles in accordance with social expectations.

Yet this picture is incomplete. We need only look at the world around us to see that social norms are often violated as well as adhered to. People rob, rape, and defraud others. They wear peculiar clothing, smoke crack, and take part in riots. They embrace alien religions, become mentally disordered, and commit bigamy. A full picture of society, therefore, must include deviance from social norms as well as conformity to them.

What exactly is deviance? Strictly speaking, the concept would include any behavior that does not conform to social norms. In practice, though, many norms are not regarded as particularly important, and nonconformity to them may be tolerated or even ignored. The sociology of deviance is therefore primarily concerned with violations that are considered offensive by a large number of people. The one characteristic shared by those who are widely regarded as deviant is **stigma**—the mark of social disgrace that sets the deviant apart from those who consider themselves "normal." Erving Goffman (1963b) perceptively remarked that the stigmatized person has a "spoiled identity" as a result of negative evaluations by others. For our purposes, then, **deviance** is behavior that violates significant social norms and is disapproved by large numbers of people as a result. This definition brings us closer to an understanding of deviance, and two additional points will clarify the concept further.

The first point is that society cannot be divided neatly into the sheep and the goats, the "normals" who conform and the "deviants" who do not. Although a majority of people usually conform to any specific norm that is important to society, most people have violated one or more important norms at some time in their lives. If we were to subtract from "normal" society all the people who have engaged in prohibited sexual acts, all the people who have ever stolen something, all the people who have suffered a mental disorder, and all the people who have used illegal drugs—to mention just a few out of hundreds of possibilities—we would have very few "normal" people left. Most people, however, escape discovery of their deviant behavior, are not stigmatized, and generally do not regard themselves as deviant at all.

The second point is that deviance is relative. No act is inherently deviant. It becomes deviant only when it is socially defined as such, and definitions vary greatly from time to time, place to place, and group to group. The heretic of one

Figure 6.1 *Deviance can indirectly strengthen social control, for when a society punishes deviants, the rules— and the penalties for breaking them— are made clear to everyone. Through- out history, in fact, many societies have applied formal negative sanctions in public, so that the entire community* *can express its solidarity against the offender. In early New England, devi- ants were often placed in the stocks, where they had to endure the taunts and censure of the populace. In mod- ern China, convicted criminals are often displayed in public before their execution.*

age may be the saint of the next; the "freedom fighter" of one group may be a "terrorist" to another; conservative views in one society may seem dangerously radical in a different society. Who and what are defined as deviant depend on who is doing the defining and who has the power to make the definition stick.

Explaining Deviance

The extent and the content of deviant behavior vary a great deal from one society to another and among different groups within a society, a fact that re- quires explanation. Psychologists may be interested in the reasons why specific people adopt the deviant practices that they do. But the sociological problem is not to explain why a particular person becomes deviant: it is to understand why deviance arises at all, why it follows specific patterns, and why some acts rather than others are defined as deviant in the first place. Four main sociological theories of deviance have been offered. Although none of them provides a com- prehensive explanation of all deviance, the theories do tend to overlap and complement one another, and bring us much closer to an understanding of the phenomenon.

Cultural-Transmission Theory

One approach is **cultural-transmission theory,** which explains deviance as be- havior that is learned in the same way as conformity—through interaction with other people. In effect, this approach draws on the insights of symbolic interac- tionism, and applies them to the process of socialization into deviance.

Early in this century, sociologists noticed that high crime rates persisted in the same neighborhoods over many years. This fact suggested that deviance might have become rooted in the local cultures and then transmitted over time from one person or even one generation to another. Edwin Sutherland (1939) produced an influential theory to explain exactly how this process of cultural transmission takes place. According to Sutherland, deviant behavior is learned through **differential association,** or social relationships oriented toward particu- lar types of people, such as criminals. This concept is really a sophisticated version of the old "bad companions" formula ("He was such a good kid until he got in with *that* crowd"). Just as people will tend to be conformists if their socialization emphasizes a respect for the prevailing norms, so they will tend to become deviant if their socialization encourages a contempt for these norms.

Since nobody is exposed exclusively to conformists or to deviants, several factors determine which influences will be the stronger. One is the *intensity* of contacts with others; a person is more likely to be influenced by deviant friends or family members than by deviant acquaintances. Another is the *age* at which the contacts take place; influences in childhood and adolescence are more powerful than those occurring later in life. Another is the *ratio* of contacts with deviants to contacts with conformists; the more one associates with deviants rather than conformists, the more likely one is to become deviant.

In short, nobody is born with the knowledge, the techniques, or the justifications that are available to the deviant. Like any other elements of culture, these things must be transmitted from one person or group to another.

Evaluation Cultural-transmission theory has an interesting implication: behavior that the dominant culture views as deviant may actually be conformist from the point of view of a subculture. For example, a Jehovah's Witness who refuses to salute the flag or swear allegiance, or who denies permission for a child to receive a blood transfusion, is regarded as deviant by the wider society—yet that person is merely conforming to the group's norms, which are based on specific passages in the Bible. Several sociologists have applied this insight to gang delinquency, arguing that mere acceptance of certain lower-class norms and values—such as those related to "toughness," "street smarts," and the search for "kicks"—can put juveniles in trouble with the law. Simply by accepting the values of their own subculture, lower-class juveniles may come to be regarded as delinquent by the society beyond. Cultural-transmission theory also helps to explain why so many criminals, drug addicts, and other deviants relapse into their former behavior after release or treatment: they rejoin their social networks of deviant associates, and renew the activities.

Yet the theory has some problems. Many people, despite their deviant associations, fail to become deviant themselves: most children raised in high-crime neighborhoods, for example, do not become criminals. Additionally, some people become deviant without any actual contact with deviants: check forgers or rapists need not have had personal instruction in their particular acts. And some forms of deviant behavior are actually learned in contact with conforming citizens. One can learn the techniques of embezzlement, for example, by taking a course in bookkeeping. Also, cultural-transmission theory explains only how deviance is learned, not how it arose in the culture or why it was defined as deviance in the first place.

Figure 6.2 Cultural-transmission theory implies that people socialized in a particular environment may become deviant simply through learning the norms of their own subculture. Raised in an area where gang activities are commonplace, a child may learn patterns of behavior that the mainstream culture defines as deviant.

Structural-Strain Theory

Another approach is **structural-strain theory,** which explains deviance as the outcome of social strains that put pressure on some people to deviate. A very simplistic version of structural-strain theory is the ancient adage that "poverty breeds crime": it supposes that the very existence of poor people within the social structure creates pressures for certain kinds of deviance.

Modern structural-strain theory uses an important concept that Emile Durkheim (1964a, orig. 1893) introduced to modern sociology—**anomie,** a condition of confusion that exists in both individual and society when social norms are weak, absent, or conflicting. Modern societies, Durkheim warned, are especially prone to anomie, for their cultural diversity creates confusion over norms and values and leaves people without clear moral guidelines. Individuals who are in a condition of anomie lack rules for behavior, for they feel little sense of social discipline over their personal desires and acts.

Robert Merton (1938, 1968) developed the concept of anomie and applied it to deviant behavior. Like Durkheim, Merton writes from a functionalist perspective, and he regards deviance as the outcome of an imbalance in the social system. Anomie may arise, he claims, when there is an imbalance between socially approved *goals* and the availability of socially approved *means* of achieving them. In the United States, for example, the population is socialized into the belief that one has to "make it" in the world by achieving financial success, or be a "failure." But not everybody can be wealthy, and some categories of the population—such as people with little education or few job skills—may find wealth difficult to achieve. Someone who accepts the goal of success but finds the approved means blocked may then fall into a state of anomie and seek success by disapproved methods such as theft or fraud, or may become deviant in other ways, such as turning to drugs. Strains within society itself thus exert pressure on some people to deviate rather than conform.

Merton claims that people may respond to a discrepancy between approved goals and approved methods of reaching them in one of five different ways, depending on their acceptance or rejection of the goals or the means (see Figure 6.3).

1. *Conformity* occurs when people accept both the approved goals and the approved means. Conformists want to achieve such goals as success, and generally use approved means—even if they are unsuccessful.

Merton's Typology of Deviance

Modes of Adapting	Accepts Culturally Approved Goals	Accepts Culturally Approved Means
Conformist	yes	yes
Innovator	yes	no
Ritualist	no	yes
Retreatist	no	no
Rebel	no (creates new goals)	no (creates new means)

Figure 6.3 *According to Merton's theory, people will conform or deviate depending on their acceptance or rejection of culturally approved goals and culturally approved means. This table illustrates the various outcomes that are possible.*

Source: Adapted from Robert K. Merton, *Social Theory and Social Structure* (New York: Free Press, 1968), p. 194.

2. *Innovation* occurs when people accept the approved goals but resort to disapproved means. This is the most common form of deviance: it occurs, for example, when a student wants to pass a test but resorts to cheating; or when a woman wants to earn money but becomes a prostitute.

3. *Ritualism* occurs when people abandon the goals as irrelevant to their lives but still accept and compulsively enact the means. The classic example is the bureaucrat who becomes obsessed with petty rules and procedures, losing sight of the objectives that the rules were designed to achieve.

4. *Retreatism* occurs when people abandon both the approved goals and the approved means of achieving them. The retreatist is the "double failure" in the eyes of society—the vagrant, the chronic narcotics addict, the "skid-row bum."

5. *Rebellion* occurs when people reject both the approved goals and means and then substitute new, disapproved ones instead. The rebel, for example, may reject the goal of personal wealth and a business career as the way to achieve it, turning instead to a goal of social equality to be achieved through revolution.

Evaluation Merton's theory of deviance is an elegant, thoughtful, and influential one. It not only locates the source of deviance squarely in social structure and culture rather than in the deviants themselves, but it also provides a plausible explanation of why people commit certain deviant acts, particularly crimes involving property. Albert Cohen (1955) pointed out, for example, that gangs are generally composed of lower-class boys who, lacking the social and educational background that would enable them to achieve success via approved channels, try to gain the respect of their peers through "hell-raising" and other forms of behavior that conform to gang norms. The gang provides people who cannot achieve a "respectable" status with the opportunity for other forms of achievement, even if these are disapproved by the wider society.

Unfortunately, structural-strain theory is less useful for explaining other forms of deviance, such as exhibitionism or mental disorder. Nor does it explain why very wealthy people, who have access to means of earning money legitimately, may resort to such crimes as embezzlement or insider trading to gain even more wealth. And because Merton shares the implicit functionalist assumption that there is a general consensus of values in society, he largely ignores the process by which some people and certain acts are defined as deviant by others— a process that often involves a conflict of values between those who have the power to apply these definitions and those who do not.

Control Theory

A third approach to the problem of deviance is **control theory,** which explains deviance as the outcome of a failure of social control. Unlike other theories of deviance, which begin with the question of why people deviate, control theory begins by asking why they conform in the first place. Control theorists suggest that deviance, not conformity, should be taken for granted: after all, life is full of temptations, and some deviant acts may be quite rewarding. People conform only because society is able to control their behavior, and if there were no such control, there might be little conformity.

This theory, too, is influenced by Durkheim's work. As we noted in Chapter 1, Durkheim found that the rate of a certain form of deviance—suicide—is related to the strength of the bonds that tie the individual to the community: the stronger the bonds, the less the likelihood of suicide. On the basis of this discovery, Durkheim advanced a more general theory of deviance: in a society with strong social solidarity, the members are likely to conform to shared norms and values, but in a society with weak bonds among the members, people are more likely to deviate. Modern control theory relies on this insight, for it holds that

Figure 6.4 *According to control theory, people may become deviant if they have loose bonds with society and therefore experience weak social control. Urban "bag ladies," who live an isolated existence on city streets, may have originally fallen into this deviant way of life because they lacked strong bonds with others. In turn, their solitary lifestyle may make further deviance more likely.*

people who are integrated into their community tend to follow its rules, whereas people who are isolated from their community may be inclined to break them.

Travis Hirschi (1969) suggests that a strong bond to society has four main elements. The first of these is *attachment*, or significant links to specific other people. Those who have affection and respect for others take the welfare and feelings of these people into account, and so are inclined to act in a responsible way. Conversely, people who are unattached need not worry about putting their social relationships at risk, and are more likely to steal, say, or to abuse drugs. The second element is *commitment*, or the "stake" that people have in society. The greater people's investment in their education, their careers, or their homes and other possessions, the more reason they have to conform so as to protect what they have achieved. Conversely, those who have little investment in society may see little risk in deviating—and perhaps a chance to benefit from doing so. The third element in the bond with society is *involvement*, or continued participation in nondeviant activities. Time and energy are limited, so a person who is generally busy—perhaps with a job, hobbies, or family life—has little opportunity to take part in deviant acts. Conversely, "idle hands do the devil's work": people who are unemployed or otherwise uninvolved in conventional activities have greater chances for deviance. The final element is *belief*, the individual's allegiance to the values and moral code of the group. If people firmly believe that certain deviant acts are wrong, participation in those acts becomes almost unthinkable to them. Conversely, those who have weak allegiance to the beliefs of the community may be more inclined to ignore its values and deviate from its norms. Hirschi concludes that a group whose members have strong mutual ties is better able to exert social control over their behavior than one whose members are not closely bonded together.

Evaluation   Control theory, like structural-strain theory, focuses on the social sources of deviance. It offers a plausible reason why some kinds of deviance are more likely to be present among certain types of people who lack close social bonds: consider, for example, the homeless "bag ladies" who live on big-city streets, carrying their possessions with them, or the hobos and drifters who ride freight cars on endless journeys around the country. Those who join certain religious cults, too, are often young, unattached people who have recently left home and are in a new environment in which they have no strong bonds with others (which is why the cults often look for potential converts in airports and bus stations). Control theory seems particularly applicable to juvenile delinquency, since delinquency tends to occur at precisely the time when young people are loosening their bonds with their parents, and tapers off later as they begin to take steady jobs and to develop stable new relationships, particularly through marriage.

However, the theory runs into some problems. It cannot easily explain the extensive criminal, sexual, drug-related, and other deviance that occurs among respectable, high-status people who appear well integrated into society. Also, the theory does not help explain why people's deviance takes the various forms that it does—why, for example, one corporate executive might turn to cocaine, another to fraud. And control theory does not really come to grips with the possibility that some people have weak bonds with society because of their deviance, and not the other way around—that is, that their behavior is so offensive that most people simply do not want very much to do with them.

Labeling Theory

Another theory confronts several of the problems that other explanations are unable to resolve. This is **labeling theory,** which explains deviance as a process by which some people successfully define others as deviant. This theory emphasizes the relativity of deviance, claiming that a person or act becomes deviant only when the "label" of deviance has been applied by others. Accordingly, labeling theorists assert that the way people are labeled as deviant, not their acts, should be the focus of sociological attention. The theory draws heavily on the insights of the interactionist perspective for its understanding of the labeling process, and in recent years has also used aspects of conflict theory to explain why some people and behaviors rather than others are called deviant.

Early labeling theorists, notably Edwin Lemert (1951, 1967) and Howard Becker (1963b), point out that virtually everyone behaves in a deviant manner at some time or other. Most of this behavior falls into the category of **primary deviance**—nonconformity that is temporary, exploratory, trivial, or easily concealed. The primary deviant may be a person who hides some income from the tax collector, an overburdened parent who sometimes becomes hysterical, an adolescent who has a passing homosexual relationship with a friend, or a youth who tries an illicit drug "to see what it's like." This behavior may go unnoticed,

"Someone once labelled me a reactionary, and it stuck."

and the individuals concerned do not regard themselves as deviants and are not regarded as such by others.

The situation changes markedly, however, if deviant acts are discovered and made public by significant other people—friends, parents, employers, school principals, or even the police and the courts. The offender is confronted by the evidence, often in a situation that Harold Garfinkel (1956) calls a "degradation ceremony." In this "ceremony" the person is accused of the deviant act, lectured to and perhaps punished, and forced to acknowledge the moral superiority of the accusers. Most important, the person is now labeled by others as a deviant— as a "nut," "whore," "queer," "weirdo," "crook," "dope addict." Other people begin to respond to the offender in terms of this label. As a result, the person consciously or unconsciously accepts the label, develops a new self-concept, and begins to behave accordingly. The label proves prophetic, and the deviance becomes habitual. The behavior now takes the form of **secondary deviance**— persistent nonconformity by a person who accepts the label of deviant. Often, in fact, the stigma that is applied to those now identified as deviants forces them into the company of other deviants, restricting their options, reinforcing their deviance, and thrusting them into a "deviant career," in which much of their behavior is interpreted by other people in the light of this single characteristic.

Evaluation   Labeling theory addresses the important question of why certain people and acts—rather than other people and different acts—are considered deviant. Many types of behavior, labeling theorists argue, become "deviant" because they offend *some* people's moral codes. Certain "moral entrepreneurs," such as religious groups or citizens' committees, try to arouse public opinion against behaviors they disapprove of, such as the sale of pornography, marijuana use, abortion, vagrancy, and the like. As Edwin Schur (1965, 1980) points out, the ensuing argument becomes a "stigma contest," a clash of competing moralities in which the winners declare themselves moral and normal and the losers immoral and deviant. In general, the decision to stigmatize or even criminalize particular acts will depend on which of the contending groups has the most wealth, power, prestige, and other resources. For example, begging in the streets is considered deviant, but living in idleness off inherited wealth is not.

Despite its broad usefulness, there are several objections to labeling theory. One is that empirical research has shown that, in many cases, labeling is not an important influence on deviant behavior (Gove, 1980). For example, some habitual shoplifters or users of pornography might never have been discovered and labeled, yet many still behave in a consistently deviant way. Another objection is that the theory ignores the fact that labeling may actually serve as an effective warning, jolting the offender out of deviance altogether. Another problem with labeling theory is that it tends to encourage an indiscriminate sympathy for the "underdog" as the helpless victim of definitions arbitrarily imposed by the powerful. But not all inmates of a prison or an asylum are there simply because somebody chose to label them, although labeling was certainly part of the process that put them there. Some deviant acts are so socially disruptive that society must impose severe sanctions if social order is to be maintained, and the extreme relativism of labeling theory sometimes obscures this fact.

It is doubtful whether any single theory could account for behavior as diverse as drug addiction, compulsive gambling, child molestation, religious heresy, juvenile delinquency, or insurance fraud. Taken together, however, the four theories do show how deviant behavior occurs as a result of social processes, though each focuses on a different aspect of the phenomenon. We turn now to an examination of crime, one of the most widespread forms of deviance in American society today.

Crime

A **crime** is an act that contravenes a law. Political authorities are likely to make behavior illegal if it meets two conditions: first, it must be considered too socially disruptive to be permitted, and second, it must be difficult to control through informal sanctions alone. Like all forms of deviance, crime is a relative matter. In medieval Iceland it was illegal to write verses of more than a certain length about another person; in the Soviet Union it has long been illegal to form a new political party; in South Africa it is illegal for a black student to attend a "white" college without a government permit. People in every society tend to regard the difference between criminal and noncriminal behavior as absolute, but these distinctions merely reflect the cultural assumptions of the time and place in question.

Types of Crime

The main types of crime in the United States can be conveniently classified into four principal categories: crimes of violence; crimes against property; crimes without victims; and white-collar and corporate crime. Our information about crime comes primarily from the annual reports of the Federal Bureau of Investigation (FBI), which compiles data provided by local police forces. The FBI regards crimes of violence and crimes against property as the most serious offenses. These acts—homicide, robbery, rape, aggravated assault, burglary, larceny, auto theft, and arson—are known as the eight "crime index" offenses, and the FBI reports concentrate on them.

Crimes of Violence Crimes of violence are the ones that Americans fear the most. The 1988 FBI report showed that, on average, a violent crime reportedly occurred in the United States every 21 seconds: a murder every 26 minutes, a forcible rape every 6 minutes, a robbery every 60 seconds, and an aggravated assault every 37 seconds. The rate of violent crime almost doubled during the 1970s, declined somewhat in the early 1980s, and rose slightly in the late 1980s. Violent crime represents only a minuscule proportion of crimes as a whole, but this is small consolation to its victims.

The fear of violent crime is heightened by anxiety about being attacked—and particularly, murdered—by a complete stranger. Actually, most people who are murdered are already acquainted with the attacker. Some 57 percent of

Figure 6.5 *An American's chances of being murdered are strongly influenced by social characteristics. According to FBI calculations, a white female has a 1-in-606 lifetime chance of becoming a murder victim; a white male has a 1-in-186 chance; a black female has a 1-in-124 chance; and a black male has a 1-in-29 chance.*

murders, in fact, are committed by a relative or acquaintance of the victim, usually in the context of a heated argument or a sexual triangle. Only 20 percent of murders occur in the course of "street" crimes—robbery, burglary, and other crimes directed against persons and property.

In international terms, the United States is an extremely violent society, with a homicide rate far exceeding that of any other industrialized nation. A single American city like Chicago, Houston, or Los Angeles records more murders in a typical year than does the whole of England, where even the police do not normally carry guns. Most other countries severely restrict private handgun ownership, but there are at least 60 million handguns in the United States—and weapons of this type are used in 44 percent of the 20,000 or so murders that occur each year. In 1980, the American handgun homicide rate was 77 times the average rate for England, Japan, Sweden, Switzerland, Australia, Israel, and Canada combined (Shields, 1981; Anderson, 1985). Why, then, does the United States permit such widespread access to handguns? One reason is the persistent belief that, since criminals have guns, law-abiding people need them for self-protection. Actually, gun-owning households are much more likely to suffer fatalities from their own weapons than from those of outsiders. One study found that only 2 percent of all slayings in gun-owning households were for self-protection; the remainder were suicides, homicides, or accidental deaths, almost all involving family members, friends, or acquaintances (Kellerman, 1986). A second reason for the proliferation of handguns is the belief, deeply held by many Americans, that gun ownership is an individual right. For granting this liberty to the individual, American society pays the price in the deviance of those who abuse it.

Crimes Against Property   Crimes against property are those offenses in which the criminal steals or damages something that belongs to someone else. These crimes are far more common than those involving violence: on average, one occurs every 3 seconds. The main forms of this offense are burglary, which involves an unlawful entry to commit a theft or other serious crime (one every 10 seconds); larceny, or theft (one every 4 seconds); motor-vehicle theft (one every 24 seconds); and arson, or maliciously setting fire to property.

Like the rate for violent crime, the property-crime rate rose sharply in the 1970s (by over one-third) but declined in the early 1980s before rising slightly in the late 1980s. The main reason for the rapid earlier rise and subsequent leveling in the violent- and property-crime rate lies in changes in the average age of the population. More than half of those arrested for violent crimes, and two-thirds of those arrested for property crimes, are between the ages of sixteen and twenty-five. Any increase or decrease in the proportion of this age group in the total population, therefore, affects the crime rate—which is what has happened over the past couple of decades. As the large "baby boom" generation—born in the period from about 1946 to 1964—passed through its youthful years, crime rates rose sharply. When this huge generation entered adulthood, the proportion of youth in the general population shrank and the crime rate dropped—a trend that sociologists predicted years ago.

The slight upturn in crime rates in the late 1980s was not expected, however. The causes of this trend are not yet clear, but another form of deviance, drug addiction, is certainly a significant factor. One reason is that hundreds of thousands of addicts have to find large sums of money to support their habits, and they frequently turn to crime to do so. A study of 354 Baltimore heroin addicts found that they had committed more than 775,000 crimes during a nine-year period (Ball et al., 1981). A second reason for the involvement of drugs in crime is that social control tends to fail over people who are under the influence

Figure 6.6 *Drugs are deeply involved in crime in several ways: users sometimes commit crimes while under the influence of drugs; addicts often commit crimes in order to pay for their drug habits; and suppliers commit crimes in the course of smuggling and distributing drugs. This photo shows the destruction of a large cache of contraband drugs.*

of mind-altering chemicals. The Justice Department reported in 1988 that 70 percent of suspects arrested for serious crimes in twelve major cities over a six-month period tested positive for recent use of illicit drugs.

Crimes Without Victims   There is an entire category of offenses from which nobody usually suffers *directly*, except perhaps the offenders themselves. These are the victimless crimes, such as gambling, prostitution, vagrancy, illicit drug use, prohibited sexual acts between consenting adults, and the like. Well over a third of all arrests each year involve offenses of this kind. The 1988 FBI report shows that there were over 828,000 arrests for public drunkenness and about 36,000 for vagrancy, 25,000 for illegal gambling, 110,000 for prostitution, 89,000 for curfew violations and loitering, and 937,000 for various drug offenses.

Victimless crime is notoriously difficult to control. One reason, of course, is that there is no aggrieved victim to bring a charge, or to give evidence, against the offender. Another reason is that the offenders often regard the laws, not themselves, as wrong. The fact that such behavior as gambling or marijuana smoking is illegal presents two additional problems. First, the prosecution of the offenders consumes an enormous amount of police effort and clogs the jails and the courts. Second, the illegal nature of these pursuits stimulates the activities of organized crime, which, ever since Prohibition, has depended for its existence on supplying illegal goods and services, such as narcotics and gambling, to others who are willing to pay for them. Indeed, the President's Commission on Organized Crime (1986) reported that organized crime is now a $100-billion-a-year enterprise—comparable in size to the American steel or textile industry.

The most notorious group in organized crime has long been the Mafia—also known as Cosa Nostra, the Syndicate, or the Mob—which has Sicilian origins and which has long been involved in such activities as gambling, drug smuggling, and prostitution. Today, the Mafia has to face competition from a number of other criminal syndicates. Recently, Chinese organized crime, based on ancient secret groups known as Triads, has penetrated the United States; it is now responsible for much of the heroin trade from Southeast Asia. Colombian organized crime, too, plays an important part in drug smuggling and distribution, particularly in the lucrative cocaine trade.

White-Collar and Corporate Crime   The phrase "white-collar crime" refers to all the crimes typically committed by high-status people, such as tax evasion, willful toxic pollution, copyright infringement, stock manipulation, price fixing, corruption of public officials, and fraud. Much of this crime takes place in the context of corporate activities. Even though individual corporate officers are involved in these offenses, fines and other sanctions are often directed instead at the corporation itself, for a corporation is, for most legal purposes, a "person." Additionally, many white-collar offenses escape prosecution because they are dealt with through regulatory agencies (such as the Securities and Exchange Commission, which scrutinizes the stock market) rather than through the criminal courts.

White-collar and corporate crime is generally regarded with more tolerance than other forms of crime, yet its economic impact is much greater. The U.S. Department of Justice estimates that this type of crime costs about $200 billion a year—about eighteen times the cost of street crime. These costs involve inflated prices, poisoned air and water, lost tax revenue, hazardous products, and the like. And this crime is by no means rare: studies have shown that about half of the leading 500 corporations have been convicted in recent years of at least one major crime (Ermann and Lundman, 1987; Simon and Eitzen, 1986; J. W. Coleman, 1988).

"I'm honest, but not scrupulously honest."

The fact that this form of crime is so prevalent, even at the highest levels of society, raises serious doubts about traditional notions of criminals and crime. It may well be that "poverty breeds crime" by giving low-status people an incentive to steal and rob, but it seems that greed can just as easily breed crime in high-status people as well. In fact, there is not the slightest evidence that criminal behavior is any more common at the lower level of society than at any other. It seems, rather, that people of different statuses have different opportunities to commit various crimes. The criminal poor are hardly in a position to embezzle trust funds or trade stocks on insider information, so they resort to high-risk, low-yield crimes such as larceny and burglary. The criminal nonpoor have no need to hold up gas stations or snatch purses, so they resort to low-risk, high-yield crimes such as tax evasion and computer fraud.

Who Are the Criminals?

At first sight it seems easy enough to establish who the criminals are: we need only look at the statistics published each year by the FBI in its *Uniform Crime Reports*. The 1988 report tells us that 48 percent of all persons arrested the previous year were under twenty-five, that males were four times more likely than females to be arrested, that persons arrested were much more likely to live in large cities than in small towns or rural areas, and that they were disproportionately likely to be black—in fact, blacks constituted a little less than 12 percent of the total population, but 29 percent of all arrestees.

Unfortunately, the official statistics may not give an accurate picture of society's "criminal element." One problem is that a great deal of crime is not reported at all, even if it is detected: Justice Department surveys indicate that the actual crime rate is about three times as high as the reported rate. A second problem is that the FBI presents data on only twenty-nine categories of crime and concentrates on the eight "crime index" offenses. White-collar crimes are hardly mentioned in the FBI reports—although the inclusion of statistics on these crimes would substantially alter our picture of the "typical" criminal, who would become significantly whiter, older, more suburban, and more "respectable."

Most significant, the crime statistics exclude the largest group of criminals—those who escape detection. And the disconcerting fact is that this category includes virtually all of us. This does not mean, of course, that there are not important differences between people who are habitually law-abiding and people who are habitually criminal, or between people who commit minor crimes and people who commit serious ones. But a large number of self-report studies, in which people were asked to give anonymous details of any crimes they had committed, indicate that close to 100 percent of Americans have committed some kind of illegal offense (Doleschal and Klapmuts, 1973). These studies have a disturbing implication for our traditional distinctions between criminal and law-abiding citizens. The "typical" criminal is not the typical criminal at all but rather the one who typically gets arrested, prosecuted, and convicted. The tiny proportion of offenders who actually experience formal negative sanctions are the product of a long process of social selection.

Selecting the Criminal

There are several stages in the process of selecting the criminal. Only a proportion of crimes are detected, only a proportion of those detected are reported to the police, only a proportion of those reported lead to an arrest, only a proportion of arrests lead to prosecution, only a proportion of prosecutions lead to conviction, and only a proportion of convictions lead to imprisonment. The chances of going from one stage to the next depend largely on two factors: the seriousness of the offense, and the social status of the offender (Hazel et al., 1980; Reiman, 1984).

The crimes that go either undetected or unreported are predominantly petty crimes against property and "white-collar" offenses such as inflated insurance claims or tax evasion. When a crime is actually detected, the social status of the offender, all other things being equal, appears to be the determinant of whether an arrest and prosecution will follow. This tendency is especially apparent in the treatment of juvenile offenders. The great majority of juveniles in the arrest statistics are lower-class males, but this does not necessarily mean they commit most delinquent acts—only that they are more likely to be arrested. Self-report studies of juveniles, in which the subjects anonymously admit any illegal offenses they may have committed, have found little or no relationship between delinquent behavior and social class (Doleschal and Klapmuts, 1973; Tittle et al., 1978).

Why, then, are lower-class youths more likely to be selected for arrest? Two classic studies suggest an answer. Irvin Piliavan and Scott Briar (1964) spent nine months riding in police cars of the juvenile bureau of a West Coast police department. They found that more than 90 percent of the incidents that came to police attention were very minor. In these cases the police were reluctant to take official action unless they felt that the offender had a basically "bad character." In making this assessment the police were guided by such cues as race, dress, and demeanor. Of those who were polite, contrite, and cooperative, less than 5 percent were arrested; but of those who were defiant, nonchalant, and uncooperative, fully two-thirds were arrested. William Chambliss (1973) studied two teenage gangs in the same town, a lower-class gang he called the "Roughnecks" and a middle-class gang he called the "Saints." The Saints committed far more delinquent acts than the Roughnecks, but it was the Roughnecks, who were perceived and labeled by the community as delinquents, who were constantly in trouble.

The process of selecting the adult criminal is especially apparent once the offender appears in court. Although every accused person has the right to coun-

Figure 6.7 *On the whole, the police are not very successful at "clearing" crimes—that is, arresting suspects and turning them over to the judicial system. Of all the serious offenses shown in this chart, only homicide, aggravated assault, and forcible rape result in an arrest in the majority of cases. The arrest rate for other crimes, such as white-collar offenses, is very much lower. Moreover, not all those arrested are actually prosecuted. The process of selecting the criminal continues in the courts, where some defendants are found guilty of lesser crimes or are acquitted. Of those convicted, only a minority are eventually imprisoned.*

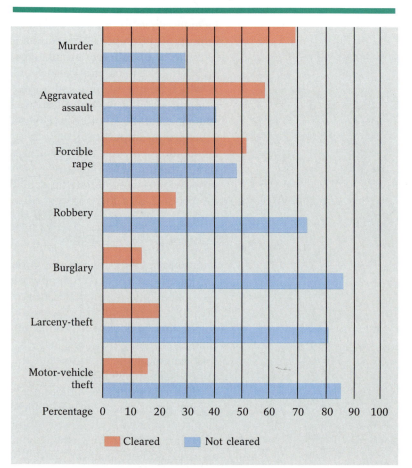

Crimes Cleared by Arrest

Source: Crimes in the United States: Uniform Crime Reports (Washington, D.C.: U.S. Government Printing Office, 1988).

sel, to a jury trial, and to appeal to higher courts, the system does not work quite this way in practice. Many people cannot afford bail and may spend weeks or months in jail awaiting trial. Actual courtroom procedure rarely follows the stylized confrontations seen in TV dramas. Over 90 percent of the people who appear in lower courts plead guilty and are sentenced on the spot—usually after an unofficial "plea-bargaining" in which the accused agrees to plead guilty to a reduced charge. Poor people, who cannot afford their own lawyers, are frequently urged to plead guilty by overworked public defenders. People who demand a jury trial and are eventually convicted tend to receive a more severe sentence than those who plead guilty: in effect, they are punished for "wasting" the court's time.

Judges also tend to take the social status of a convicted criminal into account before passing sentence, frequently reasoning that a higher-status offender has "already suffered" through damage to reputation and perhaps loss of employment. Although around 70 percent of people convicted of crime-index offenses go to prison, about 60 percent of white-collar criminals receive no jail terms, and of those who are jailed, the great majority serve one year or less. In part this discrepancy reflects the greater public fear of, and outrage at, crimes that are physically directed toward individuals or their property. But in part it also reflects the greater ability of high-status people to evade the full impact of the law.

Corrections

Corrections are the sanctions and other measures that society applies to convicted criminals—in the United States, primarily imprisonment, probation, and parole. Ideally, corrections serve several distinct purposes:

1. *Retribution.* Corrections serve to punish the offender, applying revenge on behalf of both the victim and society as a whole.

2. *Deterrence.* Through punishment, corrections serve both to deter the offender from deviating again, and to scare others who might be tempted into crime.

3. *Incapacitation.* By imposing restrictions on the freedom of the offender, corrections help prevent that person from committing further crimes, at least for the duration of the restrictions.

4. *Rehabilitation.* Corrections may serve to reform the offender by providing the skills and attitudes that make return to a law-abiding life possible and more attractive.

For most adults convicted of the serious crime-index offenses, corrections are likely to include imprisonment. This was not always the case, for prisons are a relatively recent innovation. Until two centuries ago, convicts were more likely to be executed, tortured, deported, or exposed to public ridicule in the stocks. Originally, imprisonment was intended to provide the convicted individual with the opportunity for solitary reflection and thus for penitence and rehabilitation, but this goal has certainly not been achieved in practice. In fact, the rate of **recidivism,** or repeated crime by those who have been convicted before, seems alarmingly high. Nearly three-quarters of all offenders released after serving prison time are rearrested within four years—sometimes for the same type of crime. Since other released prisoners presumably also return to crime but are not arrested, the actual crime rate among released convicts is even greater.

Clearly, prisons fail to rehabilitate. One reason, no doubt, is that relatively few resources are devoted to rehabilitation in the first place. A major reason, however, lies in the very nature of a prison, in which the authorities' custodial duties take priority over all other goals. As we noted in Chapter 4 ("Socialization"), a prison is organized as what Erving Goffman (1961) called a **total institution**—a place of residence where the inmates are confined for a set period of their lives, under the almost absolute control of a hierarchy of officials. Goffman argued that the very nature of a total institution aggravates the existing problems of the inmates, and in the long run can make it even harder for them to assume normal social responsibilities. Additionally, the prison environment guarantees differential association with other criminals—so the inmates can scarcely fail to learn about new techniques and possibilities for crime. Imprisonment may thus lead to further crime, not rehabilitation.

Imprisonment rates have been increasing sharply in the United States in recent years: on an average day in 1988, over 580,000 Americans were in prison, a record rate of about 210 per 10,000 people. More than 95 percent of inmates are male, and most have been in prison before. However, the vast majority of the 2.4 million convicted offenders undergoing corrections in the United States are not imprisoned: they are on probation or parole. Probation is a supervised period in which offenders are required to hold a job and commit no further offense, after which their case is closed; parole is a partial reduction of a prison sentence, given conditionally to convicts who have behaved well in prison. Few people believe that imprisonment does the offender any good; rather, it is used as a last-resort means of punishing criminals and protecting society from them (Currie, 1986). Several observers argue that society should

The Death Penalty

Sources: Ernest van den Haag and John P. Conrad (eds.), *The Death Penalty: A Debate* (New York: Plenum, 1983); James A. Yunker, "The Relevance of the Identification Problem to Statistical Research on Capital Punishment," *Crime and Delinquency,* 28, 96–124, 1982; Isaac Ehrlich, "The Deterrent Effect of Capital Punishment: A Question of Life and Death," *American Economic Review,* 65, 397–417, 1975; Richard M. McGahey, "Dr. Ehrlich's Magic Bullet: Econometric Theory, Econometrics, and the Death Penalty," *Crime and Delinquency,* 26, 485–502, 1980; Thorsten Sellin, *The Penalty of Death* (Beverly Hills, Calif.: Sage, 1980); U.S. Department of Justice, Bureau of Justice Statistics Bulletin, *Capital Punishment, 1987* (Washington, D.C.: U.S. Government Printing Office, 1988).

A handful of murderers in the United States receive society's ultimate negative sanction: execution. The Supreme Court struck down the death penalty in 1972, but reinstated it in 1976 on condition that judges and juries consider aggravating and mitigating circumstances. Executions began again the following year, and today some thirty-seven states have laws providing for the death penalty. Eighteen of these states permit execution by lethal injection, fourteen by electrocution, seven by gas, two by hanging, and two by firing squad.

More than 100 prisoners have been executed since 1976, and by 1988 there were over 2,000 inmates under sentence of death. Their number is increasing steadily; the courts sentence about 150 people to die each year, while overturning about 50 existing death sentences. The total number of executions has thus far been relatively low—about two dozen a year—but may increase rapidly over the next decade as a large backlog of appeals is finally dealt with. More than thirty people on death row in 1988 were juveniles at the time of their crime; three of them were fifteen when the offense was committed. Sixteen states permit executions of juveniles, with age limits ranging from seventeen to ten years of age (in Indiana), and eleven states have no age limit at all.

The usefulness and morality of the death sentence are controversial, particularly because the United States is virtually the only Western democracy that allows executions. A principal argument for the death penalty is that it will deter murder—but what is the evidence for this view? Although people on both sides of the debate have wrenched the statistics this way and that in support of their claims, there does not appear to be any consistent difference in homicide rates between states with the death penalty and otherwise similar states without it. And if the death penalty alone deterred murder, there would be hardly any homicide in the United States, which has the death penalty, and a great deal of homicide among other industrialized nations, which do not. Yet the reverse is true: the American homicide rate is by far the highest in the industrialized world.

It seems, then, that the fear of death frequently fails to act as a powerful deterrent—but why? There appear to be two main reasons. The first is that homicide, unlike most other crimes, is rarely premeditated: it usually occurs in the heat of the moment—in such situations as family arguments or bungled robberies—when the perpetrator is least likely to think about the possible consequences. In the few cases where murder is premeditated, on the other hand, the offender obviously does not expect to get caught or punished anyway. (In many

waste little energy on imprisoning petty offenders, for whom other forms of correction—like probation or community service—might be more appropriate, and should concentrate instead on incapacitating dangerous and persistent offenders by locking them up—if necessary, for very long periods indeed (Moore et al., 1985).

Incidentally, the fact that so many criminals are repeatedly rearrested does not necessarily mean that prison fails to deter people from crime: it certainly fails to deter *these* individuals, but the example of their fate no doubt provides a strong enough warning to deter most other people. As Jack Gibbs (1975) points out, the best deterrence is not necessarily the most severe punishment; rather, it is punishment that is *swift* and *certain*. If punishment follows soon after the crime, and if there is little doubt that it will follow, the crime rate will be low; but if people think they may escape punishment indefinitely, then the sanctions will have much less deterrent effect.

cases this expectation is borne out: about a quarter of murders do not lead to any arrest, and many arrests do not lead to conviction.)

The second reason the death penalty often fails to deter is that, as presently applied, no punishment is less swift or less certain. A death sentence is never carried out immediately: to minimize the chance of an innocent person's being executed, courts permit an elaborate review process that sometimes lasts a decade or more. And far from being a certain punishment for murder, the death sentence is almost certain *not* to be given or applied. Only about 5 percent of convicted murderers arrive on death row, and many of them will never be executed. Most convicted murderers are sentenced to "life" imprisonment—but a 1986 Bureau of Justice Statistics survey found that more than half of them serve less than seven years behind bars.

Who are the unlucky few who do get sentenced to death or even executed? Several factors affect the selection process. One is the specific state: 90 percent of all executions since 1976 have taken place in the South, and 75 percent have occurred in just four states—Florida, Texas, Georgia, and Lousiana. Another factor is the ability to afford a skilled lawyer: more than 90 percent of death-row inmates were so poor that they had to rely on court-appointed defenders. An-

other factor is the race of the homicide victim: people are four times more likely to die for murdering a white as for murdering a black—in fact, 96 percent of those on death row killed whites—and about 70 percent of the blacks awaiting execution murdered a white person.

All in all, risking the death penalty is a gamble in which the odds strongly favor the killer. In theory, of course, it would be possible to make death the swift and certain punishment for homicide—but that could involve the specter of about fifty executions in the United States every day of the year, something without parallel or precedent in a civilized society.

Decisions about capital punishment, then, are not really about deterrence. They are about retribution—about society's revenge on a person who takes another's life. Whether such retribution is justified is not a matter of measurable *facts;* it is a moral *judgment* for each individual to make. Some people feel that those who kill another human being should pay the supreme penalty and forfeit their own lives; others feel that human life is so sacred that society is demeaned when the state kills its citizens, however grave their offense. In any event, a large and increasing majority of Americans—some 75 percent in a recent Gallup poll—favor the death penalty.

Crime: A Conflict View

The conflict perspective draws attention to the competing interests of the deviants and their accusers by asking, Exactly whose "law and order" do legal sanctions uphold? Extending Karl Marx's contention that the state supports the powerful against the weak, the rich against the poor, and the rulers against the ruled, some conflict theorists argue that a great deal of "crime" is merely behavior that powerful groups consider a threat to their position or interests (Quinney, 1979, 1980; Chambliss and Seidman, 1982).

Conflict theorists advance a good deal of evidence to support this general view. In the early United States, for example, the law was used to deprive the Indians of their rights and lands. The legal system also upheld slavery, and later enforced racial segregation. During the 1920s and 1930s, labor unions were treated as criminal conspiracies, and employers could call on the police and courts to break workers' strikes. In the 1960s, during the Vietnam war, antiwar groups were systematically infiltrated and harassed by law-enforcement agencies. Conflict theorists see such outcomes as inevitable, for the laws tend to reflect the interests of the powerful and affluent rather than the powerless and poor. For that reason, the legal penalties for theft may be more severe than the penalties for, say, the failure of slum landlords to provide heat for their tenants in winter: those in power have more to lose from theft than the poor, and are less likely to live in unheated rental dwellings.

Conflict theorists also focus on how crimes against people and property, which are mostly committed by low-status people, are often punished with prison sentences, while crimes by people of higher status, such as embezzlement or fraud, tend to be treated more leniently. Consider the case of tax evasion, which is primarily a crime of high-income people. According to Internal Revenue Service estimates, about $200 billion of taxable income went unreported in 1984. This is a great deal of money. We might expect, therefore, that hundreds of thousands of tax dodgers would be hauled before the courts to receive severe sanctions. Yet the total number of people sentenced for tax fraud in 1984 was 1,854, of whom 1,149 were sentenced to prison, for an average term of two years. (This works out, incidentally, to roughly one prison sentence for every $174 million of tax evasion in that year.) In the same year, in contrast, some 1,291,700 people were arrested for larceny—the kinds of nonviolent stealing typically committed by lower-status people, such as shoplifting. Similarly, there is great concern about food-stamp fraud by poor people. But there is much less concern about pervasive mealtime fraud by executives who routinely dine with friends at expensive restaurants and deduct most of the costs from personal or corporate taxes as a business expense—a crime of fraud that is almost never prosecuted, even though it is probably one of the commonest in America.

Conflict theory also draws attention to "principled deviance"—socially disapproved acts that people commit out of moral conviction rather than in pursuit of personal goals. The outstanding examples of such deviance are political crimes, ranging from illegal demonstrations and draft evasion to sedition, sabotage, treason, and revolution. The people who do these things are not "typical" criminals; they include activists as different as George Washington and Fidel Castro. In many countries around the world, ranging from totalitarian communist societies to right-wing dictatorships, such people are often imprisoned or

Figure 6.8 *During the Vietnam war, several Buddhist monks burned themselves to death in public as a dramatic form of political protest. This behavior is an example of principled deviance— acts done for a moral cause rather than for personal gratification.*

even tortured or killed for their opposition to the status quo (Turk, 1982). This principled deviance and the conflict it creates can play an important part in social change—for what is deviant today can be conformist tomorrow. Anyone who sets out to change the existing norms risks being branded as a deviant, but the changes may be necessary and may not come about unless people are prepared to take this risk.

Not all deviance, of course, is simply a matter of the interests of the powerful taking precedence over those of the weak. Laws against crimes of violence, such as homicide and armed robbery, are intended to protect rich and poor alike—indeed, the poor are the primary victims of such offenses. The conflict approach is helpful because it shows how controversial questions of conformity or deviance may be influenced by the relative resources of the contending groups, and how deviance can sometimes provide the thrust for social change (Schur, 1980).

Mental Disorder

Another important form of deviance is **mental disorder,** the psychological inability to cope realistically and effectively with the ordinary challenges of life. Mentally disordered people violate social norms concerning reality, for their behavior can range from irrational depression to delusions, hallucinations, and fractured forms of thought and speech. The behavior of such people may be unpredictable, incomprehensible, or even frightening to others, making mutual social interaction difficult or even impossible. Consequently, mental disorder attracts the stigma of deviance—a stigma that may linger even if the deviant should return to normality.

How common is mental disorder in the United States? According to a 1985 report by the National Institutes of Mental Health, some 29 million Americans, or about one adult in five, suffer from such mental problems as severe anxiety and depression, although few of these people try to get professional help. These statistics are open to some question, however, for there is wide disagreement on exactly what constitutes mental disorder. Most mental disorders have no known physical cause or definitive symptoms. This means that there is rarely a simple, clinical test to determine if and how someone is mentally disordered. Instead, the decision depends on the opinion of trained observers—who frequently disagree among themselves (Eaton, 1980; Cockerham, 1981).

The Medical Model

In the past, most societies attributed mental disorder to supernatural influences: the victims were believed to be "possessed" by an evil spirit that had entered the body. Over 4,000 years ago, for example, the Egyptians chipped holes in the skulls of mentally disordered people to allow these spirits to escape; and, centuries later, the medieval Church tried to exorcise the demons, often by flogging, drowning, burning, or hanging the people they supposedly inhabited. By the eighteenth century, however, physicians began to claim that mental disorder was a medical problem—an "illness" best dealt with by doctors. A medical model was applied to the behavior: in other words, physicians came to "diagnose" and "treat" the "patient" for a specific "disease," just as they might in the case of a physical ailment. This trend accelerated in the late nineteenth century when psychiatry emerged as a specialized branch of medicine. Even so, medical science had little impact on mental disorders until the middle of the twentieth century, when newly available sedatives and tranquilizers made it possible to suppress some symptoms of disordered behavior. To this day, however, psychiatrists are unable to cure most mental disorders through any conventional medical methods, and many critics question whether the medical model is always appropriate.

Figure 6.9 *By the middle of the nineteenth century, physicians began to view mental disorder as a "disease" that they could "treat" by "medical" methods, such as suspending patients in swings and spinning them around. Treatment methods have changed a great deal since that time, but physicians are still unable to cure most mental disorders by standard medical means.*

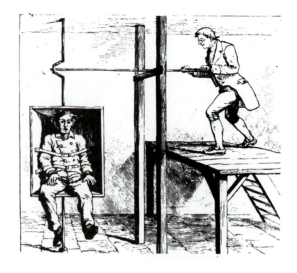

There are several problems in applying a medical model to mental disorders. One problem lies in the actual causes of the conditions. Although some disorders result from such factors as neurological damage or imbalances in brain chemistry, most of them have no known physical causes. Mental disorders are therefore rather different in this respect from the usual diseases that doctors confront. Another problem in applying a medical model to mental disorders is that their symptoms, unlike those of such physical diseases as lung cancer or acne, are culturally variable. Different cultures have different ideas of how "mad" people should act—in one culture, perhaps, they might hear voices, while in another they might run amok in public—and these ideas actually influence how deranged people behave. A judgment about someone's sanity therefore depends to an extent on the assumptions of the culture, of the subculture, and of the individual making the judgment: for example, someone who talks to spirits may be normal to one observer, eccentric to another, and a raving lunatic to a third. Indeed, eminent psychiatrists frequently testify at trials as "expert" witnesses— only to give conflicting opinions on the sanity of the accused. A final problem is that many of the more trivial disorders recognized by modern psychiatry look suspiciously like ordinary problems in living that have merely been given fancy-sounding names ("tobacco-dependence disorder" for cigarette smoking, or "isolated explosive disorder" for losing one's temper). Are such "disorders" really medical in nature (Church, 1978; Kleinman, 1979; Lipkowitz and Idupaganti, 1983; Clinard and Meier, 1985)?

This ambiguity about the medical model has generated a great deal of criticism of modern psychiatry and its assumptions. For example, Thomas Szasz (1970a, 1974) declares that "mental illness is a myth." The *behavior* called mental illness exists, of course, but it is not an *illness*—it is a learned but defective means of dealing with the world. Unable to handle their environment in any other way, some people resort to paranoid, depressive, manic, or otherwise deranged approaches to reality. Psychiatry, Szasz argues, is not really a medical science at all, but rather a pseudoscience like astrology and alchemy; its various diagnostic labels are just mumbo-jumbo that lends it a veneer of scientific respectability. This does not mean that psychiatrists cannot help people through their problems—they very often can, but probably because of their personal qualities of insight and compassion rather than their medical training. All in all, argues Szasz, the psychiatrist is just an agent of social control, much like the priest or judge—someone who interprets the social norms of the time, decides who is deviating from them, and tries to return the deviants to normality.

The potential for the psychiatrist to act as an agent of social control is perhaps clearer in the case of other cultures where different psychiatric assumptions prevail. In the Soviet Union, for example, psychiatry has sometimes been used in much the same way as Americans might use the law—as a sanction against deviance. From about 1960 until very recently, Soviet authorities committed thousands of political dissidents to mental hospitals—thus eliminating critics on the grounds that there was something wrong with them, not their society.

Becoming Mentally Disordered

How, at least in conventional American terms, do people become mentally disordered? Most sociological explanations concur with Szasz's view that some (though certainly not all) mental disorder is a learned form of behavior, unconsciously adopted by some people as a means of dealing with—or avoiding—personal pressures that threaten to overwhelm them. These pressures are assumed to arise from the social and particularly the family environment. Pathological family interaction patterns, in which the victim is subject to subtle, contradictory, and manipulative demands in an emotionally charged atmosphere, may lead certain people—particularly those who are biologically so predisposed—to "crack" under stress. In an influential statement, Thomas Scheff (1966, 1984) offers what is essentially a labeling theory of mental disorder. All of us, he says, violate norms of reality on occasion—by talking to ourselves, making irrelevant responses to questions, suffering memory lapses, irrationally fearing persecution, laughing inappropriately, losing our temper, and so on. Under pressure, some people violate these norms too often or too noticeably, and other people, suspecting that the offenders have taken leave of their senses, label them as "mentally ill." The offenders may find that this label has some advantages, for it lessens the pressures on them—it frees them, for example, from many normal social obligations, such as the duty to work, to show love to other family members, and so on. But, although the label was first applied because of a temporary inability to cope with reality, it is not as easily cast off as it was taken on, and the deviance may become habitual. Those who have been labeled as mentally ill may unconsciously adopt the behaviors that their culture teaches are appropriate for such people.

Who, then, becomes mentally disordered? Extensive sociological research has shown that mental disorder, like criminality, is not randomly distributed in the population: it, too, varies according to social status. By far the highest rates of severe disorders are found in the lowest social classes. The exact reason is a matter of debate. It could be that the pressures of lower-class life make people more susceptible to mental problems; or it could be that mental problems make people more likely to end up in lower social statuses; or it could be that lower-class people are simply more likely to be labeled as mentally disordered. Treatment, too, varies according to social class: higher-status people are more likely to be seen by private psychiatrists and given psychotherapy; lower-status people are more likely to be seen by hospital psychiatrists and to be given drugs or committed to the hospital. There are also marked differences along the lines of race and sex: blacks have higher hospitalization rates for mental disorders than whites, and women have higher rates than men (Srole et al., 1977; Dohrenwend et al., 1980; Eaton, 1985).

The number of people hospitalized for mental disorder has actually been declining—from 550,000 asylum patients in 1955 to under 120,000 today. The emptying of mental hospitals began after the discovery of the drugs that make it unnecessary to closely control or even restrain many mentally disordered people. The process was hastened by civil libertarians, who urged the release of people who had been confined against their own will, and by politicians, who called for the discharge of patients in order to cut public spending. The results have often been tragic. Tens of thousands of seriously disordered people have been "returned to the community"—where, isolated and abandoned, they live in dilapidated urban rooming houses, eke out an existence on permanent welfare, or are even to be seen mumbling, raging, and scavenging their way about the streets of the great American cities.

The Medicalization of Deviance

"Yes, yes—angst, indefinable cravings, sleeplessness, weltschmerz, and occasional outbursts of rage. Just something that's going around."

Drawing by Ed Fisher; © 1985
The New Yorker Magazine, Inc.

The application of a medical model to mental disorder is only one aspect of **medicalization,** the process by which the influence of medicine is extended over areas of life that were previously considered nonmedical. During this century, medicine has rapidly developed into one of modern society's major institutions. One effect of this trend is that physicians have extended their expertise to new areas. Consequently, many human experiences—such as pregnancy, child development, anxiety, insomnia, attempted suicide, alcoholism, addictions, voyeurism, or compulsive stealing—have gradually come to be regarded largely as medical matters, rather than as moral, religious, biological, or legal ones (Conrad and Schneider, 1980; Starr, 1982).

Obesity provides a case in point. Until a few decades ago, people who deviated from the ideal physical form by being overweight were held to have a personal problem of eating too much or exercising too little. Gradually, however, physicians have succeeded in defining obesity as a disease, to be cured by such means as scientific diets, psychotherapy, or even surgery. Another example is gender confusion, a deviant identity in which someone feels like, or wishes to be, a member of the opposite sex. This personal dilemma is now subject to medical intervention in the form of a "sex-change" operation. Similarly, repeated shoplifting—which the church might regard as immoral, or the courts as illegal—is defined by psychiatry as the "disease" of "kleptomania." One form of deviance, in fact, became a "disease" only after a drug was accidentally found to "cure" it. Hyperactive children have long been disruptive in classrooms, where their behavior was considered a discipline problem. Then researchers discovered that a stimulant drug, Ritalin, had the unexpected effect of pacifying these children. Having found the "medicine," physicians soon discovered the "disease" of "hyperkinesis"—which, despite its scientific sound, is merely the Greek word for "overenergetic." An important implication of this medicalization of deviance, however, is that offenders are *treated* as "sick" people rather than *punished* as "bad" people (Conrad and Schneider, 1980).

In this manner, medicine has greatly extended its influence as an agent of social control, with psychiatrists defining the approved norms, labeling those who deviate from them, and trying to ensure that the deviants conform once more. This process can be clearly seen in the example of homosexuality—a form of deviance that has been both medicalized and then demedicalized as social attitudes have evolved. For centuries, the Western world generally viewed homosexuality as a moral matter, as a sin that might evoke divine retribution. Then, around the end of the nineteenth century, many Western countries redefined homosexuality as a crime, punishable by imprisonment. But by the middle of the twentieth century, public opinion—encouraged by psychiatry—once again shifted, and homosexuality was viewed primarily in medical terms. Homosexuals were considered "sick," and psychiatrists tried (and failed) to change their sexual orientation in order to "cure" them. By the 1960s, however, an emerging gay liberation movement insisted that homosexuality is simply a different lifestyle. In 1974 the American Psychiatric Association accepted this view, and gave millions of homosexuals an instant cure by simply voting the "disease" out of existence (Bayer, 1981). The obvious fact that physicians cannot similarly vote away cancer or diabetes points up the difference between deviant behaviors and physical ailments.

It is thus doubtful whether deviant behaviors are medical problems in any scientific sense. Yet our taken-for-granted social reality now includes the notion that certain forms of deviance are "diseases," or at least medical "disorders" of some kind. In practice, then, the medical profession's definitions and redefinitions of deviance both shape and reflect society's changing norms and values (Szasz, 1970a, 1974; Shrag, 1978; Gross, 1978).

The Social Implications of Deviance

Deviance has a number of social consequences, some of which are functional and some of which are dysfunctional to society.

Functions of Deviance

Strange as it may seem, deviance may actually be useful to society, for—provided that it is kept within reasonable limits—it can help maintain social control and social stability in several different ways.

1. *Clarification of norms.* Paradoxically, a certain amount of deviance is actually necessary, for it helps to clarify what the limits of permissible behavior are. The existence of rule-breakers reminds us what the rules are, and the punishment of rule-breakers demonstrates to everyone how far society's tolerance extends on any specific issue at any particular time.

2. *Enhancement of solidarity.* By collectively reacting against deviants, conforming members of society reaffirm their shared norms and values, and are thus made more aware of their group solidarity. Emile Durkheim maintained that this function of deviance is so important that if there were no deviants, they would have to be invented.

Figure 6.10 *The seventeenth-century Puritans of Salem, Massachusetts, created deviants where they did not exist, in the form of witches. By the time the Puritan witchhunt was over, several women had been executed. In persecuting "witches," the Puritans reaffirmed their own solidarity as a community and enhanced their sense of righteousness. A witchhunt of a different sort occurred in the United States during the 1950s, when the late Senator Joseph McCarthy made indiscriminate charges that "Reds" were infesting various areas of American life, including the State Department. Con-* *gress set up the Committee on Un-American Activities, which tried to track down alleged communist sympathizers. These were the early days of the "cold war" with the Soviet Union, and the search for political deviants closer to home provided a focus for national solidarity against communism. Although he recklessly smeared the reputations of hundreds of people, McCarthy could never substantiate his claims. When he finally began to attack the U.S. Army, public revulsion led his colleagues in the Senate to formally censure him, and his search for "un-American" deviants came to an end.*

3. *Diversion of discontent.* Deviance may sometimes serve as a "safety valve" for individual or social discontent, allowing people to violate the rules rather than attack the institutions that the rules uphold. For example, minor forms of delinquency, such as writing graffiti on public walls, may provide a more tolerable outlet for frustrated people than outright challenges to political authority. Deviance can thus function to take the strain off the social system by preventing an excessive accumulation of discontent.

4. *Identification of problems.* Deviance can help to identify social problems by signaling some defect in the social system. The widespread bootlegging and illicit drinking that accompanied the prohibition of alcohol is a useful example: it showed that existing legislation was simply unenforceable. Other forms of deviance—such as high rates of mental disorder in a particular social group, or of truancy in a specific school—also provide a signal that something is amiss.

Dysfunctions of Deviance

Of course, deviance also has negative effects on society, which is why every society attempts to restrain deviant behavior within tolerable limits. There are several such dysfunctions.

1. *Disruption of social order.* Widespread violation of social norms can disrupt social order by making social life difficult and unpredictable. This is true for small groups as well as for the larger society. The idle worker can clog the flow of the assembly line, the psychotic can disrupt the family, the embezzler can become a threat to the commercial enterprise.

2. *Confusion of norms and values.* Extensive deviance leads to confusion over norms and values, making it difficult for people to know what behavior is expected, or even what is considered right or wrong. This is particularly true if deviants are seen to "get away with it," or if there is a growing perception that "everyone does it." Moreover, when a variety of different moralities compete in society, social tension may arise between conventional and deviant groups.

3. *Diversion of resources.* The need to control widespread deviance often diverts resources that could be more usefully directed elsewhere. For example, in the United States vast resources are devoted to the attempt to control crime and drug abuse—resources that could be channeled instead to other social needs and more productive uses, such as education or health care.

4. *Violation of trust.* An important dysfunction of deviance is that it undermines trust. Social relationships are based on the assumption that people will behave according to the accepted norms of conduct: that they will not break contracts, not exploit friendships, not molest children left in their care, not rob strangers they meet in the street. Widespread deviance undermines this trust for everyone, conformists and deviants alike. It also imposes many inconveniences on society: for example, because a handful of people hijack airliners, millions of air passengers must be searched for weapons.

Deviance, then, is not intrinsically good or bad. It can be socially useful or socially destructive, depending on the circumstances. Deviance arises from the very nature of society and the necessity for establishing and maintaining social order. Without rules there can be no rule-breakers; but where there are rules, there will always be people who are tempted—or pressured—to break them. The individual deviant may be abnormal, but deviance itself is intrinsic to social living.

Summary

1. Deviance refers to socially disapproved violations of important norms and expectations; deviants share the characteristic of stigma. Deviance is a relative matter, because the determination of who is deviant varies from one social context to another.

2. Several explanations of deviance have been offered. Cultural-transmission theory regards deviant behavior as learned through differential association with other deviants. Structural-strain theory sees deviance as arising from a discrepancy between socially approved goals and the availability of socially approved means of achieving them; those who lack the approved means may fall into a state of anomie and use disapproved means instead. Control theory sees deviance as the result of inadequate social control over the behavior of people who have weak bonds to the community. Labeling theory explains deviance as a process by which some people are able to label others as deviant.

3. The main types of crime in the United States may be classified as crimes of violence, crimes against property, crimes without victims, and white-collar and corporate crimes. Most crime data focus on the crimes of violence and crimes against property.

4. The selection of criminals is a process in which higher-status offenders are disproportionately more likely to escape sanctions, which usually take the form of corrections such as imprisonment, probation, or parole. Only a small minority of offenders is ultimately imprisoned. The prison incapacitates these offenders, but its nature as a total institution makes it ineffective at rehabilitation. Conflict theorists emphasize that much crime is actually behavior that acts against the interests of the most powerful groups in society.

5. Mental disorder represents deviance from norms of reality. The disorders are treated by psychiatrists according to a medical model. Definitions of mental disorder are culturally relative and depend in part on the assumptions of the observer. Critics charge that much mental disorder is a form of learned but socially defective behavior and that psychiatrists may serve as agents of social control over this deviance.

6. Many forms of deviance are becoming medicalized, or treated as sickness rather than as moral failings or criminal acts. This trend reflects the growing power of the medical profession, and the fact that society finds medicalization a convenient way of controlling some deviance.

7. Deviance has several functions: it clarifies norms, enhances solidarity, diverts discontent, and identifies problems. It also has dysfunctions: it disrupts social order, confuses norms and values, diverts resources, and violates trust. Its effects, therefore, can be both positive and negative.

Important Terms

stigma (115)

deviance (115)

cultural-transmission
theory (116)

differential association (116)

structural-strain theory (118)

anomie (118)

control theory (119)

labeling theory (121)

primary deviance (121)

secondary deviance (122)

crime (123)

corrections (129)

recidivism (129)

total institution (129)

mental disorder (133)

medicalization (136)

CHAPTER 7

Sexuality and Society

For centuries, the societies of the Western world have shrouded sexuality in myth, taboo, and ignorance. Even sociologists—supposedly dedicated to studying social behavior regardless of the prejudices and obstacles that might stand in their way—did not accept human sexuality as a legitimate field of research until after World War II. Yet the fact remains that every society contains two sexes, a feature that obviously has important and far-reaching implications for personal behavior and social life.

Sexuality is a significant ingredient of individual personality. Much of our leisure time is occupied with sexual acts, thoughts, feelings, and sometimes fears. Even in situations that are not defined as sexual—the street, the workplace, the grocery store, the college cafeteria—undertones and overtones of sexuality are frequently present. Social interaction is often rich in various forms of sexual expression, ranging from overt acts to the most subtle glances, gestures, and other signals.

Sexual relationships have an even greater importance in the broader societal context, especially when they are institutionalized in the form of marriage. The sexual bond between husband and wife is the basis of marriage, which, in turn, is the basis of the family, the most fundamental institution in all societies. It is small wonder, then, that every society carefully regulates the sexual behavior of its members, channeling their biological potentials into outlets that are socially regarded as natural and moral.

Some aspects of human sexuality are still imperfectly researched, partly because of continuing social inhibitions about the subject. Nevertheless, there is now sufficient scientific knowledge about sexual attitudes and behavior, in our own society and in many others, to provide an intelligent understanding of the subject. Even so, the sociological perspective on human sexuality may at first seem to run counter to common sense and everyday experience. To most people nothing seems more natural, or even more "instinctive," than their particular sexual preferences. But this popular view is simply wrong, for unlike the sexual behavior of most other animals, our sexual responses are not dictated by genes. Human sexual behavior and feelings are primarily learned through the socialization process and generally conform to the prevailing norms of the society concerned. Ideas about what is sexually appropriate or inappropriate, moral or immoral, erotic or offensive, are purely social in origin. In fact, even people who deviate from the prevailing norms of their culture tend to do so in predictable, patterned ways that are typical of each society.

Certain features of human sexuality, particularly those relating to love, courtship, and marriage, will be discussed in greater detail in Chapter 11 ("Family and Religion"). In this chapter we will concentrate more on other aspects of sexuality that seem to require some explanation, such as cross-cultural variations in sexual practices, the incest taboo, and rape, showing how sociological analysis aids our understanding.

The Nature of Human Sexuality

Researchers in several disciplines now recognize that human sexual behavior is highly flexible, so much so that we can learn to attach our erotic desires to almost anything—human beings, animals, inanimate objects such as shoes or underwear, or even the experience of pain and humiliation. Kingsley Davis (1971), one of the first sociologists to study sexual behavior, states flatly that "like other forms of behavior, sexual activity must be learned. Without socialization, human beings would not even know how to copulate." The same principle seems to apply to some higher primates as well. Harry Harlow's experiments with rhesus monkeys (discussed in Chapter 4, "Socialization") have shown that if monkeys are raised in isolation, they do not know how to mate in later life, and it is extremely difficult, especially in the case of the males, to teach them how to do so. Even monkeys must learn their sexual conduct.

The human sex drive can usefully be compared to the hunger drive. We all have an innate tendency to feel hungry periodically—but we have to learn through the socialization process what we may eat and what we may not eat, although different societies teach rather different lessons in this regard. Unlike the inhabitants of some societies, the well-socialized American who encounters a dog, rat, or spider does not for one moment consider the creature as "food": we have what seems to be an "instinctive," but what is in fact a learned, aversion to the idea. The way we come to follow our society's norms of sexual conduct is similar. We start with a basic, undirected drive and learn through the socialization process to recognize some stimuli as nonsexual, some as sexual and appropriate, and some as potentially sexual but inappropriate or even taboo. The fact that our sex drive is so flexible is, of course, the reason every society goes to such lengths to regulate it. If we all behaved "instinctively" in a rigid and predictable manner, there would be no need for the guidelines supplied by powerful norms and taboos, and they would not exist.

Drawing by Koren; © 1987 The New Yorker Magazine, Inc.

"Tonight, you're dessert!"

Sexual Behavior in Other Cultures

We can get an idea of how flexible human sexuality is by looking at sexual expression in other societies. There are two comprehensive surveys of cross-cultural variations in sexual behavior. The first is by Clellan Ford and Frank Beach (1951), who analyzed information on 190 traditional, preindustrial societies from all over the world; the second is by Edgar Gregersen, whose preliminary report (1983) draws on data from 294 such societies. Both surveys are based primarily on the reports of cultural anthropologists who lived among and studied the people concerned. The information that follows is from these surveys unless otherwise indicated.

Cultural Universals

There is a great deal of variation in the sexual practices of different societies, and much variety, too, within each society. There are, however, three **cultural universals**—practices that are found in every society.

1. *The incest taboo.* Every society that we know of, past and present, has an **incest taboo,** a powerful moral prohibition against sexual contact between certain categories of relatives. The taboo almost always applies to relations between parent and child and between brother and sister. Additionally, all societies apply an incest taboo to sex between certain other categories of relatives—but each society has its own rules in this regard, so sexual relationships that are quite acceptable to one people might be utterly outrageous to another. As we shall see later in the chapter, the incest taboo is necessary to prevent the disintegration of the family.

2. *Marriage.* Every society expects at least some sexual behavior to be expressed within the context of **marriage,** a socially approved mating arrangement between two or more people. The practice of marriage helps to regulate sexual behavior by narrowing its context and encouraging a bonding of the partners. Marriage also ensures that children will be born legitimate: the identity of a child's mother is usually known, but if a child is born outside marriage, there may be nobody to play the social role of father—a situation every society tries to avoid. In practice, the great majority of people in every society get married. Most societies frown on extramarital sex: about two-thirds of the societies in the cross-cultural samples forbid **adultery,** or sexual relations involving partners at least one of whom is married to someone else. Most societies are more lax about premarital intercourse, which may be tolerated, approved, or in some cases even required. Societies that permit extensive premarital intercourse have to make provision for children born outside marriage—for example, by assigning the social role of father to an uncle, by creating rules for adoption, or by requiring welfare agencies to help support the children.

3. *Heterosexuality.* Every society insists on some conformity to a norm of **heterosexuality,** or sexual orientation toward the opposite sex. The reason is obvious enough: without genital, heterosexual intercourse, a society could not reproduce and would soon be extinct. In practice, of course, the great majority of people learn to become heterosexual. About a third of the societies included in the cross-cultural samples totally forbid **homosexuality,** or sexual orientation toward the same sex. In the remaining societies, homosexual behavior is tolerated, approved, and occasionally required. All societies that permit very extensive homosexual practices, however, require those involved to also practice heterosexuality or **bisexuality**—sexual orientation toward both sexes—at some point in their life course. Exclusive homosexuality is never tolerated for more than a small minority, because it might otherwise significantly affect reproduction. Two predominantly homosexual societies have been recorded: the Marindanim, a New Guinea tribe, and their neighbors, the Etoro, who actually place a taboo on sex between men and women for 295 days a year. However, even these societies expect everyone to marry and practice heterosexuality some of the time (Van Baal, 1966; Kelly, 1977; Herdt, 1981).

Conceptions of Beauty

Ideas about beauty and sexual attractiveness vary a great deal from one society to another. But although much is known about conceptions of female beauty in other cultures, there is little information on how other peoples judge the attractiveness of men. The main reason, it seems, is that most societies have more

Figure 7.1 *Conceptions of beauty and adornment are culturally learned; in fact, what may be attractive in one culture may seem strange or unattractive in another. The pictures here show a woman from Kenya and a man from West Irian.*

specific ideas about female than about male beauty, for men are much more likely to be valued for characteristics other than appearance, such as wealth and power.

There are few if any universal standards of female attractiveness. Some peoples focus on the shape and color of the eyes; others are more concerned about the formation of the mouth, nose, or ears. Cultural preferences in these respects vary widely: the Mayans, for example, admired cross-eyes, while the Yapese of the South Pacific consider black teeth attractive. In some societies small, slim women are admired, but there is a strong cross-cultural tendency for men to prefer fat women; in some West African societies the sexy woman is one who is positively obese. The Thonga of eastern Africa admire a woman who is tall and powerful; the Tongans of Polynesia are more concerned that a woman's ankles be small. The Masai of eastern Africa prefer women with small breasts, whereas the Apache prefer women with very large breasts. In many tropical societies women do not cover their breasts, but this does not mean that the men are in a constant state of erotic frenzy. The breasts are simply not considered a sexual stimulus at all, and attention may focus instead on the legs, buttocks, back, or elsewhere.

Restrictiveness and Permissiveness

Societies vary a great deal in their degree of sexual **restrictiveness,** or insistence on adherence to narrowly defined sexual norms, and in their degree of sexual **permissiveness,** or acceptance of some latitude in sexual norms and conduct.

Most societies in the cross-cultural samples are more permissive than restrictive in their attitudes toward sexual behavior. Only a handful of societies, in fact, wholly disapprove of both premarital and extramarital sex. People in these restrictive societies try to keep sexual knowledge from young children, but some of them carry their prohibitions even further. Among the Arapaho Indians, for example, the sexes were strictly segregated from childhood and could not play together; in later adolescence they could meet only in the presence of chaperones. Among the Gilbertese Islanders of the Pacific, a girl who was seduced could be put to death with her seducer, and among the Vedda of Ceylon, a man seen merely talking to an unmarried woman could be killed by her relatives. In restrictive societies, punishment for adultery can also be severe, although a husband's infidelity is likely to be treated more leniently than a wife's. Many societies permit a husband to beat, mutilate, or kill an adulterous wife. The Muslim tradition, for example, calls for stoning an unfaithful wife to death.

These attitudes contrast sharply with those of more permissive societies. Among some peoples, such as the Lesu of the Pacific, sexual knowledge is fully available to young children, and the parents openly copulate in front of them. The Trukese of the Carolines encourage sexual experimentation by children, and little huts are constructed outside the main compound for this purpose. The Lepcha of the Himalayas believe that young girls will not mature without the benefit of sexual experience, and Trobriand Island parents gave their children sexual instruction at a very early age, enabling them to begin practicing at the age of six to eight for girls and ten to twelve for boys. In addition, Ford and Beach noted that over a third of the societies in their sample allow some form of what we would call adultery. The Siriono of Bolivia permit a man to have sexual relations with his wife's sisters and with his brothers' wives and their sisters. Among the Toda of southern India, married men and women are free to form sexual liaisons with others; their language contains no word for adultery. And sex hospitality, in which a husband offers his wife to guests, has been common in a number of societies—including, as we saw in Chapter 2 ("Culture"), the Eskimo.

Sexual Conduct

Even the norms for the conduct of the sexual act vary widely. For example, the position that the partners commonly adopt in the sexual act differs from one society to another. The usual position in most Western societies is for the couple to lie face to face with the male on top; in his groundbreaking study of sexual behavior, Alfred Kinsey (1948) found that 70 percent of American couples had never tried any other position. In the South Sea Islands of the Pacific, incredulous women laughingly called this approach the "missionary position," for it had been quite unknown to them until they had sex with visiting clergymen. In a survey of the evidence from 131 other societies, the anthropologist Clyde Kluckhohn (1948) found that the "missionary position" was customary or preferred in only 17 cases. Other peoples conduct intercourse from the side, from the rear, with the female on top, with the male kneeling over the female, and in other positions.

The context and content of sexual intercourse is also highly variable. Some peoples regard full nakedness as desirable or obligatory; others, as quite improper or even dangerous. The Hopi Indians insist that sex take place indoors; the Witoto of South America insist that it take place outside. The Masai of eastern Africa believe that sex in the daytime can be fatal; the Chenchu of India believe that sex at night can lead to the birth of a blind child. Some people insist on privacy; others are indifferent to the presence of observers. Some, such as the Trobriand Islanders, believe that women are sexually insatiable and expect them to take the initiative; others, such as the Chiricahua Indians, expect that a woman will remain completely passive. Kissing is unknown in some societies; the Siriono consider it a particularly disgusting act. Foreplay before sex is unknown among the Lepcha but may occupy several hours among the Ponapeans of the Pacific. Kinsey (1948) found that in the 1940s, the great majority of American males reached orgasm within two minutes of starting intercourse, but the Marquesan men of the Pacific habitually perform for several hours. Even the frequency of the sex act is related to cultural norms. The Keraki of New Guinea are reported to average once a week; Americans, two or three times a week; the Aranda of Australia, three to five times a day; and the Chagga of eastern Africa

Figure 7.2 *This picture shows a child wedding in a remote part of India. In many traditional societies, weddings are arranged by the parents as a means of creating an alliance between* *the two kinship groups involved. The wedding serves to pledge the children to each other until they can assume normal marital responsibilities at around the age of puberty.*

are alleged to manage ten episodes in a single night. Some peoples have learned to experience violence during sex as erotically exciting. The Siriono find pleasure in poking their fingers into each other's eyes; Choroti women in South America spit in their partner's face; Ponapean men tug out tufts of their mate's hair; and Apinaye women in the Brazilian jungle are reported to bite off pieces of their lover's eyebrows, noisily spitting them aside to enhance the erotic effect.

Evaluation

This cross-cultural evidence can be misleading in an important respect, for it deals only with the sexual practices of small, preindustrial societies, many of which have changed their cultural practices or have even become extinct since anthropologists first reported on them. No comparable study of modern industrial societies has been made, but it seems likely that sexual behavior in these societies, like most other aspects of their cultures, is much less variable. Since the majority of the world's population lives in industrialized or industrializing societies, it is probably safe to conclude that the sexual practices of most people in the world no longer differ radically from those of Western nations. The value of the evidence from these preindustrial societies is that it shows how the interplay between biological potentials and cultural norms can produce extraordinarily diverse kinds of sexual conduct.

The conclusion from the cross-cultural data may be disconcerting to some, but it is inescapable. If you were raised in one of these other societies, you would probably follow its rules of sexual conduct. You would do so with the full knowledge and approval of your community, and if your personal tastes should happen to run counter to the prevailing norms, you might be considered distinctly odd—even wicked. Being no less ethnocentric than peoples in other societies, you would also regard American sexual attitudes and practices as most peculiar, to say the least.

Sexual Behavior in America

The most striking feature of sexuality in America is the tension between a tradition of highly restrictive standards, on the one hand, and a modern climate that values individuality and personal freedom, on the other. As a result, there is a discrepancy between the sexuality that is portrayed in the **ideal culture**—the norms and values a society adheres to in principle—and the sexuality that is actually expressed in the **real culture**—the norms and values a society adheres to in practice.

Traditional Values

The traditional sexual values of American society, and of Western society in general, have their roots in a particular interpretation of ancient Judeo-Christian morality. Sexual activity can have two basic purposes: reproduction and pleasure. The Western tradition has strongly emphasized the former and has generally disapproved of the latter: sex was morally acceptable if the partners were married and if their primary purpose was reproduction; sex for pleasure alone, especially by unmarried partners, was considered immoral.

The tradition that the main purpose of sex is to produce children comes from the Old Testament, which urges the faithful to "be fruitful and multiply," censures those who "waste" their seed, and imposes severe penalties for nonreproductive sexual acts. Sexuality itself, however, was not regarded as sinful. The negative emphasis on sexuality, with its blanket prohibition on sex outside marriage, comes from the New Testament—not from the teachings of Jesus, who had little to say about sex, but from those of Saint Paul, who recommended total abstention from sex and tolerated marriage only on the grounds that it was "better to marry than to burn." By the early Middle Ages sex was virtually equated with sin. The Church not only insisted that priests be celibate, but even tried to limit marital sex, forbidding it on Sundays, Wednesdays, and eventually Fridays, with the result that sexual activity was prohibited for the equivalent of about five months of the year.

Subsequent centuries were marked by alternating periods of restrictiveness and relative permissiveness, with particularly restrictive attitudes occurring among the early Puritans and among the Victorians of the past century. Prudery reached a climax with the middle-class Victorians, who were unable to refer to anything remotely sexual except in the most discreet terms. Sweat became "perspiration" and then "glow"; legs became "limbs"; underwear became "unmentionables"; chicken breast became "white meat"; prostitutes became "fallen women"; pregnancy became "an interesting condition." Women were careful to cover even their ankles from the gaze of men, and some zealots actually covered the legs of their furniture from the public view. Masturbation was regarded as a dreadful vice that caused such maladies as deafness, blindness, heart disease, stunted growth, epilepsy, hair on the palms, and insanity. Some lunatic asylums even had separate wards for inmates who were believed to be victims of this "self-abuse."

Figure 7.3 *Traditional Western attitudes toward sexuality derive from a particular interpretation of Judeo-Christian morality. The Genesis account of the sin of Adam and Eve and their subsequent expulsion from the Garden of Eden, depicted in this painting by the Italian artist Masaccio, has strong sexual overtones: the human species is sinful, nakedness is shameful, and sex for pleasure's sake is immoral.*

The Incest Taboo

The question of why the incest taboo exists—and of why it is a cultural universal—offers a useful example of how sociological analysis can explain an otherwise puzzling practice. Why does every known society prohibit sexual relations between certain categories of relatives?

We have already noted that the taboo almost always applies to sex between parent and child and brother and sister. The exceptions are few and far between. Brother and sister were expected to marry in the royal families of ancient Egypt, Hawaii, and Peru, probably to prevent the royal lineage from being tainted by commoners. The Thonga of West Africa permit a father to have ritual sex with his daughter before he goes on a lion hunt; the Azande of central Africa expect their highest chiefs to marry their daughters; and the mothers of Burundi are expected to cure impotence in their adult sons by having intercourse with them. There is also evidence that brother-sister and parent-child marriages were occasionally practiced among the general population at certain periods in ancient Egypt and Iran, perhaps as a means of keeping property within the family (Ford and Beach, 1951; Murdock, 1949; La Barre, 1954; Albert, 1963; Middleton, 1962). The general cross-cultural rule, however, is that people regard sex with certain close relatives as utterly immoral and even unthinkable. Why is this the case?

A ready response might be that the taboo is instinctive, because we certainly experience our aversion to incest as though it were an "instinct." But this view is clearly wrong, for several reasons. First, no other animal observes an incest taboo, and it is highly unlikely that we, who rely less than any other species on inherited behavior, would have evolved an instinct that all other animals lack. Second, if the attitude to incest were instinctive, there would be no need for the taboo—yet every society finds it necessary to have the taboo and laws that aim—frequently unsuccessfully—to prevent the behavior. A third reason why the taboo cannot be instinctive is that definitions of incest vary from one society to another. In some societies it is incestuous to marry any cousin; in other societies all cousins may intermarry. In some societies it is incestuous to marry the child of one's father's brother or one's mother's sister, but it is obligatory to marry the child of one's father's sister or one's mother's brother, even though all these cousins are equally closely related. It would be a very strange instinct indeed that took quite different forms in different societies, scrupulously observing local and national boundaries in the process!

If the taboo is not instinctive, then might it exist to prevent the physical and mental degeneration that comes from inbreeding? This explanation sounds plausible, but for several reasons it is also incorrect. First, inbreeding does not necessarily produce degeneration: it merely intensifies certain traits, good or bad, that are already present in the related partners. Brother-sister marriages in Egypt and among the Inca resulted in no degeneration over as many as fourteen generations; indeed, the beautiful and intelligent Cleopatra was the product of such a union. Agricultural scientists use selective inbreeding, in fact, to produce healthier stock. Second, any ill effects of inbreeding usually take place too slowly and too haphazardly to be noticeable over a few generations. People living in simple, traditional societies would not be likely to link cause and effect, especially when other explanations, such as illness or witchcraft, are more readily available. Third, some peoples were apparently unaware that pregnancy is the result of sexual intercourse: the Trobriand Islanders, for example, denied that sex leads to conception, and other peoples attribute pregnancy to the work of their dead ancestors. Yet these societies have some of the most complex incest taboos ever recorded.

Then why the taboo? There are three main reasons, and they are social, not biological. The first is that early human beings—living primarily in small kinship groups of hunters and gatherers—needed to protect themselves by forming alliances with other groups. By forcing their children to marry into families outside their own, each group widened its social links and provided itself with allies in time of conflict and help in time of famine or other hazards. These groups, it has been said, faced the alternatives of marrying out or dying out.

The second reason for the incest taboo is that the family itself could not function without it, for the statuses of family members would be utterly and hopelessly confused. As Kingsley Davis (1948) points out:

> The incestuous child of a father-daughter union would be a brother of his own mother, i.e. the son of his own sister; a stepson of his own grandmother; possibly a brother of his own uncle; and certainly a grandson of his own father.

The third reason is that without an incest taboo, sexual rivalry among family members would disrupt the normal roles and attitudes of the various relatives. The father, for example, might experience role conflict as both the disciplinarian and the lover of his daughter; the mother might be jealous of both; and the child, of course, would be caught in the middle. Faced with constant conflict and tension, the family institution might simply disintegrate.

The incest taboo has developed over time because it is vital to the survival of the family and thus of society itself. Of course, neither traditional nor modern societies consciously appreciate the reasons for the taboo. They and we simply accept it as natural and moral.

Rape

The tender, romantic, and passionate intimacies of men and women are among the supreme human emotional experiences. Perhaps no other subject is so universally celebrated and even idealized in literature, art, and daily life. But the relationships of the sexes can have a darker side, one that may involve extremes of exploitation and violence.

Rape is forcible sexual intercourse against the will of the victim. It is a terrifying, brutal, and sometimes life-threatening crime, one that often leaves deep, long-term psychological scars. In the United States about 90,000 rapes are reported to the police every year, but these cases probably represent only about a tenth of the real total. One reason that rape is so underreported is that many victims are unwilling to relive the experience by submitting to police interrogation, medical examination, and court proceedings.

The fear of the crime touches virtually all women, instilling in them a wariness of male strangers and an apprehension about walking alone at night or being in deserted places. Yet, contrary to popular belief, most rapes are actually committed by an acquaintance of the victim—a family friend, a neighbor, a teacher, an employer, an ex-lover, a new dating partner. Victims of "date rape" are particularly reluctant to report the crime, for they are afraid that other people—including family, friends, and jurors—will suspect they did something to "ask for it" (Russell, 1984; Seligman et al., 1984).

"Date rape" is a threat even among American college students. One study found that 35 percent of male students said they might commit rape if they could be assured they would not be caught. Other studies of college males have found that 10 percent admit to having had sex with a woman against her will—although most of them do not regard the act as rape. These students tend to regard sexual aggression as normal, and to believe that women "don't really mean it" when they say "no" to sexual advances. They are likely to answer "true" to such statements as "Most women are sly and manipulating when they want to attract a man," "A woman will only respect a man who will lay down the law to her," and "A man's got to show the woman who's boss right from the start or he'll end up henpecked." Such attitudes seem to develop quite early: another study found that over 50 percent of male high school students believed that it is acceptable "for a guy to hold a girl down and force her to have sexual intercourse" in various situations, such as when "she gets him sexually excited"

"I know you expect something in return for the movie, the flowers, and the dinner. Wait here and I'll get you a receipt."

Figure 7.7 *When a man and a woman pass close together, they almost always turn as they do in this picture—the man toward the woman, the woman away from the man. This subtle form of body language reflects the different roles that men and women commonly play in their interaction with one another: the man as aggressor and pursuer, the woman as nonaggressive and pursued.*

or "she says she's going to have sex with him and then changes her mind" (Malamuth, 1981; Sweet, 1985).

Although many people still regard rape as an expression of unrestrained, impulsive sexual desire, the sociological and psychological research of recent years has proven this view to be a myth. Rape is a crime of violence, not of passion; it is a ritual of power and humiliation which, although socially regarded as intolerable, has its origins in approved patterns of interaction between the sexes (Chappell et al., 1977; Scully and Marolla, 1983).

The Social Context

In some cultures rape is virtually unknown, while in others it is relatively common. In a survey of 95 societies, Peggy Sanday (1982a) found that 47 percent were rape-free or almost rape-free, 17 percent were rape-prone, and 36 percent had a limited but undetermined amount of rape. The extent of rape seems to depend on cultural factors: rape-prone societies often have male gods, accord women low status, and encourage aggressiveness in boys, whereas rape-free societies believe in gods who are female or of both sexes, accord women more equality with men, and discourage male aggression. Thus the Ashanti of West Africa, who have a rape-free society, emphasize an earth goddess, treat women with great respect, and admire nurturant rather than aggressive traits. On the other hand, the Gusei of Kenya, who have a rape-prone society, emphasize male gods, treat women as inferiors, and conceive of routine sex as an assault on women. In rape as in other aspects of human behavior, the conduct of the individual is influenced by the norms of the surrounding society.

In the United States, as in many other societies, the social relations of the sexes are marked by two cultural features relevant to rape: inequality between women and men, and a tendency for men to view women as actual or potential sexual property—that is, as sex objects. A classic example of this tendency is the barrage of whistles, catcalls, and obscene suggestions that often assails a young woman walking past a group of male construction workers. Since the likelihood that the woman will respond favorably to this kind of attention is approximately zero, the behavior clearly serves some other purposes. What it actually does is to allow the men to bolster their own egos, to demonstrate their "masculinity" to their peers, and to reassert the view that the role of women is to gratify men. The woman's feelings are not at issue.

In fact, this view of women is quite prevalent in the workplace, where the sexual harassment of women is a common and serious problem. In the office or factory, as elsewhere in society, men have a virtual monopoly of power and influence. Frequently, they take advantage of this superior status to indulge in uninvited and unwanted sexual advances, ranging from ogling, leering, squeezing, pinching, bottom-patting, and the like to outright propositions accompanied by the implied or explicit threat of dismissal.

The norms of this kind of interaction require comparatively little self-control by the men; instead, it is the women who are expected to manage the situation. Many men, it seems, are convinced that any normal woman will be flattered by sexual attention in any form; women, for their part, have been socialized to receive these advances as gracefully as possible, regardless of their private response. The myth has it that they enjoy the attention, that they find it easy to deal with, and that the behavior is trivial in any case. But surveys show the reverse to be true: almost unanimously, women declare that sexual advances in the workplace make them feel powerless, trapped, defeated, intimidated, or demeaned. This reaction is understandable, for these norms of sexual harassment have a wider social significance. In all cases, the male's message is the same: Your responsibility is to satisfy me, you are not my equal, don't compete, your real value is your body.

The Nature of Rape

Rape is an extreme outcome of culturally approved activities in which one segment of society dominates another, socially and sexually. It is usually not an act of sudden impulse, for the majority of these crimes are planned in advance, with the rapist—whether a stranger or an acquaintance—carefully selecting a time, place, and victim for the attack. Nor is rape the result of any lack of alternative sexual outlets: many rapists are married, many have other sexual partners, and most could easily afford a prostitute. In fact, lust seems to have remarkably little to do with rape: a high proportion of rapists are completely impotent, and many more become sexually aroused only when they have sufficiently terrified and debased their victim through verbal and physical abuse. All the evidence indicates that the sexual aspect of rape is of secondary importance. The primary object is to humiliate and subjugate the woman, and thus to bolster the aggressor's feelings of power, superiority, and masculinity (Estrich, 1987; Brownmiller, 1975; Gordon and Riger, 1987; Scully and Marolla, 1983; Russell, 1984).

The effects of rape can be devastating for the victim, involving physical and emotional damage and the disruption of personal, social, familial, and sexual life. If the victim reports the attack to the police, the emotional trauma may be reexperienced months or years later in a courtroom, where the intimate details of the rape are dissected before an audience of strangers. Typically, defense lawyers try to shift the burden of guilt from the accused to the victim. They may try to show that the woman is "loose," implying that if she has consented to any man before, she must have been willing on this occasion also. Or, utilizing the myth that women somehow enjoy being raped, they may claim that the victim consciously or subconsciously encouraged the assault. They may even argue that she was provocatively dressed and was therefore at fault—another example of the way in which responsibility for the control of male advances is shifted to the female. Such a line of defense is unique to the crime of rape—a well-dressed man stepping from an expensive limousine would never be accused of thereby tempting someone to mug him. Even this aspect of the act and its aftermath can be fully understood only in terms of the overall patterns of sexual interaction in the society (Hilberman, 1976; Holmstrom and Burgess, 1976).

Homosexuality

Homosexuality presents a recurring issue for both society and sociology. The behavior occurs all over the world and throughout history, although its form, acceptability, and apparent extent vary greatly from one society to another. In many societies, as we have seen, homosexuality is taboo and therefore practiced in secret, while in others the behavior is more acceptable and thus more public. There is a good deal of cross-cultural evidence about male homosexuality, but much less information about female homosexuality, or lesbianism. It seems that in any given society where male homosexuality is tolerated or encouraged, it takes *one* of three quite different types: pederasty, involving a relationship between a man and a boy; or transvestism, in which certain men take on the social and sexual role of women; or homophilia, in which both partners are adult men who play otherwise conventional masculine roles. Whichever of these types predominates, the other two types tend to be rare and highly disapproved—not just by society at large, but also by most of those who practice the tolerated type of homosexuality (Gregersen, 1983).

Cross-culturally, pederasty is by far the most widespread form of socially accepted homosexual behavior, although it usually occurs in a bisexual context. Several societies, such as the Aranda of Australia, the Siwans of North Africa, and the Keraki of New Guinea, require every male to have exclusively homosexual relations with adults during adolescence but to be bisexual or heterosexual thereafter. Among the Keraki, for example, the initiation of adolescent males into adulthood requires them to take the passive role in anal intercourse for a year; when they become older, but before they get married, they initiate younger boys in like manner. The outstanding historical example of socially approved pederasty occurred in ancient Greece, where an elaborate system of sexual and spiritual relationships between adults and youths was apparently more highly valued than heterosexuality. But, like other societies that accept pederasty, the ancient Greeks regarded sex between adult men, or effeminate behavior by any males, as contemptible (Herdt, 1985; Dover, 1980).

Transvestism is cross-culturally much more rarely approved. This behavior has been accepted primarily among Asian people and North American Indian tribes, where there was often a clearly defined transvestite role with specific social duties, frequently those of tribal shaman. Clyde Kluckhohn (1948) found male homosexual behavior, generally of this type, accepted by 120 American Indian peoples and rejected by 54. A few societies that recognize the transvestite role, such as the Chukchi of Siberia, allow marriage between men. In such cases, the transvestite plays the social role of wife, while the husband is regarded as a normal heterosexual. Societies that accept transvestism generally regard pederasty as intolerable and consider homophilia almost incomprehensible.

Homophilia, involving adult males without any gender-role changes, is historically and cross-culturally very unusual. It is found almost exclusively in the industrialized world—particularly in the emerging postindustrial societies of Europe and particularly North America, where a distinct "gay" subculture is tolerated, but not encouraged, in larger cities. Homophilia is virtually unknown in simple, preindustrial societies, and there is very little evidence for it anywhere before the nineteenth century: most languages do not even have a name for this role, and our word "homosexual" was first coined in 1869. Societies that tolerate this type of homosexual behavior take a dim view of transvestism and particularly of pederasty, as do most homosexuals within these cultures.

The cross-cultural evidence on lesbianism is fragmentary, but the behavior seems to be generally less common than male homosexuality. The reason may lie in the fact that women in most societies have less freedom to experiment and deviate sexually than men, but it may also be the case that lesbian behavior is typically so discreet that visiting anthropologists may have interpreted it as mere "affection" and overlooked its real meaning. In any event, Gregersen (1983) found only five traditional societies that specifically approve of lesbianism, although the behavior is reported to be especially common in societies where men have many wives, particularly if the wives live together in harems. Lesbianism generally appears to take the homophilic form; relations between adult women and girls and relations involving gender-role reversals appear to be cross-culturally rare and are never socially approved. In general, lesbianism does not appear to arouse the strong reactions that male homosexuality sometimes does, and in practice most cultures appear to tolerate or not notice it. (The classic example of this phenomenon was a nineteenth-century British law that forbade male homosexuality but ignored lesbianism—because Queen Victoria refused to believe that women did such things!)

Western attitudes toward homosexuality have generally been negative. The reason lies yet again in the Western moral tradition that tolerates sexual acts only if they occur within marriage and can lead to reproduction. Homosexual acts are pursued for nonmarital love or pleasure and are necessarily nonreproductive. Until the global population explosion of the present century, widespread exclusive homosexuality would have been highly dysfunctional, for a society that did not encourage high birth rates might risk extinction. In societies faced with overpopulation, however, homosexuality (and contraception, masturbation, oral-genital sex, and other nonreproductive forms of heterosexual activity) are no longer dysfunctional in this respect, and so receive more acceptance than in the past.

Figure 7.8 *The nature and extent of homosexual behavior depend very much on the social context in which they arise. Large, publicly visible gay subcultures based on relationships between otherwise conventional adults are found and tolerated almost exclusively in the democratic nations of the industrialized Western world. Other societies have tolerated quite different forms of homosexual behavior.*

The Gay and Lesbian Community

How common is homosexuality in the United States? The answer to this question depends in part on the definition of homosexuality. Americans, unlike many other peoples, tend to see homosexuality and heterosexuality as "either/or" categories. Yet any attempt to divide the population into two distinct categories must fail because of the countless ambiguous cases that arise—people whose desires are homosexual but whose behavior is heterosexual; people who have heterosexual histories but whose current behavior is homosexual; people who alternate between the two forms of behavior; and so on. On the basis of his research, Kinsey recognized that sexual orientation is a continuum, with exclusive homosexuality at one end and exclusive heterosexuality at the other. Subsequent studies of the topic have been tentative and fragmentary, but they have generally indicated that 10 percent or so of the population can be considered exclusively or predominantly homosexual. Such an estimate would include somewhere in the region of 25 million Americans. There is no evidence, however, that the percentage of homosexuals in the population has increased over time, although homosexuality has certainly become more visible.

Over the past decade and a half, the gay liberation movement has substantially changed attitudes toward homosexuality, and gay men and lesbian women (the names they prefer) are able to pursue their lifestyles with relative freedom in larger cities, many of which now have local laws to guarantee their civil rights. Of course, some homosexuals attempt throughout their lives to "pass" as heterosexuals, even to the extent of marrying. On the whole, they seem successful in this attempt: according to one national poll, less than a third of Americans are sure they know a homosexual, and more than half believe they do not know any homosexuals at all (Schneider and Lewis, 1984). This is a remarkable finding, given that there are about as many substantially homosexual people in the United States as there are blacks or people aged sixty-five or over—and they, obviously, all have to be *somebody's* child, parent, cousin, coworker, teacher, neighbor, friend, or fellow student.

Most large cities contain definable areas that are occupied primarily by gays and lesbians and in which shops, restaurants, bars, hotels, churches, beaches, and other amenities cater primarily to them. Homosexuals are drawn together not only by a shared sexual orientation but also by a common social experience of stigma as deviants. As gay and lesbian people grow up, they, like anyone else, experience sexual emotions, desires, and acts that feel natural and right. Yet at some point, each maturing gay or lesbian person experiences the shock of realizing that these deep personal feelings are often despised in the society beyond, and that to express them, even in acts of love, may sometimes be a crime. Some homosexuals react to this wound to their self-concept by accepting society's attitude toward homosexuality and falling into self-hatred. Some spend a lifetime denying their homosexual tendencies, to others and perhaps even to themselves. Most, however, find ways to resolve the conflict, and many are able to do so in the gay and lesbian communities, subcultures in which they can be resocialized by learning new roles, norms, and values. The new climate helps to neutralize earlier conceptions of homosexuality as perverted or sinful, and enables gays and lesbians to build positive self-concepts (Warren, 1974; Altman, 1972, 1982; Wolf, 1979).

The great majority of gay men tend to form long-lasting, affectionate relationships, and lesbians seem to maintain even more stable and enduring relationships than heterosexuals do (Blumstein and Schwartz, 1983; Ettmore, 1980). It is true, however, that male homosexuals are more promiscuous as a group than heterosexuals. This is not surprising. Men in general are expected to be more promiscuous than women. We would therefore expect to find, and do find, that sexual relationships involving only men are more promiscuous than those involving men and women, while those involving only women are the least promiscuous of all. In the first decade or so of gay liberation, in fact, some gay men seemed to initiate their own sexual revolution, reacting to their new freedom by almost celebrating promiscuity. The appearance of AIDS has abruptly chastened that attitude, and encouraged many gay men to revert to more traditional practices of dating and settling down with a single partner. The gay community's collective response to AIDS—especially through the support services it has provided to gays, drug addicts, children, and others stricken by the disease—has cemented its bonds in a way that promiscuous sex never could.

Learning Sexual Orientation

Many people, including some homosexuals, believe that gays and lesbians are simply "born that way." But since we know that even heterosexuals are not "born that way," this explanation seems unlikely. Biological factors cannot explain the different extent of homosexuality in different societies at different times, or the changes of sexual orientation that may take place during the lifetime of an individual. Despite extensive research, no consistent evidence has been found for genetic or hormonal factors that predispose individuals toward homosexuality—or, for that matter, toward any of the other acts or preferences that occur in the vast spectrum of human sexual experience. Homosexuality, like any other sexual behavior ranging from oral sex to sadomasochism to a pursuit of brunettes, is learned (Marmor, 1980).

How do people learn their eventual sexual orientation—and, more specifically, why do some become homosexual in the face of so much discouragement in the socialization process? The question has been widely discussed and several theories have been offered.

1. *Early experiences.* A common popular view is that homosexuality is caused by early childhood experiences, particularly seduction. But while this may be true in some specific instances, it cannot provide a comprehensive explanation. Most American preadolescents and a substantial proportion of adolescents have had some homosexual experience, but only a small minority of them become exclusive homosexuals. Other people who have never had any homosexual experience in their entire lives may still privately define themselves as homosexual. Conversely, most gays and lesbians have had some youthful heterosexual experience—but it obviously did not make them heterosexual.

2. *Family environment.* Psychoanalysts have focused on the family background of homosexuals, usually in the belief that homosexuality is a form of mental disorder or "sickness" resulting from pathological family interactions. The leading proponent of this theory is Irving Bieber (1962), who claimed that homosexual males typically had domineering, possessive mothers and ineffectual or hostile fathers. Bieber's study, which was based entirely on psychiatric patients, has not been supported by subsequent studies, which have found no significant relationship between family background and sexual orientation. Other studies have found no consistent personality differences between homosexuals and heterosexuals (Hooker, 1965, 1969). Correspondingly, in 1974, the American Psychiatric Association removed homosexuality from its list of mental disorders.

3. *Social learning.* Another view comes from some psychologists, who argue that sexual orientation is learned through rewards and punishments. A person who finds a homosexual experience pleasurable may continue to repeat the experience, and a homosexual identity may result. This approach is helpful, but it still has two major defects. First, the balance of rewards and punishments in society heavily favors a heterosexual orientation, and it is difficult to see how

Figure 7.9 *A significant proportion of the population does not conform to heterosexual norms. This fact, which is often perplexing to the rest of society, presents an important question for socialization theory: How do people learn their sexual orientation?*

specific rewards in a limited context would counter this powerful social experience. Second, some homosexuals clearly do not find their orientation rewarding. They may wish to abandon their homosexual lifestyle but seem unable to do so. It is difficult to see how their sexual preference can be fully explained in terms of the punishments and rewards it offers them.

4. *Self-labeling.* A more recent approach to the problem avoids many of these difficulties. It recognizes the flexibility of the human sex drive and sees homosexual identity—or indeed any other sexual identity, including a heterosexual one—as the result of a self-definition, or label that people apply to themselves. This self-labeling usually occurs in late childhood or adolescence. At this age, young people may not even be aware that they are labeling themselves, and in some cases they may apply the label reluctantly—but their self-definition shapes their later sexual orientation.

How does this self-labeling work? Consider the quite common case of an adolescent boy who experiences a mild sexual interest in another male. It is possible for him to interpret this interest in various ways. If he thinks, "This means nothing, it's just a phase many straight people go through," then he is defining himself as heterosexual and is likely to continue on that path. If he thinks, "Hmm. This means that I'm attracted to boys as well as girls," then he is considering himself bisexual and may develop a bisexual identity in later years. And if he thinks, "I'm attracted to another male—I must be gay," then his self-labeling may propel him further in the direction of homosexuality. In short, people become trapped within their own self-definition of their sexual orientation and, particularly if other people also label them as homosexuals (or heterosexuals), they usually cannot escape from it. Regardless of social rewards or punishments, they look for no road back from their particular sexual orientation, for they believe there is none (Sagarin, 1973, 1975; Blumstein and Schwartz, 1974).

Cultural beliefs strongly influence the self-definition that the individual makes. It is quite possible to engage in homosexual acts without defining oneself as, or becoming, homosexual, provided one's culture or subculture offers this option. Among American male prison communities, in which homosexuality is very common, the dominant partner in a sexual encounter is defined as heterosexual (even though he achieves sexual gratification from his homosexual acts) and the submissive partner is defined as homosexual (even if he is unwilling and even if he is raped). The participants in the acts learn to accept these definitions,

Figure 7.10 *Conflict theorists argue that the institution of prostitution reflects, in microcosm, the power relations of the sexes. Arrests of female prostitutes are commonplace—but how often are their male clients led off in handcuffs?*

And when the police crack down on this crime, it is the prostitutes who get arrested, not their respectable clients. Prostitution thus institutionalizes the tendency to regard women as sex objects, and represents, in microcosm, the economic and political inequality of the sexes (Chapman and Gates, 1978; James, 1978; Dworkin, 1981).

Interactionist researchers have looked less at the broader societal context than at the ordinary human relationships involved in prostitution—at how the participants interact and how they understand their own behavior. One focus of research, for example, is on the resocialization that takes place as a new recruit enters the occupation. From pimps and other prostitutes, she learns various techniques: how to solicit in public, how to recognize undercover police officers, how to handle difficult customers, how to perform minimum services in the least possible time for a maximum fee. She also acquires a new set of values that help to maintain her own relative self-concept: she learns to despise her clients, to hold "respectable" women in contempt as prostitutes in disguise, to regard society as hypocritical, and to justify her own activities as socially valuable (Bryant, 1965; N. Davis, 1971; Heyl, 1977).

The three perspectives may seem contradictory, but, as is often the case, they complement each other to some extent, for each focuses on a rather different aspect of reality. The functionalist approach shows how prostitution may fulfill a certain social need; the conflict approach shows how the institution favors some groups at the expense of others; and the interactionist approach reveals the dynamics of the everyday social relationships involved. Taken together, they may provide a more comprehensive view of the topic than could be offered by any one perspective alone.

The sociological perspective on prostitution, as on all other forms of human sexual expression, offers a more acute insight into this aspect of social behavior—and with that insight, perhaps, comes a better understanding of the varied ways of men and women in our own society and elsewhere.

Summary

1. Sexuality is an important element in social life. Human sexual behavior is not innate, but is learned through the socialization process. The subject has been poorly researched until recently.

2. Human sexuality is extremely flexible; for this reason, every society makes strong efforts to regulate its expression.

3. There are three cultural universals in human sexuality: the incest taboo, marriage, and heterosexuality. Other than that, there are considerable variations in sexual practices in other societies, particularly preindustrial societies. Societies vary in their conception of beauty, their permissiveness or restrictiveness, and their norms of sexual conduct. This variation reveals the interplay of biological potentials and cultural learning.

4. Sexual behavior in the United States is marked by a contrast between real and ideal norms and values. Traditional values emphasize sex as legitimate only in the context of marriage and only if its primary purpose is reproduction, but they tolerate a double standard of behavior for males and females. The work of Kinsey and others indicates that these norms and values are extensively violated. A sexual revolution from the mid-1960s to the mid-1970s brought changes in attitudes, premarital sex, the double standard, teenage pregnancy, pornography, and sexually transmitted disease, notably herpes and AIDS. Sexual norms and values have now become more stable.

5. Some form of incest taboo is universal. The taboo is not instinctive, nor does it exist to prevent any ill effects of inbreeding. It exists to encourage alliances between groups through marriage, to prevent confusion of statuses in the family, and to prevent sexual jealousies between family members.

6. Rape is a crime of violence, not of passion, rooted in cultural norms. Many men tend to view women as sex objects, often subjecting them to sexual harassment in the workplace and elsewhere. Rape is an extreme manifestation of such established patterns of behavior, in which the aggressor bolsters his feelings of power and masculinity by abusing and humiliating the victim.

7. Where societies approve or tolerate homosexuality, it takes one of three main forms: pederasty, transvestism, or homophilia. Homosexuality has long been stigmatized in Western societies. Homosexual life, particularly in urban centers, focuses on a defined homosexual community. Several theories of causation have been offered: early experiences, family environment, social learning, and self-labeling in terms of cultural beliefs.

8. The practice of prostitution violates several traditional values and is stigmatized in the United States. Functionalist theory sees prostitution as meeting sound needs without placing too much strain on the family system; conflict theory sees it as a reflection of wider sexual inequalities; interactionist theory concentrates on the social behavior involved, such as the socialization of prostitutes.

Important Terms

cultural universals (143)

incest taboo (143)

marriage (143)

adultery (143)

heterosexuality (143)

homosexuality (143)

bisexuality (143)

restrictiveness (144)

permissiveness (144)

ideal culture (147)

real culture (147)

double standard (148)

pornography (151)

rape (155)

prostitution (162)

CHAPTER OUTLINE

CHAPTER 8

Social Stratification

For perhaps 99 percent of human history, our ancestors lived in small groups of hunters and gatherers, sharing whatever food, shelter, or other resources they had. In these societies, social inequality (other than that based on age or sex) meant only minor differences in the status of particular *individuals*. One person might have higher status than others, for example, because of some personal quality such as wisdom, beauty, or hunting skill. But as societies have become more complex over the past few thousand years, a quite different kind of inequality has appeared—inequality among entire *categories* of people. Like the layers of rock that can be seen in cliffs such as those of the Grand Canyon, the inhabitants of these societies are grouped into "strata." They generally regard people in their own stratum as equals, those in any higher stratum as in some way superior, and those in any lower stratum as somehow inferior.

To the sociologist, **social stratification** is the inequality of entire categories of people, who have different access to social rewards as a result of their status in a social hierarchy. Although there are still a few simple societies whose members are more or less equal, almost the entire human population now lives in stratified societies. A fundamental task of sociology is to find out why this is so, whether it is inevitable, and what effects this inequality has on human lives.

Stratification is perhaps the most profoundly important subject in the entire discipline. Sociologists have found that almost every aspect of our lives is strongly linked to our status in the social hierarchy: our scores on IQ tests, our educational achievements, the size of our families, our standards of nutrition, the chances that we will be arrested or imprisoned or divorced or committed to a mental hospital, our tastes in literature and art, our political opinions, the diseases we suffer, our life expectancy, even the probability of our keeping the lights on during sexual intercourse.

What this means is that people within a particular stratum share similar **life chances,** or probabilities of benefiting or suffering from the opportunities or disadvantages their society offers. By its very nature, therefore, stratification raises issues of deep moral and emotional significance—wealth and poverty, greed and misery, ambition and failure, brutality and compassion, oppression and rebellion. Throughout history it has generated bloody conflict between slave and master, peasant and noble, worker and employer, poor and rich. Today, the nuclear superpowers are divided primarily over their views on how a society's wealth should be distributed among its people. If these nations ever came into open conflict, much of the human life on earth could be wiped out.

Stratification Systems

Forms of stratification vary widely from one society to another according to how "closed" or "open" they are. In a closed, or "caste," system, the boundaries between the strata are very clearly drawn, and there is no way for people to change their statuses. In an open, or "class," system, the boundaries between the strata are more flexible, and there are opportunities for people to change their statuses. Additionally, some societies, such as the Soviet Union, claim to have no stratification, and thus to be "classless." Examples of each type of system will make these distinctions clear.

Caste

A **caste system** is a closed form of social stratification in which status is determined by birth and is lifelong. Caste membership is therefore an **ascribed status,** one that is attached to people on grounds over which they have no control, such as skin color or parental religion. A person's caste status is, obviously, the same as that of his or her parents, and there is virtually no way to change it.

What would happen, though, if someone were born to parents from two different castes? The result would be confusion—a blurring of the boundaries of caste by individuals who did not fit into the system. All caste societies therefore insist on **endogamy,** or marriage within the same social category. Endogamy is usually reinforced by a taboo against sexual relations across caste lines. Additionally, caste societies recognize and guard against **ritual pollution**—types of contact or proximity between members of different castes that are considered unclean for the superior caste. The risk of such pollution helps keep the strata physically as well as socially separate.

Caste systems were historically quite common, but only two rigid caste systems still exist in the modern world. South Africa is a caste society, with four distinct racial strata. As we saw in Chapter 2 ("Culture"), this system is faltering: its laws against interracial sex were repealed in 1985, and revolutionary violence is under way. The other system is in India.

India   Caste has been a fundamental feature of Indian life for over 2,500 years. Although the caste system was officially abolished in 1949, it still persists in rural areas, where it dominates the lives of tens of millions of people. In theory India has four main castes, or *varnas*. The highest varna is that of the Brahmans, or priests and scholars; next are the Kshatriyas, or nobles and warriors; below them are the Vaishyas, or merchants and skilled artisans; and finally there are the Shudras, or common laborers. Beyond the actual castes are the lowest of the low—the Harijans, or outcastes. In practice, the caste system actually consists of thousands of subcastes, or *jati*. These *jati* are usually linked to a particular occupation—scavenging, silkworm-raising, or even snake-charming—and everyone born into one is expected to do the same work. Intermarriage between castes is taboo, and intermarriage between *jati* is strongly disapproved.

The rules concerning ritual pollution are highly elaborate. Shudras and Harijans are often considered "untouchable": a member of a higher caste can be polluted by the slightest physical contact with them, an outrage that must be remedied by washing or other ritual cleansing. In some regions an untouchable's mere glance at a cooking pot is sufficient to defile the food, and a low-caste person's passage over a bridge can pollute the entire stream beneath. In some areas untouchables are not allowed in the villages during early morning or late afternoon because their long shadows are a ritual danger to others. Some low-caste groups are not only untouchable but also unseeable: there is one group of washerwomen who for this reason may work only at night.

Not surprisingly, the whole system breaks down in the urban areas where an increasing number of Indians live. A crowded and anonymous environment makes it difficult to ascertain other people's caste or to avoid constant ritual pollution, and industrialism shatters the old order, producing such anomalies as poor Brahmans and even wealthy outcastes. Gradually, therefore, India is moving from a caste to a class system of social inequality (Hutton, 1963; Berreman, 1973; Leonard, 1978).

Figure 8.1 *These people are members of the outcaste category that is still recognized in many parts of India. Their inherited social status is so low that they are not even included in the caste system. Members of higher strata may consider it a form of "ritual pollution" to be touched by the shadow of an outcaste—and, in some cases, even to be looked at by such a person.*

Class

A **class system** is an open form of stratification based primarily on economic statuses, which may be subject to change. The boundaries between the strata are more flexible than in a caste system, with no clear division between one class and the next. An individual's status usually depends on the occupation and income of the family breadwinner, so people sometimes move up or down the class system as their economic circumstances improve or decline. In addition, there are no formal restrictions against marriages between people from different classes. Class membership, then, is an **achieved status,** one that depends to some extent on characteristics over which the individual has some control.

Almost all societies now have class systems, although their actual shape differs from one society to another. In predominantly agricultural societies there are usually two main classes: a small and wealthy class of landowners, and a large and poor class of peasants. In industrialized societies, on the other hand, there are usually three main classes: a small and wealthy upper class, a fairly large middle class of professionals and other white-collar workers, and a large working class of less skilled blue-collar workers.

Great Britain Great Britain provides a good illustration of a class system. The country has a small upper class, a large middle class, and a working class containing somewhat more than half of the total population. Wealth is very unequally shared: a 1976 royal commission found that the richest 1 percent of the population owned a quarter of the nation's wealth, while the richest 5 percent owned nearly half of it. An important means of maintaining the system is education. About 5 percent of the nation's children go to exclusive private boarding schools whose graduates enjoy great advantages later in life. (To give one illustration of the influence of these schools, no fewer than eighteen former pupils of the most exclusive of them, Eton, have become prime ministers. Imagine the chances of a single American high school producing eighteen presidents!) The pattern is repeated at the college level. Two universities, Oxford and Cambridge, enjoy the greatest prestige, and about half their entrants come from that 5 percent of children at the private schools. Graduates of Oxford and Cambridge are disproportionately represented at the upper levels of British society (Gathorne-Hardy, 1978; Halsey et al., 1980; Sampson, 1983).

Class differences in lifestyles are far more evident in Britain than in North America, and people are much more aware of class relationships. One reason is that the British monarchy has survived into the twentieth century, along with its

Figure 8.2 *Modern British society is marked by significant class divisions. These inequalities are made more noticeable by some remaining traces of the country's feudal past, such as the monarchy and the House of Lords—a legislative assembly consisting mostly of men who inherited their titles. The roles of the queen and the lords are now mainly symbolic, but the persistence of an aristocracy is a reminder of how the society's wealth is distributed along traditional class lines.*

ritual pomp and an intricate system of prestige awards—earldoms, knighthoods, dameships. Another reason, interestingly enough, is that voice accent is the most important indicator of social class, overriding such other symbols as style of dress. There are distinct differences among and within the accents of the upper, middle, and lower classes, and anyone raised in the country is unavoidably aware of the social status of another the moment that person utters a sentence. The observant American tourist will notice that the British tend to respond to one another quite differently on the basis of accent: a salesperson may address someone with an upper-class accent as "sir" or "madam," but may call someone with a lower-class accent "mate" or "dear." Despite these peculiarities, the British system shares basic features with all class systems: unequal distribution of wealth, differences in lifestyle from one stratum to another, and reproduction of the system from one generation to the next through such means as education and inheritance (Goldthorpe, 1980; Halsey, 1986).

A Classless Society?

A **classless society** is one with no economically based strata. Can a modern society be classless? This is an important question, for such a society is the stated goal of one of the major political forces of our time—communism. Although countries such as the Soviet Union are often described as "communist" in the West, none of these societies actually regards itself as communist. The communist-ruled nations claim only to have reached the intermediate stage of socialism, in which classes have been formally abolished but some inequality among individuals still remains, pending the transition to a completely equal communist society.

The Soviet Union   How valid is the claim that Soviet classes no longer exist? Actually, there is great social and economic inequality in the Soviet Union. About 9 percent of the people belong to the Communist party, which dominates national life. However, the real elite—consisting of about 1 percent of the population—is concentrated in what the Russians call the *nomenklatura*, a listing of high officials in the government, economy, military, media, education, and science. This elite and their families have incomes several times that of ordinary citizens, and enjoy a variety of special privileges, such as better housing and medical facilities. The *nomenklatura* is also overwhelmingly old, male, and Russian, in a country where Russians constitute only half the population (there are

Figure 8.3 *Although the Soviet Union claims to have abolished classes, there are marked inequalities of power, wealth, and prestige between the ordinary citizens and the select group within the Communist party who form the country's bureaucratic elite. These huge portraits of Marx, Engels, and Lenin on a Moscow public building suggest the role of state officialdom in Soviet life.*

128 other nationalities in the Soviet Union, speaking 125 different languages) (Voslensky, 1984). Moreover, the political leadership does not face free national elections, and its policies are subject to only limited public criticism.

The Soviet Union admits that it has social inequality among individuals, but denies that it has social stratification among classes. The country certainly does not have a dominant class living partly off profits and inherited wealth, as all capitalist industrial societies do. On the other hand, there are at least three economic strata that surely *look* like classes: a large class of poor peasants and urban laborers, a smaller middle class of white-collar workers, and the tiny, affluent, privileged elite. Perhaps more to the point, members of the *nomenklatura* use their influence to get their children into elite schools and high-paying jobs, with the result that existing inequalities are becoming more structured into the system, not less. Also, the Soviet Union (like China, Hungary, and most other communist-ruled nations) increasingly uses financial rewards to encourage productivity, even though these incentives lead to greater income inequality. A totally classless society might be possible—but the Soviet Union is far from this goal, is getting no nearer to it, and has no specific plans to achieve it (Shipler, 1982; Aganbegyan, 1988).

Social Mobility

A key question about any stratification system is what chance it offers for **social mobility**—movement from one social status to another. Such movement can be either upward or downward, depending on whether people rise to higher statuses or fall to lower ones. Sociologists are especially interested in **intergenerational mobility,** or movement up or down the hierarchy by family members from one generation to the next. The amount of this movement—which occurs, for example, when a janitor's child becomes a doctor, or a doctor's child becomes a janitor—tells how rigidly inequality is structured into the society. But what factors determine how much mobility a society has?

Actually, there are two quite different kinds of social mobility, and each has its own source. The first kind is **exchange mobility,** changes in people's social statuses as they exchange places with one another at different levels of the hierarchy. For example, high-level incompetents may lose their jobs and fall to lower statuses, while more competent people at lower levels are promoted to higher statuses. The amount of this mobility depends on how closed or open the society is: in a closed system there can be little exchange mobility, but in an open system there is potential for much more.

The second kind of mobility is **structural mobility,** changes in people's social statuses as a result of changes in the structure of the economy. For example, in times of economic recession there is a general downward trend in mobility as incomes shrink and workers are laid off. College graduates, no matter how keen they are to get good jobs, may find themselves driving cabs or collecting unemployment benefits. In times of economic growth, on the other hand, there is an upward trend in mobility as incomes rise and new jobs are created. College graduates, even the less promising ones, may find many excellent jobs available for the asking. The amount of this mobility depends on economic conditions: in a static economy there is little structural mobility, but in times of economic change there may be a good deal.

Which kind of mobility is more common? The answer is that most mobility in all modern societies is structural mobility. Over the past century or so, the mechanization of agriculture and the automation of industry have steadily eliminated millions of low-status blue-collar jobs, no matter how hard those who occupied them worked. Simultaneously, the growth of service industries and of government and corporate bureaucracies has created millions of new, higher-status white-collar jobs, which had to be filled. Under such structural conditions, social mobility is *guaranteed* for a large part of the population: huge numbers of people are forced out of a lower status and pulled into a higher one by factors that have little to do with them as individuals. But despite this trend, mobility from one stratum to another is the exception rather than the rule in *all* stratified societies. Even in the most open systems, like those of the United States, Canada, and other emerging postindustrial nations, most people remain throughout their lives in the social class of their parents (Lipset and Bendix, 1959; Fox and Miller, 1965, 1966; Lipset, 1982; Grusky and Hauser, 1984).

Analysis of Class

In a caste system, people know their place because the boundaries between the strata are very sharp and rigidly maintained. In a class society, the matter is not so simple. What, for example, is your own social class? Middle class? Upper class? Lower-middle class? Working class? You may hesitate over the answer, and you may find that other people disagree about your exact social position, or that you disagree about theirs. Given that class lines are so blurred and uncertain, how do we determine the outlines of classes and who their members are?

Marx's Analysis

Karl Marx spent most of his life writing about social class. His pioneering work on the subject—voluminous, passionate, sometimes contradictory—has had such immense influence that almost all subsequent discussion of class systems has had to confront his ideas.

To Marx (1967, orig. 1876), a class consists of all those people who share a common relationship to the means of production. Those who own and therefore control the means of production—people such as slaveholders, feudal landowners, or the owners of property such as factories and capital—make up the dominant class. Those who work for them—such as slaves, peasants, or industrial laborers—are the subordinate class. The relationship between the classes involves not only inequality but also exploitation, because the dominant class takes unfair advantage of the subordinate one. The workers produce **surplus wealth**—more goods and services than are necessary to meet their producers' basic needs. But the workers do not enjoy the use of the surplus they have created. Instead, those who own the means of production are able to seize the surplus as "profit" for their own use. Often the owners have merely inherited what they own, and often they do less work than their workers—yet they enjoy much higher incomes. This, in Marx's view, is the essence of exploitation, and the main source of conflict between the classes throughout history.

Figure 8.4 *Karl Marx's views, like anyone's, were deeply influenced by the social environment. Marx wrote in England at a time when a large and impoverished working class labored for a handful of wealthy capitalists. Marx assumed that this situation would inevitably lead to revolution. But Marx did not foresee many of the changes that later occurred in industrial societies, such as the growth of a large middle class. No revolution has ever occurred in an advanced industrialized society.*

Marx wrote in an era when industry was owned and controlled by individual capitalists, and the bulk of the population comprised a poorly paid labor force living in wretched conditions. But changes in industrial societies since that time have thrown doubt on Marx's concept of class. One significant change is in the occupational structure: the middle class has expanded rapidly, and a variety of new jobs have emerged that do not seem to fit Marx's concept. Many middle-class people, for example, work not for capitalists but rather for their fellow citizens, perhaps as teachers, nurses, or civil servants. Others do not work for anybody: they are self-employed. Some blue-collar workers, too, are paid more than some white-collar professionals. An American truck driver, for example, may sometimes earn more than a high school principal—so what is their relative class status?

Another important change since Marx's time is that most industry is now run by large corporations, which are owned by thousands or even hundreds of thousands of stockholders but are controlled by salaried managers. As a result, the *ownership* and the *control* of the means of production are no longer identical. True, corporate managers and directors typically own stock in the companies that employ them, but—especially in the case of large companies—they rarely own a controlling interest. Indeed, it may be that a "new class" is appearing, consisting of well-educated experts whose high social status is based on knowledge, not ownership. It is not clear where these salaried executives, bureaucrats, scientists, and others fit in Marx's concept of class (Gouldner, 1979; Bruce-Biggs, 1979; Herman, 1981).

Weber's Analysis

Max Weber (1946) offered an influential analysis of class that confronts the limitations of Marx's view. It breaks the single concept of class into three distinct but related elements, which we may translate as economic status, or *wealth;* political status, or *power;* and social status, or *prestige.* So, instead of trying to decide whether a truck driver is of higher or lower class than a high school principal, we can rank them both on all three dimensions. In this case the truck driver might have greater wealth, whereas the principal might have superior power and prestige.

Prestige Ratings of Occupations in the United States

Occupation	Score	Occupation	Score	Occupation	Score	Occupation	Score
Physician	82	Registered nurse	62	Foreman	45	Baker	34
College professor	78	Pharmacist	61	Real estate agent	44	Shoe repairman	33
Judge	76	Veterinarian	60	Fireman	44	Bulldozer operator	33
Lawyer	76	Elementary school teacher	60	Postal clerk	43	Bus driver	32
Physicist	74	Accountant	57	Advertising agent	42	Truck driver	32
Dentist	74	Librarian	55	Mail carrier	42	Cashier	31
Banker	72	Statistician	55	Railroad conductor	41	Sales clerk	29
Aeronautical engineer	71	Social worker	52	Typist	41	Meat cutter	28
Architect	71	Funeral director	52	Plumber	41	Housekeeper	25
Psychologist	71	Computer specialist	51	Farmer	41	Longshoreman	24
Airline pilot	70	Stock broker	51	Telephone operator	40	Gas station attendant	22
Chemist	69	Reporter	51	Carpenter	40	Cab driver	22
Minister	69	Office manager	50	Welder	40	Elevator operator	21
Civil engineer	68	Bank teller	50	Dancer	38	Bartender	20
Biologist	68	Electrician	49	Barber	38	Waiter	20
Geologist	67	Machinist	48	Jeweler	37	Farm laborer	18
Sociologist	66	Police officer	48	Watchmaker	37	Maid/servant	18
Political scientist	66	Insurance agent	47	Bricklayer	36	Garbage collector	17
Mathematician	65	Musician	46	Airline stewardess	36	Janitor	17
High school teacher	63	Secretary	46	Meter reader	36	Shoe shiner	9
				Mechanic	35		

Source: James A. Davis and Tom W. Smith, *General Social Survey Cumulative File, 1972–1982.*
Ann Arbor, Mich.: Inter-University Consortium for Political and Social Research.

Figure 8.5 *This table shows the average prestige ratings, on a scale of 1 to 100, that Americans give to various occupations. The most prestigious jobs in this ranking appear to be those that yield high income or that require extensive educational credentials.*

Wealth, power, and prestige can thus be independent of each other. In practice, though, they are usually closely related. The reason is that any one of them can often be "converted" into any of the others. This is particularly true of wealth, which can readily be used to acquire power or prestige. Over the years, sociologists have used opinion polls to find out how the public in the United States, Canada, and several other industrialized societies ranks the prestige of various occupations. The results show that, as a general rule, prestige is closely linked to positions of political power and to occupations with high income (Treiman, 1977; Davis and Smith, 1983). Prestige ratings for a number of different occupations are shown in Figure 8.5.

Influenced by Weber, many sociologists now assess a person's social position in terms of his or her overall **socioeconomic status,** or **SES,** a complex of factors such as income, type of occupation, years of education, and sometimes place of residence.

Maintaining Stratification

How can stratification systems possibly survive? At first sight, it seems unlikely that any of them would last very long, because the great majority of the people are denied an equal share of what the society produces. Yet revolutions are rare events, and some of the most apparently unfair and rigid systems—like the Indian caste system—persist for centuries. Two factors, it seems, are vital in maintaining stratification: the ruling stratum's control of the resources necessary to preserve the system; and a general belief throughout the society that the inequality is actually "natural" or "right."

Control of Resources

Marx emphasized that social institutions tend to reflect the interests of those who control the economy rather than the interests of those who do not. In any society, therefore, the laws tend to protect the rich, not the poor. The established religion supports the social order, rather than preaching its overthrow. Education teaches the virtues of the present system, not its vices. Government upholds the status quo, rather than undermining it. In fact, any attempt to dislodge the ruling class is likely to be regarded as a revolutionary assault on the state as a whole, because the interests of the two are so closely identified.

This does not necessarily mean that the dominant class actually plots to ensure that government and other institutions protect its advantages. Its members achieve this effect merely by acting in their common interests. Like anyone else, high-status people form **social networks**—webs of relationships that link the individual directly and indirectly to other people. Because the social networks of the dominant stratum have much greater resources of wealth, power, and prestige than those of other strata, the elite have far more "leverage" in society, despite their fewer numbers. They influence, control, or occupy the commanding heights of the economic and political order, and their actions tend to preserve the advantages of their class as a whole (Collins, 1974, 1979; Bourdieu, 1977).

"Tom Willoughby, meet Howard Sylvester—
one of us."

A stratification system therefore survives for as long as the resources of those who benefit from it outweigh the resources of those who are disadvantaged by it. Change may come about if members of the lower stratum successfully mobilize their own resources. Typically, they do this by forming a social movement—such as the labor movement or the civil rights movement—that organizes such resources as their votes, funds, access to the media, ability to cause demonstrations and strikes, and so on. In extreme cases social movements aim at revolution, using violence as a resource. World history, particularly of the past two hundred years, has seen the revolutionary overthrow of several ruling classes—from the French Revolution of the eighteenth century to the Russian, Chinese, Cuban, Iranian, and Nicaraguan revolutions of the twentieth century.

Revolutions are exceptional, however, and even violent class conflict is unusual. Although the ruling elite can use its ultimate resource—force—to maintain its advantage, this is rarely necessary. Instead, over time, the existing inequality becomes a tradition, to be taken for granted as "the way things are." In short, it gains **legitimacy,** the generally held belief that a given political system is valid and justified. Stratification thus tends to be widely accepted and even defended—not just by members of the privileged higher strata, but often by members of the lower strata as well.

Ideology

An **ideology** is a set of beliefs that explains and justifies some actual or potential social arrangements. Karl Marx explored the role of ideologies in legitimating social stratification, and his views are now widely accepted, even by sociologists who reject some of his other ideas. Marx's argument was simple. The dominant ideology in any society is always the ideology of the ruling class, and it always justifies that class's economic interests. Of course, other ideologies may exist in a society, but none can ever become dominant unless the class that holds it, and whose own interests it justifies, becomes the dominant class. In a society controlled by capitalists, therefore, the dominant ideology will be capitalism, not communism. In a society controlled by communists, the dominant ideology will be communism, not capitalism. In a society controlled by slaveholders, the dominant ideology will justify slavery, not freedom for all.

It is obvious why members of the upper stratum might regard the dominant ideology as "natural," but what about members of the lower stratum? Their acceptance of the ideology is what Marx called **false consciousness,** a subjective understanding that does not accord with the objective facts of one's situation. Members of the lower stratum fail to realize that their individual life chances are linked to their common circumstances as an oppressed group. Instead of blaming the system, they attribute their low status as slaves, peasants, outcastes, or laborers to luck, fate, nature, the will of God, or other factors beyond their control. Only if they gain **class consciousness**—an objective awareness of the lower stratum's common plight and interests as an oppressed group—do they begin to question the legitimacy of the system. They then develop a new ideology, one that justifies their own class interests and consequently seems revolutionary to the dominant stratum. At that point, according to Marx, class conflict will begin.

An ideology is a complex belief system, often containing religious, political, economic, and other ideas. The Indian caste system provides a good example of an ideology in operation, for it is legitimated by the Hindu religion. According to Hindu doctrine, everyone is reincarnated through a series of lifetimes, and one's status in the next lifetime depends on how well one observes the required behavior in the present one. Failure to live up to the duties of one's caste may result in reincarnation as a member of a lower caste, or even as an animal. This ideology thus serves the interests of the upper stratum—while giving the lower strata powerful reason to accept their own status.

Another example comes from the feudal system of medieval Europe, in which, generation after generation, a great mass of peasants worked for a tiny aristocracy of hereditary landowners. Feudalism was legitimated by the political and religious doctrine of the divine right of kings, which held that the monarch derives authority directly from God. When the king delegated some of this authority to the feudal lords, it followed logically that the peasants were under a divine imperative to obey the lords also. The Church lent full support to this system. The whole social order thus seemed unchallengeable because it had been ordained by God—a view that the peasants appear, on the whole, to have accepted as unquestioningly as their masters did.

Stratification in modern industrial societies is also legitimated by ideologies that tend to be accepted without question by members of all classes. In America, for example, inequality is justified as a means of providing incentives and rewarding achievement. It is believed that people have equal opportunity to improve their status: everyone is supposed to have the same chance to get rich by working hard. Actually, most Americans do work very hard, but most stay in the same class all their lives. Yet those who do not get rich (that is, most of us, and especially those who started out from low-status families) tend to blame only themselves or their bad luck: the well-socialized American who becomes a failure in the class system does not blame the system itself. Such "failure," however, is *inevitable* for a large part of the population, because the American

Figure 8.6 *In the feudal system of late medieval Europe, stratification was based on the ownership of land. The peasants spent their lives working for a landowning aristocracy, who in turn made financial contributions to a hereditary monarch. The entire system was legitimated by the ideology of the "divine right of kings"—the notion that feudalism had divine approval because the king ruled through the will of God.*

system—like a caste system, feudalism, colonialism, or any other form of stratification—presupposes the existence of a large lower stratum that has to be filled by somebody.

Control of resources and the power of ideology thus help maintain stratification. But why are most societies stratified at all? Both functionalist and conflict theorists have offered answers to this question.

Stratification: A Functionalist View

In keeping with their assumption that features of society have functions, or effects, that contribute to the stability and survival of society as a whole, functionalists argue that stratification must have some useful social function, particularly since it is so widespread. In a classic statement, Kingsley Davis and Wilbert Moore (1945) contend that some form of stratification is a social necessity.

Davis and Moore point out that some vital social roles require scarce talents or prolonged training. If a society is to function effectively, it must fill these roles with talented, skilled people. Because the roles often involve stress and sacrifice, people must be attracted to them by rewards—such as wealth, power, or prestige. Thus, a society that values surgeons more than priests will give higher status and rewards to the surgeons, and one that values senators above garbage collectors will give higher status to the senators. This unequal distribution of social rewards is functional for the society as a whole because the ablest individuals are drawn to the most demanding roles. Social stratification, however, is the inevitable result.

This explanation has been much criticized, primarily on the grounds that stratification systems do not work so neatly in practice. Some people who have no apparent value to society, such as the jet-setting inheritors of family fortunes, are highly rewarded. Some people whose roles are of limited value, such as movie or football stars, are more highly rewarded than people who play vital roles, such as prime ministers and presidents. Yoko Ono, for example, is worth over $150 million, but it is not immediately clear that her social value is *that* much greater than that of, say, your sociology professor. Above all, every society contains many people who have low rewards wholly or partly because their status is ascribed (outcastes in India, blacks in the United States) and many who have high rewards for the same reason (wealthy aristocrats in Britain, whites in South Africa). In all societies, as we have seen, the rate of intergenerational mobility from one stratum to another is actually rather low. Thus, stratification does not necessarily ensure that the ablest people fill the most demanding roles. It ensures that most people stay more or less where they are.

Actually, the theory of Davis and Moore shows how inequality among *individuals*—not stratification among whole *categories* of people—might be functional as a way of matching skilled people with demanding roles. But even when people do gain high status through their own efforts, they, like the poor, tend to pass this status on to their descendants. Inequality thus spreads with the passage of time, until the ultimate stratification system bears little resemblance to its origin, whether it was functional or not. At that point, in fact, stratification may have dysfunctions, or negative social effects. One dysfunction is that stratification, by denying people equal access to social roles, prevents a society from making the best use of its members' talents. A second dysfunction lies in the strain that stratification can cause—leading, perhaps, to disruption rather than stability in the social order.

Stratification: A Conflict View

Conflict theorists reject the functionalist view of society as a balanced system whose various features contribute to overall social stability. Instead, they regard tension and competition as a powerful factor in shaping culture and social structure. The conflict approach derives from Marx's work, but has been much modified by later conflict theorists.

Marx held that stratification exists only because some groups become rich and powerful, and then preserve and enhance their own interests at the expense of other classes. He saw class conflict as the key to historical change: every ruling class is eventually overthrown by the subordinate class, which then becomes the new ruling class. This process repeats itself until a final confrontation between workers and capitalists in industrial society: the capitalists would grow fewer as a result of their endless competition, the middle class would disappear into an ever larger and more impoverished working class, and a successful revolution would inevitably result. The triumphant workers would then create a new socialist society in which the means of producing and distributing wealth would be owned by the public, for the good of all. Socialism would lead ultimately to a communist society, in which inequality, alienation, conflict, oppression, and human misery would be things of the past. This is a powerful vision—so powerful that, long after Marx's death, it continues to provoke revolutionary zeal against class systems in many parts of the world.

American sociologists tended to neglect Marx's theories until the 1960s, primarily because his predictions about the future of industrial capitalism and its class system were so hopelessly inaccurate. Recognizing these flaws, many modern conflict theorists have tried to modify some of Marx's insights and apply them to the changed conditions of the contemporary world. For example, Ralf Dahrendorf (1959) downplays competition between classes, and focuses instead on struggles among other groups in society, such as unions and employers. He argues that much inequality today is shaped not by who owns or does not own property, but rather by who gives orders and who takes them. Others, like Randall Collins (1974, 1979), emphasize how different groups jockey for posi-

"Everybody loves money. Too bad there isn't enough to go around."

Drawing by Bernard Schoenbaum; © 1987 The New Yorker Magazine, Inc.

tion by acquiring such resources as educational credentials, which they can then use to secure jobs and other advantages for themselves. In any case, Marx's failure as a prophet does not necessarily invalidate his basic insight: that conflict over scarce resources leads to the creation of caste and class systems, and that in every case the interests of the dominant class are served by the ideology and power of the state. The implication is that stratification is not a functional necessity at all—although it is certainly convenient for those who happen to benefit from it.

But does the conflict approach provide a complete explanation for stratification? People, after all, grow up to be unequal in talents, skills, determination, perseverance, thrift, and so on. Surely, then, they will tend to achieve unequal rewards. And if there is no validity to the functionalist argument, then why do all societies—even communist-ruled ones—offer greater social rewards to people with rare and valued talents?

A Synthesis?

The conflict and functionalist views of stratification are not necessarily incompatible. Gerhard Lenski (1966) combines aspects of both in an influential theory that shows why some types of societies are more stratified than others. He claims that the basic resources a society needs for survival are allocated much the way the functionalists claim—that is, to meet basic social needs by matching roles with rewards. This seems an efficient procedure, so it happens to some extent in every society. But Lenski maintains that a society's surplus resources are mostly allocated the way the conflict theorists claim—through struggle among different groups. The resulting inequalities may sometimes be functional, but most societies become much more stratified than they need to be.

As we noted in Chapter 3 ("Society"), there has been a general historical trend of **sociocultural evolution,** the tendency for societies' social structures and cultures to grow more complex over time. Lenski uses this idea to show that societies are stratified largely according to how much surplus wealth they have. *Hunting and gathering* societies generally lack a surplus, and so have no stratification: there is no way for people to become wealthier than others, let alone to pass their status on to their descendants. In the more productive *horticultural* societies and *pastoral* societies, there is a limited surplus, which permits some inequality of wealth among specific families. These societies are usually not stratified, however, because there is insufficient surplus to support entire castes or classes. In *agricultural* societies, on the other hand, a considerable surplus is possible, and the picture changes radically. Rigid strata invariably emerge, with wealth, power, and prestige concentrated in the hands of a hereditary, landowning aristocracy, usually headed by a monarch.

Industrial societies produce unprecedented wealth, and in the early stages of industrialism there is often a vast gap between the rich and the poor, as a rural peasantry is transformed into an urban work force living in slums and shantytowns. In the more advanced industrial societies, however, there is usually less inequality—even though there is more surplus wealth than ever. Why should this be? The reason is that industrialism creates a multitude of jobs that require a skilled, educated, and mobile labor force. As a result, structural social mobility causes the lower class to shrink and the middle class to expand. In response to demands from this large, rising class, governments become more democratic, and new social inventions, such as social-security programs and progressive income taxes, limit extremes of poverty and wealth. Lenski therefore expects that the long-term trend in most industrialized societies may be toward greater equality. This trend may well continue in the emerging *postindustrial* societies, where the middle class is expanding even further as technological innovations steadily create more new white-collar jobs. For the present, however, postindustrial societies still contain noticeable class divisions.

Stratification in the United States

The founders of the United States declared in ringing tones that "all men are created equal," and this value has been a central one in American culture ever since. Yet, from the moment of its birth, the United States has been a stratified society. For nearly a century after the Declaration of Independence, the nation had a caste system in the form of racial slavery. Like caste in India, the American version insisted on endogamy (through laws against intermarriage and taboos on sex across caste lines) and had strict rules about ritual pollution. These rules persisted until the middle of the twentieth century, in the form of segregation laws designed to prevent blacks from ritually polluting whites in such public facilities as restrooms, restaurants, and buses. Moreover, for decades after the founding of the new republic, the vote was restricted to adult white males who owned property. Women were not permitted to vote until early in this century, and until recently were generally paid much less than men for doing the identical job. And despite its professed commitment to human equality, the United States today contains over 600,000 millionaires—while over 32 million people, including one child in every five, live below the official poverty line. Thus, the world's leading postindustrial society remains a visibly stratified one, marked by a very unequal distribution of wealth, power, and prestige.

Wealth

The most obvious sign of stratification in the United States is its unequal distribution of wealth. Wealth actually contains two components—*assets* (property such as real estate and stock) and *income* (earnings such as salaries and wages). Although both kinds of wealth usually become more equally shared in the most economically advanced societies, the United States seems to be an exception to this trend. For at least the past quarter century there has been little equalization of wealth in the form of assets, and none in the form of income. Moreover, the economic inequalities between the rich and the poor are enormous.

Assets   The bulk of the nation's wealth in the form of assets is owned by a tiny minority of the population. It is difficult to get precise data on the subject, but, using various sources, the Office of Management and the Budget (1973) reported that the poorest fifth of Americans owned only 0.2 percent of the national wealth, while the richest fifth owned 76 percent. More recently, the Bureau of the Census (1986b) calculated that the top 12 percent of American families own 38 percent of the nation's assets. There is an important difference, too, in the assets of the poor and those of the rich. The wealth of the poor consists mostly of items that depreciate in value and produce no income, such as household goods. The wealth of the rich consists largely of assets that may appreciate in value and produce income, such as real estate and stocks. In fact, the Bureau of the Census (1984) reported that 46 percent of all corporate stock is owned by 1 percent of the population.

Who are the highly wealthy? Their numbers are small: only about 0.3 percent of Americans are millionaires, and many of these owe this status to huge but unexpected increases in the value of their own homes. But if the gap between the poor and those with assets of a million dollars yawns wide, it is nothing compared to the gulf between the "just millionaires" and those who form the real elite of the wealthy. Our best peek at the super-rich comes from *Forbes* magazine's regular survey of the 400 wealthiest Americans, which draws on a variety of public and private sources of information. Its 1988 survey included 400 people worth over $225 million, 185 of whom were worth at least $500 million, and 51 of whom were worth at least $1 billion. In addition, there were 98 family groups with assets of between $300 million and $6.5 billion. In the recipe for all this success, one ingredient stands out: rich parents. All of the 98 families and 154 of the 400 individuals inherited all or part of their wealth.

Income   The annual income of Americans is also very unequally distributed. As Figure 8.7 shows, there is a huge gap between the incomes of the very rich and the very poor. The bottom fifth of American families receives only 4.6 percent of total income, while the highest fifth receives 43.7 percent. These shares are similar to those at the end of World War II, over four decades ago.

Who receives the highest incomes? Their numbers are few. Less than 5 percent of American individuals and families earn more than $50,000 a year, and less than 1 percent earn more than $100,000. Only about 12,000 people—less than .005 percent of the population—receive more than $1 million a year. These high-income people consist primarily of two overlapping groups. The first includes those living off earnings from businesses, stocks, and other capital investments. These assets of the wealthy produce income in such forms as rents, interest, dividends, and capital gains.

The second major group of high-income earners are executives of major corporations. In a 1985 survey of corporate incomes, *U.S. News and World Report* found that the highest officials of 202 of the largest corporations were paid over half a million dollars each. In fact, 51 of this group were paid over $1 million a year, and 6 received more than $2 million. And these salaries are not the full story, since the highest executives may receive bonuses and other "perks" worth far more than their salaries. In contrast, the median family income of all Americans is just over $31,000, a figure that often includes the earnings of two or more family members. More than 70 percent of American individuals and households earn less than this amount.

Figure 8.7 *The distribution of income— salaries, wages, and other earnings— has remained virtually unchanged for many years. The highest-earning fifth of American families has consistently earned over 40 percent of the national income, while the poorest fifth has consistently received around 5 percent.*

Percentage Share of Total Income Received by Each Fifth and Top 5 Percent of Families, 1958 to 1987

Year						

| | Percent Distribution of Aggregate Income | | | | | |
Year	Lowest Fifth	Second Fifth	Middle Fifth	Fourth Fifth	Highest Fifth	Top 5 Percent
1987	4.6	10.8	16.9	24.1	43.7	16.9
1986	4.6	10.8	16.8	24.0	43.7	17.0
1984	4.7	11.0	17.0	24.4	42.9	15.7
1982	4.7	11.2	17.1	24.3	42.7	16.0
1980	5.1	11.6	17.5	24.1	41.5	15.6
1978	5.2	11.6	17.5	24.1	41.5	15.6
1976	5.4	11.8	17.6	24.1	41.1	15.6
1974	5.4	12.0	17.6	24.1	41.0	15.3
1972	5.4	11.9	17.5	23.9	41.4	15.9
1970	5.4	12.2	17.6	23.8	40.9	15.6
1968	5.6	12.4	17.7	23.7	40.5	15.6
1966	5.6	12.4	17.8	23.8	40.5	15.6
1964	5.1	12.0	17.7	24.0	41.2	15.9
1962	5.0	12.1	17.6	24.0	41.3	15.7
1960	4.8	12.2	17.8	24.0	41.3	15.9
1958	5.0	12.5	18.0	23.9	40.6	15.4

Source: U.S. Bureau of the Census.

Despite these marked disparities in assets and income, however, overall living standards have generally been improving. The real median income of Americans has more than doubled over the past three decades, and the proportion of the population that lives in poverty has declined, with some sharp fluctuations, from about 27 percent in the late 1940s to under 14 percent at the end of the 1980s.

Power

Like wealth, power is very unequally shared in the United States. The historical extension of voting rights to the poor, to blacks, and to women represents progress in one direction, but this has been offset by the growth of huge federal bureaucracies and influential private interest groups, leading to a concentration of power at the upper levels of government and the corporate economy. American voters can periodically elect or dismiss their political leaders, but the electorate is only one of several sources of influence over day-to-day government decisions. Americans generally suspect that they are excluded from much of the important decision making in the society: opinion polls regularly show large majorities agreeing that government is run for the benefit of a few private interests looking after themselves.

Indeed, if everyone had equal access to power, we might expect high office-holders to represent a cross-section of the American people. In fact, these officials are overwhelmingly white, middle-aged, male, Protestant, and, perhaps most significant, wealthy—for in the United States, as elsewhere, wealth is readily convertible to power. No matter what administration is in office, most cabinet members are very wealthy men. Money is no disadvantage to those seeking election to public office in the United States, either: in 1988, almost a third of the senators were millionaires.

Sociologists have debated not *whether* power is unequally shared but, rather, *how* unequally it is shared. Some, such as C. Wright Mills (1956) and Michael Useem (1986), argue that the United States is dominated by an elite of high officials in government and corporations. They claim that this elite operates informally and behind the scenes, making most of the important decisions that affect economic and political life. Other sociologists, such as David Riesman (1961) and Robert Dahl (1982), take a more pluralistic view. They claim that a variety of powerful interest groups struggle for advantage, sometimes privately and sometimes publicly, but tend to counterbalance each other in the long run. It is difficult to prove or disprove either of these views, but it is significant that the ordinary voter does not figure in the elite model and is a marginal element in the pluralistic model. Several studies have also shown that there is a tight-knit "establishment" or "governing class" of high-income individuals in government and corporate life that has a strong informal influence, especially in economic and foreign affairs (for example, Dye, 1986; G. Moore, 1979; Useem, 1978, 1979, 1986; Domhoff, 1983).

Prestige

Differences in prestige seem less significant in the United States than differences in wealth and power. Some people have high prestige—the wealthy, the powerful, and a variety of other "celebrities," such as stars from the worlds of sport and entertainment. Others have low prestige—essentially the poor, the deviant, and other social rejects. On the whole, however, Americans treat one another in a way which, by international standards, is remarkably equal and informal. A beggar in the street may be viewed with distaste, or the occupant of a chauffeured limousine with envy, but there is much less of the deference toward "superiors" and arrogance toward "inferiors" that is typical of most other strati-

Figure 8.8 *In the United States, prestige often depends on "conspicuous consumption"—the socially noticeable display of desired material goods.*

fied societies. In many stratified societies in the past, such displays were actually required, with members of the lower strata being expected to kneel, bow, curtsey, doff their hats, or offer other submissive gestures to their superiors.

Inequalities in prestige can be sustained only if the symbols that imply prestige are unequally distributed. But unlike power and wealth, which show no signs of becoming more equally shared, the symbols of prestige have become available to an increasing number of Americans. These symbols are mainly of a material nature—houses, cars, color TV sets, designer clothes, and respectable jobs. The main reason for the more general distribution of the symbols of prestige lies in a radical change in the nature of jobs since the beginning of the century. The United States has become a predominantly middle-class society, in which the bulk of the jobs make possible a broadly similar lifestyle and the prestige that goes with it. Additionally, there is a fundamental belief in America that every individual is, at least potentially, as good as anyone else—a belief less strongly and less widely held in many other stratified societies.

The American Class System

How many classes are there in the United States, and who belongs to them? There is no definitive answer to this question, for various observers may draw the boundaries of class in different ways. Just as we can create many ways of measuring off the length of a piece of wood—by inches, millimeters, and so on—so we can create many ways of categorizing an unequal population into classes.

Sociologists have used three basic methods of analyzing the American class system. One, the "reputational" method, is to ask people to describe stratification as they see it in their own community. The second, the "subjective" method, is to ask people what class they think they belong to. The third, the "objective" method, is to rank people into classes according to such measures of socioeconomic status as income and occupation. These methods all yield fairly similar results, and most sociologists would probably accept that the United States contains an upper class of about 1 to 3 percent of the population; an upper-middle class of 10 to 15 percent; a lower-middle class of about 30 to 35 percent; a working class of about 40 to 45 percent; and a lower class of about 20 to 25 percent (Rossides, 1976; Vanfossen, 1979; Gilbert and Kahl, 1982; Kerbo, 1983).

Figure 8.9 *Although "hard work" is supposed to be the key to success in American society, many people achieve success not by working harder than others but by having better ideas. Henry Ford made a fortune when he mass-produced the Model-T Ford; Steven Jobs achieved wealth by creating the Apple, the first personal computer.*

Consider specific high-status jobs. Even if "everybody" had an equal chance to become a U.S. senator, only 100 people in the entire society can occupy that status at the same time. Even if "anybody" could become president of one of the leading 10,000 corporations, only 10,000 out of tens of millions of Americans could have the jobs. Or consider the prospects of getting rich. If we define the "rich" as, say, the top 30 percent or so of taxpayers (currently those making more than $25,000 a year), then, automatically, over 70 percent cannot be rich. Or, if "rich" means only the top 5 percent of taxpayers (those making more than $50,000 a year), there will be no room in this category for the remaining 95 percent. And if we confine "rich" to the top 1 percent (those earning over $100,000), more than 99 percent are excluded. Few gamblers would be impressed with such odds. In fact, the prospects are worse than these numbers suggest, because many of the high-status positions are already "reserved" for the children and heirs of the wealthy. People do not all have equal opportunity to rise to the top: those already close to the heights have but a short way to travel; those nearer the bottom face a longer and harder journey.

By contrast, short-distance mobility within a particular class is much more common: over half the men in the United States are upwardly mobile within their class of origin. In most cases, however, they move to a status only somewhat above their fathers'—for example, from factory worker to factory supervisor, or from high school teacher to college professor. So, although the chances of streaking ahead and leaving others behind are small, the chances for rising together with most of the people at one's own level are quite good. Why should this be the case?

The reason is that the United States has a great deal of upward structural mobility—the kind where economic growth creates a higher proportion of upper-status jobs from one generation to the next, ensuring that most people will be upwardly mobile to some degree. Over the course of this century the middle class has expanded, radically changing the shape of stratification in America—from a pyramid, with most statuses at the bottom, to an egg, with most bunched in the middle. Moreover, increasing prosperity has affected almost every job. An auto mechanic, for example, has much the same relative social status as a blacksmith had a couple of generations ago—but enjoys an incomparably higher standard of living.

Some people, however, are more upwardly mobile than others. What are their characteristics? Two factors have overriding importance. The first is social-class background: the higher the social class of your parents, the higher your ultimate position is likely to be. The second factor is education. The higher your level of education, the better your prospects for upward mobility—especially if you have a college degree. Of course, social class influences educational achievement—almost two-thirds of white-collar sons have at least a year of college, compared with one-third of blue-collar sons. But those blue-collar sons who do attend college are able to use their education to "cancel" the effects of their social-class background (J. Davis, 1982).

What else, beyond class and education, affects individual mobility? Several factors have been identified—some under the control of the individual, some not. These include childhood nutrition, health, place of residence, age at marriage, the status of one's spouse, willingness to postpone gratification, race, sex, height, physical appearance (especially among women), intelligence, and career field. Character traits are presumably important, too, and might include shrewd judgment, willingness to take risks, innovative imagination, skill at negotiating, and so on. In most successful careers, too, there is a random element of luck—basically, of happening to be in the right place at the right time (Jencks et al., 1979).

How does intergenerational mobility in the United States compare with rates in other Western industrialized societies? Studies have repeatedly found that there is very little difference among these societies—no matter what their ideologies on the subject may be. All these nations have been undergoing roughly similar changes in occupational structure, so rates of structural mobility are much the same from one country to another, with Israel, Canada, and the United States enjoying rather higher rates than the others. The United States differs from most other societies in one principal respect: a much higher proportion of people from working-class backgrounds manage to reach professional status. Although only 1 working-class American male in 10 rises this far, the rates in other industrial societies are much lower—1 Japanese in 14, 1 Swede in 30, 1 Frenchman in 67, 1 Dane in 100, 1 Italian in 300. The reason for the contrast is that a far higher percentage of working-class children graduate from high school and college in the United States than anywhere else in the world, enabling them to use education as a passport to better jobs and higher statuses (Fox and Miller, 1965, 1966; Blau and Duncan, 1967; Lipset, 1972, 1982; Grusky and Hauser, 1984).

Of course, intergenerational mobility is not always upward. About a quarter of American men are downwardly mobile relative to their fathers, usually by only a short distance. Again, the class system works in favor of the upper classes: people starting out near the top have a great deal more cushioning for a fall than those starting out near the bottom. For tens of millions of working Americans, the loss of a few thousand dollars of income—perhaps caused by the illness, unemployment, or death of a breadwinner—can plunge an entire family into grinding hardship.

What does all this mean for your own chances of upward mobility? If past patterns of economic growth persist, you can expect the following. You, and most people similar to you, will enjoy upward mobility as the developing post-industrial economy improves living standards and creates new, higher-status jobs—including, no doubt, positions nobody has yet thought of, in industries that do not yet exist. You will probably experience occasional negative patches, when recessions threaten downward mobility. You will have to work hard to keep up with people at your own level, because most of them will be working hard, too. For whatever reasons, a few of you will be downwardly mobile relative to the group, and a few of you will be upwardly mobile relative to the group, moving by one means or another into the small number of very high statuses that are available. Overall, you will benefit not just from your own efforts but also from each other's, because in the final analysis the whole economy is driven by the energy of the individuals who sustain it. Collectively, you will help shape the social forces that, in turn, will help shape your own careers.

Poverty

Millions of American adults and children live in poverty. For these impoverished people, life may be marked by illiteracy and ignorance, insecurity and homelessness, disease and early death, the stunting of human lives and potential. Yet many Americans, accustomed to life in a generally affluent, optimistic society, tend to ignore the existence of poverty or even to blame the poor themselves for their plight. To people in other nations, however, the existence of so much poverty in the midst of such wealth may seem to undermine America's claim to the superiority of its system and to moral leadership in the world.

What Is Poverty?

Basically there are two ways to define poverty. The first is in terms of **relative deprivation,** the inability to maintain the living standards customary in the society. This approach assumes that people are poor only in relation to others who are not poor. Accordingly, the poor are simply defined as the lowest income-earners in society—say, the bottom fifth or the bottom tenth. The implication is

CHAPTER 9

Racial and Ethnic Stratification

One of the most fascinating aspects of our species is the extraordinary physical and cultural diversity of its members. Yet this diversity is frequently a source of conflict and inequality, because human relationships are all too often shaped by the differences rather than the similarities between groups.

Social distinctions are commonly made among people on the basis of their inherited physical characteristics or their learned cultural traits. As a result of these social distinctions, the groups in question come to regard themselves, and to be regarded and treated by others, as "different." Those people who share similar physical characteristics are socially defined as a "race," and those who share similar cultural traits are socially defined as an "ethnic group."

Throughout history, relationships among racial and ethnic groups have been marked by antagonism, inequality, and violence. Over the course of the twentieth century alone, millions of people have been slaughtered, and many millions more subjected to humiliation, cruelty, and injustice, for no apparent reason other than their membership in some despised group. In the United States, a country formally committed to human equality, the physical and cultural differences among various groups still have a strong influence on their members' social status.

Race and Ethnicity as Social Facts

Although "race" and "ethnicity" have such an impact on intergroup relations, the two words are often misused in ordinary speech, and we must examine their meaning more closely.

Race

There are over 5 billion people in the world, and they display a wide variety of skin colors, hair textures, limb-to-trunk ratios, and other characteristics, such as distinctive nose, lip, and eyelid forms. These physical differences have resulted from the adaptations that human groups have made to the environments in which they lived. For example, populations in tropical areas tend to have dark skin, which protects them against harmful rays from the sun. Populations in high altitudes tend to have large lung capacity, which makes breathing easier for them. Populations in very cold climates tend to have relatively short limbs, which enable them to conserve body heat. Although the human animal can be traced back in the fossil record for well over 3 million years, the racial differences that we see today are of comparatively recent origin—50,000 years at the most.

As a biological concept, the word "race" is almost meaningless. There is certainly no such thing as a "pure" race. Different populations have been interbreeding for thousands of years, and a continuum of human types has resulted.

Figure 9.4 *Population transfer—often involving the expulsion of the unwanted group—is a drastic but not uncommon event in race and ethnic relations. In 1838, some 16,000 Cherokee were forced to march a thousand miles in winter from their homeland in Carolina and Georgia to be "resettled" in Oklahoma. Some 4,000 of them died during the ordeal. The American artist Robert Lidneux depicted their journey in this picture,* Trail of Tears.

pluralism at present, with different groups, such as American Hispanics and French Canadians, asserting pride in their own cultural traditions. *Legal protection of minorities* has been entrenched in the laws of both countries through civil-rights and similar legislation. *Population transfer* was used extensively against the Indians of North America, who were often forced to leave their traditional territories and to settle on remote reservations. The United States and Canada both practiced *continued subjugation* of their minorities, with the most extreme example being that of slavery in the Southern states. *Extermination* was used against American Indians in both countries, and tribes such as the Mohicans, Pequots, and Yana were in fact hounded out of existence.

Some racial and ethnic groups, then, are able to live together in conditions of equality and mutual respect, but others are in a state of constant inequality and conflict. Clearly, there is no inherent reason why different groups should be hostile to one another. Stratification along racial and ethnic lines has social causes. But what are these causes? How and why do racial and ethnic inequalities develop?

Intergroup Relations: A Functionalist View

Functionalist theorists generally try to explain persistent social features in terms of their positive effects on society as a whole. As we saw in Chapter 8 ("Social Stratification"), functionalists argue that social inequality can serve the function of rewarding scarce talents. We might expect, then, that since racial and ethnic inequalities are a common feature of societies, functionalists would look for some resulting social benefits. In practice they have rejected such reasoning, and have concentrated instead on the dysfunctions, or negative effects, that racial and ethnic antagonisms have on society. They point out that in the long run, racial and ethnic inequality will always tend to be dysfunctional for a society— partly because it prevents the society from making full use of the talents of all its members, and partly because, sooner or later, it inevitably generates hostility and even violence.

Functionalists do contend, however, that a certain amount of group consciousness and loyalty can be functional under certain conditions. As we saw in Chapter 2 ("Culture"), most human groups tend to display **ethnocentrism,** the tendency to judge other cultures by the standards of one's own. Some measure of ethnocentrism is almost unavoidable in any racial or ethnic group. To most people, it is self-evident that their own norms, religion, attitudes, values, and cultural practices are right and proper, while those of other groups may seem inappropriate, peculiar, bizarre, or even immoral. Within limits, such ethnocentrism can be functional for the group's survival, for these attitudes ensure its members' solidarity and cohesion. People who believe that their group and its way of life are "best" will have faith and confidence in their own cultural tradition, will discourage penetration by outsiders, and will unite to work for their common goals (Coser, 1956; Levin and Levin, 1982). The difficulty is, of course, that under certain conditions, ethnocentric attitudes can lead to the exploitation and oppression of other groups.

In general, a functionalist theory of race and ethnic relations is poorly developed: it can show why hostile relations may be dysfunctional, but it does not really explain why racial and ethnic inequalities develop in the first place.

Intergroup Relations: A Conflict View

From the conflict perspective, racial and ethnic inequalities have the same source as any other form of social stratification: they stem from competition among different groups for the same scarce resources—wealth, power, and prestige. The victorious group in this conflict becomes the dominant group, while any other contenders become minority groups.

For racial or ethnic antagonisms and inequalities to develop, three basic conditions must usually be met (Noel, 1968; Cox, 1976; Vander Zanden, 1983):

1. *Identifiable groups.* There must be two or more identifiable social groups. Unless people are aware of differences between the groups and are able to identify people as belonging to one group rather than another, conflict between them cannot develop.

2. *Competition for resources.* There must be competition between the groups for valued resources, such as power, land, or jobs. In this situation, members of one group will be inclined to secure their own interests by denying members of other groups full access to these resources.

3. *Unequal power.* The groups must be unequal in power, enabling one of them to make good its claim over scarce resources at the expense of the other group or groups. At this stage inequalities become structured into the society.

From this point on, events follow a fairly predictable course. The more the groups compete, the more negatively they view one another. The dominant group develops contemptuous beliefs about the supposed inferiority of the minority group or groups and uses these beliefs to justify its continued supremacy. Attempts by the minority group to assert its own interests are likely to be regarded as threatening by the dominant group, and further oppression may follow.

From the conflict perspective, the disputes among racial and ethnic groups are not really about racial or ethnic differences; they are about the use of such differences to create and preserve inequality in the competition for scarce resources. Thus, wherever different groups compete for the same resources—blacks and whites for power and wealth in South Africa, settlers and indigenous tribes for possession of the Brazilian hinterland, Israelis and Palestinians for the same piece of territory—intergroup hostility is the result, particularly if the groups remain unequal and one of them is able to exploit or victimize the other.

In a classic study, Richard LaPiere (1934) illustrated the practical difference between the two concepts. He traveled around the United States with a Chinese couple, stopping at over 250 restaurants and hotels on the way. In only one instance were they refused service—that is, discriminated against. Six months later, LaPiere wrote to each of the establishments he had visited and asked if they were willing to serve "members of the Chinese race." Over 90 percent of the replies indicated that Chinese would not be welcome—that is, there was prejudice against them. Yet the prejudice was not necessarily translated into discrimination. LaPiere's study is one of many examples of sociological research that reveal a marked discrepancy between what people say and what they do (Deutscher, 1973).

Sources of Prejudice

A major focus of the work of social scientists, particularly in the decade after World War II, has been the sources of prejudice. What are the characteristic features of prejudiced thought, and how and why do people become prejudiced?

Stereotypes Prejudiced thought always involves the use of a **stereotype**—a rigid mental image that summarizes whatever is believed to be typical about a group. Like ethnocentrism, stereotyped thinking is an almost unavoidable feature of social life. You probably have your own stereotype, for example, of what an Australian aborigine or an Eskimo is like. The essence of prejudiced thinking, however, is that the stereotype is not checked against reality. It is not modified by experiences that contradict the rigid image. If a prejudiced person finds that an individual member of a group does not conform to the stereotype for the group as a whole, this evidence is simply taken as "the exception that proves the rule" and not as grounds for questioning the original belief.

The "Authoritarian Personality" Do some people have personality patterns that make them more prone to prejudice than others? A classic study by Theodore Adorno and his associates (1950) concluded that many prejudiced people have an **authoritarian personality**—a distinctive set of traits, centering on conformity, intolerance, and insecurity. Those who have this personality pattern, Adorno found, are submissive to superiors and bullying to inferiors. They tend to have anti-intellectual and antiscientific attitudes; they are disturbed by any ambiguity in sexual or religious matters; and they see the world in very rigid and stereotyped terms. The authoritarian personality, Adorno claimed, is primarily a product of a family environment in which the parents were cold, aloof, disciplinarian, and themselves bigoted. Although a number of objections have been raised to Adorno's findings—including the possibility that the authoritarian personality may exist among radicals as well as conservatives—it is now generally accepted that some people are psychologically more prone to prejudiced thinking than others.

Irrationality Another consistent feature of prejudiced thought is that it is irrational—illogical and inconsistent. Prejudiced people are not concerned about genuine group characteristics; they simply accept any negative statement that feeds their existing hostility. In one study, Eugene Hartley (1946) found that people who were prejudiced against one minority group tended to be prejudiced against others. Nearly three-quarters of those who disliked Jews and blacks also disliked such people as the Wallonians, the Pireneans, and the Danireans. Some prejudiced people even urged that members of the latter three groups be expelled from the United States. As it happens, however, the Wallonians, the Pireneans, and the Danireans were fictitious names concocted by Hartley! His study convincingly demonstrates the irrationality of prejudice, for it shows that prejudiced people may be hostile toward groups they could never have met or even have heard of.

Scapegoating Another factor that can contribute to prejudice is **scapegoating**—placing the blame for one's troubles on some relatively powerless individual or group. Scapegoating typically occurs when the members of one group feel threatened but are unable to retaliate against the real source of the threat. Instead, they vent their frustrations on some weak and despised group—and thereby gain the sense that they are superior to someone at least. One contemporary example comes from Great Britain, where there has been chronic unemployment among working-class white youths. Unable to strike at the real source of their problem—the "system"—some of these youths have taken to assaulting Pakistani immigrants, whom they believe to be competing for the few available jobs at the same level. Such attacks have become so common that there is now a word for them: "Paki-bashing."

Figure 9.6 *A century ago, Chinese immigrants to the western United States often served as scapegoats for the frustrations of low-status whites, who saw them as competitors for jobs. This engraving depicts a lynching in protest of "cheap-labor foreigners."*

Social Environment The sources of prejudice mentioned thus far appear to be primarily psychological. But as we noted in Chapter 4 ("Socialization"), people's personalities—including their thoughts and feelings—develop in, and are shaped by, their social context. Certain environments, therefore, may tend to encourage or discourage prejudice. In general, if groups interact regularly on terms of equality and cooperation, there is likely to be little prejudice among their members. Conversely, if there is inequality, competition, and minimal contact between groups, prejudice can develop unchecked. Prejudice, therefore, cannot be attributed solely to the psychological quirks of individuals, for it is often simply a matter of conformity to the norms of one's own group.

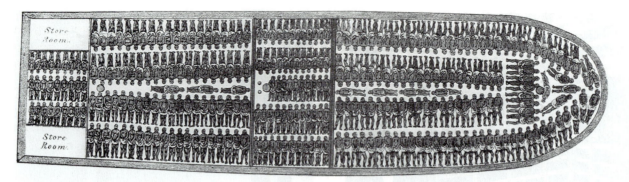

Figure 9.8 *This old print shows the "cargo" layout on one of the decks of a slave ship that plied the Africa-America route before the Civil War. On board, the slaves were chained wrist to wrist and ankle to ankle for the two-month voyage. To prevent the risk of mutiny and suicide among the captives, they were frequently kept in this position for days or weeks on end, lying in their own blood and excrement and unable even to sit up. For years an intense debate raged between two groups of slave-traders: the "tight packers," who held that profits would be greater if as many slaves as possible were crammed aboard, and the "loose packers," who argued that so many slaves died during the voyages that it would be better to allow the captives a little more space. Dragged to America in chains to be subjected to slavery and then to decades of segregation and legal discrimination, black Americans have had an experience utterly different from that of any other racial or ethnic group in the society.*

The first Africans were brought in shackles to North America in 1619, and within a few decades the demand for their labor had created a massive slave trade that ultimately transported some 400,000 captives across the Atlantic. On arrival in the United States, the slaves were sold at public auction and set to work, mostly on plantations. The original culture of these African people had little relevance in this new situation, and their old traditions, language, and religion soon fell into disuse and eventually disappeared.

At first, the slaveholders justified slavery, not by racist attitudes, but rather by their frankly admitted need for cheap labor in the cotton and tobacco fields. In time, however, the practice of slavery led to the creation of a racist ideology that justified the continued subjugation of the slaves by depicting blacks as sub-human: they were said to be innately irresponsible, promiscuous, stupid, lazy— and happy with their subordinate status. The experience of slavery set the stage for the subsequent interaction between black and white in the United States.

The Northern states began to outlaw slavery in 1780, but it persisted in the South until it was ended by the Civil War and legislation that followed Lincoln's emancipation of slaves in 1863. Thereafter, segregation remained the norm, and was gradually encoded into law. Throughout the country, including supposedly liberal metropolitan areas of the North, segregation in hotels, restaurants, and other public facilities was common. In 1954, however, the Supreme Court ruled in the historic *Brown* v. *Board of Education* case that segregated schools were inherently unequal and ordered nationwide school desegregation "with all deliberate speed." From that time on, the courts and the federal government began to dismantle the system of racial segregation and discrimination. Yet progress toward greater equality was painfully slow until the emergence of a powerful civil rights movement and a series of violent and costly riots in Northern cities during the 1960s. As conflict theory would suggest, this heightened tension between the competing groups generated rapid changes. In particular, the principle of racial equality was enshrined in the law of the land through a series of civil rights acts that prohibited legal discrimination.

How has the black minority fared since the changes of the 1960s? In some respects there have been important gains. The gap between blacks' and whites' average years of schooling has narrowed rapidly—from three years in 1960 to less than half a year today. More than 7,000 blacks now hold local elective office; among them are over 250 mayors, including those of several of the nation's largest cities. Black workers are no longer concentrated in a handful of menial jobs: in the early 1960s, for example, one of every three working black women was a maid, but today, only one in twenty does that job. In fact, a substantial part of the black population—perhaps a third—has "made it" to the American middle class, and their jobs, incomes, family structure, and general lifestyle are similar to those of their white counterparts (Davis and Watson, 1982; L. Williams, 1985; Landry, 1987).

But in other respects blacks have made little progress, or have even lost ground. Institutionalized discrimination still persists throughout the United States—perhaps more so in the North (where about half the black population now lives, mostly in urban ghettos) than in the South, which in many ways has adjusted more readily to the changing relationships between the races. As a result of informal social and economic barriers to residential integration, most blacks live in neighborhoods that are overwhelmingly black, and most black children, despite busing programs, still attend predominantly black schools. Although black college enrollment doubled between 1960 and 1980, the percentage of blacks in college is beginning to slip once more. Blacks remain underrepresented, too, at the higher levels of the political system: in 1988 only 3 percent of members of Congress were black, and there was no black senator or governor. Most important of all, the economic position of blacks has actually worsened relative to that of whites. In 1970, the median black family income was 61 percent that of whites; today, it is about 56 percent that of whites (Reid, 1983; Farley, 1984; Bureau of the Census, 1988, 1986c; Tolchin, 1988).

The fact is that despite the success of many blacks, the great majority have been left behind, and a hard core of these form an "underclass" of impoverished people who have little hope that their lives will ever improve. Almost one-third of all blacks live below the poverty line—a rate three times that of the white population. Many of these people are trapped in an unending cycle of broken homes, welfare, joblessness, violence, crime, and drug abuse. Half of the black births in America today are to unmarried women. One in every two black children lives in poverty, and one in every two lives in a home without a father. One in six black males is arrested by the age of nineteen, and homicide is the leading cause of death of black males between the ages of fifteen and nineteen. Unemployment rates for blacks are typically double those of whites, and in some urban areas the rate for black teenagers is over 50 percent. The persistence of this underclass seems a constant reproach to the proclaimed ideals of the United States, and it remains a powderkeg in the society's future.

Given that there is less prejudice and discrimination in the United States now than there was two decades ago, why has a significant part of the black population remained trapped at the bottom of the stratification system? To explain this phenomenon, some writers are now emphasizing the economic factors that have resulted in the intertwining of race and class in the United States. For example, Thomas Sowell (1981, 1983) points out that blacks are unique among minorities in that they came to the United States as slaves and were denied basic civil rights until the 1960s. Moreover, they have traditionally been a people of the rural South who began to migrate to large cities, mostly in the North, only a generation or so ago. Blacks have thus been isolated from the economic mainstream for most of their history in the United States, and in this sense are relatively "recent," unskilled immigrants to the industrialized areas of the nation. But unlike immigrants earlier in this century, blacks arrived at a time when the manufacturing base of the cities was disappearing as some blue-collar jobs van-

Certainly, white ethnics are often perceived to be distinct groups by the rest of society—a perception that is sometimes expressed, none too flatteringly, in "Polish" jokes, in stereotypes of drunken, priest-ridden Irish, or in popular misconceptions of Italians' overweight mothers or their links to organized crime. Additionally, white ethnics are generally underrepresented at the upper levels of the educational, economic, and political worlds; the most progress seems to have been made by the Irish, perhaps because they spoke English as a native language from the first generation (Greeley, 1976, 1977; Alba and Moore, 1982). Even so, white ethnic groups now perceive their identity as a potential source of pride and strength, and this has lent further impetus to the society's growing acceptance of pluralism as a whole.

Affirmative Action

In the United States, the removal of legal discrimination did not eliminate other patterns of discrimination which, over the generations, have become structured into social and economic life. Federal and local governments have therefore turned to other means to correct these historical imbalances. One important approach is the attempt to integrate education by busing black children into the schools of predominantly white areas. Another major tool is "affirmative action," or positive steps to ensure that racial minorities (and women) are not informally discriminated against in access to higher education, employment, or promotion.

Affirmative action does not mean that unqualified people must be given preference over others simply because of their minority-group status; nor does it mean that specific numerical quotas are set. Essentially, the program sets goals and timetables for the hiring of minorities in government agencies and other large organizations that receive federal contracts or funds. For example, an affirmative-action goal for a particular factory might be to hire more minority workers until the composition of its work force more or less reflects that of the surrounding neighborhoods from which the workers are drawn. Such goals serve only as targets, and there are no sanctions against employers as long as they can demonstrate good-faith efforts to meet them. Actually, very few affirmative-action goals are fully reached, but even so, the program has greatly expanded opportunities for minorities and women.

Affirmative-action programs are controversial for the obvious reason that what is "affirmative action" to one group is "reverse discrimination" to another—the white males who must face new, government-mandated competition for jobs and other privileges. When a 1988 *Newsweek* poll asked "Because of past discrimination, should qualified blacks receive preference over equally qualified whites in such matters as getting into college or getting jobs?" only 14 percent of whites answered yes, compared with 40 percent of blacks.

The Future

Race and ethnic relations in the United States are in constant flux. Indeed, if current migration patterns and birth rate trends persist, the United States could be one-quarter Asian and one-third Hispanic within a century. In any event, there is some indication that American intergroup relations are improving, but the process still has a long way to go. According to Milton Gordon (1961, 1977), there are three main options that are open to the United States in race relations.

1. *Anglo-conformity* assumes that it is desirable to maintain modified English institutions, language, and culture as the dominant standard in American life. In practice, "assimilation" in the United States has, historically, always meant Anglo-conformity.

2. *Melting pot* is a rather different concept, involving a totally new blend, culturally and biologically, of all the racial and ethnic groups in the United

States. Given enough time, the melting pot may be the society's ultimate destiny, but in practice, it has been of limited significance in the American experience.

3. *Cultural pluralism* assumes a series of distinct but coexisting groups, each preserving its own tradition and culture, but each loyal to broader national unity. In practice, there has always been a high degree of cultural pluralism in the United States, but this pluralism has been based on inequality rather than equality.

Current indications are that, for the foreseeable future at least, American race and ethnic relations will be conducted primarily within a pluralist framework. Pursuit of cultural pluralism can be a dangerous course, however, for it presumes some degree of ethnocentrism on the part of the participating groups, and it can provide a workable solution only if it is based on equality, respect, and interdependence. But if Americans can achieve that, then finally, after three centuries, the "American dilemma" may be resolved.

Summary

1. Social inequality sometimes follows lines of race and ethnicity. A race is regarded as socially distinct because its members inherit common physical characteristics; an ethnic group is regarded as socially distinct because its members share a common cultural heritage.

2. A minority group is one that is differentiated from the rest of the population and treated unequally. Minorities are socially visible; suffer social disadvantages; have a consciousness of kind; are generally born into the group; and generally marry within the group.

3. Six possible patterns of race and ethnic relations are assimilation; pluralism; legal protection of minorities; population transfer; continued subjugation; and extermination. All have been attempted in North America.

4. Functionalists point out that while racial and ethnic inequality and ethnocentrism may be functional from the point of view of the groups that benefit from them, they may be dysfunctional in the long run if they lead to hostility and violence.

5. Conflict theorists see racial and ethnic inequalities as a form of social stratification based on competition for scarce resources, with the most powerful group becoming the dominant one. Conflict may also be a source of social change in this situation.

6. Racial and ethnic inequalities are justified by the ideology of racism, which holds that some groups are inferior to others. As the European colonial experience shows, racism arises when one group wants to justify its dominance or exploitation of another.

7. Prejudice is an inflexible attitude, usually negative, toward other groups; discrimination is unequal treatment of others on the grounds of group membership. Prejudice is not necessarily translated into discrimination. Sources of prejudice include stereotyping, authoritarian personality, irrationality, scapegoating, and certain social contexts. Discrimination can be legal or institutionalized; the latter is the more difficult to eliminate.

8. The United States has never been a "melting pot" for all its peoples. Some minorities have been treated unequally because they were unlike the majority or because of the economic circumstances of their arrival and settlement. Important minorities in the modern United States are blacks, Hispanics, Indians, Asians, and "white ethnics." The groups have progressed at different rates.

9. The United States has, with some success, tried to eliminate institutionalized discrimination through such tools as affirmative action.

10. There are signs that American race and ethnic relations are improving. The most likely trend in the foreseeable future is cultural pluralism, in which different groups preserve their own culture.

Important Terms

race (195)
ethnic group (195)
minority group (195)
genocide (197)
ethnocentrism (199)
ideology (200)
racism (200)
self-fulfilling prophecy (200)
prejudice (201)
discrimination (201)
stereotype (202)
authoritarian personality (202)
scapegoating (203)
legal discrimination (204)
institutionalized discrimination (204)

CHAPTER *10*

Gender and Age Stratification

Societies can be stratified in many different ways—according to caste, class, race, language, religion, and a host of other features. Yet only two such characteristics are used in all societies: sex and age. These distinctions are universal, for they are based on ascribed statuses that arise inevitably from the human condition: our species contains males and females, and we all grow older from the time of birth to the moment of death.

Every society treats men and women in different ways and expects different patterns of behavior from them. Throughout history, men have generally been the dominant sex and women have been subordinate to them. Both men and women have usually taken this inequality for granted as a "natural" state of affairs, passing it down from generation to generation as part of their culture.

Similarly, all societies give different rights and responsibilities to people of various age categories and require them to play different social roles. Here, however, the patterns of inequality are not so consistent. Traditional societies are usually dominated by the old, but in modern societies, the middle-aged become the dominant category, and the old sometimes take on the characteristics of a disadvantaged minority.

Sex and age inequalities may affect your own life in profound ways. For example, a male college graduate in the United States can expect to enjoy lifetime earnings of about $1.5 million more than a female graduate. And a young person can expect that his or her income (and the power and prestige that go with it) will be relatively low in early adulthood, will rise through middle age, and will then decline markedly in later life. In this chapter we will examine these inequalities, using the general principles that we have already applied to other forms of structured social inequality.

Gender and Society

Throughout the world, the first question parents ask at the birth of a child is always the same: "Is it a boy or a girl?" The urgency of the question reveals the great importance that all human societies attach to the differences between men and women.

This division of the human species into two fundamental categories is based on **sex**—the biological distinction between males and females. All societies, however, elaborate this biological fact into secondary, nonbiological notions of "masculinity" and "femininity." These concepts refer not to sex but to **gender**—the culturally learned differences between males and females. In other words, male or female is what, by birth, you *are;* but masculine or feminine is what, with appropriate socialization, you may *become.* Gender thus refers to purely social characteristics, such as differences in hair styles, clothing patterns, occupational roles, and other culturally learned activities and traits.

The members of any society tend to assume that their particular version of masculinity and femininity is as much a part of "human nature" as the biological

Figure 10.1 *Unlike sex, which is a biological given, gender can be expressed in many different ways. Most Americans would regard this female body builder as being "masculine"; conversely, these Fulani tribesman of North Africa have a manner and appearance that most Americans would consider "feminine." A wide range of gender roles is possible, for these roles are culturally created.*

distinctions between males and females. Each society expects men and women to play specific **gender roles**—the behavior patterns, obligations, and privileges that are considered appropriate for each sex. And because the social statuses of the sexes are generally unequal, these gender roles tend to reflect (and to reinforce) whatever sexual stratification already exists.

Over the past quarter century or so, however, millions of people have challenged the traditional relationship of the sexes, particularly in the emerging postindustrial societies of North America and Western Europe. Growing numbers of women in these societies have been entering economic life, and in doing so have earned not just income but also independence. The result of this shift has been important changes in the status of women—changes that have opened up new risks as well as new possibilities.

How Different Are the Sexes?

Just how different are the sexes? Are there any inborn behavioral differences between men and women—and, if so, how significant are these differences? To answer this question, sociologists have drawn on evidence from three other disciplines: biology, which tells us about the physical differences between men and women and their possible effects on behavior; psychology, which tells us about the nature and origins of possible personality differences between the sexes; and anthropology, which tells us about variations in gender roles among the many cultures of the world.

Biological Evidence

Men and women are different in their *genes*, which provide the inherited blueprint for their physical development. Females have two similar chromosomes (XX), while males have two dissimilar chromosomes (XY). Except in the area of short-term feats of physical strength, the male's lack of a second X chromosome makes him in many respects the weaker sex. Male infants are more likely than females to be stillborn or malformed. Throughout the life course, the death rate for men is higher than it is for women. Women are more resistant than men to most diseases and seem to have a greater tolerance for pain and malnutrition.

Men and women also have differences in their *hormones,* chemical substances that are secreted by the body's various glands. The precise effects of hormones have not been fully determined, but it is known that they can influence both physical development and emotional arousal. Both sexes have "male" as well as "female" hormones, but the proportion of male hormones is greater in men and that of female hormones is greater in women. The present consensus among researchers is that hormonal differences probably do have some influence on the behavior of men and women but that this influence varies greatly—not only among individuals, but also within the same person over time (Teitelbaum, 1976; Weitz, 1977; Shaffer, 1981).

Additionally, there are obvious differences in the sexes' *anatomy,* or physical structure and appearance. The most important of these distinctions, of course, is in the reproductive systems and their consequences. A man's biological involvement in reproduction begins and ends with a brief act of insemination. Women, on the other hand, bear and suckle children, and as a result their personal, social, and economic activities may be periodically restricted. Also, men are generally more physically powerful than women, at least in short-term feats of exertion. Their greater strength gives men the potential to dominate women by force, a fact that helps to explain why there has never been a society in which women have had political status superior to that of men.

Psychological Evidence

Although there are many differences among both individual men and individual women, the typical personality patterns of adult men and women are clearly dissimilar in many ways. For example, men tend to be more aggressive and to have greater mathematical ability; women tend to be more nurturant and more emotional. But are these differences inborn or learned? In the case of adults, this question cannot be answered, since it is impossible to untangle the effects of biological and social influences on personality. Psychologists have therefore focused much of their research on very young infants, reasoning that the earlier sex-linked differences in behavior appear, the more likely they are to be the result of inborn factors.

Many studies of young infants have found sex-linked personality differences early in life. Even in the cradle, for example, male babies are more active than females; female babies smile more readily and are more sensitive to warmth and touch than males. But these are only general tendencies. Many male babies show traits that are more typical of female babies, and vice versa. These and other findings seem at first sight to indicate some inborn personality differences between the sexes, but it is possible that even these early variations are learned. From the time children are born, parents and others treat them in subtly different ways according to their sex. In fact, experiments have shown that if adults are told that a girl infant is a boy, they will respond to her as if she were a boy—for example, by commenting on the infant's sturdiness and playing with her vigorously. But if they are told the same child is a girl, they are likely to remark on her prettiness and to touch her more gently. Infants may therefore learn to behave differently even in the first few weeks of life (Condry and Condry, 1976; Unger, 1979; Shaffer, 1981).

Some of the most important research on the psychology of gender concerns children who for some reason have been reared as a member of the opposite sex. (This situation may arise when mentally disturbed parents raise a boy as a girl or vice versa; or when genital deformities result in a baby's being mistakenly assigned to the wrong sex; or when, on the recommendation of psychiatrists, a boy who lacks a penis—usually as a result of a circumcision accident—is raised as a transsexual female.) If a child is biologically a boy but is raised as a girl, what happens? If gender were determined by biological factors, it should be impossible to socialize a child into the "wrong" role. But research by John Money and his associates indicates that children can easily be raised as a member of the opposite sex. In fact, beyond the age of about three or four, they strongly resist attempts to change their "false" gender and have great difficulty making the adjustment, in exactly the same way as a girl or boy raised in the "right" role would do. Money concludes that humans are "psychosexually neuter at birth" and that gender is independent of biological sex (Money et al., 1973, 1975).

Over the past two decades, psychologists have published more than 16,000 articles on the psychology of the sexes. The present consensus among researchers is that there are probably some predispositions toward differences in the behavior of the sexes at birth, but that these differences are not clear-cut and can be overridden by cultural learning. Also, the differences so far discovered are relatively insignificant, and hardly justify the elaborate gender-role distinctions or sexual inequalities found in many societies (Sherman, 1978; Maccoby, 1980; Hyde, 1985; Epstein, 1988).

Cross-Cultural Evidence

If gender were largely determined by inborn differences, then we would expect the statuses and roles of men and women to be much the same in all cultures. On the other hand, if these social characteristics vary a great deal from one culture to another, then gender must be much more flexible than has usually been assumed in the past.

Anthropologists have reported on a number of societies whose gender characteristics diverge from our own. In an early study, Margaret Mead (1935) investigated three tribes in New Guinea. In one tribe, the Arapesh, both men and women seemed gentle, passive, and emotionally warm. In contrast, the neighboring Mundugumor tribe were a headhunting people who expected both sexes to be aggressive and even violent. In the third tribe, the Tchambuli, the women were domineering and wore no ornaments, while the men were gossipy, artistic, and nurturant toward children. Since then, other anthropologists have described societies in which women seem aggressive, men seem passive, or there appear to be minimal differences in the roles of men and women (D'Andrade, 1966; Friedl, 1975; Schlegel, 1972, 1977; O'Kelly and Carney, 1986).

Such cases, however, are exceptional, and the overall cross-cultural tendency points to a very strong pattern of male dominance. Even in those modern industrialized societies that have formal commitments to sexual equality, male dominance persists. The Soviet Union, for example, has entrenched sexual equality in its constitution for over half a century, but high political status is still almost exclusively a male preserve. The same pattern applies even to the democratic nations of the Western world. In Scandinavia, only 23 percent of the members of the national legislatures are women; in West Germany, 10 percent; in Italy, 7 percent; in France, 5 percent; in the United States, 5 percent; in New Zealand, 4 percent; in Britain, 4 percent.

The fact that politics is primarily "man's work" points to another cross-cultural feature. All societies have at least some **division of labor,** the specialization by individuals or groups in particular economic activities. There are many ways that labor can be divided, but one method is universal—to allocate tasks according to sex. Around the world, men generally take on tasks that require vigorous physical activity or travel away from the home, such as hunting or herding. Women, on the other hand, are responsible for tasks that require less concentrated physical effort and can be performed close to home, such as child-rearing or food preparation. Beyond these basic patterns, however, there is great cross-cultural variation in the kind of labor that is considered appropriate for men and the kind considered appropriate for women (see Figure 10.2).

Figure 10.2 *There is a great cross-cultural variation in the tasks that are considered appropriate for men and women. In many cases, in fact, the division of labor is quite unlike our own. The general tendency, however, is for men to be responsible for tasks involving strenuous effort or travel, and for women to be responsible for tasks that can be performed near the home. The data in this table came from a classic survey of 224 traditional, preindustrial societies.*

**The Division of Labor by Sex:
A Cross-Cultural Comparison in Traditional Societies**

Activity	Number of Societies in Which Activity Is Performed by:				
	Men Always	Men Usually	Either Sex Equally	Women Usually	Women Always
Pursuing sea mammals	34	1	0	0	0
Hunting	166	13	0	0	0
Trapping small animals	128	13	4	1	2
Herding	38	8	4	0	5
Fishing	98	34	19	3	4
Clearing land for agriculture	73	22	17	5	13
Dairy operations	17	4	3	1	13
Preparing and planting soil	31	23	33	20	37
Erecting and dismantling shelter	14	2	5	6	22
Tending fowl and small animals	21	4	8	1	39
Tending and harvesting crops	10	15	35	39	44
Gathering shellfish	9	4	8	7	35
Making and tending fires	18	6	25	22	62
Bearing burdens	12	6	35	20	57
Preparing drinks and narcotics	20	1	13	8	57
Gathering fruits, berries, nuts	12	3	15	13	63
Gathering fuel	22	1	10	19	89
Preserving meat and fish	8	2	10	14	74
Gathering herbs, roots, seeds	8	1	11	7	74
Cooking	5	1	9	28	158
Carrying water	7	0	5	7	119
Grinding grain	2	4	5	13	114

Source: Adapted from George P. Murdock, "Comparative Data on the Division of Labor by Sex," *Social Forces,* 15 (May 1935), pp. 551–553.

The general conclusion from the cross-cultural evidence is that there is a strong general pattern in dominance, personality, and work—but there are enough exceptions to prove that gender roles are potentially quite flexible. The specific content of "masculinity" and "femininity" is primarily a social product, learned anew by each generation. No society relies on "nature" to produce its particular gender roles, whatever they may be. Even so, most societies are marked by striking inequalities between men and women. Why is this?

Gender Inequality: A Functionalist View

Functionalist theorists start from the assumption that all societies encourage gender differences because these distinctions have some positive effects for society as a whole. They point out that, at least in traditional, preindustrial societies, it was highly functional for men and women to play different roles.

The human infant is helpless for a longer period after birth than any other animal, and has to be looked after. It is convenient if the mother, who bears and suckles the child and who may soon become pregnant with another, stays home to provide child care. To the extent that she stays at home, domestic duties tend to fall on her as well. Likewise, it is convenient if the male, who is physically more powerful and who is not periodically pregnant or suckling children, takes

spread unemployment. By the 1980s, much of this generation had settled down and married, pushing up the costs of rent and home ownership. During the 1990s, there will be a middle-aged bulge in the population structure. And finally, when this baby-boom generation retires early in the next century, American society will be largely oriented toward a huge dependent group of the elderly. Providing for their support, housing, and health care will be one of the biggest challenges American society has ever faced—and the responsibility, however it is exercised, will fall squarely on the generation containing most readers of this book (Pifer and Bronte, 1986; Wynne, 1986).

The elderly are now established as a highly effective political lobby, and are staking their claim to a greater share of the society's resources. The possible implications of this trend—which include a potential for fresh conflict among the age strata—are most clearly seen in the Social Security system, under which benefits for those who are retired are paid for by those who are working. In 1945 there were thirty-five workers to one Social Security recipient; by 1955 the ratio was seven to one; by 1985, about three to one. Within the foreseeable future there may be two workers supporting every retiree, and the burden may be heavier still if the retired people of the future are able to secure more generous benefits—and if they live longer. To ease this financial burden somewhat, the age at which people will be entitled to draw their Social Security benefits will be raised to sixty-seven years by the end of the century.

Early in the next century, the cohorts of the baby boom are likely to try to redefine what it means to be old. Well-educated, used to affluence, committed to self-fulfillment, they will anticipate a longer life, better health, more generous benefits, a more satisfying retirement. Today, members of this generation are moving into positions of economic and political power and influence, and the sheer weight of their numbers will influence decisions about the allocation of resources among different age groups, from the present until well after the year 2000. A basic challenge for the entire society will be to ensure that no major age stratum—the young, working adults, or the aged—is denied a fair share of those resources.

Summary

1. All societies treat their members unequally according to ascribed statuses of sex and age. These structured social inequalities are specific forms of the general phenomenon of social stratification.

2. Sex refers to the biological distinctions between men and women; gender refers to culturally learned notions of masculinity and femininity. Gender roles are the learned patterns of behavior expected of the sexes in a specific society.

3. The biological differences between the sexes are anatomical, genetic, and hormonal. Apart from reproductive functions, these differences have few inevitable implications for gender roles. There is probably some predisposition toward minor psychological differences in the sexes at birth, but people can be socialized into a variety of gender roles. The general cross-cultural trend is toward male dominance and female subordination, although some cultures are unlike our own.

4. In the functionalist view, gender-role differences were useful in traditional societies, and some theorists argue that this is still the case. In the conflict view, traditional gender roles reflect a conflict of interest between men and women, and will change as women gain more power by playing economic roles beyond the home. Sexism is an ideology that upholds sexual stratification. Both men and women are inclined to regard sexual inequalities as being rooted in biology. Members of the subordinate stratum are in a state of false consciousness in this respect.

5. There are distinct gender-role differences in the United States, expressed in personality traits and in the division of labor. Although gender roles have changed in recent decades, men are expected to have more dominant personalities and to play the more important economic roles. Routine patterns of male-female interaction, such as conversation, uphold traditional relationships. Agencies of socialization such as the family, the schools, and the mass media, reinforce the existing patterns. Although most women now work, they are concentrated in "pink collar" jobs; the minority who are in the professions hit an "invisible ceiling" in promotions. One proposed remedy for the discrepancy in pay between male-dominated jobs and female-dominated jobs is to pay different jobs according to their "comparable worth."

6. Gender roles have changed, but with some unforeseen consequences. In particular, women find themselves with two jobs, at home and at work, and poverty has become "feminized" as a result of changes in family structure and low female earnings.

7. The life course is a social as well as a biological process; all societies define stages of life and assign different rights and responsibilities to people in various age categories. In general, preindustrial societies gave high status to the aged; industrial societies give them low status.

8. In the functionalist view, the changed status of the elderly results from a process of mutual disengagement. In the conflict view, the status of the elderly results from competition among different age strata for valued social rewards. Ageism is the ideology that justifies the unequal treatment of different age groups, particularly with regard to the elderly.

9. Social gerontology studies the relationship between aging and society. The meaning of aging may vary from one cohort to another, and relationships among age strata are affected by a society's age structure.

10. The position of the aged in the United States has improved in recent years, although they may still have such problems as ill health, isolation, and loss of independence. Poverty was once a significant problem for the aged, but is now predominantly a problem of children. America is "graying" as a result of changes in population structure. The result may be renewed competition among age strata for society's resources.

Important Terms

sex (217)

gender (217)

gender roles (218)

division of labor (220)

ideology (224)

sexism (224)

false consciousness (226)

rites of passage (234)

extended family (235)

nuclear family (235)

ageism (238)

social gerontology (239)

cohort (239)

age structure (240)

CHAPTER *11*

Family and Religion

In this chapter we examine two universal institutions, the family and religion. These institutions are found in one form or another in every human society, and they are surely the most ancient institutions of all. The remains of prehistoric human settlements reveal clear evidence of family dwellings, and graves from tens of thousands of years ago give signs of funeral ceremonies in the form of flowers and artifacts that were buried with the dead, presumably to accompany them on the journey to an afterlife.

In the modern world, both institutions are under a great deal of pressure, at least in their traditional forms. There are those who prophesy—sometimes with dismay, sometimes with relish—the collapse of both institutions. Consider the American family. Most Americans begin sexual activity before marriage. One in every five births is to an unmarried mother, usually a teenager. One in every four pregnancies ends in abortion. One adult in five lives alone. About half of all American marriages end in divorce. New alternatives to traditional marriage, such as living together, are becoming more common. Or consider American religion. Church membership and attendance are significantly lower than they were a generation ago. Mainline churches are accused of having lost their message; fundamentalist churches are accused of dogmatism and intolerance. Prominent television evangelists are exposed as hypocrites. New religions, ranging from Scientology to the Hare Krishna movement, appear with regularity. Millions participate in practices that are not endorsed by traditional religion, such as astrology, tarot-card reading, or channeling.

Using the sociological perspective, we will look first at the family and then at religion, and in each case we will trace and analyze the changes that these institutions are experiencing.

The Family Institution

What exactly is a family? Our ideas on the subject may tend to be ethnocentric, for they are often based on the middle-class "ideal" family so relentlessly portrayed in TV commercials, one that consists of a husband, a wife, and their dependent children. This particular family pattern, however, is far from typical. A more accurate conception of the family must take account of the many different family forms that have existed or still exist both in America and in other cultures. Such a conception would have to include, for example, a Kenyan union consisting of one husband and several wives—or an American unmarried mother with her dependent children. To cover all the possibilities, we say that the **family** is a relatively permanent group of people related by ancestry, marriage, or adoption, who live together, form an economic unit, and take care of their young. If this definition seems a little cumbersome, it is only because it has to include such a great variety of family forms.

Most of us spend our lives in two families in which we have quite different

Figure 11.1 *The family is the most basic of all social institutions, and each family begins with a human mating. Because of its social importance, societies expect this mating to be a formal, publicly acknowledged event. There-fore, every society insists that a marriage be marked by a wedding or other socially recognized ritual. Such a ritual offers a public indication of the new status of the marital partners, and of their responsibility for any offspring.*

statuses and roles: a **family of orientation,** the one into which we are born as son or daughter, and a **family of procreation,** the one which we create ourselves as father or mother. In every society, a family is expected to be formed through **marriage,** a socially approved mating arrangement between two or more people. Social recognition of a marriage is usually marked through some culturally pre-scribed ritual, such as a wedding by a religious official, a registration of the union by a judge or other government servant, or a formal exchange of gifts between the families of the partners. The partners in a marriage are expected to have a sexual relationship, and are also expected to honor the economic rights and duties involved in the sharing of a household.

Every society distinguishes between offspring born in wedlock and those born out of wedlock. **Legitimate birth** is birth to a mother and father who are married to each other; **illegitimate birth** is birth to a mother who is not married to the father. All societies encourage legitimacy, because it enables them to automatically allocate the social roles of mother and father to specific persons who are then responsible for the care and protection of the young. Illegitimacy, on the other hand, can present a social problem, because although the mother is known, there may be nobody to take on the social role of father.

The family is a unit within a much wider group of relatives, or kin. **Kinship** is a social network of people related by common ancestry, adoption, or marriage. A kinship network is a highly complicated affair, as you will know if you have ever tried to construct your own family tree. If you include distant relatives such as in-laws and second cousins, it can easily run to hundreds of people. In many traditional societies, kinship is the basis of social organization, but in modern societies the family tends to become isolated from all but the closest kin. Many of us do not even know the names of our second cousins or similarly distant relatives. Frequently, even close kin gather only for a few ceremonial occasions such as Thanksgiving or funerals.

The Family: A Functionalist View

As functionalists emphasize, the family institution is a universal one because it performs vital functions in all societies.

1. *Regulation of sexual behavior.* No society allows people to mate at random. The marriage and family system provides a means of regulating sexual behavior by specifying who may mate with whom and under what circumstances they may do so.

2. *Replacement of members.* A society cannot survive unless it has a system for replacing its members from generation to generation. The family provides a stable, institutionalized means through which this replacement can take place.

3. *Socialization.* People do not become fully human until they are socialized, and the primary context for this socialization is the family, starting at birth. Although in modern society many socialization functions have been taken over by other institutions, the family remains the earliest and most significant agency of socialization.

4. *Care and protection.* People need warmth, food, shelter, and care. The family provides an environment in which these needs can be met. In particular, the productive members of the family can take care of those who, by reason of their youth, age, or infirmity, are unable to take care of themselves.

5. *Social placement.* Our family background is the most significant single determinant of our place in society. We inherit from our family of orientation not only material goods but also our social status. We belong to the same racial or ethnic group and usually to the same religion and social class that our parents belong to.

6. *Emotional support.* Human beings have a need for affection, nurturance, intimacy, and love. The family is the primary social context in which emotional needs can be fulfilled and the deepest personal feelings can be expressed. In this sense the family may function as "a haven in a heartless world," the place of ultimate emotional refuge and comfort (Lasch, 1977).

All these functions are necessary. Of course, the family is not the only conceivable means through which they could be fulfilled. Yet the family fulfills them so effectively that it takes primary responsibility for them in every culture.

The Family: A Conflict View

While conflict theorists do not dispute that the family has important social functions, they believe that the functionalist analysis does not tell the whole story. In particular, they note that the family is the principal institution in which the dominance of men over women has been expressed.

In many societies women have been treated for practical and legal purposes as the property of their husbands (or, if unmarried, of their fathers). As recently as the late 1960s, many American statutes made married women legally incompetent to enter into contracts, rent cars, or get credit without their husband's signature—in much the same way that minors cannot exercise certain privileges without the approval of a parent or guardian. Even more strikingly, husbands had absolute sexual rights over their spouses, and it is only recently that some states have made it illegal for a husband to rape his wife. Traces of the old traditions are also to be found in our contemporary wedding ceremony: in the standard form of vows, the bride solemnly promises to "obey" the groom, and it is her father who "gives her away" to her new husband, as though some piece of property were being transferred. (We can see the implications of this symbolic interaction more clearly if we imagine its opposite—the mother of the groom giving him away to the bride, and he then vowing to obey his wife for the rest of his life.) Male dominance is still very much the pattern in most societies, but in the Western postindustrial societies, these traditional inequalities are now steadily diminishing.

Conflict theorists also point out that the sociological research of the past two decades has revealed an astonishing amount of family violence—between spouses, between parents and offspring, and among the offspring themselves. About a fifth of all murders in the United States are committed by a relative of the victim—in half of the cases, by the spouse. The police detest "disturbance calls"—usually family fights—because of the vicious and dangerous nature of so many of these conflicts; indeed, more police are killed intervening in these disputes than in almost any other type of situation they face. Surveys suggest that each year around 7 million couples go through a violent episode in which one spouse tries to cause the other serious pain or injury. Wives assault their husbands as often as husbands assault their wives, and spouses are equally likely to kill each other. Although wives are rarely a match for their husbands in a fistfight, they are more likely to use lethal weapons (notably kitchen knives). In most nonfatal physical violence between the spouses, however, wives are very much the victims, for wife-beating is a widespread and very serious problem. Child abuse—involving such acts as burning children with cigarettes, locking them up in closets, tying them up for hours or days, or breaking their bones—is alarmingly common, and probably causes many of the 2 million runaways that happen each year. And the sexual abuse of children—now recognized as a national epidemic—is rarely a matter of molestation by a stranger. It is usually perpetrated by one family member on another (Gelles and Cornell, 1983, 1985; Gelles, 1987; Finkelhor, 1983, 1984; Russell, 1984, 1986).

One source of this violence may lie in the dynamics of the family as an intimate environment: close relationships are likely to involve more conflict than less intimate ones, since there are more occasions for tension to arise and more likelihood that deep emotions will be provoked. Another source may lie outside the family, for violence is frequently a response to frustration. If the person affected cannot strike back at the source of the problem—the arrogance of an employer, say, or the lack of a job—the aggression may be readily redirected at family members. Perhaps most important, violence between husband and wife takes place in a general social context that has traditionally emphasized male dominance and female subservience (Straus and Hotaling, 1980).

Family Patterns

Each society views its own patterns of marriage, family, and kinship as self-evidently right and proper, and usually as God-given as well. Much of the current concern about the fate of the modern family stems from this kind of ethnocentrism. If we assume that there is only one "right" family form, then naturally any change in that particular form will be interpreted as heralding the doom of the whole institution. It is important to recognize, therefore, that there is an immense range in marriage, family, and kinship patterns; that each of these patterns may be, at least in its own context, perfectly viable; and above all, that the family, like any other social institution, must inevitably change through time, in our own society as in all others.

A Cross-Cultural Perspective

The family patterns of other cultures challenge many of our assumptions about the nature of marriage, family, and kinship (Murdock, 1949; Ford and Beach, 1951; Stephens, 1963; Fox, 1965; Murstein, 1974).

As we saw in Chapter 7 ("Sexuality and Society"), every society has an **incest taboo,** a powerful moral prohibition against sexual contact between certain categories of relatives. However, different societies have quite different ideas about who the incest taboo should apply to. In the United States, all fifty states prohibit marriage between a person and his or her parent, grandparent, uncle or aunt, brother or sister, and niece or nephew; an additional twenty-nine states regard marriage between first cousins as incestuous, but the remainder do not. Many societies, however, do not make any distinction between siblings (brothers and sisters) and cousins. In these societies there are usually no separate words for "brother" and "cousin": they are regarded as the same kind of relative, and the incest taboo is therefore extended to first, second, third, and even more distant cousins as well. And, although certain societies consider it incestuous to marry a child of one's mother's sister, or of one's father's brother, they may expect—or even require—that one should marry a child of one's mother's brother, or of one's father's sister.

In modern, industrialized societies it is generally assumed that marriage is founded on romantic love between the partners and that the choice of a mate should be left to the individual. But this concept of romantic love is entirely unknown in many societies and is considered laughable or tragic in many others. In most traditional societies, marriage is regarded as a practical economic arrangement or a matter of family alliances, not a love match. In these societies, therefore, marriage is negotiated by the parents of the partners, often with little or no consideration of their children's wishes. If love is a feature of these marriages at all, it is expected to be a result and not a cause of the union. The economic aspect of these marriages is especially apparent in those societies in which an intending groom must pay a bride-price to his prospective father-in-law. This practice is especially widespread in sub-Saharan Africa, where nearly all the tribes expect a groom to exchange cattle for the bride.

In all Western nations, the law insists on **monogamy**, a marriage involving one spouse of each sex. However, this ideal is held by a minority of the societies of the world. In a survey of evidence from 238 mostly preindustrial societies, George Murdock (1949) found that only 43 prohibited **polygamy**, a marriage involving a spouse of one sex and two or more spouses of the opposite sex. In 4 of the remaining societies a woman was permitted to have more than one husband, and in all the rest a man was allowed to have more than one wife, a ratio that reflects the superior power and privileges of the male partner in the family institution.

Figure 11.2 *The ideal that a husband should have more than one wife is still widely held in many parts of the world, and historically it has been the favored marriage form in most societies. This photograph, from Upper Volta, West Africa, shows a family consisting of one husband, two wives, and their children. In most traditional societies, a large family is considered an economic asset.*

In modern industrialized societies, we generally assume that married partners should be adults of much the same age, although certain exceptions are made for an older man and a younger woman. Some societies offer strikingly contrasting patterns. The Kadara of Nigeria marry infants to one another. The Chuckchee of Siberia, believing that parental care is the best way of cementing the marriage bond, allow adult women to marry males of only two or three years of age; the new wives then look after the boys until they are old enough to assume their husbandly duties. And among the Tiwi of Australia, adult males marry females even before they are conceived, annulling the marriage if the newborn turns out to be the wrong sex.

In most traditional, preindustrial societies, the family system takes the form of the **extended family,** one in which more than two generations of the same kinship line live together, either in the same house or in adjacent dwellings. The head of the entire family is usually the eldest male, and all adults share responsibility for child-rearing and other tasks. The extended family can be very large: sometimes it contains several adult offspring of the head of the family, together with their spouses and children. We are more familiar with the **nuclear family,** one in which the family group consists only of the parents and their dependent children, living apart from other relatives. The nuclear family occurs in some preindustrial societies, and is the usual type in virtually all modern industrialized societies. In fact, the growing dominance of the nuclear family is transforming family life all over the world.

The Transformation of the Family

As one society after another has industrialized over the course of the past two centuries, there has been a major, global change in family patterns—a change that involves a fundamental shift in people's loyalties. Essentially, people have come to focus less on their responsibilities toward their extended kin and more on their own needs and those of their family of procreation. Marriage is now viewed less as an economic arrangement or a kinship alliance, and more as a companionship based on the emotional commitment of two individuals. This shift in loyalties has had dramatic effects on family life. In particular, the extended family has tended to be replaced by the nuclear family (Laslett, 1971, 1977; Laslett and Wall, 1972; Shorter, 1975; Stone, 1977; Gordon, 1983).

Why has the nuclear family become the dominant type? The answer is that the extended family is well suited to the conditions of preindustrial society, where every able-bodied family member is an economic asset. But the nuclear family is far better adapted to the conditions of the modern world, for several reasons.

1. *Geographic mobility.* Life in a modern society offers and sometimes requires geographic mobility—workers are expected to go where the jobs and promotions are. They cannot do so if obligations to various kin tie them to a particular area and prevent prolonged separation from relatives.

2. *Social mobility.* Unlike traditional, preindustrial societies, modern societies offer people the chance to achieve new and often higher social statuses. As a result of social mobility, various family members may eventually come to have lifestyles that are quite different from one another. Consequently, the bonds of common interests and shared experience that once bound the extended family together are loosened or, in some cases, even shattered.

3. *Loss of family functions.* In an industrialized, urban environment, formal organizations and institutions—corporations, schools, hospitals, welfare agencies, day-care centers, and the media—take over many of the functions that were once the prerogative of the extended family. People no longer have to rely on the support network provided by their kin, and instead seek a new foundation for married life—close companionship with a single spouse.

Figure 11.3 *These two paintings illustrate the dramatic transformation that has taken place in the family. The first picture is* The Hatch Family, *painted in 1871 by the American artist Eastman Johnson. It shows a typical extended family of the time, with several generations living in the same household and with the family members evidently sharing a strong sense of mutual involvement. The second picture is* Meet the Megabytes, *painted in 1986 by the American artist Kinuko Craft. It portrays a nuclear family of the modern age, consisting of parents and their dependent offspring—and with each member obviously "into" his or her own interests as an individual. This shift in loyalties—from obligations to kin toward self-fulfillment as individuals—has profoundly changed the nature of family life.*

4. *Advantages of small families.* In a modern society, children become an economic liability rather than an asset. The parents get no financial benefits to compensate for the vast expense of clothing, feeding, and educating their offspring. People therefore find it convenient to restrict the size of their households, preferring to live in independent units away from other relatives.

5. *Individualism.* An outstanding feature of industrial societies, and especially of the emerging postindustrial societies, is individualism. As we noted in Chapter 2 ("Culture"), people in these societies are increasingly concerned with self-fulfillment as a personal goal. Individual desires become more important than traditional obligations. Whether the issue is marriage or divorce, they ask: "What's in it for me?" rather than "What does my kin group expect me to do?" As Betty Yorburg (1983) observes:

> Married women will go out to work even against opposition from their husbands. They will leave unhappy marriages, sometimes without their children, especially in the middle or upper classes. Husbands will leave their economically dependent wives. . . . The presence of children no longer preserves marriages. . . . The oldest child will no longer give up educational or other personal goals to support needy brothers and sisters or aged parents and grandparents. Young people will choose marital partners or live together in heterosexual or homosexual relationships with or without the approval of parents.

Yet although the nuclear family is functional in modern society, it suffers from a number of dysfunctions as well—and this is the key to understanding some of its present difficulties. In the extended family, the individual could turn for support to an array of relatives. Today the married partners can turn only to each other, and sometimes demand more from one another than either can provide. If members of an extended family were for some reason unable to play their roles, other members could take them over. In the nuclear family, on the other hand, the death, prolonged illness, or unemployment of a breadwinner can throw the entire family into severe crisis. In the extended family, people rarely had expectations of romantic love with their spouses; marriage was a practical, common-sense affair. In the nuclear family, far higher expectations exist, and if they are not fulfilled—and often they cannot be—discontent and unhappiness may result.

Marriage and Family in America

"Love and marriage," an old popular song tells us, "go together like a horse and carriage." A compelling assumption in American society is that everyone will fall in love, will marry, will have children, and will have an emotionally satisfying lifetime relationship with the chosen partner. It is probably true that most of us fall in love at some point; it is certainly true that nearly all of us marry and have children; but it is likely that a great many of us—perhaps the majority—find that married life falls below our expectations. To find out what can go wrong and why, we must look in more detail at romantic love, courtship, marriage, and marital breakdown and divorce.

Romantic Love

The American family, like those in most modern industrialized societies, is supposed to be founded on the romantic love of the marital partners. Happily enough, romantic love defies a clinical definition. It is a different kind of love, though, from the love you have for your parents or your dog. It involves physical symptoms, such as pounding heart and sexual desire, and psychological symptoms, such as obsessive focus on one person and a disregard for any resulting social or economic risks. Our culture encourages us to look for this love—to find that "one and only," perhaps even through "love at first sight." Behavior of this kind is portrayed and warmly endorsed throughout American popular culture, by books, magazines, comics, records, popular songs, movies, and TV.

Romantic love is a noble ideal, and it can certainly help provide a basis for the spouses to "live happily ever after." But since marriage can equally well be founded on much more practical considerations, why is romantic love of such importance in the modern world? The reason seems to be that it has the following basic functions in maintaining the institution of the nuclear family (Goode, 1959):

1. *Transfer of loyalties.* Romantic love helps the young partners to loosen their bonds with their family of orientation, a step that is essential if they are to establish an independent nuclear family. Their total absorption in one another facilitates a transfer of commitment from existing family and kin to a new family of procreation.

2. *Emotional support.* Romantic love provides the couple with emotional support in the difficulties that they face in establishing a new life on their own. This love would not be so necessary in an extended family, where the relatives are able to confront problems cooperatively.

3. *Incentive to marriage.* Romantic love serves as bait to lure people into marriage. In the modern world, people have considerable choice over whether they will get married or not. A contract to form a lifelong commitment to another person is not necessarily a very tempting proposition, however: to some, the prospect may look more like a noose than like a bed of roses. Without feelings of romantic love, many people might have no incentive to marry.

Figure 11.4 *Romantic love, captured in this idealized painting, is a culture trait found primarily in the industrialized societies of the world. Although Westerners take romantic love for granted, it is unknown in many other societies, where far more practical considerations determine who will marry whom. The painting is* The Storm *(1880), by the French artist Pierre Auguste Cot.*

To most of us, particularly to those who are in love, romantic love seems to be the most natural thing in the world, but as we saw earlier, it is a purely cultural product, arising in certain societies for specific reasons. In a different time or in a different society, you might never fall in love, nor would you expect to.

Courtship and Marriage

A courtship system is essentially a marriage market. (The metaphor of the "market" may seem a little unromantic, but, in fact, the participants do attempt to "sell" their assets—physical appearance, personal charms, talents and interests, and career prospects.) In the matter of mate selection, different courtship systems vary according to how much choice they permit the individual. The United States probably allows more freedom of choice than any other society. In this predominantly urban and anonymous society, young people—often with access to automobiles—have an exceptional degree of privacy in their courting. The practice of dating enables them to find out about one another, to improve their own interpersonal skills in the market, to experiment sexually if they so wish, and finally to select a marriage partner.

Who marries whom, then? Cupid's arrow, it turns out, does not strike at random. Despite the cultural emphasis on love as something mysterious and irrational, the selection of marital partners is actually fairly orderly and predictable. In general, the American mate-selection process produces **homogamy**, marriage between partners who share similar social characteristics. In general, spouses tend to be of similar age, social class, religious affiliation, and educational level, and they are also much more likely to marry within their own racial or ethnic group than outside it. The reason is not hard to find, for there is considerable parental and peer pressure for young people to restrict their social contacts to those who are "suitable"—which usually means "similar."

Of course, homogamy provides only the general framework in which specific people choose their specific mates. In selecting their partners, people are influenced by psychological as well as social factors. Some researchers claim that people want partners whose personalities match their own in significant respects. In this "birds of a feather" view, conservatives may be attracted by other conservatives, or alcoholics may tend to seek out other alcoholics. But other researchers claim that people look for partners whose personality traits are different from, but complementary to, their own. In this "opposites attract" view, dominant people may look for passive mates, or those who love to eat may link up with those who love to cook. Both views are probably valid, depending on the psychological "chemistry" of the couple in question—a chemistry that may well change over the course of the relationship.

Marital Breakdown

The divorce rate in the United States is believed to be the highest in the world, and statistics on the subject are often quoted as conclusive evidence of the decay of the family. This evidence indicates that about 50 percent of recent marriages will end in divorce, the average duration of these ill-fated unions being around 7 years.

Divorce constitutes official social recognition that a marriage has failed, and it can be a traumatic experience for all concerned. Most states now offer a "no fault" divorce on grounds of simple incompatibility, but there is still room for fierce resentment over the custody of offspring and child-support payments. Children are present in over 70 percent of the families that break up through divorce: more than a million children are involved every year. The children inevitably suffer through the divorce of their parents—particularly during the first year or two—but many people believe that it may be even more emotionally disturbing for them to remain in a home where the marriage is deeply unhappy. Both divorcing parties may also be in for a difficult time emotionally. Divorce ruptures one's personal universe; it is no coincidence that men are much more likely to be fired from their jobs after divorce, nor that the death rate for divorced people is significantly higher than that for married people, at all age levels (Weiss, 1975; Emery et al., 1984).

The ex-wife may face severe economic problems, especially if she has to raise young children. In the past, when most wives were not expected to work outside the home, courts frequently awarded alimony to divorced women; but now that women are considered capable of earning their own living, they receive alimony in only about 15 percent of divorce settlements. Courts award child custody to mothers rather than to fathers in 90 percent of cases, however, and usually require that the fathers provide child support. But many divorced women find that they have low earning power—particularly if they have spent their entire married lives as housewives and have no job skills or experience— and a majority of divorced fathers default on their child-support payments. More than half of American children in families where the father is absent live below the poverty line, and many single mothers become long-term welfare recipients.

Who gets divorced? The social characteristics of divorce-prone partners have been well established. Divorces are especially common among urban couples, among those who marry very young, among those who marry after only short or shallow acquaintance, and among those whose relatives and friends disapprove of the marriage. In general, the people who are most likely to get divorced are those who, statistically, would be considered the least likely to marry. And the greater the wife's ability to support herself, the more likely she is to leave an unhappy marriage. Partners who have been married before are more likely to become involved in subsequent divorce. Most divorces take place within the first few years of marriage—and the longer a marriage has lasted, the less likely it is to end in divorce (Carter and Glick, 1976; Goode, 1982; Fisher, 1987).

Figure 11.5 *As this chart shows, from the 1940s to the 1980s, the rate of divorce increased steadily, while the rate of marriage fluctuated during this time. The divorce rate is now one-half the marriage rate. This ratio is distorted, however, by the fact that the population that is eligible for divorce is a huge one, containing everybody who is married, while the population that is eligible for marriage is much smaller, consisting primarily of unmarried people between the ages of eighteen and thirty. The ratio is therefore not as alarming as it seems to be.*

Different social factors influence the marriage and divorce rate. The divorce rate may be pushed up, for example, by laws that make divorces easier to get, or by better employment opportunities for women. The marriage rate, on the other hand, may be influenced by such factors as the proportion of young adults in the population, or by current social attitudes toward alternatives to marriage, such as living together.

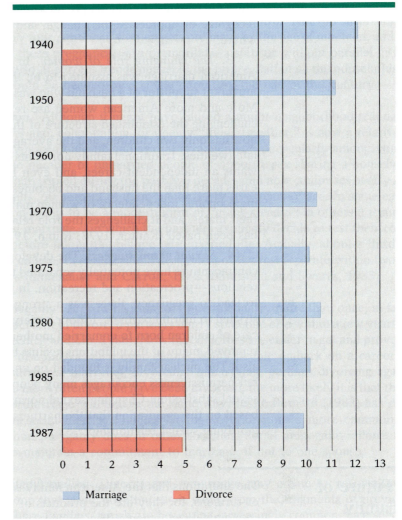

Marriage and Divorce Rates: 1940–1987
Per 1,000 population

Source: U.S. Bureau of the Census, 1988.

Causes of Marital Breakdown

There are many causes for the collapse of modern American marriages, but the following seem to be the main ones.

1. *Stress on the nuclear family.* As we have seen, the nuclear family is highly vulnerable if the breadwinner is for any reason unwilling or unable to meet economic obligations. In addition, the spouses in a nuclear family have a very strong mutual dependency and may make heavy demands on one another for emotional support. The failure of one partner to meet the expectations of the other jeopardizes the marriage in a way that would hardly be possible under the extended family system.

2. *The fading of romantic love.* Americans are thoroughly socialized into the expectation that romantic love will "conquer all" and make their marriage happy ever after. But the heady joys of romantic love are usually short-lived, and the excitement of the earlier relationship is lessened or even lost in the daily routines of job and housework, diapers and dishwashing, mortgages and bills.

Figure 11.6 *All religions recognize the sacred, a realm of experience so awesome that it cannot be approached except through rituals, or formal, stylized procedures. These photographs show Hindus in India purifying themselves in the sacred waters of the Ganges; a Muslim in Yemen kneeling in the direction of Mecca to pray; and Buddhists in China performing a purification ritual before entering a temple to worship.*

have been a Southern Baptist or a Hindu. Similarly, if your parents are Catholic, you are probably Catholic; if they are Mormon, you too are probably a Mormon. As a result of all this variety of belief, there are a large number of people who are convinced that theirs is the one true faith and that all others are misguided, superstitious, even wicked. Where does this leave sociologists who study religion? Can and should they make judgments in these matters?

The answer is that sociology is not and cannot be concerned with the truth or falsity of any religion. Like other empirical sciences, such as economics or chemistry, sociology is simply not competent to investigate the supernatural or to play umpire between competing faiths. Individual sociologists may be personally committed to a religious viewpoint—as indeed many of the leading contemporary sociologists of religion are. But sociological research is necessarily directed at the social rather than the theological aspects of religion. Regardless of whether or not a supernatural power exists, religion, like any other institution, has social characteristics that can be studied by the methods of social science.

Types of Religion

Sociologists who study religion have tried to bring some conceptual order to their field by classifying different religions into a series of basic types. One useful classification is that of Reece McGee (1975), who divides religions into four main categories according to their central belief: simple supernaturalism, animism, theism, and transcendent idealism. These are merely artificial categories, of course, and not all religions will fit neatly into this classification.

Simple supernaturalism is a type of religion that does not recognize specific gods or spirits, but does assume that supernatural forces influence human events for better or worse. This type of religion is fairly common in very simple preindustrial societies. The Melanesian Islanders of the South Pacific, for example, believe in "mana," a diffuse, impersonal force that may exist in both people and natural objects. Some forms of simple supernaturalism still linger in the Western world: for example, the gambler's belief in "luck," a soldier's reliance on a protective charm such as a rabbit's foot, or a baseball player's adherence to particular rituals to preserve a winning streak.

Animism is a type of religion that recognizes active, animate spirits operating in the world. These spirits may be found both in people and in natural phenomena such as rivers, mountains, and the weather. The spirits of animistic religion may be benevolent or evil, or they may even be indifferent to human beings, but they are not gods, for they are not worshiped. People must take account of these spirits, however, and shamans or "witch doctors" may try to influence them by the use of **magic,** or rituals intended to harness supernatural power for human ends. Animistic religions have been particularly common among the tribes of Africa and the Americas, but some animism persists in the Western world in rituals such as exorcism, and in such occult forms as spiritualism and black magic.

Theism is a type of religion that centers on a belief in gods. A god is presumed to be powerful, to have an interest in human affairs, and to be worthy of worship. Cross-culturally, the most common form of theism is **polytheism,** a belief in a number of gods. A second form of theism is **monotheism,** the belief in a single supreme being. Although there are only three monotheistic religions in the modern world—Judaism, Christianity, and Islam—they have the greatest number of adherents.

Transcendent idealism is a type of religion that centers not on the worship of a god but rather on sacred principles of thought and conduct. Its goal is to reach an elevated state of consciousness, and in this way to fulfill one's human potential to the utmost. Religions of transcendent idealism are characterized by reverence for such principles as life, truth, and tolerance of other beliefs. This type of religion is found predominantly in Asia; the best-known example is Buddhism, which is concerned with the attempt to become "at one with the universe" through many years of meditation. During the past quarter century, some versions of these Eastern religions have attracted interest in the West, especially among young people.

Most religions do not try to win converts, and their adherents are usually indifferent toward the religions of others. Several of the major world religions, however, have tried to win converts at some point in their history. A common feature of these world religions is that they provide a convincing **theodicy,** an emotionally satisfying explanation for such great problems of earthly existence as human origins, suffering, and death. We are born, live a brief span of years, often suffer, and then die. This universal sequence can easily seem purposeless and bleak, but a theodicy gives it meaning by explaining or justifying the presence of evil and misfortune in the world.

Theodicies can explain human problems in many ways. The Hindu doctrine of reincarnation deals with suffering and evil by extending the life span indefinitely: one's present existence becomes merely a tiny link in an endless chain, in

There is no shortage of historical evidence to support Marx's view that the dominant religion in any society legitimates the interests of the ruling class. In fact, it is difficult to find a contrary example. The most striking instances occurred in those ancient societies in which the rulers were believed to be divine, or at least descended from gods. The pharaohs of ancient Egypt, for example, were regarded by their subjects as sacred—which made rebellion against them virtually unthinkable. Somewhat more subtle, though just as effective, were the religious ideologies that upheld the Indian caste system or the late European feudal system. As we saw in Chapter 8 ("Social Stratification"), Hindu doctrine threatens that Indians who try to change their caste status will be reincarnated as a member of a lower caste, or even as an animal, while the feudal system drew legitimacy from the notion of the "divine right" of kings to rule as God's representatives on earth.

Religion often serves to legitimate political authority when one society conquers and then rules another society whose people have a different religion. In such cases, the conquered people often assume (and are usually taught) that their new rulers have a superior god or gods. In time, the subject people tend to change their allegiance to the religion of their conquerors. Both of the two largest world religions, Christianity and Islam, were spread largely through conquest. Christianity was originally disseminated through western Europe as the official religion of the Roman empire, and then was carried to other continents when Europeans seized and colonized vast territories elsewhere in the world, particularly in Africa and the Americas. Similarly, Islam was spread around the Mediterranean, the Middle East, and the Near East through wars of conquest. Indeed, both religions have enjoyed immense success in societies that their adherents have dominated politically, while making relatively little headway elsewhere.

Figure 11.9 *Religion can become deeply involved in social conflict, particularly when the dominant religion is closely allied to the state. Between the thirteenth and the seventeenth centuries, the European clergy caused as many as half a million people to be tortured and murdered on the grounds of witchcraft or heresy. The victims ranged from old, widowed women to political and social deviants—Jews, Muslims, heretics, and critics of the political and religious leaders of the time. Typically, the "witches" were tortured until they confessed, after which they were burned to death. Fear of witchcraft helped to divert the attention of the wretched peasantry from the real source of many of their problems—corrupt popes and tyrannical princes—by shifting the responsibility to imaginary demons in human form. Much has changed in the centuries since then—but there are still zealots, in every faith, who create God in the image of their own bigotry.*

However, Marx's view of religion as the "opium of the people" may have been too narrow, for religion can be involved in social conflict in other ways as well. Sometimes, in fact, a group may actually be inspired by religion to challenge the existing order. Religion plays this part in social conflict because religious doctrines can provide a moral standard against which existing social arrangements may be judged—and perhaps found wanting. These challenges rarely come from the dominant religious organizations, for they and their leaders are usually too closely linked to the social and political establishment. Instead, the challenges tend to come from religious movements near the fringes of society, or from dissident groups within the dominant religion. In many of the highly unequal and impoverished societies of Central and South America, for example, the Catholic Church has long been associated with the military, social, and economic elite. Yet in recent years a minority of priests and nuns has embraced "liberation theology," which blends Christian compassion for the poor with an explicit commitment to political change through class struggle. Similarly, religion has persistently inspired criticism of the existing order in the United States, too—sometimes by liberals, sometimes by conservatives. (The role of one religion, Islam, in social conflict is discussed in the box on page 268.)

Religious Organizations

Religious organizations can be conveniently divided into one of four basic types: the ecclesia, the denomination, the sect, and the cult. This classification represents only artificial categories designed to fit most situations, but it does help draw our attention to important differences in beliefs, practices, and membership (Weber, 1963; Niebuhr, 1929; Troeltsch, 1931; Johnstone, 1988).

The **ecclesia** is a religious organization that claims the membership of everyone in a society or even in several societies. One does not "join" an ecclesia; one is a member by virtue of one's citizenship. A powerful, bureaucratized organization with a hierarchy of full-time officials, it gives complete support to the state authorities and expects the same from them in turn. People who are born into a society with such an "official" religion become members almost automatically. The Roman Catholic Church was such an organization for centuries until Protestantism began to compete with it in several countries. Strictly speaking, there is probably no true ecclesia in the modern world, but there are some religious organizations that approximate one in varying degrees, such as Islam in Iran and Saudi Arabia, and the Catholic Church in Ireland and Spain.

The **denomination** (or "church") is one of two or more well-established, relatively tolerant religious organizations that claim the allegiance of a substantial part of the population. The denomination does not demand official support from the state and may even be at odds with it on occasion. Like the ecclesia, it has a formal, bureaucratic structure, with trained clergy and other officials. A given denomination will have been around a long time—certainly for many decades—and is "respectable," drawing its members primarily from the middle and upper classes. Many of the members are born into the faith, but the denomination usually accepts almost anyone who wants to join. In North America, this type of organization includes the Greek Orthodox, Russian Orthodox, and Roman Catholic churches; the Methodist, Episcopal, and similar large Protestant churches; and, in most respects, the Orthodox, Conservative, and Reform branches of mainstream Judaism.

The **sect** is an exclusive and uncompromising religious organization, usually one that has split off from a denomination for doctrinal reasons. Particularly in the period soon after the founding of a sect, its adherents are generally recruited by conversion. The sect is less socially "respectable" than the denomination, and its members are usually of lower socioeconomic status. Intolerant of other religious organizations, it is dogmatic and fundamentalist, believing that its particular interpretation of the Scriptures is the literal and only route to salvation.

Fundamentalism and Conflict in the Islamic World

Islam is one of the world's major religions; it claims the allegiance of a fifth of the entire human population. Over the past decade, religious fervor has erupted in the Islamic world in general and in the Middle East in particular. It has led, for example, to a revolution in Iran, to the assassination of Anwar Sadat, the president of Egypt, and to fierce resistance to the Soviet invasion of Afghanistan. This fervor has been inspired by fundamentalism, a commitment to, and reliance on, the traditional basics of religious doctrine.

To many Westerners, Islamic fundamentalism seems like an almost scandalous return to a medieval morality. It conjures forth images of women behind veils, of adulterers being stoned, of thieves having their hands cut off, or public floggings and executions, of martyrdom in holy wars, and, in extreme cases, of political fanaticism exemplified in aircraft hijackings and terrorist bombings. This picture is rather distorted, for it is based on what is newsworthy rather than what is typical. In a way that is difficult for most Westerners to comprehend, Islam is a comprehensive way of life, continuously and intensely pervading belief and behavior, public conduct and private experience. The very word "Islam" means "submission" to the will of Allah, who demands personal integrity, social justice, and brotherhood among all believers.

Why has Islamic fundamentalism intensified at all—especially at a time when we might expect the societies involved to be moving forward, toward modernization, rather than backward, toward tradition? Sociologists have observed that fundamentalist revivals, in whatever religion, take place in times when social changes have led to turmoil, uncertainty, and the erosion of familiar values. When people find themselves confused, threatened, or even appalled at changing conditions, they may see a "return to basics" as a solution. It is not surprising, therefore, that Islamic fundamentalism has surged in societies like Iran, which have experienced wrenching social change as a result of their new oil wealth. Some of these societies had previously remained culturally fairly static for generations—in some cases, for centuries. Then, in less

than the space of a single life span, they were thrust into a world of airports and highways, schools and television, factories and power plants. As part of this process, some of the Islamic societies have been flooded with foreign advisers, officials, and entrepreneurs. In the view of the fundamentalists, these foreigners, especially those from the West, are a profoundly immoral and corrupting influence.

Muslims look with particular horror at America's sexual permissiveness, at the relative assertiveness and immodesty of American women, at the high rates of illegitimacy, abortion, and divorce, at the preoccupation with pleasure, drugs, alcohol, pornography, and material possessions, and at the search for individual self-fulfillment at the expense of obligations to kin and community. The fundamentalists regard Americans essentially as barbarians—but as barbarians whose economic, technological, and military influence threatens the integrity of Muslim societies and traditions. Their own governments, they claim, are often used as mere pawns in America's geopolitical strategy against the Soviet Union, a strategy in which the interests of ordinary Muslims count for nothing.

Despite their antipathy to the United States, the fundamentalists are concerned mainly with conditions in their own countries. Most Muslims are desperately poor, for their nations' oil wealth has often been unequally shared, creating a new elite whose extravagant lifestyle arouses deep resentment in the populace. The fundamentalists aim at nothing less than the replacement of their rulers by Islamic governments, in which the distinction between the religious and the secular would disappear. Their inspiration comes from the 1979 Iranian revolution, in which the shah, a deeply unpopular ruler who was perceived as an American puppet, was deposed through a movement led by Shiite Muslim clergy. In many Islamic societies, Shiite fundamentalists now form an unofficial opposition to the political and social establishment. Islamic fundamentalism, like all religious movements, thus arises out of specific social and cultural conditions and may then, in turn, influence the subsequent course of social change.

Sources: Edward Said, *Orientalism* (New York: Pantheon, 1979); Barry Rubin, "Iran's Year of Turmoil," *Current History*, January 1983, pp. 28–31; Roy Mottahedah, *The Mantle of the Prophet: Religion and Politics in Iran* (New York; Simon and Schuster, 1985).

The sect also tends to be indifferent or even hostile to political authority, which it often regards as too worldly and corrupt. Sects usually have no trained clergy, and rituals of worship emphasize emotion, spontaneity, and extensive participation by the congregation. Most sects tend to be short-lived, but some gradually become denominations—always with an accompanying loss of fervor and a gain in social respectability. Contemporary North American sects include the Jehovah's Witnesses, the Assembly of God, the Amish, and Hassidic Jews.

The **cult** is a loosely organized religious movement that is independent of the religious tradition of the surrounding society. Unlike the sect, which attempts to revive or reinterpret older doctrines, the cult emphasizes the new, drawing symbols and rituals from beyond the religious mainstream. The cult tends to be the most temporary of all forms of religious organization. It usually has few coherent doctrines and imposes minimal demands on believers: like the denomination but unlike the sect, it is open to almost anyone who wishes to participate. Cults are often centered on specific prophets or other leaders and generally lack trained officials. They appeal to people who, disenchanted with traditional religion, participate primarily for the personal benefits or experiences the cult offers them. In North America, contemporary cults currently include such loosely structured groups as believers in channeling, spiritualism, or transcendental meditation.

Since the ecclesia hardly exists and cults have relatively few adherents in modern societies, sociologists usually focus on denominations and sects. Although there is immense variety within each category, the overall differences between the two types of organization seem more significant. Denominations and sects are not static, however: their membership, rituals, and beliefs are in a constant flux, and this process is a vital element in religious change. Sects are continually formed as groups break off from denominations in search of doctrinal purity that the parent body seems to have lost. Most of these new sects wither and die; a few retain the intensity of conviction that first inspired them; and some survive over the generations, only to grow steadily more prosperous but less committed to the faith—occasionally, in fact, to become denominations from which new sects break off.

The Methodists, for example, started out as a spontaneous, unrestrained sect of the poor, but today they are among the most affluent and respectable of all Protestant denominations. Similarly, the Mormons were once an oppressed sect, persecuted in state after state until they settled in the area that became Utah. But as the Mormons became more prosperous and successful, they abandoned some earlier fundamentalist teachings (notably that permitting polygamy, which they gave up in order to gain statehood for Utah). The status of the organization now seems to be transitional between that of a sect and a denomination. The Seventh-Day Adventists, too, began as a sect prophesying the end of the world on a specific date. That day having come and gone, they are presently developing from a sect into a denomination with an increasingly middle-class membership and a trained clergy.

Religion in the United States

At the time of its founding, the United States seemed to be an infertile ground for religion. Many of the nation's leaders—including George Washington, Thomas Jefferson, and Benjamin Franklin—were not Christians, did not accept the authority of the Bible, and were hostile to organized religion. The attitude of the general public was one of apathy: in 1776, only about 5 percent of the population were participating members of churches. Yet, in the two centuries since then, religion has come to be one of the most highly regarded of all American institutions, claiming the adherence of the vast majority of the people.

Some Characteristics

The part played by religion in American life is different in many respects from that of religion in other societies, for the American institution has several distinctive characteristics.

1. *Freedom of religion.* The United States has no official, "established" religion; indeed, the Constitution forbids any formal or legal assumption that any particular faith is more or less "true" than any other. Of course, the line between government and religion is not always clearly drawn, and in some cases (particularly involving minors), the state does interfere in the exercise of religious freedom. Courts, for example, have shown little sympathy for sects that claim biblical authority to give children a purely religious education, to deny them vaccinations or medical treatment, or to severely beat them. No religion, however, can be declared illegal simply because of its beliefs and practices. On the whole, Americans are fairly tolerant of religious diversity, particularly among the main denominations.

2. *Breadth of religious commitment.* The overwhelming majority of Americans appear to have some commitment to religion. Seven out of ten Americans belong to a religious organization, and in an average week about 40 percent of the population attends a church or synagogue. But whether this commitment is deep as well as broad is another matter. Thus, a 1982 Gallup poll found that only a quarter of those professing Christianity claim to lead a very Christian life. A 1985 Gallup poll found that although eight out of ten teenagers say they consider the Ten Commandments to be "valid rules for living today," two-thirds of them are unable to name more than half of the commandments. And although about 90 percent of the population claim to be Christian, most of them cannot even name the four gospels that contain Jesus's message.

3. *Religiosity as a value.* President Eisenhower once commented that it did not matter what religion a person believed in, as long as he or she had one. This is a characteristically American view, reflecting the high value placed on religiosity itself. Many Americans tend to use religion primarily for social rather than religious purposes, finding in their church a source of community, and in its beliefs, a justification for the American values of good neighborliness, self-help, individualism, hard work, and anticommunism. There is an implicit cultural assumption that Americans should be religious—not necessarily by attending church or synagogue, but at least by expressing a belief in God and in religious principles.

Figure 11.10 *As this graph suggests, Americans are especially likely to believe in God or a universal spirit.*

Belief in God or Universal Spirit

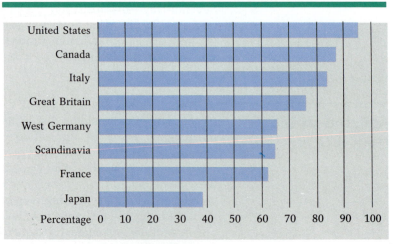

Source: Princeton Religious Research Center, 1986.

4. *Religious pluralism.* The United States is probably the most religiously diverse society in history. In most societies there are only a handful of significant religious organizations. In Canada, for example, 90 percent of the population is Christian; half of them are Catholic and half are Protestant, and three-quarters of the Protestants belong to two denominations, the Anglican Church and the United Church of Canada. The United States is also about 90 percent Christian, but the largest denomination, the Catholic Church, has only about 28 percent of total church allegiance. Some 57 percent of Americans are Protestant, but they are fragmented into so many denominations and sects that none of them can claim even a tenth of the total religiously affiliated population. Although about two dozen organizations account for the preference of almost the entire religious population, there are currently over 1,300 distinct denominations, sects, and cults (Stark and Bainbridge, 1985).

5. *Religious innovation.* The United States does not rely on imports for its diverse religious organizations, for American culture has long been a producer of new sects and cults. Most have been short-lived and are long since forgotten. However, a few religious groups founded over the course of the past century or so have thrived, such as the Christian Scientists, the Jehovah's Witnesses, the Mormons, the Seventh-Day Adventists, and the Assembly of God. Currently there is a vast array of new religious organizations, ranging from minor groups such as the Divine Light Mission and the Church of the Psychedelic Venus to relatively established groups, such as the Church of Scientology, the Hare Krishna movement, and the Unification Church ("Moonies"). This profusion is hardly surprising, for it emerges in a postindustrial society whose hallmark is social diversity. Americans are increasingly apt to pick and choose among religious organizations, rather like consumers looking for a particular product to suit their own needs. Only time will tell whether some of the new religions, like others before them, will grow into denominations—or whether they will go the way of most new religions, into oblivion.

6. *Fundamentalism.* The United States is quite unlike all other advanced industrialized societies in that it has a strong, vital, broadly based Protestant fundamentalist movement. Fundamentalists hold that every word of the Bible is literally true; they claim that the individual can be saved only by being "born again" through a personal relationship with Jesus Christ, and they vigorously oppose permissive trends in the society at large. Fundamentalist organizations enjoyed rapid growth during the 1980s, largely because of their domination of

Figure 11.11 *The Hare Krishna movement is one of several new religious organizations that combine elements from both Western and Eastern religious traditions.*

CHAPTER *12*

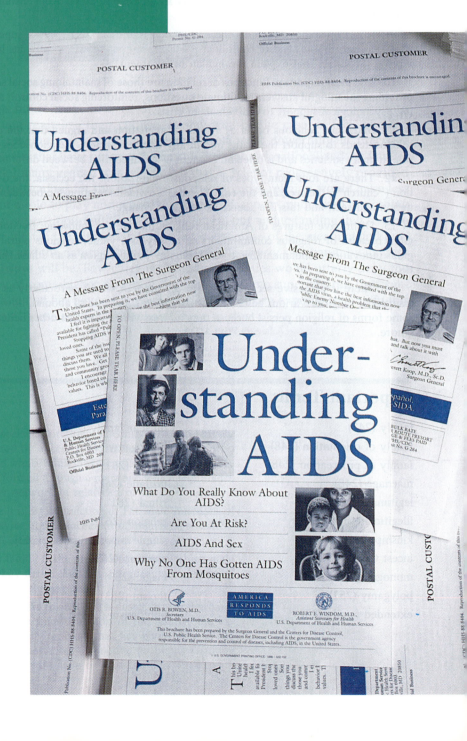

Education and Medicine

In this chapter we examine two of the most prominent institutions of modern society, education and medicine. These institutions existed in only rudimentary form in preindustrial societies. In those societies, schooling had little practical use, and was undertaken only by those with the time and money to pursue the cultivation of the mind for its own sake. The rest of the population began their working lives at adolescence or even earlier, and most people acquired all the knowledge they needed through ordinary, everyday contacts with parents and other kin. Similarly, the social arrangements for dealing with sickness were relatively uncomplicated in preindustrial societies, often involving only two roles: the sick person and the healer. The latter was typically also the priest, shaman, or witch doctor, who relied primarily on magical rituals both to identify and to treat disease.

In the modern world, on the other hand, education and medicine have become highly bureaucratized complexes that consume an immense amount of society's resources. With the rise of industrialism, mass elementary schooling came to be seen as desirable and, eventually, as necessary. By the 1930s, secondary education was becoming common and even compulsory in industrial societies, and since the 1950s there has been a sharp rise in the proportion of high school graduates who go on to college, and even to graduate school. Similarly, medicine has now become a highly elaborate and specialized activity, with participants playing dozens of roles such as those of brain surgeon, anesthetist, druggist, and hospital administrator, linked with various organizations such as nursing homes, insurance companies, medical schools, and pharmaceutical corporations. In fact, education and medicine have become two of the largest industries in the United States, with pervasive influences on social life.

The Educational Institution

In its broadest sense, "education" is almost synonymous with "socialization," since both involve the passing on of culture from one person or group to another. The distinguishing feature of education in modern societies, however, is that it has become an institutionalized, formal activity. These societies deliberately organize the educational experience, make it compulsory for people in certain age groups, train specialists to act as educators, and provide locations and equipment for the teaching and learning process. For our present purposes, then, **education** is the systematic, formalized transmission of knowledge, skills, and values.

In terms of the number of people involved, education is the largest single industry in the United States. If we include students, teachers, and administrators and other staff, more than one American in five currently participates in the institution—a figure without parallel anywhere else in the world. The reasons for this remarkable emphasis on education lie in a peculiarly American attitude toward, and use of, the institution.

mia) are now controllable. In the less developed nations, progress has been much slower as a result of limited financial resources, overpopulation, unsanitary living conditions, and widespread poverty. Disease patterns there are consequently more similar to those that today's industrial societies experienced many decades ago.

Another important effect of the germ theory was a shift in the focus of medicine: doctors became absorbed in the study of disease rather than the care of the sick. As the body of medical knowledge grew, a gulf developed in the communication between physician and patient (Twaddle, 1979; Thomas, 1983). Physicians enjoyed growing prestige, which they were quick to exploit. A powerful and highly trained profession emerged, insisting on the sole legal right to practice medicine.

The Medical Profession

The rising status of physicians over the past 150 years has resulted not just from increased medical knowledge and improved techniques but also from deliberate, organized attempts by doctors to advance their own interests. In the mid-nineteenth century the public regarded physicians with suspicion. Medical schools awarded credentials indiscriminately to almost any white male who applied. In fact, formal qualifications were not even needed, and many people simply declared themselves physicians and proceeded to practice medicine. Quacks and charlatans abounded, lending a bad reputation to even the most dedicated doctors. This chaotic situation changed in the United States when some physicians formed the American Medical Association (AMA) and campaigned vigorously to have their occupation recognized not just as a job, but as a profession.

Professionalization

A **profession** is an occupation requiring extensive, systematic knowledge of, or training in, an art or science. Because their job requires knowledge that is unavailable to the general public, members of a profession are able to claim special privileges. Professionals in every field form associations to protect their interests, primarily by insisting on the sole legal right to perform the work. This right is based on a license to practice the profession. Because the licensing process is usually directly or indirectly controlled by existing members, they are able to restrict entry to their ranks. In comparison with other workers, professionals are able to command high fees and prestige, and they enjoy far more autonomy in their work.

Since the early twentieth century, physicians' prestige has risen spectacularly. The exalted status of doctors distinguishes their job from most others and insulates them from normal workplace relationships. In their professional duties, doctors do not take orders from their clients (the patients) or their employers (such as hospital administrators). A physician's performance can supposedly be evaluated only by another physician, for outsiders are considered incompetent to make such judgments. Unlike most workers, doctors can generally insist on the right to set the fees for their own services, since people are reluctant to question doctors' opinions of what procedures are needed and what they should cost. As a result, American physicians enjoy higher average incomes than any other professionals (over $108,000 a year in 1988). No other profession enjoys quite this combination of prestige, autonomy, and income. It is hardly surprising that the professionalization of medicine has served as a model for many other occupations, ranging from lawyers and architects to engineers and realtors.

Yet, as Paul Starr (1982) has pointed out, current social trends may bring the status of the medical profession more into line with that of other occupations. One important factor is that power in medicine is gradually passing from physicians to bureaucratic organizations, such as government departments and the large corporations that own more and more of the nation's laboratories, clinics, nursing homes, and hospitals. A second factor is that medicine is influenced by forces beyond the institution itself. Government, employers, unions, insurance companies, and similar interest groups all have a stake in changing the health care system, particularly in ways that will help contain costs or deliver services fairly. These social forces are likely to undermine doctors' unusual professional autonomy—if only because doctors are increasingly paid by large organizations.

The Medicalization of Society

The growth of a powerful and highly regarded medical profession has had a social impact far beyond the scientific battle against disease. Some sociologists suggest that we are witnessing a **medicalization of society,** a process in which the domain of medicine is extended over areas of life that were previously considered nonmedical (Freidson, 1970; Conrad and Schneider, 1980). There are four main indications of this trend in the United States.

1. *The growth of the medical institution.* The medical institution has grown steadily in size and social importance during this century, consuming an ever greater share of society's resources and thus diverting them from other goals. The number of doctors, nurses, and hospital beds has continued to climb, far outpacing increases in population size. The pharmaceutical industry has now become one of the largest in the economy. Health insurance has become a major personal or social cost. Medicine attracts a significant share of all funds available for scientific research. American health expenditures now account for over a tenth of the gross national product, and medicine, employing 7 percent of the work force, is the second largest industry after education. All these indicators suggest that the medical institution is of large and growing social and economic importance.

2. *Medicalization of life events.* Many events of life that were once considered natural and inevitable have now been redefined as medical and modifiable, even if they do not involve "disease" in any clinical sense. Less than a century ago, for example, most births in North America took place—as they still do in many parts of the world—without medical supervision, let alone hospitalization. Today, birth has become a major (and expensive) medical event. In fact, the claims of medicine now go much further—before birth, to such issues as

Figure 12.11 *More and more areas of society are becoming medicalized, or brought under the domain of the medical institution and its members. Pregnancy, childbirth, and infant care are cases in point. These have been regarded as "natural" rather than "medical" matters throughout history (and are still nonmedical for millions of people in the less developed countries). In modern industrialized societies, however, it is automatically assumed that these processes warrant medical consultation and even intervention.*

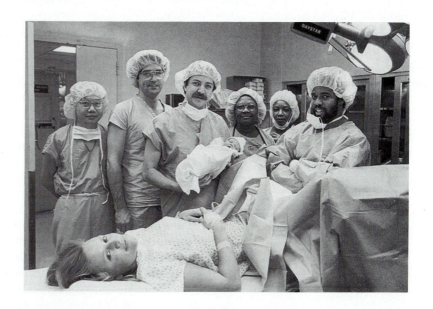

A Right to Die?

Technological innovations have greatly extended the scope of modern medicine, permitting an increasing medicalization of life events. This narrative, by Dr. Alvin Feinstein, highlights some of the social and ethical implications of this trend.

Source: Dr. Alvan R. Feinstein, "The State of the Art," *Journal of the American Medical Association,* 255, March 21, 1986, p. 1488.

Her chief complaint is that she wants to die and that the doctors will not let her.

She is 96 years old. She has attended the burial of her husband, two daughters-in-law, and all the people who were close friends throughout her lifetime. A woman of fierce and independent spirit, she never wanted to live with her children, to be supported by them or to be what she calls "a burden." After being widowed 24 years ago, she achieved those goals for a long time because she was in good health and her modest fiscal needs were met by the interest of the trust fund left by her husband.

Until 11 years ago, she lived alone and maintained her own apartment. She spent her time walking, talking with neighbors, reading, watching television, playing card games, attending religious services and traveling to visit children, grandchildren, and great-grandchildren in different cities. At age 85, however, she began to dislike shopping and cooking for herself; and she began to worry about living 60 miles away from her nearest relative. She moved, in a city where a son and grandchildren lived, into an apartment residence building that was the "congregate setting" of a geriatric center. The setting provided her with lunch, dinner, a social life and her own small apartment, in which she prepared her own breakfast.

On her 90th birthday, although in excellent mental and physical health, she began complaining that she had become too old. Her stated desire was to die in her sleep, preferably not on a night before she was scheduled to visit her great-grandchildren. When hospitalized with an episode of pneumonia that winter, she said, "My time has come." She bid a loving goodbye to each child, grandchild and great-grandchild who came to see her, and gave them a farewell blessing. When she recovered—thanks to intravenous fluids and antibiotics—she was surprised and somewhat dismayed, but she resumed her former life, remaining independent and perky.

During the next few years, she grew progressively more frail. She began having episodes of faintness, due to paroxysms of atrial fibrillation, but the episodes were brief, and the symptoms would vanish when she lay down briefly. She began walking with the aid of a cane. Although she would no longer travel long distances alone, her mind remained clear and her life independent. With each winter, however, she was rehospitalized with another bout of pneumonia. Each time she was sicker than before; each time she was prepared and wanted to die; and each time she received vigorous therapy and recovered.

During an episode three years ago, however, she had a spell of faintness while in the bathroom of her hospital room. Uncertain that she could successfully get back to her bed, she treated the symptom in her usual manner. She lay down calmly on the floor, closed her eyes and waited. In that position, and with a rapid irregular pulse, she was found by a nurse who promptly issued an emergency "Code" alarm. By the time the doctors and equipment arrived, she actually felt much better; but the excitement of the aggregated "team" convinced her she must be moribund. When she failed to die, she became angry and depressed. "I want to die, and I am ready to die," she said, "but the doctors won't let me."

After she returned to her small apartment she became less depressed as she became persuaded that she needed to live

fertility, conception, prenatal care, or abortion; after birth, to such matters as postnatal care, pediatrics, and child development generally. Throughout life, many common physical difficulties—such as getting too fat or being unable to sleep—are now translated into medical diagnoses, such as obesity or insomnia, and treated accordingly. Medicine can even intervene in the physical appearances of age and sex: those who want to look younger can have plastic surgery or hair transplants, and individuals who would rather be of the opposite sex can have a "sex change" operation. Death, too, has become a medical event as well as a biological and social one: it usually takes place in a clinical setting, where physicians sometimes make judgments about whether to keep people alive or let them die—or even to hasten their deaths.

at least another year to attend the religious confirmation of her youngest granddaughter. During that year, she became more frail, but her mind stayed clear and her spirits high. She traveled four hours in each direction by private car to go to the confirmation cermony, and she took special pleasure in participating in it. During the trip, she laughed, sang, and joked, exchanging stories of the old days with a brother-in-law whom she seldom sees and who had come a long distance to ride with her to the ceremony.

Several days after her return home, she had a stroke. She became confused and disoriented. Although physically able to function, she could no longer take care of herself. She could not cook or successfully make her way alone to and from the dining room. When lucidity transiently drifted in, she would complain unhappily and bitterly about having a "companion," who had been hired to be with her during waking hours, and about having become a "a burden."

About a week later, she re-entered the hospital with another, more severe stroke. She was conscious, seemed aware of her surroundings, and could state the names of her family visitors, but she made no other conversation. Moving her eyes toward the sky, she seemed to be pleading with God to take her at long last. When she developed anorexia, fever and pneumonia, her children asked the house staff to let her alone, but they and the attending physicians insisted that they could not "do nothing." Before one of her sons—a physician at a medical school in a distant city—could arrive to dispute the doctors' plan, she was given intravenous antibiotics, fluids and other vigorous support.

She recovered, left the hospital and now resides in a nursing home. She can still recognize her family visitors, say their names, and engage in trivial conversation, but her mind is substantially destroyed. She does not know where she is or how long she has been there. She cannot read, watch television, walk alone, use a telephone or play card games. She retains bladder and bowel continence, but she cannot dress heself, feed herself or transfer from bed to chair to bathroom.

She is no longer aware of her plight, and expresses no suggestion of despair, but everything she wanted to avoid has happened. In a semivegetating state, she has lost her functional and mental independence; and she is about to become a financial as well as a physical burden. Because she has the trust fund, the government will not pay for the costs of the nursing home; but the trust fund interest is not large enough to cover the charge of $80 a day. She had hoped to leave the trust-fund principal to her grandchildren, but now it will be gradually transferred to the nursing home.

As her visitors deal with the agony of her vegetation, they wonder why this problem has been created. Since the preservation of her life helps no one, and is desired neither by her nor by those who love her most dearly, why could her doctors not be content to let her die in peace and serenity? Why did they pursue a vigorous therapy that would benefit no one except their own satisfaction in thwarting death, regardless of the consequences?

I do not know the answers to these questions. But I, the physician son of this woman, weep for my mother and for what has happened to my profession.

3. *The medicalization of deviance.* We noted in Chapter 6 ("Deviance") that many behaviors once considered sinful, criminal, or immoral are now regarded as medical problems instead. As a result, people who might formerly have been called "wicked" are now diagnosed as "sick"—which implies, for the most part, that they should be treated rather than punished. The deviant behaviors that have been largely medicalized include alcoholism, drug addiction, certain disciplinary problems of childhood and adolescence, exhibitionism and other forms of unconventional sexuality, attempted suicide, child abuse, spouse-beating, and compulsive stealing. Again, none of these behaviors is self-evidently "medical." They have become so only because physicians—and particularly psychiatrists—have successfully claimed authority over them.

The Leading Causes of Death in the United States

Death rates per 100,000 people

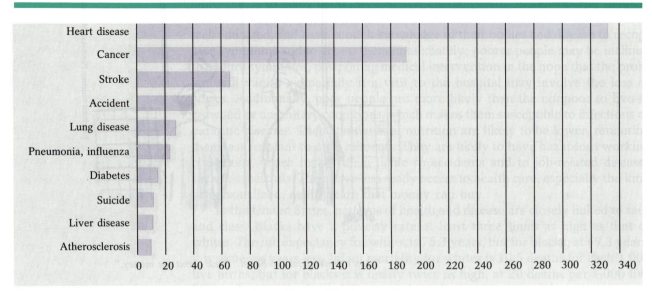

Source: Bureau of the Census, 1988.

Figure 12.15 *Most of the major killer diseases in the modern United States are degenerative conditions resulting from aging or environmental influences. Only influenza and pneumonia* *are caused by germs—and a high proportion of deaths from these diseases occur among people whose immunity has been weakened by age or other disease.*

The causes of these diseases are many and complex, but fundamentally they arise from the relationship between individuals and their natural and social environment. In other words, the diseases involve interactions among such factors as genetic background, climate, diet, nutrition, weight, stress, occupation, physical activity, use of alcohol, tobacco, and other drugs, radiation, and chemical pollution of air, water, and food. The ideal of the total elimination of such diseases may prove to be a mirage, for new environmentally caused diseases are likely to appear as long as human technology and lifestyles continue to change. Many of our contemporary ailments are, in truth, the "diseases of civilization." But although they often cannot be cured, they can be prevented. Unfortunately, modern medical practice focuses primarily on the treatment rather than on the prevention of disease—for example, on surgery for failed hearts rather than on preventing the habits that led those hearts to fail in the first place. We have grown accustomed to the idea that we become sick, and that doctors make us well. In all too many cases, however, the truth is that we make ourselves sick, and that doctors can do little or nothing to make us better.

A prime example of this truth is tobacco use. The dangers of smoking are well known, yet some 50 million Americans still smoke—33 percent of adult men and 28 percent of adult women. Each year, Americans smoke over 620 billion cigarettes, and about 350,000 of them die of smoking-related causes. Similarly, many Americans decline to use automobile seat belts, even though the practice drastically reduces the chance of death or serious injury in an accident.

The Epidemiology of Smoking and Disease

Does smoking contribute to disease? And why is the question controversial? It is sometimes difficult to establish a link between a particular disease and specific social or cultural factors. This is especially true when no infectious agent is involved, or when a long time passes between exposure to the cause and the final appearance of any symptoms. In such instances, years of research and statistical analysis may be needed before an unambiguous link can be shown. This is the case for the relationship between smoking, a practice deeply embedded in modern social, cultural, and economic life, and lung cancer, one of the major killer diseases of the twentieth century. The evidence for a causal connection rests on convincing statistical correlations, documented in a series of reports by the Surgeon General of the United States.

The statistical picture shows the following consistent links between cancer and smoking:

1. During this century, increased rates of smoking have been followed by increased rates of lung cancer.

2. The majority of lung-cancer victims—82 percent of them—have a history of smoking.

3. Men smoke more than women, and are more likely than women to get lung cancer.

4. As smoking has become more common among women, female lung-cancer rates have risen.

5. The longer people smoke, the higher their risk of lung cancer; and if they give up smoking, their risk is less than if they continue.

6. The more men smoke, the greater their chances of getting lung cancer: those who smoke less than one pack a day are ten times more likely to die of lung cancer than nonsmokers, but those who smoke more than one pack a day are thirty times more likely to die in this way.

Smoking has also been found to correlate strongly with other cancers: compared with nonsmokers, smokers are four times more likely to get cancer of the mouth and five times more likely to get cancer of the larynx. In addition, smoking appears to increase susceptibility to other diseases as well. Smokers are six times more likely to die of bronchitis or emphysema than nonsmokers. Asbestos workers who smoke have ninety times more risk of contracting lung cancer than people exposed neither to asbestos nor smoking. Smoking is associated with pregnancy problems, including lower birth weight, stillbirth, spontaneous abortion, and infant mortality. Smokers have shorter life expectancy than nonsmokers: for example, a 32-year-old smoker can expect to die seven years earlier than a comparable nonsmoker. Also, there is growing evidence that smoking causes disease in nonsmokers who inhale other people's smoke.

The tobacco industry has consistently refused to accept these statistical correlations as proof that smoking causes cancer and other health problems. Why? The fact that one variable correlates with another does not prove that one causes the other, or even that they are related at all. The link between them might be spurious—that is, it might be merely coincidental, and not imply any causal relationship. But no other plausible factor has been suggested to explain this particular correlation, or the fact that increases or decreases in one variable—smoking—lead to corresponding increases or decreases in the other—lung cancer and other diseases. The statistical correlations also have to be evaluated against a background of other facts. Most cancers are caused by environmental agents, and it seems reasonable to conclude that repeatedly inhaling the hundreds of chemicals that are present in cigarettes might eventually cause lung cancer. In any event, the evidence that smoking is dangerous to health, and often fatally so, has been sufficient to convince virtually everyone except the tobacco industry and some addicts of the drug.

Source: From the Surgeon General's reports, 1983, 1984.

Many complain about and often exceed speed limits, although observing a limit of 55 mph would save 4,500 lives and prevent 90,000 severe head injuries each year. Millions eat themselves into cholesterol-induced heart disease, and still encourage their children to eat junk food. Millions become addicted to alcohol, barbiturates, cocaine, heroin, and other drugs whose dangers are common knowledge. Millions risk AIDS by engaging in unsafe sexual practices, convincing themselves that this time, with this partner, they will get away with it.

Having exposed themselves to the dangers of injury and disease, Americans then turn to the medical institution for help when the damage is done. The message of the sociological study of medicine is that it would be much cheaper, and far more effective, for individuals and society to make those changes that would prevent disease from occurring in the first place.

Summary

1. Education is the systematic, formalized transmission of knowledge, skills, and values. American education has a unique combination of characteristics: commitment to elementary and high school education for all, a utilitarian emphasis on education, and a strong tradition of community control.

2. Education has several important social functions: cultural transmission, social integration, personal development, screening and selection, innovation, and a number of latent functions.

3. The conflict perspective emphasizes that educational credentials are a valuable resource in the competition for jobs. Individuals' educational achievement is strongly influenced by their social-class background. The schools thus reinforce existing inequalities.

4. American schools are organized as formal, bureaucratic structures. They place great emphasis on competition for such rewards as grades. By treating pupils differently according to their supposed abilities, teachers may cause a self-fulfilling prophecy under which pupils perform according to the teachers' expectations.

5. There are discrepancies in the average educational achievement of people from different social classes and races. Class and race distinctions overlap, and the racial differences are the product of class differences. Several specific factors account for these class differences: costs of education, family expectations, cultural background, language problems, teacher attitudes, labeling of students, the effects of IQ testing, and peer-group influence.

6. Attempts have been made to equalize educational opportunity in the belief that this will lead to greater social equality. The Coleman report, however, found that student achievement is primarily determined by class background. Partly for this reason, controversial measures such as busing have been used to integrate the schools.

7. American schools are charged with allowing academic standards to decline. There are several reasons for this decline, and reform efforts are now focused on curricula and teachers.

8. The United States is becoming a "credential society," in which competition for jobs has raised the required qualifications to unnecessarily high levels.

9. Medicine is the institution focused on disease and its social implications. Disease may be endemic or epidemic, acute or chronic. Sickness is a social as well as an individual matter, for disease has a social impact, and social factors influence disease.

10. Epidemiology is the science of the distribution of disease in populations.

11. The Hippocratic theory, based on a balance of four "humors," dominated Western medicine for centuries. It was followed by the germ theory, which revolutionized medicine by emphasizing infectious microorganisms.

12. Physicians have formed a profession, which helps ensure high earnings, prestige, and great autonomy in the workplace. The success of medicine has led to the medicalization of society.

13. Health-seeking behavior is influenced by cultural factors, such as ethnic-group membership. Sociologists recognize a difference between illness (a personal, subjective condition), disease (a physical, objective condition), and sickness (a social, behavioral condition). Relationships between patients and physicians are complex, and diagnoses are sometimes "negotiated" by the participants.

14. According to the concept of the sick role, sickness is a form of deviance; sick people are exempted from social duties only if they want to get well and cooperate by seeking competent help. The functions of medicine are the maintenance of health, the treatment of disease, research and innovation, and social control.

15. The conflict view of medicine emphasizes that inequalities of health follow the lines of stratification, and that health care systems reflect the power relations in society.

16. Despite the successes of medicine, serious disease is still widespread in modern societies. It is now recognized that many diseases are caused not by germs, but rather by environmental conditions and lifestyles.

Important Terms

education (277)

manifest function (280)

latent function (280)

social mobility (281)

self-fulfilling prophecy (283)

medicine (292)

endemic disease (292)

epidemic disease (293)

acute disease (293)

chronic disease (293)

epidemiology (294)

profession (298)

medicalization of society (299)

illness/disease/sickness (303)

sick role (305)

CHAPTER *13*

The Economic and Political Systems

In this chapter we look at two closely related institutions, the economic system and the political system. These institutions are focused, respectively, on wealth and power. Yet the link between them is so intimate that they were once considered different branches of the same academic discipline, called "political economy." For the purposes of our present analysis we will treat them separately, at the same time recognizing that each institution profoundly influences the other. The reason for this relationship, as we have noted in previous chapters, is that wealth can be readily "converted" into power, or vice versa. A sociological analysis enables us to trace these connections, particularly as they operate in the United States—the most economically advanced and politically powerful country on earth.

The Economic Institution

The human animal must have food and shelter in order to survive: these are basic necessities. Beyond these fundamental requirements, people in all societies feel that they have "needs" for certain other goods and services as well—in one society, these needs may include bows and arrows, a dugout canoe, and the attention of a witch doctor; in another society, they may include a color TV set, a well-stocked wardrobe, and the skills of an auto mechanic. Whether they are biological or social, human needs can usually be satisfied only by human effort. Most goods and services are scarce. People must work to produce them and must find some way of distributing them among the various members of the society. This activity, which is basic to our species, is the substance of economic life. The **economic system** is the institutionalized means of producing and distributing goods and services.

Economic activity is significant not only because it sustains life. Throughout this book we have noted the central importance of economic production for human culture and social structure as well. The principal means of production that a society uses strongly influences the size and complexity of the society and the character of its cultural and social life. Changes in the means of economic production are therefore inevitably accompanied by sweeping changes elsewhere in society. We have also noted the close link between economic inequality and other forms of social inequality—between different social classes, different racial and ethnic groups, different age groups, and even between men and women. Economic activity, too, is a vital part of our everyday existence, for our jobs usually provide our incomes and define our social status. Work is therefore a significant source of personal and social identity: in fact, one of the first questions we ask a person we have just met is "What do you do?" The answer to that single question enables us to predict, with a good deal of accuracy, a person's social class, income, level of education, type of residential neighborhood, and various other social traits.

The Sociology of Work

The work people do depends largely on their society's basic subsistence strategy: in one society, perhaps, work means herding camels; in another, it might mean serving hamburgers. Different economies offer people different kinds of jobs, and thus, indirectly, a variety of social and cultural styles. Sociologists are therefore interested in the way the occupational structure of a society develops and changes, and the effects this structure has on human existence.

Primary, Secondary, and Tertiary Sectors

Any economy contains three basic sectors, with the proportion of the labor force in each sector depending on the society's basic subsistence strategy. The **primary sector** is the part of the economy that involves the gathering or extracting of undeveloped natural resources—for example, fishing, mining, forestry, or agriculture. The **secondary sector** is the part of the economy that involves turning the raw materials produced by the primary sector into manufactured goods—for example, houses, furniture, automobiles, canned foods. The **tertiary sector** is the part of the economy that involves providing services—for example, medicine, laundering, teaching, broadcasting. Over the course of sociocultural evolution, the economic emphasis shifts steadily from the primary to the secondary and then to the tertiary sector, with profound effects on the nature of work and, indeed, on society as a whole.

In *preindustrial* societies, virtually the entire population is engaged in the primary sector—hunting and gathering, tending herds or gardens, or plowing and harvesting fields. In *industrial* societies, most of the work force is engaged in "blue-collar" jobs in the secondary sector, producing manufactured goods in workshops and factories. In *postindustrial* societies, most of the work force is engaged in the tertiary sector—providing services and processing information in locations like restaurants, hospitals, and offices.

In the 1950s, the United States became the first country in the world to have more than half its labor force engaged in the tertiary sector, and this trend still continues. Today, American farm workers, who represented almost 40 percent of the work force at the turn of the century, comprise less than 3 percent of all workers; the industrial work force is shrinking rapidly, and now comprises less than 29 percent of all workers; and over 68 percent of workers are employed in providing services or handling information. Predictably, a shift of this magnitude does not take place without wrenching social changes.

Figure 13.1 *The three main sectors of work in an economy are exemplified in these photographs. Primary industry involves gathering or extracting raw materials; secondary industry involves manufacturing goods; and tertiary industry involves providing services. Over the course of economic development, the proportion of workers in secondary and, later, tertiary industry grows larger.*

The Division of Labor

Another important trend in the course of economic development is a refinement in the **division of labor,** the specialization by individuals or groups in particular economic activities. This specialization occurs in all societies because it is highly functional. By assigning particular people to do specific jobs, the division of labor helps ensure that they will become more expert at their work, and thus enhances the efficiency of economic life.

In *preindustrial* societies there is little division of labor. These societies allocate some tasks according to age or sex, but there are very few full-time, specialized roles, and most people do much the same kinds of work. The great bulk of the population works in food production.

In *industrial* societies, the division of labor becomes highly elaborate. One reason is that many new jobs are created by the very diversity of industrial production. But another reason is that industrialism creates an entirely new form of the division of labor—the high degree of specialization found in factories where each individual contributes only a minute part to the final product.

In *postindustrial* societies, the division of labor reaches its highest degree of complexity. Economic and technological development in these societies creates a series of new specialties and subspecialties, like computer designer, computer programmer, computer analyst, computer technician, computer operator. The contrast between the occupational structure of postindustrial societies and the less complex societies of the past is striking.

In the simplest preindustrial society, the number of specialized occupational roles—if any exist at all—can probably be counted on the fingers of one hand. Even in the early stages of industrialism in the United States, the 1850 census recorded a grand total of 323 occupations. In the postindustrial United States today, in contrast, the Department of Labor records over 20,000 jobs, including such highly specialized occupations as blintz roller, alligator farmer, oxtail washer, corset stringer, ear-muff assembler, gherkin pickler, chicken sexer, singing messenger, tamale-machine feeder, braille proofreader, environmental epidemiologist, and nuclear-criticality safety engineer. This list, of course, includes only legitimate occupations. It leaves out such jobs as dope pusher, pimp, pickpocket, counterfeiter, and con artist, all of which include many further subspecialties. But what does all this occupational diversity mean for modern society?

Figure 13.2 *In a traditional, preindustrial society, there is hardly any division of labor except on the grounds of age and sex. People wear similar clothes, reside in similar dwellings, share similar ideas, and experience much the same lives. Such a society, Durkheim argued, is held together by "mechanical solidarity," or the basic similarity of its members. A diversified modern industrialized society, on the other hand, is held together by "organic solidarity," or the dissimilarity of people who have to depend on one another's specialized skills. These two pictures—one of a village in rural Kenya and one of a single street in Manhattan—give some idea of what this distinction can mean for the everyday life of the society.*

Specialization and Society

In his important work *The Division of Labor in Society* (1893), Emile Durkheim concluded that increased specialization has two significant and related effects: it actually changes the very nature of the bonds that hold society together, and it encourages individualism at the expense of community—perhaps to a dangerous degree.

Traditional societies, Durkheim argued, are held together by **mechanical solidarity,** a form of social cohesion that is based on the similarity of the members. Because these societies are small and because everyone does much the same work, the members are all socialized in the same pattern, share the same experiences, and hold common values. These values, which are mainly religious in nature, form a "collective consciousness" for the community, a set of norms, beliefs, and assumptions shared by one and all. There is little individuality—for people think of themselves primarily in terms of their membership in, and loyalty to, the group. The society consists basically of a collection of kinship groups, all with similar characteristics.

Modern societies, on the other hand, are held together by **organic solidarity,** a form of social cohesion based on the differences among the members, which make them interdependent. People in modern societies play a variety of economic roles, have quite different experiences, hold different values, and socialize their children in many varying patterns. Consequently, they think of themselves as individuals first and as members of a kinship or wider social group second. The modern society thus consists of a series of interconnected individuals, each with different characteristics. Because they are now interdependent, however, they must rely on one another if their society is to function effectively.

The basis for social solidarity is no longer the *similarity* of the members but rather their *differences*.

According to Durkheim, the end result of this division of labor, with its emphasis on differences and individuality, may be **anomie**—a condition of confusion that exists in both individual and society when social norms are weak, absent, or conflicting. As anomie spreads, people feel ever more detached from their fellows. Having little commitment to shared norms, they lack social guidelines for personal conduct and are inclined to pursue their private desires without regard for the interests of society as a whole. Social control of individual behavior becomes ineffective, and the society is threatened with extensive deviance, disorganization, or even disintegration as a result.

How valid do Durkheim's concerns seem today? He was probably correct in his view that the division of labor would lead to growing individualism and the breakdown of shared commitment to social norms. Indeed, we have touched on this issue at several points in this book. For example, in Chapter 2 ("Culture") we noted that self-fulfillment is becoming an important value in the postindustrial United States; in Chapter 6 ("Deviance"), that crime and other forms of deviant behavior seem much more widespread in modern societies than in traditionalist ones; in Chapter 11 ("Family and Religion"), that people are increasingly inclined to judge family issues in terms of their own desires rather than their obligations to their kin, and that loyalty to traditional religion is being eroded in the most economically developed societies. In short, it seems plausible that there is widespread anomie in modern societies—but not enough to cause the social breakdown that Durkheim feared. Moreover, many people look favorably on the growth of individualism, with all it implies for personal freedom and the exercise of choice over one's own destiny.

Work and Alienation

Work is a central part of our existence. Whether we see work as a source of fulfillment and satisfaction or as a cause of boredom and indignity, whether we view it as enjoyable in itself or simply as a means of earning a living, it is the activity that occupies most of our waking adult lives. Sociologists are therefore deeply interested in how people experience their work.

Karl Marx took up this question and made it a central part of his analysis of industrial societies. He believed that the capacity for labor is one of the most distinctive human characteristics. All other species, he argued, are merely objects in the world; human beings alone are subjects, because they consciously act on and create the world, shaping their lives, cultures, and personalities in the process. In modern societies, however, people have become estranged from their work, and thus from nature, from other human beings, and from themselves.

Marx referred to this sense of estrangement as **alienation**—the situation in which people lose their control over the social world they have created, with the result that they find themselves "alien" in a hostile environment. In his view, an important source of alienation in modern societies is the extreme division of labor. Each worker has a specific, restricted, and limiting role that makes it impossible to apply the full human capacities of the hands, the mind, and the emotions to work. The worker has diminished responsibility, does not own the tools with which the work is done, does not own the final product, does not have the right to make decisions—and is therefore reduced to a minute part of a process, a mere cog in a machine. Work becomes an enforced activity, not a creative and satisfying one. Marx claimed further that this situation is aggravated in capitalist economies, in which the profit produced by the labor of the worker goes to someone else.

chip in Japan, its circuit boards in Singapore, its keyboard in Taiwan, its disks in Germany. The combined effects of international competition and technological development may lead to a wave of what the economist Joseph Schumpeter has called "creative destruction"—the reallocation of resources from old industries to the enterprises of the future, in ways that may change the face of economy and society. The ubiquitous microchip, after all, was not even invented in 1970; who knows what the innovation of the day, or its implications, will be in 2000?

Capitalism and Socialism

There are now two basic economic systems in the world. One is **capitalism,** an economic system in which the means of production and distribution are privately owned. The other is **socialism,** an economic system in which the means of production and distribution are publicly owned. In practice there is great variety in these two kinds of economy, ranging from the most capitalist societies, such as the United States and Canada, through intermediate societies, such as Britain, Sweden, and Yugoslavia, to the most socialist societies, such as China and Albania. There is also great variety in the political systems that are associated with both capitalism and socialism, for democratic and authoritarian forms of government are found in each type of economy. For example, Sweden is socialist but democratic, while Cuba is socialist but authoritarian; Switzerland is capitalist and democratic, but South Africa is capitalist and authoritarian.

The Concept of Property

The chief bone of contention between advocates of each system is the ownership of property. In everyday speech we think of "property" as objects. Strictly speaking, however, **property** is the set of rights that the owner of something has in relation to others who do not own it. Property is established in a society through social norms, often expressed in law, that define the conditions under which people may own objects. Ownership of property may take one of three forms:

1. *Communal ownership* exists when property belongs to the community as a whole and may be used by any member of the community. Communal ownership of land is frequently found in small preindustrial societies—it was the traditional form, for example, among most American Indian tribes.

2. *Private ownership* exists when property belongs to specific persons. Private property is recognized in all societies. In some it may be restricted to a few household possessions; in others it may include assets worth millions of dollars. (Corporations are regarded as "persons" for legal purposes, so corporate ownership is a form of private ownership.)

3. *Public ownership* exists when property belongs to the state or some other political authority that claims the property on behalf of the people as a whole. A good deal of property in all modern societies (such as highways and schools) is publicly owned.

The main reason the ownership of property is such a controversial matter is that those who own the means of producing and distributing goods and services—means such as land, factories, and capital funds—are potentially in a position of power over those who do not. The debate between the advocates of capitalism and socialism hinges on this issue. Advocates of capitalism contend that the interests of all are served best if there is a minimum of public ownership of the means of production and distribution. Advocates of socialism argue that private ownership leads to exploitation and inequality, which can be avoided if the means of production and distribution are publicly owned. The issue is so important that it has divided the major industrialized societies of the modern world into two opposing, armed camps.

Figure 13.3 *A great deal of property in modern societies—such as most American high schools—is socialized, or publicly owned. Capitalists and socialists differ, even among themselves, on the question of how much public ownership of property is desirable.*

Capitalism

In its ideal form, capitalism contains two essential ingredients. The first is the deliberate pursuit of *personal profit* as the goal of economic activity. The second ingredient is *market competition* as the mechanism for determining what is produced, at what price, and for which consumers.

Why is the pursuit of profit and an atmosphere of unrestricted competition so necessary for capitalism? The theory is that under these conditions, the market forces of supply and demand will ensure the production of the best possible products at the lowest possible price. The profit motive will provide the incentive for individual capitalists to produce the goods and services the public wants. Competition among capitalists will give the public the opportunity to compare the quality and prices of goods, so that any producers who are inefficient or who charge excessive prices will be put out of business. The "invisible hand" of market forces thus ensures the greatest good for the entire society. Efficient producers are rewarded with profits, and consumers get quality products at competitive prices. For the system to work, however, there should ideally be a minimum of political interference in market forces. The government should therefore adopt a policy of *laissez faire*, meaning "leave it alone."

The United States conforms most closely to the ideal model of capitalism. But since the Great Depression, when the capitalist system seemed in danger of total collapse, it has been generally accepted that the federal government must supervise many details of economic activity. For example, the government sets minimum prices for some commodities and puts ceilings on the prices of others. It intervenes in international trade and concerns itself with the balance of payments with other countries. It protects some natural resources and encourages the exploitation of others. It lays down minimum wage standards, provides for unemployment benefits, and sometimes supervises labor-management relations. It tries to ensure the safety of the workplace and of manufactured goods. It regulates the level of production and consumption through its fiscal policies. It also has the authority to safeguard competition in the marketplace by preventing the growth of a **monopoly,** a single firm that dominates an industry, or of an **oligopoly,** a group of a few firms that dominates an industry.

Modern American capitalism is thus unlike the classical model in many respects. It has certain drawbacks, too, that are common to all capitalist systems: marked social inequality, a large and impoverished lower class, and repeated cycles of prosperity and recession, employment and unemployment. No capitalist society has yet found a way out of these dilemmas. Nevertheless, for those who can afford them, American capitalism has certainly delivered the goods. With just over 5 percent of the world's population, the United States accounts for over 20 percent of its output.

Socialism

In its ideal form, socialism also contains two essential ingredients: the fulfillment of *social needs* as the goal of economic activity, and reliance on *centralized planning* as the mechanism for determining what is produced, at what price, and for which consumers. Socialism thus rests on entirely different assumptions from those of capitalism. The pursuit of private profit is regarded as fundamentally immoral, because one person's profit is another person's loss, and the ultimate result of capitalism is social inequality. In addition, competition among different firms producing similar products is regarded as a waste of resources.

Socialism proposes that production should be designed to serve social needs, and whether it is profitable or not is of secondary importance. It is therefore necessary for the means of production to be taken into public ownership and run in the best interests of society as a whole. Similarly, the means of distribution of wealth must be publicly owned to ensure that goods and services flow to those who need them rather than only to those who can afford them. To this end, the government must regulate the economy in accordance with long-term national plans, and it must not hesitate to establish artificial price levels or to run important industries at a loss if necessary.

In actuality, there are two very divergent forms of socialism in the modern world—one practiced in authoritarian, communist-ruled societies, mostly in Eastern Europe and Asia, and one practiced in democratic, pluralist societies, mostly in Western Europe. These versions differ markedly in their degree of centralized control of the economy, and in the liberties their citizens enjoy.

Soviet-Style Socialism   Soviet-style socialism exists in the Soviet Union and other countries that are ruled by communist parties, such as Bulgaria and Vietnam. In every case, the governments of these societies seized power through revolution or other use of force. These countries are often called "communist" in the United States, but they never describe themselves that way. Although they are ruled by communist parties, they consider themselves to be in a stage of socialism, a preparatory step toward their true goal. That goal is **communism,** a hypothetical egalitarian political and economic system in which the means of production and distribution would be communally owned.

Since no communist society has ever existed, and since the writings of Marx and other advocates of communism are somewhat vague in their vision of one, it is not entirely clear what a communist society would look like. In general, however, it would have some of the characteristics of the communal-ownership pattern that is currently found only in primitive societies. The role of the state would shrink; there would be an abundance of goods and services; people would no longer regard property as "private"; and wealth and power would be shared in harmony by the community as a whole. Under socialism, people are paid according to their work, but under communism, individuals would contribute according to their abilities and receive according to their needs. The history of human alienation and strife would be over, and each person would be able to fulfill his or her human potential to the full. The major problem with such a

Figure 13.4 *These Russian women are relaxing after the ordeal of a day spent shopping. Because of fundamental inefficiencies in the country's economy, there are chronic shortages of consumer items of every kind. The women—who like many Russians, take string bags with them when they leave home so that they can carry back any suitable consumer items that suddenly become available—may have to wait for hours in line to make a single purchase. Some communist-ruled countries, such as Hungary, have more efficient economies because they rely far less on bureaucratic central planning. Current reforms in the Soviet Union are intended to loosen centralized control of the economy and to provide incentives for greater productivity.*

society is that nobody seems to know quite how to arrive there. It is now clear that the Soviet Union and other communist-ruled societies are "stuck" in the socialist stage and have virtually no idea of how to get beyond it.

The economy of the Soviet Union conforms in some respects, however, to the ideal socialist model. The means of production and distribution—land, machines, factories, capital funds, banks, retail outlets, and so on—are publicly owned. Citizens are permitted private ownership of personal items, such as household goods and automobiles, but until recently could not engage in speculative investment or own wealth-producing property. The economy is closely regulated in accordance with national economic plans that are designed to meet specified national goals. Critics allege that overly centralized planning leads to inefficiency. The new Soviet leadership, under Mikhail Gorbachev, is responding to these charges with a sweeping *perestroika,* or restructuring, designed to loosen bureaucratic controls.

Every Soviet citizen is guaranteed health care, a job, and a home, so people have no real fear of medical costs, unemployment, or destitution. In all Soviet-style societies, however, there are significant differences in income between ordinary workers and those in managerial or other executive positions. The Soviet Union and most of these countries are now experimenting with "incentive payments" to encourage higher productivity—a practice not very different from offering them greater "profit" for working harder. Actually, productivity is relatively poor, giving the Soviet Union one of the lowest standards of living of all industrialized societies.

It is important to recognize that when Marx advocated communism, he had in mind the concept of communism outlined above, not the Soviet version of socialism. Much of the antagonism to Marxist thought in the United States stems from a confusion between Marx's ideas and contemporary Soviet practice. On the basis of his writings, however, it seems highly unlikely that Marx would have regarded modern Soviet society with much enthusiasm.

Democratic Socialism Many of the countries of Western Europe, such as Denmark and Austria, practice one form or another of **democratic socialism,** a political and economic system that aims to preserve individual freedom in the context of social equality achieved through a centrally planned economy.

Under democratic socialism—also known as the "welfare state"—the state takes ownership of only strategic industries and services, such as railways, airlines, mines, banks, radio, TV, telephone systems, medical services, colleges, and important manufacturing enterprises such as chemicals and steel. Private ownership of other means of production is permitted, even encouraged, but the economy is closely regulated in accordance with national priorities. High tax rates are used to prevent excessive profits or an undue concentration of wealth. A measure of social equality is ensured through extensive welfare services. In Great Britain, for example, college education and medical services are available free of charge, and about a quarter of the population lives in heavily subsidized public housing.

Most of the countries of Western Europe have had periods of both socialist and nonsocialist rule since World War II, as their electorates have periodically switched allegiance from one political party to another. Currently, most of these countries have been moving in a more capitalistic direction—for example, by selling off nationalized industries (such as British Airways and British Telecom) to private owners once more. Several less developed countries elsewhere in the world, like India, Nigeria, and Argentina, are also shifting away from a centrally planned economy and toward one driven by free enterprise. The reason seems to be that, while socialist societies may distribute wealth more evenly than capitalist ones, they are less efficient at creating wealth in the first place. The twentieth century has provided overwhelming evidence that socialist economies are more bureaucratized and less productive than capitalist ones (Berger, 1986).

Corporate Capitalism

The modern American economy, as we have seen, is no longer based on the competitive efforts of innumerable private capitalists. Although there are hundreds of thousands of businesses, a mere 500 of them account for three-quarters of the gross national product. The economy is now dominated not by the individual entrepreneur but rather by the **corporation,** a legally recognized organization whose existence, powers, and liabilities are separate and distinct from those of its owners or employees.

Corporations are owned by thousands or even hundreds of thousands of stockholders, and some of these stockholders are other corporations. In theory, the stockholders control the corporation by electing a board of directors and by voting on company policies at annual stockholders' meetings. In practice, the widely dispersed stockholders rubber-stamp decisions that have already been made for them. The day-to-day running of the corporation is in the hands of the management, which not only supervises company operations but also makes most of the major policy decisions, which in turn are usually approved by the board.

The size and economic power of the major corporations are immense. The largest 100 corporations own 49 percent of all the manufacturing assets in the United States, and the largest 200 corporations own 61 percent of these assets (Bureau of the Census, 1986a). Some of the largest corporations, such as Exxon and General Motors, have budgets that are larger than those of every country in the world other than the United States and the Soviet Union.

The largest American corporations are linked together through **interlocking directorates,** social networks consisting of individuals who are members of several different corporate boards. The directors of the board of General Motors, for example, sit on 29 other corporate boards. The members of those boards, in turn, sit on the boards of an additional 650 corporations. The total directorate of the leading corporations resembles a tightly spun web, making the influence of these organizations all the more concentrated (Mintz and Schwartz, 1981, 1985; Dye, 1986; Useem, 1980, 1986). The domination of the American economy by

Figure 13.5 *Thanks largely to the way that corporate capitalism creates both products and the public demand for them, Americans have become the world's greatest consumers. Indeed, these two figures could only be American, and would be instantly recognized as such almost anywhere in the world. Actually, the pair—entitled* Couple with Shopping Bags—*were created, in vinyl, by the contemporary American artist Duane Hanson.*

large corporations has several important consequences. One of them is that these corporations are able to apply political leverage on national policy, winning favors for themselves, influencing the country's tax structure, and successfully promoting the growth of oligopolies in particular industries. In fact, about 60 percent of manufacturing in the United States is oligopolistic, with a handful of firms controlling most of the output of such products as automobiles, cigarettes, and steel.

In the past, corporations concentrated their efforts in one country. Today, many have also established an international presence, often diversifying into various industries in the process. A **multinational corporation** is a corporate enterprise which, although headquartered in one country, conducts its operations through subsidiaries that it owns or controls around the world. ITT, for example, employs over 400,000 workers in sixty-eight countries. Exxon operates in nearly a hundred countries, and its fleet of oil tankers constitutes a navy as large as Great Britain's. General Motors is active in thirty-nine countries, where it sells over $80 billion worth of products every year. In fact, some of these corporations are substantially wealthier than many of their host countries. The multinationals are already responsible for more than a quarter of total world economic production, and they are expected to account for over half by the end of the century—one of the most remarkable trends in the modern world (Modelski, 1979; Heilbroner, 1982).

About 300 of the largest 500 multinationals are headquartered in one country, the United States. The international influence of these organizations, therefore, is primarily an American one. Decisions made by a small group of people in the United States can mean prosperity or unemployment in nations thousands of miles away. Multinational corporations dominate the economies of many less developed countries, influencing the level of wages, the kind of crops that are grown, or how national resources are allocated.

American-based multinationals have an impressive record of interference in the affairs of the host countries, with activities ranging from bribery of local officials to outright attempts to overthrow foreign governments, including those of Iran in 1953, Guatemala in 1954, and Chile in 1970. When these and similar facts became public in the mid-1970s, Congress demanded extensive investigations of illicit corporate activity. Exxon, it was soon discovered, had paid nearly $60 million to government officials in fifteen nations, including $27 million to several Italian political parties. Lockheed had distributed nearly $200 million in bribes and payoffs in several countries, and the resulting scandals implicated the prince of the Netherlands, the prime minister of Japan, military leaders in Colombia, and cabinet members in Italy. Overwhelmed by the size of their task, federal investigators offered corporations immunity in return for full confessions. In all, more than 500 major American corporations, most of them multinational, admitted giving bribes or other questionable payments to government officials in order to obtain benefits for themselves (Sampson, 1973; Hougan, 1976; Hersh, 1982).

The multinationals do offer many useful resources to the less developed countries. They encourage economic growth by importing the necessary capital and technology, and they create new industries and markets all over the world. But their motives are purely selfish—to exploit cheap labor and resources on an international scale for the benefit of a handful of stockholders in wealthy countries. Their activities have had a significant impact within the United States, too, for the multinationals export not only capital but also jobs: if an item can be manufactured more cheaply in Hong Kong than Detroit, the multinationals may close down their American plant, open one in Asia, and import the finished item back to the United States. They are also able to shift assets and operations around the world—recording losses in high-tax nations and profits in low-tax nations, or evading safety regulations or labor laws in one country by moving to another that lacks them. The multinationals are joining nation-states as the major actors on the international stage, for they inevitably develop worldwide interests and the "foreign policies" that go with them. Dedicated to the pursuit of profit and subject to the authority of no one nation, run by a tiny elite of managers and directors who have a largely fictional responsibility to their far-flung shareholders, they represent a disturbing and growing concentration of global influence and power (Ball, 1975; Vernon, 1977; Evans, 1981; Bornschier and Hoby, 1981).

The Political Institution

Over 2,000 years ago the philosopher Aristotle observed that we are political animals. We are indeed, and necessarily so, for politics is an inevitable consequence of social living. In every society some valued resources are scarce, and politics is essentially the process of deciding "who gets what, when, and how" (Lasswell, 1936).

The **political system** is the institutionalized means through which some individuals or groups acquire and exercise power over others. Here, we will focus primarily on these processes as they occur at the level of the **state,** the supreme political authority in society. Max Weber (1946), who laid the foundations of modern political sociology, pointed out that the state is the only authority that can successfully claim a monopoly on the right to use force within a given territory. Of course, the state may choose to delegate some of its powers to other agencies, such as local authorities, the police, or the military. In the final analysis, however, the state can override all other agencies and is thus the central and most vital component of the political order. The "state," incidentally, is not quite the same thing as the "government." The state is an impersonal social authority, whereas the government is the collection of individuals who happen to be directing the power of the state at any given moment.

Politics is about power—about who gets it, how it is obtained, how it is applied, and to what purposes it is put. As Weber defined it, **power** is the ability to control the behavior of others, even in the absence of their consent. The exercise of power may be either legitimate or illegitimate. As we noted in Chapter 8 ("Social Stratification"), **legitimacy** is the generally held belief that a political system is valid and justified. Power, therefore, is considered legitimate only if people generally recognize that those who apply it have the right to do so—perhaps because they are elected government officials, perhaps because they are an aristocracy whose commands are never questioned, perhaps because they are believed to be inspired by God. According to Weber, **authority** is the form of power whose legitimacy is recognized by those to whom it is applied. Power is considered illegitimate, on the other hand, if people believe that those who apply it do not have the right to do so—perhaps because they are acting illegally, perhaps because they hold no public office, perhaps because they are newly successful revolutionaries who have not yet entrenched their regime. To Weber, **coercion** is the form of power whose legitimacy is denied by those to whom it is applied.

A simple example will illustrate this distinction more fully. If a judge rules that you must pay a fine, you will probably obey: if you do not, the judge has the power to make you suffer other negative consequences. If an armed mugger in the street demands your money, you will likewise probably obey: the mugger also has the power to make you suffer negative consequences if you refuse. But you regard the judge's demand as legitimate. It rests on judicial authority, and you recognize that the judge has the *right* to fine you even if you disagree with and resent the decision. You do not accept, however, that the mugger has any *right* whatever to take your money. You hand it over simply because you are being coerced.

Power based on authority is usually unquestioningly accepted by those to whom it is applied, for obedience to it has become a social norm. Power based on coercion, on the other hand, tends to be unstable, because people obey only out of fear and will disobey at the first opportunity. For this reason every political system must be regarded as legitimate by its participants if it is to survive. Most people must consider it desirable, workable, and better than any alternatives. If the bulk of the citizens in any society no longer consider their political system legitimate, it is doomed, for its power can then rest only on coercion, which will fail in the long run.

Types of Authority

Max Weber distinguished three basic types of legitimate authority: traditional authority, legal-rational authority, and charismatic authority. Each type is legitimate because it rests on the implicit or explicit consent of the governed. A person who can successfully claim one of these types of authority is regarded as having the right to compel obedience, at least within socially specified limits.

Traditional Authority **Traditional authority** is a type of authority in which power is legitimated by ancient custom. Chieftainships and monarchies, for example, have always relied on traditional authority, and historically it has been the most common source of legitimation of power. Traditional authority is generally founded on unwritten laws and has an almost sacred quality. The competence or policies of a particular ruler are not really at issue in such a system, so long as he or she has a legitimate claim to the throne or other traditional ruling status.

People obey traditional authority because "it has always been that way": the right of the king to rule is not open to question. Claim to traditional authority is usually based on birthright, with the status of ruler generally passing to the eldest son of the incumbent. In some cases the power of the ruler over the

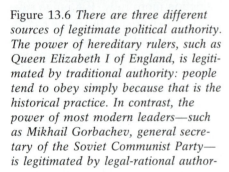

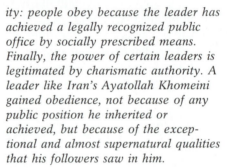

Figure 13.6 *There are three different sources of legitimate political authority. The power of hereditary rulers, such as Queen Elizabeth I of England, is legitimated by traditional authority: people tend to obey simply because that is the historical practice. In contrast, the power of most modern leaders—such as Mikhail Gorbachev, general secretary of the Soviet Communist Party— is legitimated by legal-rational author- ity: people obey because the leader has achieved a legally recognized public office by socially prescribed means. Finally, the power of certain leaders is legitimated by charismatic authority. A leader like Iran's Ayatollah Khomeini gained obedience, not because of any public position he inherited or achieved, but because of the excep- tional and almost supernatural qualities that his followers saw in him.*

subjects seems virtually unlimited, but in practice there are always informal social norms setting the boundaries within which power can be exercised. But when a society begins to modernize, support for systems based on traditional authority wanes, and some people look for a more rational alternative.

Legal-Rational Authority   **Legal-rational authority** is a type of authority in which power is legitimated by explicit rules and procedures that define the rights and obligations of the rulers. The rules and procedures are typically found in a written constitution and set of laws that, at least in theory, have been socially agreed upon. This form of authority is characteristic of the political systems of most modern societies.

Legal-rational authority stresses a government of laws, not of specific rulers. The power of an official in a country such as the United States, Canada, or the Soviet Union derives from the office the person holds, not from personal charac- teristics such as birthright. Officials can exercise power only within legally de- fined limits that have been formally set in advance. Americans thus acknowl- edge the right of a president or even of a minor bureaucrat to exercise power, provided that person does not exceed the specific boundaries of authority that attach to his or her respective office.

Charismatic Authority   **Charismatic authority** is a type of authority in which power is legitimated by the unique and remarkable qualities that people attri- bute to a specific leader. Weber called this extraordinary quality "charisma," from a Greek word meaning "gift of grace." Typical charismatic leaders include such figures as Jesus, Joan of Arc, Hitler, Gandhi, Napoleon, Mao, Castro, Julius Caesar, Alexander the Great, Churchill, and the Ayatollah Khomeini. The char- ismatic leader is seen as a person of destiny who is inspired by unusual vision, by lofty principles, or perhaps even by God. The charisma of these leaders is itself sufficient to make their authority seem legitimate to their followers. Whether they can also lay claim to traditional or legal-rational authority is of little relevance to their popular appeal.

Charisma is a spontaneous, irrational phenomenon that often poses a threat to systems based on traditional or legal-rational authority. Revolutions are commonly led by charismatic figures who win personal allegiance and are regarded as the symbol of radical changes to come. Yet charismatic authority is inherently unstable. It has no traditions or rules to guide conduct, and because it rests on the unique characteristics of a particular individual, it is undermined if the leader fails or dies. For this reason, systems based on charismatic authority are usually short-lived. Many of them collapse. Others gradually evolve into legal-rational systems based on bureaucratic rules and procedures, or—more commonly in the past than today—into traditional systems in which power passes to the descendants of the original leader.

The State

As we have seen, the state is the supreme political authority in society. Yet in most parts of the world, the state is a relatively recent historical development. Only two centuries ago, most of the peoples of the world lived under the often informal authority of local rulers. But since then, the state has emerged as the main source of social authority, successfully claiming a monopoly of the legitimate use of force within a given territory. That territory comprises a nation—a geographically distinct collectivity of people under the authority of a single state.

In modern societies, the responsibilities of the state steadily expand as it comes to regulate more and more areas of social life, such as welfare, education, medicine, public transport, scientific research, and economic planning.

In the United States, for example, this growth can be measured in the extraordinary rise in government expenditures. Just under two centuries ago, George Washington's administration spent an average of $20,000 a day. In 1934, Franklin Roosevelt became known as a "big spender" when his administration spent $18 million a day. By 1988, Ronald Reagan's administration was spending well over $2.7 billion a day—Reagan, in fact, was the first president to have an annual budget over $1 trillion. The size of the government bureaucracy has shown a corresponding increase. A century and a half ago, the federal government employed 5,000 people. Today it employs nearly 3 million civilians, and the total of all federal, state, and local government employees exceeds 16 million people.

The State: A Functionalist View

From the functionalist perspective, the emergence of the state and its dominant position in modern societies can be explained in terms of the functions that it serves in the maintenance of the social system as a whole (Parsons, 1969). Four major functions of the state can be identified.

1. *Enforcement of norms.* In small, traditional communities, norms are usually unwritten and are generally enforced by spontaneous community action. In a highly complex and rapidly changing modern society, such a system would be unworkable. The state accordingly takes the responsibility for codifying important norms in the form of laws.

2. *Arbitration of conflict.* The state provides an institutionalized process for deciding "who gets what, when, and how." Conflict over the allocation of scarce resources and over national goals must be kept within manageable limits. The state acts as arbitrator, or umpire, between conflicting interests, establishing means for resolving disputes and determining policies.

CHAPTER *14*

Human Ecology

In the modern industrialized world, we often feel insulated from nature, and confident that our technology can give us mastery over the natural environment. We easily forget that we too are animals, ultimately as dependent on the environment for our survival as any other species.

Ecology is the science of the relationship between living organisms and their environments. The discipline emerged as a natural science in the late nineteenth century and is still primarily the domain of biologists. In the twentieth century, however, social scientists have systematically applied ecological principles to the study of human societies and populations. This research has gained urgency from a growing awareness of an "ecological crisis," brought about by the impact of industrialization and population growth on the global environment.

Sociologists are particularly interested in **human ecology**, the interrelationship between human groups and their natural environment. We have already seen in Chapter 3 ("Society") that the ecological approach is a useful means of analyzing social arrangements, for the subsistence strategy that a society uses to exploit its environment has important effects on social structure and culture. In particular, the subsistence strategy strongly affects the size and distribution of a population. If all societies still relied on hunting and gathering for their subsistence, world population would have leveled off at around 10 million people, living mostly in small, isolated groups. But the industrial mode of production permits a small part of the population to feed the rest, and thus makes possible large, concentrated populations, including cities of millions of people.

Directly or indirectly, global industrialization has contributed to three issues that we will examine in this chapter—rapid population increase, the urbanization of the human population, and the destruction of the natural environment.

Population

By this time tomorrow, about a quarter of a million more human beings will have been born. Some 50,000 years ago, when our ancestors lived in small bands of hunters and gatherers, there was 1 person for every 200 square miles of the earth's surface—but if current rates of population growth persist, within less than a thousand years there will be 100 people for each square yard! Of course, such an absurdity will not occur, if only because, one way or another, population growth is going to stop long before that point is reached. But already, the world has a population of over 5.1 billion people, a number that will rise beyond 6 billion by the end of this century and will probably exceed 8 billion well within the lifetime of most of today's students.

This population growth represents one of the most critical social problems in the modern world, with potential consequences in terms of sheer human misery that are almost unimaginable. At least 10 million people die every year from the effects of starvation, at least 500 million more are undernourished or malnourished, and most of the remaining human population lives in conditions of pov-

Figure 14.9 *These contrasting pictures suggest the differences between small-scale, traditional communities and the large-scale urban environment of today. The first picture,* Peasant Dance, *by David Teniers the Younger, was painted in the seventeenth century. The work captures the features of what Tönnies called the* Gemeinschaft—*its intimacy of interpersonal relationships and sense of community solidarity. The second picture,* The Subway, *was painted in 1950 by the American artist George Tooker. This work reflects some features of the* Gesellschaft—*its anonymity and lack of shared commitment. But while there is some truth in both of these portraits, the features of each are exaggerated. It is unlikely that the peasant community was always so sociable, and the modern city is hardly so impersonal.*

Classical Views   Classical sociological views of the city, published in the late nineteenth and early twentieth century, tended to take a rather pessimistic view: urban life was seen as imposing severe strains on human relationships. Ferdinand Tönnies (1855–1936) distinguished between the **Gemeinschaft,** a "community" in which most people know one another, and the **Gesellschaft,** an "association" in which most people are strangers to one another. For Tönnies, urbanization implied that the community with strong interpersonal bonds is replaced by an association of individuals, most of whose relationships are temporary and impersonal. Similarly, Louis Wirth (1938) argued that three distinctive features of the city—its size, population density, and social diversity—combine to create a style of life that is very different from that of small communities. The *size* of the city produces an anonymous existence, for the individual becomes almost insignificant in a mass environment. The *density* of the city forces people into contact with one another, but only in terms of highly specific roles—like mail carrier or merchant—and not as whole people. Relationships therefore become rational and calculated rather than warm and affectionate. The *social diversity* of the city produces an awareness of many different viewpoints and lifestyles, and so tends to break down the individual's unquestioning allegiance to traditional values. In short, the close-knit rural community cannot be reproduced in the impersonal city, where in Wirth's words, "the clock and the traffic signal are symbolic of the basis of our social order."

Modern Views Modern sociologists are inclined to take a more benign view of the city, emphasizing the opportunities it offers. For example, Herbert Gans (1962a, 1962b, 1968) rejects the view that the city is essentially impersonal. He argues that the city, despite its size, is really a mosaic of different groups and neighborhoods. The individual resident, he claims, experiences city life within these much smaller and more manageable environments, not in the anonymous city as a whole. Other research has supported Gans's view. For example, Gerald Suttles (1970) has shown that strong feelings of community solidarity exist in slum neighborhoods, where residents are often acutely aware of the identity, membership, and boundaries of their communities. Likewise, Claude Fischer (1984) claims that the city actually gives people a sense of belonging because it contains a variety of subcultures that support and cater to interests that cannot be satisfied anywhere else. In other words, there are enough people devoted to particular kinds of politics, music, art, recreation, drugs, sexual practices, or religious cults for groups to emerge that support these interests and values. So urban life may help create private worlds that give people a sense of intimacy and belonging despite the anonymity and impersonality of the wider city environment.

It seems, then, that a fair reassessment of urban life must take account of both its drawbacks and its advantages. There is little doubt that urban life can be more impersonal and isolating than life in a traditional rural community. The city cuts people off from the beauty of the natural environment and exposes them to too many people, too much noise, and too much pollution. It immerses them in social problems such as poverty, racial conflict, drug addiction, and crime.

But rural life is not all wine and roses. The traditional community lacks many of the comforts and amenities of the city. Large urban populations can support a cultural life of a richness and diversity never found in a small community. The city allows occupational specialization and therefore greater opportunities for fulfilling talents. Its anonymity is something for which many people are grateful. The close relationships of the small community can too often mean that everyone pries into everyone else's affairs. Nonconformists thrive in the more tolerant atmosphere of the city, where behavior that might scandalize a traditional community is ignored or may even be accepted. The city provides a more cosmopolitan outlook, in contrast to the relatively narrow, conservative, and provincial outlook of the small community. Urban living thus offers a much greater opportunity for intellectual and personal freedom.

The American City and Its Problems

The United States is one of the most urbanized societies in the world. Yet the first U.S. census in 1790 recorded only twenty-four urban places, of which only two had populations of more than 25,000. Today, two out of every three Americans now reside in urban areas of at least 1 million people, more than 50 percent of the population lives on 1 percent of the nation's land mass, and less than 3 percent live or work on farms.

The Metropolis

The fact that most Americans live in urban areas does not mean that they necessarily live in the central cities. In fact, slightly more Americans reside in the suburbs of metropolitan areas than the central cities themselves, and many others live in urban areas with relatively small populations. At present, the Bureau of the Census recognizes 281 metropolitan areas of 50,000 or more, containing just over three-quarters of the American population. The bureau also recognizes eighteen megalopolises, containing adjacent metropolises that have developed

Various efforts have been made to revitalize the central cities, but the results have been mixed. During the 1950s and 1960s, massive "urban renewal" projects razed many city neighborhoods—including, in some cases, "ethnic villages"—and replaced them with high-rise office buildings and luxury apartments. Most of these "renewed" urban areas are arid, uninteresting places to live in or even to walk about in. With buildings that lack any architectural diversity or human scale, they seem cold and colorless. Yet a lesson has been learned from these disasters, and many cities are now beginning to "recycle" older buildings by putting them to new uses. Twenty years ago, deteriorating or abandoned central-city facilities, such as old markets or docklands, would have been targeted for "urban renewal," to be demolished and replaced by featureless high-rise buildings. Instead, careful recycling has produced such immensely successful projects as Ghirardelli Square in San Francisco, the rehabilitated Skid Row in Sacramento, Harborside in Baltimore, South Street Seaport in Manhattan, and Quincy Market in Boston—lively and colorful market areas that attract millions of visitors every year. Unlike so many other urban-planning episodes, these renovations have not neglected the human element that is essential to bringing a great city to life.

Society and Nature

Other animals can sustain themselves directly from the environment—for example, by grazing on vegetation or preying on other species. Human beings, however, rely on tools for their subsistence, whether these are as simple as a hunting knife or as complex as a modern agricultural enterprise backed by fertilizers, combine harvesters, irrigation networks, storage and transportation facilities, and electric power. As a result, we have had an extraordinary impact on nature. Yet the difference between ourselves and other creatures can be a deceptive one, leading us to believe that our technology has given us mastery over the natural environment. In fact, the technology of large-scale industrialization poses two major problems. First, it generates pollution of the natural environment, threatening or destroying life in a chain reaction that can run from the tiniest microorganism to human beings. Second, it depletes natural resources such as wood, oil, and minerals, many of which are in short supply and cannot be replaced. The question that arises is whether a world population that will double in about forty years—and thus produce twice as many people to consume and pollute, perhaps more profligately than they do at present—can be supported by the environment.

Life on earth exists only in the biosphere, a thin film of soil, air, and water at or near the surface of the planet. Within this biosphere all living organisms exist in a delicate balance with one another and with the environmental resources that support them. A fundamental ecological concept is the **ecosystem,** a self-sustaining community of organisms within its natural environment. An ecosystem may be as small as a drop of pond water or as large as the biosphere itself, but the same principle of mutual interdependence always applies. Energy and inorganic (nonliving) matter are both essential for life. The energy is derived directly or indirectly from the sun, and the inorganic matter from the soil and the air. Green plants convert the sun's energy and the inorganic nutrients into organic, living matter. The plants are eaten by animals, many of which are consumed in turn by other animals in highly complex food chains. Finally, insects, bacteria, fungi, and other decomposers break down the dead bodies of plants and animals, releasing the nutrients back into the ecosystem and completing the cycle.

We may think nothing of the bacteria in the soil, but if we destroy them, we destroy ourselves, for all life depends on these lowly creatures. We poison insects at our peril, for insects are an element in a food chain that may ultimately

Figure 14.12 *Over the centuries, our technological innovations have had ever greater potential for environmental damage. Preindustrial societies drew their energy directly from such natural resources as wind and water. In the modern world we rely extensively on electricity derived from much more sophisticated sources, such as nuclear reactors. Such advances yield greater resources of energy, but they do so at greater risk to the environment.*

concentrate the poison in the bodies of animals, including ourselves, for whom it was never intended. In preindustrial societies people traditionally treated nature with respect, considering themselves a part of, rather than set apart from, the natural world; this attitude was typical, for example, among the Indian tribes of North America in precolonial times. In industrialized societies our attitude is different. We consider ourselves the lords of creation and see nature primarily as a resource for exploitation. As our "needs" increase, our capacity for exploitation expands. We do not see our ravaging of the environment as "ravaging" at all; it is "progress" or "development." We are so used to exploiting natural resources and dumping our waste products into the environment that we frequently forget that resources are limited and exhaustible and that pollution can disrupt the natural order on which our survival depends.

Pollution

Over the past quarter century, pollution of the environment has begun to threaten the ecological balance of the planet and the health of many of its species, including ourselves. One important source of environmental pollution is the widespread agricultural use of hundreds of chemical poisons in the form of herbicides and insecticides, which, as we have noted, can be transmitted and concentrated through the food chain until they turn up, sometimes years later, in the bodies of other organisms. Serious though the spread of pesticides may be, it is only a minor aspect of the problem of chemical pollution. Over 60,000 synthetic chemicals are now on the market, where they are used—often to our great benefit—in such areas as medicine, food processing, and manufacturing. However, more than half of these chemicals are classified by the Environmental Protection Agency as either potentially or definitely harmful to human health.

Figure 14.13 *During the early days of nuclear power, experts and public alike foresaw the "Uranium Age," an era of unlimited energy and abundance. This prototype automobile of the 1950s is the "uranium powered" Ford Nucleon, which was supposed to draw its energy from a little reactor at the rear of the vehicle.*

Some resources, of course, are plentiful: the United States, for example, has coal deposits that will last for centuries and can be burned to generate energy as other resources fail. But the use of a resource cannot be considered in isolation from its potentially complex environmental impacts. As we have seen, the burning of coal produces acid rain, which has a drastic effect on another resource, forests. Most of the trees that are to be cut for housing in the year 2030 are already growing, and in many cases already dying. And the carbon dioxide from increased coal burning would contribute to the "greenhouse effect" that would scorch the Great Plains and shift the world's "breadbasket" northward—to the vast tracts of currently empty land in Canada and the Soviet Union. Other apparently simple solutions to energy production—such as the use of winds, tides, or sunlight—still appear, after years of intensive research, to be too inefficient or uneconomic for large-scale use at present. Moreover, nuclear energy—particularly since the two serious accidents at Three Mile Island and Chernobyl—is now so controversial that few new plants are likely to be built.

Given the interrelationship among technology, ecology, and resources, can global industrialization continue indefinitely? Some writers, such as William Ophuls (1977), glumly foresee a new era of scarcity, in which economic growth would be replaced, at best, by economic stability—and at worst, by economic shrinkage. Others, such as Julian Simon (1981), are highly optimistic that we can continue on our present path, relying on technological innovations to solve problems in the future as they have in the past. Yet nobody denies that the planet has a finite amount of resources or that it can tolerate only a limited amount of pollution. If world population continues to grow rapidly, if industrialism spreads around the world, and if pollution and resource depletion continue at an increasing rate—and all these things are happening—where is human society headed? The most optimistic answer to these questions would be that, one way or another, sweeping social changes await us.

Species Extinction

The march of industrial civilization is having a devastating effect on the other life forms of the planet. In fact, in the latter part of the twentieth century we are witnessing a catastrophic extinction of other species: not by the dozens, or the hundreds, or even the thousands—but by the millions. This quiet apocalypse probably represents the greatest ecological disaster in the long history of life on earth. Indeed, if some different creature were to have the calamitous effects on other plants and animals that we ourselves do, we would undoubtedly consider it the most noxious and virulent pest ever to crawl upon the face of the earth.

All over the world, and especially in the less developed societies, the pressure of the human population and its technologies is devastating natural ecosystems. This pressure takes many forms—urbanization and highway construction;

transformation of virgin land into farmland; chemical pollution of fresh water; dredging and landfill in coastal areas; uncontrolled hunting and poaching, especially of African wildlife; deliberate and accidental poisoning of wildlife with pesticides; disruption of predator-prey relationships; strangulation of millions of birds and fish with discarded styrofoam pellets, plastic bags, and other synthetic flotsam; dam construction and irrigation; and massive deforestation.

Biologists estimate that there are anywhere between 5 million and 30 million species on earth. Of these, only about 1.6 million have been classified. The rest—plants, insects, fish, reptiles, birds, and even some mammals—are still almost complete mysteries to us. They have never been named, cataloged, or studied, yet many are becoming extinct even before we know of their existence. This wholesale extinction of life forms occurs primarily in the tropical rain forests, a primordial green girdle stretching around parts of Central and South America, the Congo Basin in Africa, and Indonesian islands in the Pacific. These forests cover less than 6 percent of the planet, yet they contain most of its species. Under pressure from ranchers and peasants, the rain forest is being cut down and burned. More than 40 percent of the original rain forest has disappeared since World War II, and at present 100 acres fall to axes and bulldozers every minute. If this process continues, more than a million species will be extinct by the end of the century, and millions more will be lost in the decades that follow (Ehrlich and Ehrlich, 1981; Forsythe and Miyata, 1984; Myers, 1984; Caufield, 1985).

Figure 14.14 *These two photographs show the early steps in the permanent destruction of the tropical rain forest— an ecosystem that contains the most abundant life on the planet. First, a road is bulldozed through the virgin forest. Soon thereafter, farmers or ranchers move in and burn the jungle to the ground, destroying all animal habitats and plant life. The newcomers then try to convert the land to agricultural purposes—but within a few years, it becomes barren wasteland, and the farmers move on to repeat the process elsewhere. Despite the luxuriant appearance of the jungle, the soil in these areas is very poor. The rain forest has evolved over 60 million years in such a way that decaying materials are immediately broken down by humidity and fungi and returned to the plants, so virtually all the nutrients are held in the vegetation itself. Once the forest cover is gone, rainfall soon leaches the remaining nutrients from the soil, leaving a moonscape in place of abundant life.*

Drawing by Modell; © 1988 The New Yorker Magazine, Inc.

"Here come the pests."

Actually, there are many practical reasons why human society should protect other life forms. Tropical forests are a stabilizing factor in the global climate, for they absorb vast amounts of atmospheric carbon dioxide. Many plants are medically valuable: most anticancer compounds, for example, come from plants of the rain forest, and this pharmaceutical cornucopia is still mostly untapped. Wild species are a "storehouse" for agricultural scientists who interbreed them with domestic species in order to create more fruitful or hardier strains. Many species among the millions of uncataloged plants will surely prove to be edible, and could become major crops in the future. And the trees and the flowers, the beasts of the field and the fowls of the air, are an aesthetic treasure, capable of delighting our senses and giving us some vision of what we are so carelessly destroying.

There is another argument for protecting other life forms, however, and it has nothing to do with any direct benefit to ourselves. The breathtaking diversity of species has evolved in delicate and precarious balance over many millions of years. Most of the plants and animals with which we share the earth have been here a great deal longer than we have. For a fleeting moment in planetary history, our technology has given us domain over them. In awe, respect, and humility, we might just let them be.

Summary

1. Human ecology refers to the interrelationship between human groups and their natural environment. Rapid population growth in a context of limited resources is one of the most serious social problems in the modern world. Much of this population growth has taken place in urban areas.

2. Demography is the study of population composition and change. The principal factors involved in demographic change are the birth rate, the death rate, and the migration rate. Population growth rate, which is exponential, is also influenced by the age structure of the population concerned.

3. Malthus pointed out that population tends to grow faster than the food supply. This problem has been averted in advanced industrial societies, but now threatens less developed societies, where population has exploded because death rates have declined while birth rates have remained high. In these societies cultural values concerning large families have been slow to change.

4. The theory of demographic transition holds that birth rates will decline once developing societies become more industrialized, but the poorest nations may have great difficulty in reaching an adequate level of industrialization.

5. Despite low birth, death, and growth rates, U.S. population increases will tax natural resources and will place a disproportionate burden on other societies.

6. There are three possible strategies for reducing birth rates: family planning, antinatalism, and economic improvements.

7. A city is a permanent concentration of fairly large numbers of people who do not produce their own food. Urbanization is one of the most significant trends in the modern world. In the less developed countries, cities contain an affluent center surrounded by slums. In fully industrialized societies, cities contain a central city and suburbs, which together form a metropolis. When metropolises merge, they form a megalopolis.

8. The ecological approach attempts to explain the appearance and growth of cities in terms of influences from both the social and natural environment.

9. Classical theories of urban life focused on the drawbacks of city life. Tönnies saw the city as an association rather than a community, and Wirth stressed the impersonality of urban life. Modern theories focus more on the opportunities of city life. Gans sees the city as a mosaic of communities, and Fischer stresses the city's subcultural diversity.

10. The United States is a highly urbanized society, with most people living in metropolitan areas. Suburbs have expanded rapidly and now contain more people than central cities do. The central cities face continuing problems, largely as a result of the flight of middle-class residents and their local tax money to the suburbs.

11. Industrial technology can have dramatic ecological effects. It is leading to extensive pollution of air, water, and land, with disruptive effects on the health of organisms and the climate of the planet. It is also leading to the rapid depletion of resources. Additionally, the combined effects of pollution and habitat destruction are causing a mass extinction of other species.

Important Terms

ecology (349)

human ecology (349)

demography (350)

birth rate (350)

death rate (350)

migration rate (350)

growth rate (350)

doubling time (351)

zero population growth (351)

age structure (352)

developed country (353)

less developed country (353)

demographic transition (354)

urbanization (358)

city (358)

metropolis (360)

megalopolis (360)

community (361)

Gemeinschaft (362)

Gesellschaft (362)

ecosystem (366)

CHAPTER *15*

Social Change

"Everything changes," observed the ancient Greek philosopher Heraclitus. It was he who pointed out that a man cannot step twice into the same river—for he is not quite the same man, nor is it quite the same river. This principle applies to every phenomenon known to us, from the dance of subatomic particles to the expansion of the universe, from the growth and decay of living organisms to the development of individual personality. Societies, as we are only too well aware in the modern world, also change. Yet, although social change is one of the major concerns of sociology, the question of how, why, and in what specific ways societies change remains one of the most intriguing and difficult problems in the discipline.

Social change is the alteration in patterns of culture, social structure, and social behavior over time. No society can successfully prevent change, not even those that try to do so, although some societies are more resistant to change than others. But the rate, nature, and direction of change differ greatly from one society to another. Over the past 200 years, the United States has changed from a predominantly agricultural society into an industrial and then a postindustrial one. In the same period, the society of the BaMbuti Pygmies of the Central African forests has changed hardly at all. Why? What caused the great civilizations of the past to flourish, and what led to their ruin? Why did civilization arise in India long before it appeared in Europe? Why did industrialism emerge in Europe rather than in India? Does social change take place in a haphazard manner, or are recurrent patterns to be found in all societies? Are all human societies moving toward similar social forms and a common destiny, or will they differ in the future as much as they have in the past?

These are important questions, and they are as old as sociology itself. The man who first coined the term "sociology," Auguste Comte, believed that the new science could lay bare the processes of social change and thus make it possible to plan the human future in a rational way. Almost without exception, the most distinguished sociologists of the nineteenth and twentieth centuries have grappled with the problem of social change. As yet, however, sociology has failed to fully meet the challenge. Many theories have been offered, but none has been able to win general acceptance. As Wilbert Moore (1960) comments: "The mention of 'theory of social change' will make most social scientists appear defensive, furtive, guilt-ridden, or frightened."

Why does the study of social change present such problems? One reason is that social change involves not only the past and present, but also the future—and the future, of course, cannot be known with certainty. Indeed, accurate prediction of the future course of history involves an insuperable logical flaw. If we knew what was to happen, we would be able to prevent it from happening—in which case the prediction would be false. A second reason for the difficulty is that social change usually involves a complex of interacting factors—environmental, technological, personal, cultural, political, religious, economic, knowledge to work with, and merely to produce a bow and arrow was a considerable intellectual achievement. We are no cleverer than our "primitive" ancestors; we simply have more knowledge to build on. As Ralph Linton (1936) remarked, "If Einstein had been born into a primitive tribe which was unable to count beyond three, lifelong application to mathematics probably would not have carried him beyond the development of a decimal system based on fingers and toes." Inventions occur exponentially: the more inventions that exist in a culture, the more rapidly further inventions can be made.

Diffusion   **Diffusion** is the spread of cultural elements from one society to another. Diffusion may result from many factors, such as travel, trade, conquest, migration, or telecommunications. Diffusion may involve not only material artifacts like arrows or computers, but also aspects of nonmaterial culture, like norms and values. Ideas, for example, may arise in one cultural context, become "detached" from that context, then have an independent effect in another time or place. For instance, the ban on artificial birth control by the Catholic Church and some other Christian groups stems ultimately from the stern morality of the ancient Israelites. The Israelites were a small tribe, subject to a high infant death rate and surrounded by enemies, so they placed great value on large families. This value was transmitted to early Christianity, and, many centuries later, the "immorality" of artificial birth control became part of the official doctrine of several churches in modern countries where quite different conditions prevail. And this diffusion from the past carries still further potential for social change in the future. For example, in those Catholic countries where condoms are hard to obtain, a vital barrier to the spread of AIDS is lacking. Similarly, religious opposition to birth control is encouraging rapid population growth in impoverished nations in Latin America and elsewhere—thus worsening a problem of overpopulation and poverty that may, in time, lead to other political and economic changes.

Population

Any significant decrease or increase in population size or growth rates may affect or even disrupt social life. A population that grows too slowly or even declines in numbers faces the danger of extinction. A population that grows too large puts impossible demands on resources. The result, as it has so often been in history, may be mass migration, usually resulting in cultural diffusion and sometimes in wars as the migrants invade other territories. Or the result may be upheaval and conflict over scarce resources within the society itself. The problem of population decrease is not one that most societies have to face today, but as we have seen, overpopulation is one of the most pressing social problems in the contemporary world. If global population continues to increase at anything like its current rate, demands for food, living space, and other natural resources may become insupportable. Extensive social changes would follow, including an abrupt population decline as the death rate soars due to malnutrition, disease, and, quite probably, even wars.

Changes in the demographic structure of a population also cause social changes. For example, as the post-World War II "baby boom" generation ages, the United States will become "top heavy" with old people, resulting in still further social changes. Medical science will focus increasingly on the problems of the aged, and geriatrics will become a growth area in medicine. New provision will have to be made for the elderly, probably through an extension of old-age homes and similar facilities. Younger workers may find that an increasing part of what they earn goes in taxes to support the growing ranks of the retired, and funeral homes will enjoy an unprecedented boom.

Technology

A major source of social change is **technology,** the practical applications of scientific or other knowledge. Over the generations, such cultural artifacts as the knife, the wheel, the plow, gunpowder, irrigation, screws, windmills, dams, the compass, clocks, the printing press, steam engines, vaccinations, pesticides, television, rockets, lasers, and nuclear reactors have dramatically influenced our social and sometimes our natural surroundings. Modern civilization depends on our ability to translate knowledge of nature into a multitude of gadgets, contraptions, processes, implements, and techniques: aircraft and antibiotics, computers and plastics, assembly lines and telecommunications, synthetic fabrics and skyscrapers.

Technological Innovation   A recent U.S. Air Force recruitment slogan declares "Technology is taking over the world. Keep up with it or you're going to be left behind." As the slogan correctly implies, technological innovation and social change are intimately connected, particularly in the modern world. The slogan also implies that technological innovation is desirable. Many people in modern societies, in fact, seem to implicitly assume that technological development and human progress are much the same thing. But although some observers see advanced technology as the key to a brighter future, others wonder if it may sometimes be more of a curse than a blessing. Modern technology has certainly offered admirable achievements, but it has also created dismaying problems.

Most technological innovations are based on existing scientific knowledge and technology. The more advanced a society is in this respect, therefore, the faster the pace of technological change is likely to be. And the more rapid the technological change, the more rapid is the social change that it generates. A mere sixty-six years elapsed between the first faltering flight of the Wright

Figure 15.2 *The rate of technological change in modern societies is without precedent. This glider, piloted by Orville Wright, was considered something of a marvel in 1908; the space craft that allowed this astronaut to walk in space is already obsolete. One reason for the rapid pace of technological innovation is that each advance builds on previous ones. The greater the accumulation of technology, therefore, the faster the rate of innovation tends to be.*

3. *Multinational corporations.* A **multinational corporation** is a corporate enterprise which, though headquartered in one country, conducts its operations through subsidiaries that it owns or controls around the world. The less developed countries often welcome the multinationals because they are a source of investment and jobs. Yet their presence has its drawbacks, for these organizations soon develop immense political and economic influence in the host countries. Development becomes concentrated in a few industries that are oriented to the needs of outsiders; profits are frequently exported rather than reinvested; and local benefits go mainly to a small ruling elite whose interests are tied to those of the foreigners rather than to those of their own people.

The world-system model implies that international inequalities can be resolved only if the less developed countries are able to achieve liberation and real autonomy over their destinies. But this model also has some shortcomings. One problem is that some third-world countries are actually industrializing very rapidly. Singapore, Hong Kong, Taiwan, Venezuela, and South Korea, for example, are behaving in the way modernization theory suggests they should—so successfully that some developed countries are considering trade barriers to protect their own industries from this new competition.

It seems that both the modernization and world-system approaches may be valid in certain respects. The modernization model does help us make sense of the historical fact of industrialization and of the various internal adjustments that societies undergo during this process. The world-system model reminds us that countries develop in a context of fierce international political and economic competition—a competition whose outcome favors the stronger parties. In combining aspects of these approaches, we are using the three general theories of social change outlined earlier: sociocultural-evolution theory (to provide the general context for transition to industrialism), functionalist theory (to show how societies maintain stability through modernizing adjustments), and conflict theory (to explain who gets ahead the fastest in world competition for resources).

Revolutions

A **revolution** is the violent overthrow of an existing political or social system. Revolutions are among the most unusual and dramatic of all forms of social change, for they may bring about, often in a fairly short time, a radical reconstruction of the society.

Unlike a **coup d'état**—the restricted use of force to replace one set of leaders with another, usually consisting of military officers—a revolution generally involves mass violence. Sociologists have long been interested in the conditions that give rise to such a situation, and several factors have been identified (Brinton, 1960; B. Moore, 1966, 1979; Gurr, 1970; Davies, 1962, 1971; Skocpol, 1979). If all the following conditions are present, a revolution is a distinct possibility, although not a certainty. Each situation has its own unique characteristics that may affect the chances for revolution to occur.

1. *Widespread grievance.* There must be a widespread awareness that valued resources, such as wealth and power, are unfairly distributed. Unless a large part of the population feels a continuing sense of grievance, a revolution is unlikely.

2. *Rising expectations.* People must be aware that there are alternatives to the existing system. To be poor or oppressed is not in itself sufficient grounds for revolution. If it were, most of the world would be in revolt at this moment, since well over half the global population is impoverished and is denied democratic rights. Revolutions generally occur in the context of rising expectations: people who have accepted the situation in the past must sense that it is their right to have something better in the future.

Figure 15.10 *Of all the various types of social movements, the ones that can have the greatest social impact are revolutionary movements. The revolutionaries in America and in Iran (shown here toppling equestrian statues of, respectively, George III and the shah) radically altered the history and culture of their societies. Many other revolutionary movements, of course, are unsuccessful.*

3. *Blockage of change.* Alternative channels to change must be blocked, and significant groups in society must feel that they have no access to power. Revolutions are more likely if the rulers refuse to accept change or keep the pace of change too slow, while suppressing efforts by other groups to bring about change.

4. *Loss of legitimacy.* Existing political institutions must usually be weak or even on the verge of breakdown. The ruling elite in prerevolutionary situations is often divided. The system is failing to "work," and the legitimacy of the form of government is being eroded, so that the system is maintained by coercion. In many revolutionary situations the government is so weak that prolonged or widespread bloodshed is not needed to bring it down: it frequently collapses at the first push.

5. *Military breakdown.* A breakdown of the state's military apparatus must occur, with the result that the armed forces cannot or will not repress the uprising; frequently, in fact, members of the military change sides and join the rebels. The military is often in a demoralized condition before the revolution breaks out—perhaps because it has been defeated in war, or perhaps because it senses public resentment at its role in maintaining the despised rulers in office. If the military falters, the regime may fall.

Revolutions are almost always led, not by members of the oppressed class, but rather by well-educated members of the middle class. A revolution does not need the support of the majority of the people; it is sufficient if those who support the government are in a minority and most other people are apathetic.

ther would attack the other. However, the United States cannot be said to be at peace with the Soviet Union, because each society has the plans and the means to reduce the other to smoldering rubble within thirty minutes. Rather, these two societies are in a state of hostility, a sort of limbo between peace and war. In fact, the Soviet Union and the United States, which together have less than 11 percent of the world's population, account for 23 percent of its armed forces, 60 percent of its military expenditures, 80 percent of its weapons research, and 97 percent of its nuclear warheads and bombs (Sivard, 1986). Whether their mutual hostility turns to war or peace is perhaps the most vital question affecting the course of global social change—and, indeed, the future of humanity.

Why War?

Since warfare is highly unpleasant for the combatants, why is warfare such a common phenomenon? An answer frequently offered, it seems, is that we humans are naturally warlike. As we noted in Chapter 2 ("Culture"), many people assume that "human nature" includes some kind of an aggressive "instinct," and popular writers have advanced this view widely. Thus Konrad Lorenz (1966), an expert in animal behavior, claimed that humanity shares an aggressive drive with lower animals, and Robert Ardrey (1970), a playwright, argued that we are descended from "killer apes" and so are destined to do battle with one another. An obvious problem with this approach is that one could just as easily make the reverse argument. Most people and societies are *not* at war most of the time—so on this evidence we could say that human nature includes a "peaceful instinct," and that we are destined to cooperate with one another! In fact, we are all capable of both aggression and friendship, war and peace—but we are not biologically driven to them. Some people seem willing to fight, some people do not. Some societies, like the Jalé of New Guinea or the Yanamamö of South America, seem warlike. Other societies seem peaceful: Sweden and Switzerland, for example, have chosen to be neutral and have stayed out of all wars for a century and a half. Human society has survived thus far, not because we are a fundamentally aggressive species, but because we are a fundamentally sociable and cooperative one (Otterbein, 1970, 1973; Montagu, 1973, 1978; Fried, Harris, and Murphy, 1986).

Then why war? The answer is that war occurs as a result of a political decision. There can be no war between nations unless the leaders of at least two societies with conflicting interests decide that they prefer war to any alternative means of settling their differences. The soldiers themselves go to war—frequently not knowing what they are fighting for, and usually terrified of meeting the enemy in battle—because a legitimate political authority is determined on that course of action. War is actually a highly structured social activity. It cannot be sustained without a strong political authority that can persuade or even force people to risk their lives for a purpose beyond themselves (Barnet, 1970; Falk and Kim, 1980).

Many factors may influence the decision to go to war—the personalities of the leaders; the influence of nationalist, religious, or other ideologies; the extent of popular support for war; the anticipated economic gains or losses; the ambitions or advice of the military; perceptions or misperceptions of the other side's motives and intentions; the expected reaction of the international community; and, of course, expectations about the likely outcome of the conflict. But one factor that seems particularly likely to encourage war is preparations for it. A military build-up by country X may make country Y feel threatened, leading Y to begin a defensive build-up. Country X perceives the new build-up as a hostile move and increases its armaments, proving to Y that its suspicions about X were right all along and that more arms are needed—and so on. In general, militarized nations tend to fight with other militarized nations, and countries that prepare for war tend to become engaged in war (Naroll, 1966; Blainey, 1973; Wallace, 1979). At times, however, even countries that are totally unprepared for war find themselves in one.

Development of War

The history of war is largely the story of the development of ever more technologically advanced weapons and the means of delivering them. The first weapons were rocks, clubs, spears, and swords, wielded or thrown by human beings. Gradually, ways were found to strike further, more accurately, and with greater force—with slings, catapults, bows and arrows, crossbows. The invention of gunpowder and similar explosives led to the musket, the rifle, the cannon, the grenade, the bomb. These weapons were mounted on land vehicles, ships, and eventually aircraft. Today, missiles can travel thousands of miles from one continent to another and deliver their warheads with an accuracy that can be measured in feet and seconds. Ever since weapons first appeared on the scene, defenses have also evolved in such forms as shields, armor, fortresses, antiaircraft guns, electronic jamming devices, antimissile missiles, and so on. One effect of innovations in military technology is to make killing—even mass killing—impersonal. A few centuries ago, war meant soldiers physically attacking one another. Today, a handful of people can obliterate a city thousands of miles away by deciding to push a button or turn a key.

Figure 15.11 The history of warfare is marked by constant technological developments that have greatly extended the range and destructive force of weaponry. The first illustration shows an assault on a fifteenth-century city in France. The second illustration captures the "star wars" imagery of weapons systems that are being planned for the new century.

Over the centuries, the number of people involved in, and killed by, warfare has also increased dramatically. Alexander the Great set out to conquer the world as he knew it with an army of less than 40,000 men. William the Conqueror invaded England with 50,000 men. The Napoleonic Wars involved hundreds of thousands of soldiers. In the American Civil War, nearly 2 million men were under arms. During World War I, some 65 million troops were mobilized, and 19 million people were killed. The carnage of that pointless and dreadful conflict so stunned the world that people called it "the war to end all wars," for they knew humanity would never commit such folly again. World War II followed a mere twenty-one years later—and this time, almost 100 million people took up arms, and an estimated 38 million soldiers and civilians were killed. All told in this century, there have been over forty wars that resulted in 100,000 deaths or more, with a total loss of life of about 84 million people (see the table on the next page). Today, the major powers maintain huge standing armies, even though they are not at war. The United States has 2.2 million people in its armed forces, the Soviet Union has 3.8 million, and China has over 4 million. Of course, in nuclear war, the size of armies would be irrelevant, for the entire civilian populations of the countries concerned would be brought into the arena of battle—along with much of the rest of the world's population.

To a visitor from another planet, it would seem that the modern world is obsessed with preparation for "defense" (it is never called "offense"). Many countries spend more of their budgets for military purposes than they do for education or medical care. Altogether, the international military establishment employs an estimated 100 million people. Over the past thirty years, global spending for military purposes has consumed more than $15 trillion (that is, $15,000,000,000,000). This represents a colossal diversion of funds from socially useful goals: for example, three hours' worth of these expenditures would suffice to save, through immunization, the 3.5 million children around the world who die each year from preventable infectious diseases (Sivard, 1987).

Superpower Hostility

The United States and the Soviet Union—the two greatest powers the world has ever known—confront one another with suspicion and hostility. This fact is not particularly surprising. Powerful nations are often rivals, for the simple reason that they frequently have conflicting goals within a common sphere of influence. The hostility between the two contemporary superpowers is greatly increased, however, by the fact that they also represent quite different ways of life. Although both societies claim to offer the best hope for the human future, the Soviet Union is a totalitarian society that advocates communism, while the United States is a democratic society that advocates capitalism.

Whenever two societies are in a state of hostility, each tends to "demonize" the other—that is, to attribute all manner of wickedness to the opposing side. For example, Iranians tend to demonize Iraqis, and Iraqis tend to demonize Iranians; Israelis tend to demonize Syrians, and Syrians tend to demonize Israelis. What is often striking to outside observers is the similarity of each side's images of the other. Thus, the United States and the Soviet Union both view their own country as peace-loving and the other country as war-mongering. Each nation believes the other is liable to start a major war, and each claims to build up its own military defenses to forestall the other's aggression. Each society claims that the other seeks world domination, in the form of either communist "enslavement" or capitalist "exploitation." Each country charges the other with trying to enforce its political will on its immediate neighbors, and of unjustified meddling in distant lands. Each sees the other side as unreasonable, untrustworthy, and fundamentally treacherous. Relying on fragments of limited information from their schools and mass media, the peoples of both countries think of each other largely in terms of negative stereotypes (Shipler, 1985).

Figure 15.12 *This table gives some idea of the appalling loss of life that has occurred through war in the twentieth century. The table lists only major conflicts; if the death toll in minor wars were also included, the total number of fatalities would probably be about 100 million—and the century is by no means over yet.*

Twentieth-Century Wars With Deaths of 100,000 or More

Location	Date	Identification of Conflict	Deaths
Latin America			
Bolivia	1932–35	Paraguay vs Bolivia	200,000
Columbia	1949–62	"La Violencia"; civil war	300,000
Mexico	1910–20	Liberals & Radicals vs Govt.	250,000
Europe			
Greece	1945–49	Civil war; UK intervening	160,000
Poland	1919–20	USSR vs Poland	100,000
Spain	1936–39	Civil war; Italy, Portugal & Germany intervening	1,200,000
Turkey	1915	Armenians deported	1,000,000
USSR	1904–05	Japan vs Russia	130,000
	1918–20	Civil war; Allied intervention	1,300,000
Europe and Other			
	1914–18	World War I	19,617,000
	1939–45	World War II	38,351,000
Middle East			
Iraq	1961–70	Civil war; massacres	105,000
	1982–88	Iran attack following Iraq invasion	1,000,000
Lebanon	1975–76	Civil war; Syria intervening	100,000
Yemen, AR	1962–69	Coup; civil war; Egypt intervening	101,000
South Asia			
Afghanistan	1978–88	Civil war; USSR intervening	500,000
Bangladesh	1971	Bengalis vs Pak; India invad.; famine & massacres	1,500,000
India	1946–48	Muslims vs Hindus; UK intervening; massacres	800,000
Far East			
Cambodia	1970–75	Civil war; NV, US intervening	156,000
	1975–78	Pol Pot Govt. vs people; famine and massacres	2,000,000
China	1928	Muslim rebellion vs Govt.	200,000
	1930–35	Civil war	500,000
	1937–41	Japan vs China	1,800,000
	1946–50	Civil war	1,000,000
	1950–51	Govt. executes landlords	1,000,000
	1956–59	Tibetan revolt	100,000
Indonesia	1965–66	Abortive coup; massacres	500,000
	1975–80	Annexation of East Timor; famine & massacres	100,000
Korea	1950–53	Korean War; UN intervening	2,889,000
Vietnam	1945–54	War of independence from France	600,000
	1960–65	Civil war; US intervening	300,000
	1965–75	Peak of Indo-China War; US bombing	2,058,000
Africa			
Algeria	1954–62	Civil war; France intervening	320,000
Burundi	1972	Hutu vs Govt.; massacres	100,000
Ethiopia	1974–88	Eritrean revolt and famine	545,000
Mozambique	1981–88	Famine worsened by civil war	400,000
Nigeria	1967–70	Civil war; famine & massacres	2,000,000
Rwanda	1956–65	Tutsis vs Govt.; massacres	108,000
Sudan	1963–72	Christians vs Arab Govt.; massacres	300,000
Tanzania	1905–07	Revolt against Germany; massacres	150,000
Uganda	1971–78	Civil war, Idi Amin coup; massacres	300,000
	1981–85	Army vs people; massacres	102,000
Zaire	1960–65	Katanga secession; UK, Belgium intervening	100,000
			84,342,000

Source: Adapted from Ruth Leger Sivard, *World Military and Social Expenditures 1987–1988* (Washington, D.C.: World Priorities, 1988).

nuclear weapons. Over the next two decades, a sizable number of other countries will have the ability to make nuclear bombs, including such nations as Libya, Iran, and North Korea—three nations whose current leaders are often viewed in the West as lunatics. Once there are enough nuclear powers in the world, it may become possible for one of them to use a warhead on another country anonymously. For example, a fanatical leader of a minor nation could launch a nuclear cruise missile from a fishing vessel at the capital city of a major power. Additionally, the proliferation of nuclear weapons greatly increases the probability that terrorists will eventually capture a bomb and use it to threaten a major power in pursuit of their goals (Meyer, 1984).

Nuclear war could also begin by accident—say, by the misfiring of a missile, particularly in a time of crisis. Actually, there have been at least thirty-two serious nuclear-weapon accidents involving American planes, missiles, or vessels, including some in which nuclear bombs crashed to the ground unexploded or were lost at sea. The Soviet Union has doubtless had accidents of its own, but few details are known (Cox, 1977). More worrisome is the possibility that war may break out as a result of false alarms, of which there have been many American (and no doubt Soviet) instances over the years. During the 1950s, a flock of Canadian geese picked up by radar led Americans to believe that a Soviet bomber attack was under way. In 1960, a meteor shower was interpreted as an assault by enemy missiles. In 1961, an early-warning station misinterpreted a moon echo as a launch against the United States, and in response American bombers flew off toward Russia for two hours before being recalled. In 1978, a technician inadvertently loaded a war-games tape into an operational system, causing a Soviet missile attack to be displayed at the American Strategic Air Command. In 1980, a 46-cent computer chip failed, and led to a warning of a submarine strike on the American mainland. In each case, the error was caught in time, thanks to cross-checking and the human element that is built into the warning system (Wicker, 1982).

The Effects of Nuclear War

In an all-out war, the nuclear powers would strike at targets of military, economic, and industrial significance. Because so many of these targets are in or near urban areas, many or most of the large cities in both societies would be hit by nuclear warheads. The immediate effects on these populated areas would depend in part on the number and power of the striking warheads. For simplicity's sake, let us consider the effects primarily in terms of a single (and relatively small) 1-megaton explosion. Such an explosion would destroy or flatten most structures within about five miles of ground zero, the point of explosion. The radiant heat from the explosion would ignite most flammable material, including oil- and gas-storage facilities, within five miles of ground zero, and the light from the bomb could cause temporary flash blindness to observers as much as fifty miles away. The "fallout radiation," consisting of particles of debris carried up in the mushroom cloud and made radioactive by the explosion, is a poison that can be eaten, breathed, or absorbed through the skin. Some of the fallout returns to earth within minutes and lands close to ground zero, but much of it is carried away in a plume downwind of the explosion. This fallout may remain in the atmosphere for days, weeks, months, or even years until it settles to earth or is brought down by rain.

In short, the immediate effects of a single 1-megaton nuclear bomb would be the social and physical destruction of the affected area and the pulverizing, broiling, and irradiating of many or most of the inhabitants. In practice, major cities might be hit by 20 or more megatons in the course of a full-scale nuclear war. What would be the aftermath for any who survived?

Figure 15.15 *A nuclear explosion has several immediate effects on the surrounding area. First, a blinding flash, a wave of radiant heat, an electromagnetic pulse, and a burst of lethal radiation all travel from ground zero at the speed of light. A moment later, a violent blast wave spreads out, crushing and flattening objects in its path. Combustible materials in the area burst into flame, and separate fires can merge into major conflagrations. Finally, radioactive particles are carried up into the atmosphere.*

Moments after an all-out attack, somewhere in the region of 80 million Americans would be dead, and about 50 million more would die during the next few weeks, primarily as a result of injuries, burns, radiation sickness, disease, starvation, and exposure to the elements. The Soviet Union, which is a less urbanized society with a more dispersed population, would probably suffer a somewhat lower number of deaths. In all likelihood, many tens of millions more would be dead in the countries of Eastern and Western Europe. In addition to the loss of life, the attack would profoundly damage both the physical and the social structure of the target societies (Schell, 1982; Katz, 1982; Tucker and Gleisner, 1982).

The first psychological response to nuclear attack, if the experience of Hiroshima is anything to go by, would be profound shock. The familiar world would be gone—relatives and friends dead or missing, homes destroyed, city centers vaporized, services and power sources lacking, nearly all social values stripped of their meaning. In a study of the aftermath of the Hiroshima bombing, Robert Lifton (1967) found that the survivors did not panic. Rather, they seemed emotionless: they simply moved, slowly and dully, away from the center of the destruction, many of them seeming to be walking in a dream, as though they were not really alive. Lifton suggests that this reaction was simply a closing of the mind to prevent the surrounding horror from penetrating it. The human response to such a grotesque scene of death and destruction is not rage, panic, depression, fear, or mourning, but merely mental paralysis.

"In my plan, the atomic bomb is used only for emphasis."

there can be no certainty of victory. On the other hand, if one of the parties gains (or appears to be gaining) superiority, war becomes more likely—either because the superior power is tempted to take advantage of its position, or because the inferior one is tempted to strike before its own position deteriorates further. As a matter of historical fact, that is precisely the situation that precipitated many wars of this century, most notably World War I (Diehl, 1985).

Additionally, the arms race introduces instability into the balance of power, for each new weapon or defense seems to offer one side or the other a chance to gain or maintain some temporary advantage. In practice, therefore, reliance on nuclear deterrence means a continuation of the arms race and the constant threat of annihilation. Nuclear weapons do not guarantee that war cannot happen—only that it will be calamitous if it does. The obsessive focus on the threat of weapons as the way to avoid war also blinds us to the central question: Is *anything* that the Soviet Union or the United States values so important that it justifies risking the destruction of both societies, the murder of hundreds of millions of people, and the jeopardizing of our very species?

Arms Control

An alternative to deterrence based on a continuing arms race, therefore, is **arms control**—mutually agreed limitations on the nature, numbers, and uses of weapons and defenses. But for arms control to be successful, certain conditions must be met. First, both sides have to be willing to give up the possibility of gaining further advantages over the other in their military technology. Second, both sides must trust one another sufficiently to enter the agreement at all—and trust is in short supply between any contending powers, as a result of their tendency to demonize the other side as villainous, evil, and treacherous. So a third condition is needed, in the form of some means of verifying that the other side is indeed keeping its word, and not illicitly hoarding old weapons or developing new ones. In the past, various spying techniques, notably satellite reconnaissance, made it easy for both superpowers to count submarines as they were built or land-based missiles as they were installed in their silos. But today, the construction of thousands of small, mobile, and easily hidden cruise missiles is making accurate inspection and verification exceedingly difficult—providing yet another example of how military technologies may create more problems than they solve.

Despite the difficulties, a number of significant arms-control treaties have already been achieved. Many countries, including the United States and the Soviet Union, have signed multilateral agreements restricting the testing, spread, and potential use of nuclear weapons. Of course, a treaty is only as good as the willingness of each party to abide by it, in letter and in spirit. That willingness is influenced by the prevailing attitudes in Washington and Moscow, and both countries have adopted a ''hard line'' at different times. The Reagan administration accelerated the arms race in the hopes of gaining superiority over the Soviet Union. In particular, President Reagan called for the construction of a complex and costly ''star wars'' missile defense system. During the same period, the Soviet Union under Mikhail Gorbachev was unusually conciliatory. The Soviet leader has even called for the elimination of all nuclear weapons by the end of the century. Eventually, in 1988, the two leaders signed a treaty to eliminate a large stock of short- and medium-range missiles. However, these missiles represented only a tiny fraction of the warheads available to the superpowers, and both began to redeploy other weapons to replace those that were being dismantled. Even so, the treaty marked a significant step away from war and toward peace.

Disarmament

Ideally, successful experience of arms control would eventually lead toward **disarmament,** or the steady reduction in the nature, numbers, and uses of weapons and defenses. In effect, disarmament means putting the arms race into reverse. If the process were to occur, it would almost certainly be a gradual one—partly because so much money is currently spent on military purposes that rapid disarmament would jolt the economies of the superpowers and indeed of the world, and partly because disarmament requires increasing trust between the parties involved. In all probability, therefore, the process would begin with a freeze on the manufacture and deployment of nuclear weapons; then, if tension eased and a climate of trust developed, existing bombs, warheads, and delivering systems would be scrapped in a series of carefully verified stages.

The prospect of the United States and the Soviet Union getting rid of all or most of their nuclear weapons may seem remote. But it is not impossible, for neither country has much to gain from the alternative—continued diversion of economic and human resources into an ever more costly and indefinitely prolonged arms race. Again, a major stumbling block to disarmament is the issue of trust, for each country finds it difficult to believe that the other would really abandon its supposed ambitions for ''world domination.'' Americans, for example, are generally unaware of just how threatened the Soviet government and people feel. After all, the Soviet Union is a much less affluent and technologically advanced society than the United States, and so is worse equipped to prepare for war. Worldwide, the Soviet Union has far fewer allies—and far fewer military bases—than the United States. Moreover, the Soviet Union suffers the particular disadvantage of having to maintain a huge army to protect its long border with its unfriendly neighbor, China. And whereas the United States has only one nuclear enemy, the Soviet Union faces missiles pointed at it by every other nuclear power in the world—the United States, Great Britain, France, and China. And the Soviet Union's sense of menace is further increased by the fact that its principal enemy is the only nation in the world that has ever used nuclear weapons.

"It's a great treaty, but do we trust us?"

International Peace-Making

An important element in any peace process is the international community and its mechanisms for restraining conflict among its members. Trade, travel, and telecommunications have made the nations of the modern world more interdependent than ever before. Yet today's societies entered the nuclear age with political institutions inherited from a previous era. The human population is spread among a series of sovereign independent states—most of them with their own armed forces—and so there is a built-in potential for warfare whenever two nations have conflicting interests. Before the twentieth century, there were few institutionalized ways for hostile nations to achieve peaceful settlements. Today, the structure of international peace-making is still rudimentary, but it offers infinitely better prospects for helping nations to avoid war.

Particularly in a world where all nations face a common threat of direct or indirect involvement in nuclear warfare, some reliable method is needed to limit conflicts among sovereign states. If we anticipate that some benign and fair "world government" will take on the task, we are likely to be disappointed; but if we look for progress along that continuum that runs from war to peace, the prospects are much more encouraging. Already, two vital elements for international peace-making are in place. The first is the United Nations, which provides a forum for world opinion and a mechanism for conflict resolution. The second is a growing body of international law that specifies the rights and obligations that nations have toward one another—particularly with respect to aggression. Over the years, the United Nations has intervened successfully in a number of wars (for example, in Korea and in the Middle East) and in several situations that might have led to war (for example, in the superpower crises involving Cuba and Berlin).

A major difficulty with international peace-making, of course, is that compliance with the resolutions of the United Nations and the rulings of its World Court are voluntary, for no country is willing to surrender its sovereignty to an international body. The United Nations is most effective, in fact, when both superpowers are able to agree on a course of action and mobilize their blocs to support it. Even so, the organization provides an influential forum for world opinion, and, while it does not always prevent war, it surely helps make it less likely.

Collective Action

Ultimately, the prospects for peace depend on the collective action of ordinary people. This may seem paradoxical at first, for individuals often feel powerless in the face of distant governments and mighty arsenals. Yet if sociology has a central lesson, it is that societies, together with all the social institutions and social behavior they contain, are continuously created and re-created by the acts of countless individuals, whether these individuals realize their role in the grand sweep of history or not. If a modern society goes to war, it is not just because the leaders have opted for war, but because the people have implicitly or explicitly done so also—or at least, they have not opted for peace. In the United States the public actually places informal, unspoken restraints on the ability of the leaders to wage war. For example, although the United States has tactical nuclear weapons that it could have used in local conflicts such as the Korean and Vietnam wars, it has not employed these devices—primarily because such a resort to nuclear weapons would be unacceptable and immoral to the American people. Similar restraints operate in other countries, although they are felt most strongly in democracies.

As we noted earlier, historically significant change is often brought about by the organized efforts of social movements. National and international movements that demand the elimination of nuclear weaponry are now a persistent feature of the Western world. In 1982, for example, more than 2 million Americans signed a petition calling for a nuclear freeze, and resolutions endorsing the proposal were passed by hundreds of town meetings and at least one legislature in each of twenty-three American states. Often, significant pressure for peace comes from the acts of a handful of individuals. In 1981, an American doctor and a Russian doctor founded International Physicians for the Prevention of War, a group that focuses on the medical consequences of nuclear warfare. Within five years, the organization had over 150,000 members in forty-nine countries, and it had won a Nobel prize for peace. Similarly, a small group of Japanese activists conceived the idea of "nuclear free zones"—places that formally refuse to allow nuclear weapons inside their boundaries. Within a few years, nineteen countries had explicitly prohibited the presence of nuclear weapons on their soil, and more than 3,400 communities—cities, counties, and provinces—in twenty-four countries had declared themselves "nuclear free" (Bentley, 1984).

None of these movements, however, has achieved any lasting success. One reason is that they are largely restricted to the Western world. There is no antiwar movement in the Soviet Union that can freely campaign against government policies, so Westerners are discouraged by the lack of visible evidence that the Soviet people also want peace, or can pressure their government into searching for it. But in this respect, the unfolding of sociocultural evolution offers good grounds for hope. As we noted in Chapter 3 ("Society"), the Soviet Union is still an industrial society, not a postindustrial one. As the Soviet Union attempts to

Figure 15.16 *Two decades ago, the United States underwent the highly traumatic experience of an ugly and apparently pointless war in Vietnam. The end of the war was greatly hastened by an antiwar movement that included large numbers of young people, particularly college students.*

achieve a transition to a postindustrial economy, the leadership increasingly has to tolerate the free flow of ideas and information—particularly through computers and telecommunications—that is the lifeblood of a postindustrial economy. Already the new Soviet leadership is eliminating many controls over dissidents and the media, in an effort to create greater *glasnost,* or "openness." This trend does not mean that the Soviet Union will soon become democratized in the Western sense—but once the faucet of liberty is opened, it could prove exceedingly difficult to shut off, and the Soviet Union could be irrevocably embarked on a course that would give its people a greater say in their own destiny.

A striking example of collective action to stop war occurred during the 1960s, when the United States became embroiled in the longest and most humiliating military conflict in its history. Vietnam was involved in civil war between the north, ruled by communists, and the south, ruled by an undemocratic regime that called for American help. Determined to "fight communism," the United States stumbled into an obscure but vicious conflict on behalf of peasants who seemed largely indifferent to the outcome of the fighting and to America's ideology. At first, American public opinion gave patriotic support to the war. But as the nation became more deeply involved, the Vietnam war became a quagmire that drained its energy, strength, credibility, treasure, and blood. As casualties mounted and troops became more demoralized, the war began to tear American society apart, dividing neighbor from neighbor, friend from friend, family members from one another. Some sons volunteered for war, some were drafted, some became conscientious objectors, some evaded the draft by going into hiding or fleeing the country. Those who fought and those who refused to fight branded each other with such names as traitor, brute, coward, dupe. Altogether, more than 2 million young Americans went to this unfamiliar place to fight an unwanted war for uncertain ends. Some 57,000 of them were killed, and about 300,000 wounded. To some extent, the war divides Americans still, but there is now a general consensus that, somehow, a terrible mistake was made. The memory of that mistake places an informal social restraint on American leaders, for there is intense public resistance to any prospect of "another Vietnam" in the jungles of Central American or anywhere else.

The Vietnam war came to an end largely as a result of the antiwar movement, a social movement that consisted disproportionately of young people, including many college students. When the antiwar movement first challenged the war, it received little support from politicians or the press, and its goals seemed almost hopeless. But the tide of public opinion gradually began to shift. In the 1968 presidential primaries, an antiwar candidate backed by student volunteers did unexpectedly well and President Johnson decided not to run for reelection. From that point on, political debate on the war focused not on how to stay in it, but on how to get out of it. Through collective action, ordinary people with few resources other than their own determination had changed a national consensus for war to a national consensus for peace.

A fundamental insight of sociology is that once people no longer take their world for granted, but instead understand the social authorship of their lives and futures, they can become an irresistible force in history. Whether we choose to destroy our civilization or save it is a collective decision—and it is one that may well be made within the lifetimes of most readers of this book. If more and more nuclear weapons are built, and if more sophisticated means of delivering them are devised, and if more and more nations get control of these vile devices, then we surely risk our own destruction. If ways are found to reverse that process, then we can divert unprecedented energy and resources to the real problems that face us, including poverty, disease, overpopulation, injustice, oppression, and the devastation of our natural environment. We may hope and trust that our ultimate choice will be to enhance the life on the bright and lovely planet on which all five billion of us share our adventure.

Summary

1. Social change is the alteration in patterns of culture, social structure, and social behavior over time. The process is universal but occurs at different rates and in different ways. Social change is difficult to analyze because it involves so many factors, including future unknowns.

2. Some specific sources of change are the influences of the physical environment; cultural innovation, which takes the forms of discovery, invention, and diffusion; population dynamics, such as population growth; technology, which generates changes in culture and society, sometimes causing a culture lag; and social movements, in which large numbers of people work together to bring out change.

3. The most useful general theories of change are sociocultural-evolution theory, functionalist theory, and conflict theory. Early evolutionary theory was faulty, but modern sociocultural-evolution theory helps explain the evolution of societies from simple to more complex forms. Functionalist theory focuses mainly on social order, but Parsons saw change as a process by which the social equilibrium is altered so that a new equilibrium results. Conflict theorists see competition and tension as intrinsic to society and as the main source of social change. Marx emphasized class conflict, but later theorists have focused on social conflict in general. Taken together, the theories can help explain various aspects of change.

4. The societies of the world may be roughly divided into developed countries and less developed countries, according to their degree of industrialization and economic growth. The modernization model explains development as a process of diffusion of certain characteristics from the developed to the less developed societies. The world-system model explains differences in development as a result of global patterns of inequality and exploitation.

7. Revolutions are rare events, generally requiring several preconditions: widespread grievance, rising expectations, blockage of change, loss of legitimacy, and military breakdown. During this century the United States, fearing communist influence, has generally opposed revolutions.

8. War is a social phenomenon that has social causes. The development of war has been marked by increasingly sophisticated weapons that involve an ever larger population in the arena of conflict.

9. Today the United States and the Soviet Union are hostile superpowers that are embarked on an arms race in which each side tries to gain temporary superiority. The arms race is driven by both international factors and by a domestic linkage between industry and the military.

10. Nuclear strategy has long been based on the concept of mutually assured destruction. New weapons, however, may encourage either side to contemplate limited use of nuclear weapons, or even a major strike at the opponent's missiles. Nuclear war is possible: through deliberate calculation, through miscalculation, through superpower involvement in local conflicts, through proliferation or even terrorism, and through error or accident. A nuclear explosion causes highly destructive immediate effects. Long-term effects would place the survival of the affected societies in jeopardy, and perhaps endanger the species itself.

11. There are various prospects for peace: continued reliance on nuclear deterrence; arms control; disarmament; international peace-making; and collective action by concerned citizens.

Important Terms

social change (375)

discovery (377)

invention (377)

diffusion (378)

technology (379)

technological fix (380)

automation (381)

technological determinism (381)

culture lag (382)

collective behavior (382)

social movement (382)

resource mobilization (382)

sociocultural evolution (386)

developed country (390)

less developed country (390)

modernization (391)

world system (393)

neocolonialism (393)

multinational corporation (394)

revolution (394)

coup d'état (394)

war (397)

peace (397)

arms race (402)

military-industrial complex (402)

arms control (410)

disarmament (411)

Glossary

Absolute deprivation The inability to afford minimal standards of food, clothing, shelter, and health care.

Achieved status One that depends to some extent on characteristics over which the individual has some control.

Acute disease One of short duration; generally the victim either recovers or dies.

Adultery Sexual relations involving partners at least one of whom is married to someone else.

Ageism The belief that one age category is in some respects inferior to other age categories and that unequal treatment of them is therefore justified.

Age structure The relative proportions of different age categories in a population.

Agents of socialization Significant individuals, groups, or institutions that provide structured situations in which socialization takes place.

Aggregate A collection of people who happen to be in the same place at the same time, such as the passengers in a bus or a crowd in a street.

Agricultural society A society relying for its subsistence primarily on the cultivation of crops through the use of plows and draft animals.

Alienation The situation in which people lose their control over the social world they have created, with the result that they find themselves "alien" in a hostile social environment.

Animism A type of religion that recognizes active, animate spirits operating in the world.

Anomie A condition of confusion that exists in both individual and society when social norms are weak, absent, or conflicting.

Applied research Systematic inquiry that tries to find practical uses for existing knowledge.

Arms control Mutually agreed limitations on the nature, numbers, and uses of weapons and defenses.

Arms race A process in which each side continually attempts to gain or maintain superiority in weaponry.

Art Unique, skilled, and creative cultural products intended to inspire or entertain.

Ascribed status One that is attached to people on grounds over which they have no control.

Authoritarianism A form of government in which the rulers tolerate little or no public opposition, and generally cannot be removed from office by legal means.

Authoritarian personality A distinctive set of traits, centering on conformity, intolerance, and insecurity.

Authority The form of power whose legitimacy is recognized by those to whom it is applied.

Automation The replacement of workers by nonhuman means of production.

Basic research Systematic inquiry that is concerned with establishing new knowledge.

Bias The tendency, often unconscious, to interpret facts according to one's own values.

Bilateral system One in which descent and inheritance are traced through both sides of the family.

Birth rate The annual number of births per thousand members of a population.

Bisexuality Sexual orientation toward both sexes.

Bureaucracy A hierarchical authority structure that operates under explicit rules and procedures.

Bystander apathy The reluctance of people to "get involved" in an apparent emergency affecting a stranger in public.

Capitalism An economic system in which the means of production and distribution are privately owned.

Case study A complete and detailed record of an event, group, or social process.

Caste system A closed form of social stratification in which status is determined by birth and is lifelong.

Category A number of people who may never have met each other but who share similar characteristics, such as age, race, or sex.

Charismatic authority A type of authority in which power is legitimated by the unique and remarkable qualities that people attribute to a specific leader.

Chronic disease One of long duration; the victim may not die, but usually does not recover.

City A permanent concentration of relatively large numbers of people who do not produce their own food.

Class consciousness An objective awareness of the lower stratum's common plight and interests as an oppressed group.

Classless society One with no economically based strata.

Class system An open form of stratification based primarily on economic statuses, which may be subject to change.

Coercion The form of power whose legitimacy is denied by those to whom it is applied.

Cohort A category of people who are born during the same period, such as a period of one, five, or ten years.

Collective behavior Relatively spontaneous social action that occurs when people try to work out common responses to ambiguous situations.

Colonialism The formal political and economic domination of one nation by a more powerful nation: in effect, the subordinate country is "owned" by the dominant one.

Communism A hypothetical egalitarian political and economic system in which the means of production and distribution would be communally owned.

Community A social group with a common territorial base and a sense of shared interests and "belonging."

Conflict perspective A view of society that focuses on social processes of tension, competition, and change.

Contagion theory An explanation of crowd behavior as a loss of individuality resulting from the infectious spread of emotion and action through the group.

Control group The subjects in an experiment who are exposed to all the experimental conditions except the independent variable.

Controls Ways of excluding the possibility that some other factors might be influencing the relationship between two variables.

Control theory An approach that explains deviance as the outcome of a failure of social control.

Convergence theory The hypothesis that the similar problems faced by capitalist and socialist societies may influence their evolution toward a common ultimate form.

Corporation A legally recognized organization whose existence, powers, and liabilities are separate and distinct from those of its owners or employees.

Corrections The sanctions and other measures that society applies to convicted criminals—in the United States, primarily imprisonment, probation, and parole.

Correlation A relationship between two variables that occurs regularly.

Counterculture A subculture whose values, norms, and lifestyle are fundamentally at odds with the dominant culture.

Coup d'état The restricted use of force to replace one set of leaders with another, usually consisting of military officers.

Crime An act that contravenes a law.

Crowd A temporary collection of people who are in close enough proximity to interact with one another.

Cult A loosely organized religious movement that is independent of the religious tradition of the surrounding society.

Cultural anthropology The study of the ways of life of other peoples, particularly in small-scale, traditional societies.

Cultural deprivation Deficiencies in home, family, and neighborhood background that hinder the ability to compete in the larger culture.

Cultural integration The tendency for norms, values, beliefs, practices, and other characteristics to complement one another.

Cultural relativism The recognition that one culture cannot be arbitrarily judged by the standards of another.

Cultural-transmission theory An approach that explains deviance as behavior that is learned in the same way as conformity—through interaction with other people.

Cultural universals Practices that are found in every society.

Culture An entire way of life.

Culture lag A delay between a change in material culture and the adjustment of nonmaterial culture to the change.

Death rate Annual number of deaths per thousand members of a population.

Democracy A form of government in which it is recognized that ultimate authority belongs to the people, who have the right to participate in the decision-making process and to appoint and dismiss their rulers.

Democratic socialism A political and economic system that aims to preserve individual freedom in the context of social equality achieved through a centrally planned economy.

Demographic transition The tendency for birth rates to drop and population to stabilize once a society has achieved a certain level of economic development.

Demography The study of the size, composition, distribution, and changes in human population.

Denomination One of two or more well-established, relatively tolerant religious organizations that claim the allegiance of a substantial part of the population.

Dependent variable A variable that is influenced by another variable—in other words, it is affected.

Detached observation A method in which the researcher remains as aloof as possible, and the subjects may not even know they are being studied.

Developed country A highly industrialized and comparatively affluent society.

Deviance Behavior that violates significant social norms and is disapproved by large numbers of people as a result.

Differential association Social relationships oriented toward particular types of people, such as criminals, through which deviant behavior is learned.

Diffusion The spread of cultural elements from one culture to another.

Disarmament The steady reduction in the nature, numbers, and uses of weapons and defenses.

Discovery A new perception of an aspect of reality that already exists.

Discrimination Unequal treatment of people on the grounds of their group membership.

Disease An objective pathology of the body, such as an infection.

Division of labor The specialization by individuals or groups in particular economic activities.

Double standard An unspoken expectation that restrictive rules of sexual conduct should be applied strictly to women, but leniently to men.

Doubling time The period it takes for a population to double its numbers.

Dramaturgy A method of analyzing social interaction as though the participants were actors on a stage.

Dyad A group containing two people.

Dysfunction A negative consequence that may disrupt the social system.

Ecclesia A religious organization that claims the membership of everyone in a society or even in several societies.

Ecological approach One that analyzes social and cultural elements in the context of the total environment in which a society exists.

Ecology The science of the relationship between living organisms and their environments.

Economic system The institutionalized system for producing and distributing goods and services.

Ecosystem A self-sustaining community of organisms within its natural environment.

Education The systematic, formalized transmission of knowledge, skills, and values.

Egalitarian marriage A system in which the husband and wife have a more or less equal say in family matters.

Emergent-norms theory An explanation of crowd behavior as the result of norms that arise in the course of social interaction among crowd members.

Endemic disease One that is always present in a large part of a population.

Endogamy Marriage within the same social category.

Epidemic disease One affecting a significant part of a population in which it is normally uncommon.

Epidemiology The study of the origin, distribution, and means of transmission of disease in populations.

Ethnic group A category of people who, as a result of their shared cultural heritage, are regarded as socially distinct.

Ethnocentrism The tendency to judge other cultures by the standards of one's own.

Ethnography An anthropological report about some aspects of a people's way of life.

Ethnomethodology The study of how people construct and share their definitions of reality in their everyday interactions.

Exchange mobility Changes in people's social statuses as they exchange places with one another at different levels of the hierarchy.

Exogamy Marriage outside a particular social category.

Experiment A method for studying the relationship between two variables under carefully controlled conditions.

Experimental group The subjects in an experiment who are exposed to the independent variable.

Expressive leadership The kind of leadership necessary to create harmony and solidarity among group members.

Extended family One in which more than two generations of the same kinship line live together.

Fad A temporary form of conduct that is followed enthusiastically by large numbers of people.

False consciousness A subjective understanding of one's situation that does not accord with the objective facts.

Family A relatively permanent group of people related by ancestry, marriage, or adoption, who live together, form an economic unit, and take care of their young.

Family of orientation The family into which we are born.

Family of procreation The family that we create ourselves.

Fashion A currently valued style of appearance and behavior.

Fecundity The potential number of children that could be born to a woman of childbearing age.

Fertility The actual number of children the average woman is bearing.

Folkways The ordinary usages and conventions of everyday life.

Formal organization Large secondary groups that are deliberately and rationally designed to achieve specific objectives.

Function A positive consequence for a whole social system.

Functional equivalent A social or cultural feature that has the same effect as another, and may in that sense serve as a substitute for it.

Functionalist perspective A view of society that focuses on the way various parts of society have functions, or positive effects, that maintain the stability of the whole.

Fundamentalism A commitment to, and reliance on, the traditional basics of religious doctrine.

Gemeinschaft A "community" in which most people know one another.

Gender The culturally learned differences between males and females.

Gender roles The behavior patterns, obligations, and privileges that are considered appropriate for each sex.

Generalizations Statements that apply not just to a specific case but to most cases of the same type.

Generalized other The attitudes and viewpoint of society as a whole.

Genocide The extermination of entire populations.

Gesellschaft An "association" in which most people are strangers to one another.

Group A collection of people interacting together on the basis of shared expectations about each other's behavior.

Growth rate The difference between the number of people added to, and the number of people subtracted from, a population, expressed as an annual percentage.

Hawthorne effect The contamination of an experiment by the subjects' assumptions about what the experimenter is trying to discover.

Heterosexuality Sexual orientation toward the opposite sex.

High culture Creations of a relatively profound and serious nature that appeal to, and are supported by, a fairly small and elite group.

Homogamy Marriage between partners who share similar social characteristics.

Homosexuality Sexual orientation toward the same sex.

Horticultural society A society relying for its subsistence primarily on the hoe cultivation of domesticated plants.

Human ecology The interrelationship between human groups and their natural environment.

Hunting and gathering society A society relying for its subsistence on such wild animals and vegetation as its members can hunt or gather.

Hypothesis A tentative statement that predicts a relationship between variables.

Ideal culture The norms and values a society adheres to in principle.

Ideal type An abstract description constructed from a number of real cases in order to reveal their essential features.

Ideology A set of beliefs that explains and justifies some actual or potential social arrangements.

Illegitimate birth Birth to a mother who is not married to the father.

Illness The subjective sense that one is not well.

Incest taboo A powerful moral prohibition against sexual contact between certain categories of relatives.

Independent variable A variable that influences another variable—in other words, it acts as a cause.

Industrial society A society relying for its subsistence primarily on mechanized production.

Ingroup Any group one belongs to and identifies with.

Institution A stable cluster of values, norms, statuses, roles, and groups that develops around a basic social need.

Institutionalized discrimination Unequal treatment, on the grounds of group membership, that is entrenched in social customs.

Instrumental leadership The kind of leadership necessary to organize a group in pursuit of its goal.

Interactionist perspective A view of society that focuses on the way in which people act toward, respond to, and influence one another.

Interest group A group or organization that attempts to influence political decisions that might have an impact on its members or their goals.

Intergenerational mobility Movement up and down the hierarchy by family members from one generation to the next.

Interlocking directorates Social networks consisting of individuals who are members of several different corporate boards.

Internalization of norms The unconscious process of making conformity to the norms of one's culture a part of one's personality, so that one usually follows social expectations automatically, without question.

Invention The combination or new use of existing knowledge to produce something that did not exist before.

Kinship A social network of people related by common ancestry, adoption, or marriage.

Labeling theory A theory that explains deviance as a process by which some people successfully define others as deviant.

Latent function An unrecognized and unintended consequence of some element in a social system.

Law A rule that has been formally enacted by a political authority and is backed by the power of the state.

Leader Someone who, largely by virtue of certain personality characteristics, is consistently able to influence the behavior of others.

Legal discrimination Unequal treatment, on the grounds of group membership, that is upheld by law.

Legal-rational authority A type of authority in which power is legitimated by explicit rules and procedures that define the rights and obligations of the rulers.

Legitimacy The generally held belief that a given political system is valid and justified.

Legitimate birth Birth to a mother and father who are married to each other.

Less developed country A comparatively poor society that has not achieved a predominantly industrial mode of production.

Life chances Probabilities of benefiting or suffering from the opportunities or disadvantages one's society offers.

Life course The biological and social sequence of birth, childhood, maturity, old age, and death.

Life expectancy The number of years that the average newborn in a particular population can be expected to live.

Life span The maximum length of life possible in a particular species.

Linguistic-relativity hypothesis Holds that speakers of a particular language must necessarily interpret the world through that language's unique vocabulary and grammar.

Lobbying The tactic of directly persuading decision makers.

Looking-glass self A self-concept derived from a social "mirror" in which we can observe how others react to us.

Magic Rituals intended to harness supernatural power for human ends.

Manifest function An obvious and intended consequence of some element in a social system.

Marriage A socially approved mating arrangement between two or more people.

Mass A collection of people who are concerned with the same phenomenon without being in one another's presence.

Mass hysteria A form of collective behavior involving widespread anxiety, caused by some unfounded belief.

Mass media The various forms of communication that reach a large audience without any personal contact between the senders and the receivers: newspapers, magazines, books, television, radio, movies, videos, and records.

Master status The position most important in establishing an individual's social identity.

Material culture All the artifacts, or physical objects, human beings create and give meaning to—such as wheels, clothing, schools, factories, cities, books, spacecraft, totem poles.

Matriarchy A system in which the wife has the greater authority in family matters.

Matrilineal system One in which descent and inheritance pass through the female side of the family.

Matrilocal residence The custom in which married partners settle in or near the household of the wife's father.

Mechanical solidarity A form of social cohesion based on the similarity of the members.

Medicalization of society A process in which the domain of medicine is extended over areas of life that were previously considered nonmedical.

Medicine The institution concerned with the maintenance of health and the treatment of disease.

Megalopolis A virtually unbroken urban tract consisting of two or more central cities and their surrounding suburbs.

Mental disorder The psychological inability to cope realistically and effectively with the ordinary challenges of life.

Methodology A system of rules, principles, and procedures that guides scientific investigation.

Metropolis An urban area containing a city and its surrounding suburbs, and forming an economic and geographic unity.

Metropolitan Statistical Area (MSA) Basically, any area that contains a city (or a combination of a city and its surrounding suburbs) that has a total population of 50,000 or more.

Migration rate The annual difference between the number of immigrants (people entering) or emigrants (people leaving) per thousand members of the population.

Military-industrial complex An informal system of mutual influence between the Pentagon, which buys armaments, and the major U.S. corporations that sell them.

Millenarian movement One that prophesies a cataclysmic upheaval within the immediate future.

Minority group People whose physical appearance or cultural practices are unlike those of the dominant group, making them susceptible to different and unequal treatment.

Mob An emotionally aroused crowd intent on violent or destructive action.

Modernization A process of economic, social, and cultural change that facilitates the transition from preindustrial to industrial society.

Monogamy Marriage involving one spouse of each sex.

Monopoly A single firm that dominates an industry.

Monotheism The belief in a single supreme being.

Mores Strong norms that are regarded as morally significant, and violations of which are considered a serious matter.

Multinational corporation A corporate enterprise which, though headquartered in one country, conducts its operations through subsidiaries that it owns or controls around the world.

Natural sciences Disciplines that study physical and biological phenomena.

Negotiated reality An organization that derives its existence and character from the social interaction through which the members continuously create and recreate it.

Neocolonialism The informal political and economic domination of some societies by others, such that the former are able to exploit the labor resources of the latter for their own purposes.

Neolocal residence The custom in which marriage partners establish a new residence separate from the kin of either spouse.

Nonmaterial culture Abstract human creations—languages, ideas, beliefs, rules, customs, myths, skills, family patterns, political systems.

Nonverbal communication The exchange of information through nonlinguistic symbols such as signs, gestures, and facial expressions.

Norms Shared values or guidelines that describe the behavior appropriate in a given situation.

Nuclear family One in which the family group consists only of the parents and their dependent children, living apart from other relatives.

Objectivity An interpretation that eliminates the influence of personal values and experience.

Oligarchy Rule by the few.

Oligopoly A group of a few firms that dominates an industry.

Operational definition A definition that states a variable, for the purposes of research, in terms that can be measured.

Organic solidarity A form of social cohesion based on the differences among the members, which make them interdependent.

Outgroup Any alternative group that one does not belong to or identify with.

Panic A form of collective behavior in which people faced with an immediate threat react in a fearful, spontaneous, and uncoordinated way.

Paradigm A shared set of concepts, methods, and assumptions about a scientific discipline.

Participant observation A method in which the researcher becomes directly involved in the social behavior under study.

Particular other Specific other people such as parents.

Pastoral society A society relying for its subsistence primarily on domesticated herd animals.

Patriarchy A system in which the husband has the greater authority in family matters.

Patrilineal system One in which descent and inheritance pass through the male side of the family.

Patrilocal residence The custom in which marriage partners settle in or near the household of the husband's father.

Peace Sustained amicable relations between politically organized groups.

Peers People of roughly equivalent age and other social characteristics.

Permissiveness Acceptance of some latitude in sexual norms and conduct.

Personality The fairly stable patterns of thought, feeling, and action that are typical of an individual.

Pluralist model A view of the political process that sees many competing interest groups as having access to government and shaping its decisions.

Political party An organization whose purpose is to gain legitimate control of government.

Political system The institutionalized system through which some individuals or groups acquire and exercise power over others.

Polyandry Marriage between one wife and more than one husband.

Polygamy Marriage involving a spouse of one sex and two or more spouses of the opposite sex.

Polygyny Marriage between one husband and more than one wife.

Polytheism A belief in a number of gods.

Popular culture Creations of a relatively less serious and less intellectually demanding nature that appeal primarily to, and are supported by, a large audience of typical members of the society.

Pornography Pictorial and written material intended to arouse sexual excitement.

Postindustrial society A society relying for its subsistence primarily on the production of services and information.

Power The ability to control the behavior of others, even in the absence of their consent.

Power-elite model A view of the political process that sees power as being held by, and exercised primarily in the interest of, a privileged few.

Prejudice An irrational, inflexible attitude toward an entire category of people.

Primary deviance Nonconformity that is temporary, exploratory, trivial, or easily concealed.

Primary group A small number of people who interact over a relatively long period on a direct, intimate basis.

Primary sector The part of the economy that involves the gathering or extracting of undeveloped natural resources—for example, fishing, mining, forestry, or agriculture.

Priority dispute An argument about who made a particular discovery first.

Profane Anything that is regarded as part of the ordinary rather than the supernatural world; as such it may be considered familiar, mundane, even corrupting.

Profession An occupation requiring extensive, systematic knowledge of, or training in, an art or science.

Propaganda Information or viewpoints that are presented with the deliberate intention of persuading the audience to adopt a particular opinion.

Property The set of rights that the owner of something has in relation to others who do not own it.

Prostitution The relatively indiscriminate exchange of sexual favors for economic gain.

Protestant ethic A disciplined, moral commitment to regular, conscientious work and deferred gratification.

Psychosis A profound mental disturbance involving such a severe break with reality that the affected person cannot function in society.

Public opinion The sum of the decisions of the members of a public on a particular issue.

Race A category of people who are regarded as socially distinct because they share genetically transmitted physical characteristics.

Racism The belief that one racial or ethnic group is inferior to another and that unequal treatment is therefore justified.

Random sample A sample chosen in such a way that every member of the population in question has the same chance of being selected.

Rape Forcible sexual intercourse against the will of the victim.

Rationalization The way in which traditional, spontaneous, rule-of-thumb methods of social organization are replaced by abstract, explicit, carefully calculated rules and procedures.

Real culture The norms and values a society adheres to in practice.

Recidivism Repeated crime by those who have been convicted before.

Reference group A group to which people refer when making evaluations of themselves and their behavior.

Relative deprivation The inability to maintain the living standards customary in the society.

Religion A system of communally shared beliefs and rituals that are oriented toward some sacred, supernatural realm.

Research design The actual plan for the collection and analysis of data.

Resocialization Learning that involves a sharp break with the past and socialization into radically different norms and values.

Resource mobilization The ability to organize and use available resources, such as time, money, people, and skills.

Respondents The actual subjects of a survey.

Restrictiveness Insistence on adherence to narrowly defined sexual norms.

Revolution The violent overthrow of an existing political or social system.

Rites of passage Formal ceremonies that mark an individual's transition from one age status to another.

Ritual A formal, stylized procedure, such as prayer, incantation, or ceremonial cleansing.

Ritual pollution Types of contact or proximity between members of different castes that are considered unclean for the superior caste.

Role A set of expected behavior patterns, obligations, and privileges attached to a particular social status.

Role conflict A situation in which two or more of a person's roles have contradictory requirements.

Role expectation The generally expected social norms that prescribe how a role ought to be played.

Role performance The actual behavior of a person playing a role.

Role strain A situation in which contradictory expectations are built into a single role.

Role-taking Pretending to take or actually taking the roles of other people, so that one can see the world and one's self from their viewpoints.

Rumor Information that is transmitted informally from anonymous sources.

Sacred Anything that is regarded as part of the supernatural rather than the ordinary world; as such it inspires awe, reverence, and deep respect.

Sample A small number of individuals drawn from a larger population.

Sanctions Rewards for conformity and punishments for nonconformity.

Scapegoating Placing the blame for one's troubles on some relatively powerless individual or group.

Science A body of knowledge obtained by logical, systematic methods of research.

Secondary deviance Persistent nonconformity by a person who accepts the label of deviant.

Secondary group A number of people who interact on a relatively temporary, anonymous and impersonal basis.

Secondary sector The part of the economy that involves turning the raw materials produced by the primary sector into manufactured goods—for example, houses, furniture, automobiles, canned foods.

Sect An exclusive and uncompromising religious organization, usually one that has split off from a denomination for doctrinal reasons.

Secularization The process by which religion loses its social influence.

Self The individual's conscious experience of a distinct personal identity that is separate from all other people and things.

Self-fulfilling prophecy A prediction that leads to behavior that makes the prediction come true.

Self-fulfillment The commitment to achieving the development of one's individual personality, talents, and potential.

Sex The biological distinction between male and female.

Sexism The belief that one sex is inferior to another and that unequal treatment is therefore justified.

Sickness The condition of those who are socially recognized as unwell.

Sick role A pattern of behavior expected of someone who is ill.

Simple supernaturalism A type of religion that does not recognize specific gods or spirits, but does assume that supernatural forces influence human events for better or worse.

Small group A group that contains few enough members for the participants to relate to one another as individuals.

Social change The alteration in patterns of culture, social structure, and social behavior over time.

Social class A category of people of roughly equivalent status in an unequal society.

Social construction of reality The process by which people create their understanding of the nature of their environment.

Social control A set of means of ensuring that people generally behave in expected and approved ways.

Social gerontology The study of the social aspects of aging.

Social inequality The unequal sharing of such social rewards as wealth, power, and prestige.

Social interaction The process by which people act toward or respond to other people.

Socialism An economic system in which the means of production and distribution are publicly owned.

Socialization The process of social interaction through which people acquire personality and learn the way of life of their society.

Social mobility Movement from one social status to another.

Social movement A large number of people who have joined together to bring about or resist some social or cultural change.

Social networks Webs of relationships that link the individual directly and indirectly to other people.

Social psychology The study of how personality and behavior are influenced by the social context.

Social sciences Disciplines that study various aspects of human behavior.

Social stratification The inequality of entire categories of people, who have different access to social rewards as a result of their status in a social hierarchy.

Social structure The pattern of relationships among the basic components in a social system.

Society A population that occupies the same territory, is subject to the same political authority, and participates in a common culture.

Sociocultural evolution The tendency for societies' social structures and cultures to grow more complex over time.

Socioeconomic status (SES) A complex of factors such as income, type of occupation, years of education, and sometimes place of residence.

Sociology The scientific study of human society and social behavior.

Sport Competitive physical activity guided by established rules.

Spurious correlation A correlation that is merely coincidental and does not imply any causal relationship whatsoever.

State The supreme political authority in society.

Status A position in society.

Status inconsistency A situation in which an individual's status or statuses appear contradictory.

Stereotype A rigid mental image that summarizes whatever is believed to be typical about a group.

Stigma The mark of social disgrace that sets the deviant apart from those who consider themselves "normal."

Structural mobility Changes in people's social statuses as a result of changes in the structure of the economy.

Structural-strain theory An approach that explains deviance as the outcome of social strains that put pressure on some people to deviate.

Structure A set of interrelated components such as head, limbs, a heart, and so on.

Subculture A group that shares in the overall culture of the society but also has its own distinctive values, norms, and lifestyle.

Subjectivity An interpretation based on personal values and experiences.

Surplus wealth More goods and services than are necessary to meet their producers' basic needs.

Survey A method for systematically obtaining standardized information about the attitudes, behavior, and other characteristics of a population.

Symbol Anything that can meaningfully represent something else.

Symbolic interaction The interaction between people that takes place through such symbols as signs, gestures, and language.

Taboo A powerful social belief that some specific act is utterly loathsome.

Technocracy Rule by technical experts whose specialized knowledge and recommendations are relied upon by those who are officially responsible for decisions.

Technological determinism The view that the technology available to a society is an important determinant of its culture, social structure, and even of its history.

Technological fix The use of technology to solve problems, including those that prior technology has created.

Technology The practical applications of scientific or other knowledge.

Terrorism The use of violence against civilian targets for the purpose of intimidation to achieve political ends.

Tertiary sector The part of the economy that involves producing services—for example, medicine, laundering, teaching, broadcasting.

Theism A type of religion that centers on a belief in gods.

Theodicy An emotionally satisfying explanation for such great problems of earthly existence as human origins, suffering, and death.

Theoretical perspective A broad assumption about society and social behavior that provides a point of view for the study of specific problems.

Theory A statement that organizes a set of concepts in a meaningful way by explaining the relationship among them.

Thomas theorem "If people define situations as real, they are real in their consequences."

Total institution A place of residence where the inmates are confined for a set period of their lives, under the almost absolute rule of a hierarchy of officials.

Totalitarianism An authoritarian form of government in which the rulers recognize no limits to their authority and are willing to regulate virtually any aspect of social life.

Traditional authority A type of authority in which power is legitimated by ancient custom.

Transcendent idealism A type of religion that centers not on the worship of a god but rather on sacred principles of thought and conduct.

Triad A group containing three people.

Urbanism The nature and meaning of city life.

Urbanization The process by which population is concentrated in the cities.

Urban legend A realistic but untrue story with an ironic twist concerning a recent alleged event.

Value-freedom The absence of personal values or biases.

Value judgment An opinion based on personal values or biases.

Values Socially shared ideas about what is good, right, and desirable.

Variable Any characteristic that can change or differ—for example, from time to time, from place to place, or from one individual to another.

Verstehen Subjective interpretation of a social actor's behavior and intentions.

War Sustained military conflict between politically organized groups.

World system A network of unequal economic and political relationships among the developed and the less developed countries.

Zero population growth (ZPG) A situation in which population size would remain stable.

References

Acuña, Rodolfo. 1988. *Occupied America: A History of Chicanos.* 3rd ed. New York: Harper & Row.

Adams, Herbert L. 1982. "Survivors of nuclear war: Infection and the spread of disease," in Eric Chivian et al. (eds.). *Last Aid: The Medical Dimensions of Nuclear War.* San Francisco: Freeman.

Adams, Ruth, and **Susan Cullen.** 1982. *The Final Epidemic: Physicians and Scientists on Nuclear War.* Chicago: University of Chicago Press.

Adorno, Theodore W., et al. 1950. *The Authoritarian Personality.* New York: Norton.

Aganbegyan, Abel. 1988. *The Economic Challenge of Perestroika.* Bloomington, Ind.: Indiana University Press.

Akers, Ronald L. 1985. *Deviant Behavior: A Social Learning Approach.* 3rd ed. Belmont, Calif.: Wadsworth.

Alba, Francisco. 1980. *The Population of Mexico.* New Brunswick, N.J.: Transaction Books.

Alba, Richard D., and **Gwen Moore.** 1982. "Ethnicity in the American elite." *American Sociological Review,* 47, pp. 373–383.

Albert, Ethel M. 1963. "Women of Burundi: A study of social values," in Denise Paulme (ed.), *Women of Tropical Africa.* Berkeley, Calif.: University of California Press.

Allen, Michael Patrick. 1974. "The structure of interorganizational elite cooptation: Interlocking corporate directors." *American Sociological Review,* 39, pp. 393–406.

Altman, Dennis. 1972. *Homosexual: Oppression and Liberation.* New York: Avon.

_____. 1982. *The Homosexualization of America: The Americanization of the Homosexual.* New York: St. Martin's Press.

_____. 1986. *AIDS in the Mind of America.* Garden City, N.Y.: Doubleday/Anchor.

Amin, Samir. 1976. *Unequal Development: An Essay on Social Formations of Peripheral Capitalism.* New York: Monthly Review Press.

Anderson, Jervis. 1985. *Guns in American Life.* New York: Random House.

Apple, Michael W. 1982. *Education and Power: Reproduction and Contradiction in Education.* London: Routledge & Kegan Paul.

Ariès, Philippe. 1962. *Centuries of Childhood: A Social History of Family Life.* New York: Knopf.

Asch, Solomon. 1955. "Opinions and social pressure." *Scientific American,* 193, pp. 31–35.

Astin, Alexander W. 1977. *Four Critical Years.* San Francisco: Jossey-Bass.

_____. 1985. *Achieving Educational Excellence.* San Francisco: Jossey-Bass.

_____, et al., 1987. *The American Freshman: Twenty Year Trends.* Los Angeles: Cooperative Institutional Research Program.

Atchley, Robert C. 1988. *Social Forces in Later Life.* 5th ed. Belmont, Calif.: Wadsworth.

Baldassare, Mark. 1986. *Trouble in Paradise: The Suburban Transformation in America.* New York: Columbia University Press.

Bales, Robert F. 1953. "The equilibrium problem in small groups," in Talcott Parsons et al. (eds.), *Working Papers in the Theory of Action.* Glencoe, Ill.: Free Press.

_____, and **Fred L. Strodtbeck.** 1951. "Phases in group problem solving." *Journal of Abnormal and Social Psychology,* 46, pp. 485–494.

Ball, George W. (ed.). 1975. *Global Companies: The Political Economy of World Business.* Englewood Cliffs, N.J.: Prentice-Hall.

Ball, John C., et al. 1981. "The criminality of heroin addicts when addicted and when off opiates," in James Inciardy (ed.), *The Drugs-Crime Connection.* Beverly Hills, Calif.: Sage.

Balswick, Jack. 1988. *The Inexpressive Male.* Lexington, Mass.: Lexington Books.

Barnaby, Frank C. 1977. "Hiroshima and Nagasaki: The survivors." *New Scientists,* 75, pp. 472–475.

Barnet, Richard. 1970. *Roots of War.* New York: Penguin.

_____, and **Ronald Muller.** 1974. *Global Reach: Power and the Multinational Corporations.* New York: Simon and Schuster.

Barthel, Diane. 1988. *Putting on Appearances: Gender and Advertising.* Philadelphia: Temple University Press.

Bayer, Ronald. 1981. *Homosexuality and American Psychiatry: The Politics of Diagnosis.* New York: Basic Books.

_____. 1988. *Private Acts, Social Consequences: AIDS and the Politics of Public Health.* New York: Free Press.

Becker, Howard S. 1963. *Outsiders: Studies in the Sociology of Deviance.* New York: Free Press.

_____, et al. 1968. *Making the Grade: The Academic Side of College Life.* New York: Wiley.

Beier, Ruth. 1984. *Science and Gender: A Critique of Biology and Its Theories on Women.* New York: Pergamon Press.

Bell, Alan P., and **Martin S. Weinberg.** 1978. *Homosexualities: A Study of Diversity Among Men and Women.* New York: Simon and Schuster.

Bell, Daniel. 1973. *The Coming of Postindustrial Society.* New York: Basic Books.

Bellah, Robert N. 1970. *Beyond Belief.* New York: Harper & Row.

Beres, Louis René. 1982. *Apocalypse: Nuclear Catastrophe in World Politics.* Chicago: University of Chicago Press.

Berg, Ivar. 1970. *Education and Jobs: The Great Training Robbery.* New York: Praeger.

Berger, Peter L. 1963. *Invitation to Sociology: A Humanistic Perspective.* New York: Doubleday.

—————. 1969. *A Rumor of Angels: Modern Society and the Rediscovery of the Supernatural.* New York: Doubleday.

—————. 1979. *The Heretical Imperative: Contemporary Possibilities of Religious Affirmation.* New York: Doubleday.

—————. 1986. *The Capitalist Revolution.* New York: Basic Books.

Berlin, Brent, and **Paul Kay.** 1969. *Basic Color Terms: Their Universality and Evolution.* Berkeley, Calif.: University of California Press.

Berman, Marshall. 1982. *All That Is Solid Melts into Thin Air: The Experience of Modernity.* New York: Simon and Schuster.

Bernard, Jesse. 1982. *The Future of Marriage.* 2nd ed. New Haven: Yale University Press.

Berreman, Gerald D. 1973. *Caste in the Modern World.* Morristown, N.J.: General Learning Press.

Berry, Brian J. C. 1981. *Comparative Urbanization.* New York: St. Martin's Press.

Best, Raphaela. 1983. *We've All Got Scars: What Boys and Girls Learn in Elementary School.* Bloomington: Indiana University Press.

Biddle, Wayne. 1986. "How much bang for the buck?" *Discover* (September), pp. 50–65.

Bieber, Irving, et al. 1962. *Homosexuality: A Psychoanalytic Study.* New York: Basic Books.

Bingham, Roger. 1981. "Outrageous ardor." *Science,* 81, pp. 56–61.

Bingham, Richard D., et al. (eds.). 1987. *The Homeless in Contemporary Society.* Newbury Park, Calif.: Sage.

Blainey, Geoffrey. 1973. *The Causes of War.* New York: Free Press.

Blankenship, Ralph (ed.). 1977. *Colleagues in Organization: The Social Construction of Professional Work.* New York: Wiley.

Blau, Peter, and **Otis Dudley Duncan.** 1967. *The American Occupational Structure.* New York: Wiley.

—————, and **Marshall W. Meyer.** 1973. *Bureaucracy in Modern Society.* 3rd ed. New York: Random House.

Alan Bloom. 1987. *The Closing of the American Mind.* New York: Simon and Schuster.

Blumstein, Philip, and **Pepper Schwartz.** 1974. "The acquisition of sexual identity: The bisexual case." Paper presented at the Annual Meetings of the American Sociological Association, August 25–29, Montreal, Canada.

—————. 1983. *American Couples.* New York: Morrow.

Bonacich, Edna. 1972. "A theory of ethnic antagonism: The split-labor market." *American Sociological Review,* 37, pp. 547–559.

Bornschier, Volker, and **Jean-Pierre Hoby.** 1981. "Economic policy and multinational corporations in development: The measurable impact in cross-national perspective." *Social Problems,* 28, pp. 363–377.

Boswell, James. 1980. *Christianity, Homosexuality, and Social Tolerance.* Chicago: University of Chicago Press.

Bourdieu, Pierre. 1977. *Reproduction in Education, Society, and Culture.* Beverly Hills, Calif.: Sage.

Bowen, Howard R. 1977. *Investment in Learning: The Individual and the Social Value of American Higher Education.* San Francisco: Jossey-Bass.

Bowlby, John. 1969. *Attachment and Loss.* Vol. 1. New York: Basic Books.

—————. 1988. *A Secure Base: Parent-Child Attachment and Healthy Human Development.* New York: Free Press.

Bowles, Samuel, and **Herbert Gintis.** 1976. *Schooling in Capitalist America.* New York: Basic Books.

Boyer, Ernest L. 1983. *High School.* New York: Harper & Row.

—————. 1985. *College: The Undergraduate Experience in America.* New York: Harper & Row.

Bozett, Frederick W. (ed.). 1987. *Gay and Lesbian Parents.* New York: Praeger.

Brinton, Crane. 1960. *The Anatomy of Revolution.* New York: Random House.

Brown, Seyom. 1987. *The Causes and Prevention of War.* New York: St. Martin's Press.

Brownmiller, Susan. 1975. *Against Our Will: Men, Women, and Rape.* New York: Simon and Schuster.

—————. 1984. *Feminity.* New York: Linden Press/Simon and Schuster.

Bruce, Steve. 1988. *The Rise and Fall of the New Christian Right.* New York: Oxford University Press.

Bruce-Biggs, B. (ed.). 1979. *The New Class?* New Brunswick, N.J.: Transaction Books.

Bryant, James H. 1965. "Apprenticeships in prostitution." *Social Problems,* 12, pp. 278–297.

Bullough, Vern L., and **Bonnie Bullough.** 1979. *Prostitution: An Illustrated Social History.* New York: Crown.

Bureau of the Census, 1986a. *Statistical Abstract of the United States: 1986.* Washington, D.C.: U.S. Government Printing Office.

—————. 1986b. "Household wealth and asset ownership: 1984." *Current Population Reports,* Series P-70, no. 7. Washington, D.C.: U.S. Government Printing Office.

—————. 1986c. "Money income of households, families, and persons in the United States: 1984." *Current Population Reports,* Series P-60, no. 151.

—————. 1988. *Statistical Abstract of the United States, 1988.* Washington, D.C.: Government Printing Office.

Butler, Robert. 1975. *Why Survive? Being Old in America.* New York: Harper & Row.

Calder, Nigel. 1980. *Nuclear Nightmares: An Investigation in Possible Wars.* New York: Viking.

Califano, Joseph A. 1985. *America's Health Care Revolution.* New York: Random House.

Campbell, Bernard. 1985. *Human Ecology.* Hawthorne, N.Y.: Aldine de Gruyter.

Cargan, Leonard. 1982. *Singles: Myths and Realities.* Beverly Hills, Calif.: Sage.

Carr, Raymond. 1984. *Puerto Rico: A Colonial Experiment.* New York: New York University Press/Vintage.

Carter, Hugh, and **Paul C. Glick.** 1976. *Marriage and Divorce: A Social and Economic Study.* Cambridge, Mass.: Harvard University Press.

Castells, Manuel. 1977. *The Urban Question.* Cambridge, Mass.: MIT Press.

Caufield, Catherine. 1985. *In the Rainforest.* New York: Knopf.

Chafetz, Janet Saltzman. 1984. *Sex and Advantage: A Comparative, Macro-Structural Theory of Sex Stratification.* Totowa, N.J.: Rowmann and Allanheld.

Chagnon, Napoleon A. 1967. "Yanamamö social organization and warfare," in Morton Fried et al. (eds.), *War: The Anthropology of Armed Conflict and Aggression.* New York: Doubleday.

—————. 1977. *Yanamamö: The Fierce People.* 2nd ed. New York: Holt, Rinehart and Winston.

Chambliss, William J. 1973. "The Saints and the Roughnecks." *Society,* 11, pp. 24–31.

_____, and **Robert Seidman.** 1982. *Law, Order, and Power.* 2nd ed. Reading, Mass.: Addison-Wesley.

Chang, Pao-Min. 1983. *Continuity and Change: A Profile of Chinese Americans.* New York: Vantage.

Chapman, Jane Roberts, and **Margaret Gates** (eds.). 1978. *The Victimization of Women.* Beverly Hills, Calif.: Sage.

Chappell, Duncan, et al. (eds.). 1977. *Rape: The Victim and the Offender.* New York: Columbia University Press.

Cheek, William F. 1970. *Black Resistance Before the Civil War.* Beverly Hills, Calif.: Glencoe Press.

Cherlin, Andrew. 1986. *Marriage, Divorce, and Remarriage.* Cambridge, Mass.: Harvard University Press.

Chirot, Daniel. 1977. *Social Change in the Twentieth Century.* New York: Harcourt Brace Jovanovich.

_____. 1986. *Social Change in the Modern Era.* 2nd ed. San Diego, Calif.: Harcourt Brace Jovanovich.

_____, and **Thomas H. Hall.** 1982. "World-system theory," in Ralph H. Turner and James F. Short (eds.), *Annual Review of Sociology,* 8. Palo Alto, Calif.: Annual Reviews.

Chivian, Eric, et al. (eds.). 1982. *Last Aid: The Medical Dimensions of Nuclear War.* San Francisco: Freeman.

Church, Joseph. 1978. "Two flew over the cuckoo's nest." *New York Times Book Review,* March 26, p. 11.

Clark, Candace. 1983. "Sickness and social control," in Howard Robboy and Candace Clark (eds.), *Social Interaction: Readings in Sociology.* 2nd ed. New York: St. Martin's Press.

Clayton, Richard R., and **Harwin L. Voss.** 1977. "Shacking up: Cohabitation in the 1970s." *Journal of Marriage and the Family,* 39:2, 273–283.

Clendening, Logan (ed.). 1942. *Sourcebook of Medical History.* New York: Dover Publications.

Clinard, Marshall B., and **Robert F. Meier.** 1985. *Sociology of Deviant Behavior.* 6th ed. New York: Holt, Rinehart, and Winston.

Cockburn, Andrew. 1982. *Inside the Soviet Military Machine.* New York: Random House.

Cockerham, William C. 1981. *Sociology of Mental Disorder.* Englewood Cliffs, N.J.: Prentice-Hall.

_____. 1986. *Medical Sociology.* 3rd ed. Englewood Cliffs, N.J.: Prentice-Hall.

Cockroft, James D., et al. (eds.). 1972. *Dependence and Underdevelopment.* Garden City, N.Y.: Anchor.

Cohen, Albert K. 1955. *Delinquent Boys: The Culture of the Gang.* New York: Free Press.

Cohen, Bernard. 1980. *Deviant Street Networks: Prostitution in New York City.* Lexington, Mass.: D. C. Heath.

Cohen, Stanley. 1987. *Folk Devils and Moral Panics.* 2nd ed. Oxford: Basil Blackwell.

Coleman, James S., et al. 1966. *Equality of Educational Opportunity.* Washington, D.C.: U.S. Government Printing Office.

_____, and **Thomas Hoffer.** 1986. *Public and Private High Schools: The Impact of Communities.* New York: Basic Books.

_____, **Thomas Hoffer,** and **Sally Kilgore.** 1982. *High School Achievement: Public, Catholic, and Private Schools Compared.* New York: Basic Books.

Coleman, James W. 1988. *The Criminal Elite: The Sociology of White Collar Crime.* 2nd ed. New York: St. Martin's Press.

Collins, Randall. 1971a. "A conflict theory of sexual stratification." *Social Problems,* 19, pp. 3–12.

_____. 1971b. "Functional and conflict theories of educational stratification." *American Sociological Review,* 36:6, 1002–1019.

_____. 1974. *Conflict Sociology: Toward an Explanatory Science.* New York: Academic Press.

_____. 1979. *The Credential Society.* New York: Academic Press.

_____. 1985. *Sociology of Marriage and the Family: Gender, Love, and Property.* Chicago: Nelson Hall.

_____. 1988. *The Discovery of Society.* 4th ed. New York: Random House.

Condry, John, and **Sandra Condry.** 1976. "Sex differences: A study of the eye of the beholder." *Child Development,* 47, pp. 812–819.

Conrad, Peter, and **Joseph W. Schneider,** 1980. *Deviance and Medicalization: From Badness to Sickness.* St. Louis: Mosby.

Cooley, Charles Horton. 1902. *Human Nature and the Social Order.* New York: Scribner's.

Coser, Lewis A. 1956. *The Functions of Social Conflict.* Glencoe, Ill.: Free Press.

Cowgill, Donald O. 1986. *Aging Around the World.* Belmont, Calif.: Wadsworth.

Cox, John. 1977. *Overkill.* New York: Thomas Crowell.

Cox, Oliver C. 1976. *Race Relations: Elements and Social Dynamics.* Detroit: Wayne State University Press.

Crick, Francis. 1988. *What Mad Pursuit: A Personal View of Scientific Discovery.* New York: Free Press.

Crosbie, Paul V. (ed.). 1975. *Interaction in Small Groups.* New York: Macmillan.

Cumming, Elaine, and **William E. Henry.** 1961. *Growing Old: The Process of Disengagement.* New York: Basic Books.

Currie, Elliott. 1986. *Confronting Crime: An American Challenge.* New York: Pantheon.

Cushman, John. 1986. "Experts see risk in troop carrier." *New York Times,* September 21, pp. 1, 36.

Dahl, Robert. 1961. *Who Governs?* New Haven: Yale University Press.

_____. 1981. *Democracy in the United States.* 4th ed. Boston: Houghton Mifflin.

_____. 1982. *Dilemmas of Pluralist Democracy: Autonomy vs. Control.* New Haven: Yale University Press.

Dahrendorf, Ralf. 1958. "Toward a theory of social conflict." *The Journal of Conflict Resolution,* 11, pp. 170–183.

_____. 1959. *Class and Class Conflict in Industrial Society.* Berkeley, Calif.: Stanford University Press.

Dalphin, John. 1981. *The Persistence of Social Inequality in America.* Cambridge, Mass.: Schenkman.

Daly, Martin, and **Margo Wilson.** 1988. *Homicide.* Hawthorne, N.Y.: Aldine de Gruyter.

D'Andrade, Roy G. 1966. "Sex differences and cultural institutions," in Eleanor E. Maccoby (ed.), *The Development of Sex Differences.* Palo Alto, Calif.: Stanford University Press.

Darley, John M., and **Bibb Latané.** 1968. "Bystander intervention in emergencies: Diffusion of responsibility." *Journal of Personality and Social Psychology,* 8, pp. 377–383.

Davies, James C. 1962. "Toward a theory of revolution." *American Sociological Review,* 27, pp. 5–18.

_____ (ed.). 1971. *When Men Revolt—and Why.* New York: Free Press.

Davies, Mark, and **Denise B. Kandel.** 1981. "Parental and peer influences on adolescents' educational plans: Some further evidence." *American Journal of Sociology,* 87, pp. 363–387.

Davis, Cary, Carl Haub, and **JoAnne Willette.** 1983. *U.S. Hispanics: Changing the Face of America.* Washington, D.C.: Population Reference Bureau.

Davis, George, and **Glegg Watson.** 1982. *Black Life in Corporate America.* New York: Doubleday/Anchor.

Davis, James A., and **Tom W. Smith.** 1983. *General Social Survey File, 1972–1982.* Ann Arbor, Mich.: Inter-University Consortium for Political and Social Research.

Davis, Karen. 1975. *National Health Insurance.* Washington, D.C.: Brookings Institute.

Davis, Kingsley. 1932. "The sociology of prostitution." *American Sociological Review,* 2, pp. 744–755.

_____. 1940. "Extreme social isolation of a child." *American Journal of Sociology,* 45, pp. 554–564.

_____. 1947. "Final note on a case of extreme isolation." *American Journal of Sociology,* 50, pp. 432–437.

_____. 1948. *Human Society.* New York: Macmillan.

_____, and **Wilbert E. Moore.** 1945. "Some principles of stratification." *American Sociological Review,* 10, pp. 242–249.

_____. 1976. "Sexual behavior," in Robert K. Merton and Robert Nisbet (eds.), *Contemporary Social Problems.* 3rd ed. New York: Harcourt Brace Jovanovich.

Davis, Nanette J. 1971. "The prostitute: Developing a deviant identity," in James M. Henslin (ed.), *Studies in the Sociology of Sex.* New York: Appleton-Century-Crofts.

Dear, Michael J., and **Jennifer R. Welch.** 1987. *Landscapes of Despair: From Deinstitutionalization to Homelessness.* Princeton, N.J.: Princeton University Press.

De Mause, Lloyd (ed.). 1974. *The History of Childhood.* New York: Psychohistory Press.

DeSpelder, Lynne Anne, and **Albert Lee Strickland.** 1983. *The Last Dance: Encountering Death and Dying.* Palo Alto, Calif.: Mayfield.

Deutscher, Irwin. 1973. *What We Say, What We Do: Sentiments and Acts.* Glenview, Ill.: Scott, Foresman.

Diehl, Paul F. 1984. *The New Politics of Science.* New York: Pantheon.

Dohrenword, Bruce P. 1980. *Mental Illness in the United States: Epidemiological Estimates.* New York: Praeger.

Doleschal, Eugene, and **Norah Klapmuts.** 1973. *Toward a New Criminology.* Hackensack, N.J.: National Council on Crime and Delinquency.

Domhoff, G. William. 1967. *Who Rules America?* Englewood Cliffs, N.J.: Prentice-Hall.

_____. 1971. *Higher Circles: The Governing Class in America.* New York: Random House.

_____. 1983. *Who Rules America Now?* Englewood Cliffs, N.J.: Prentice-Hall.

Donnerstein, Edward, et al. 1987. *The Question of Pornography.* Chicago: Free Press.

Dover, K. J. 1980. *Greek Homosexuality.* Cambridge, Mass.: Harvard University Press.

Doyle, James A. 1983. *The Male Experience.* Dubuque, Iowa: Wm. C. Brown.

Drew, David E. (ed.). 1978. *Competency, Careers, and College: New Directions for Education and Work.* San Francisco: Jossey-Bass.

Drew, Elizabeth. 1983. *Politics and Money: The New Road to Corruption.* New York: Macmillan.

Dubos, René. 1959. *Health as Mirage.* New York: Doubleday.

_____. 1969. *Man, Medicine, and Environment.* New York: Mentor.

Duffy, John. 1976. *The Healers: The Rise of the Medical Establishment.* New York: McGraw-Hill.

Dunn, John, and **Carol Kendrick.** 1983. *Siblings: Love, Envy, and Understanding.* Cambridge, Mass.: Harvard University Press.

Dunn, Judy. 1988. *The Beginnings of Social Understanding.* Cambridge, Mass.: Harvard University Press.

Durkheim, Emile. 1954, originally published 1912. *The Elementary Forms of Religious Life.* Joseph W. Swain (trans.). Glencoe, Ill.: Free Press.

_____. 1964a, originally published 1893. *The Division of Labor in Society.* George Simpson (trans.). Glencoe, Ill.: Free Press.

_____. 1964b, originally published 1897. *Suicide.* Glencoe, Ill.: Free Press.

Duverger, Maurice. 1954. *Political Parties.* New York: Wiley.

Dworkin, Andrea. 1981. *Pornography: Men Possessing Women.* New York: Putnam.

Dye, Thomas R. 1986. *Who's Running America?* 4th ed. Englewood Cliffs, N.J.: Prentice-Hall.

Eaton, William W. 1985. *The Sociology of Mental Disorders.* 2nd ed. New York: Praeger.

Eckholm, Eric. 1986. "Significant rise in sea level now seems certain." *New York Times,* February 18.

Ehrlich, Paul R. 1968. *The Population Bomb.* New York: Macmillan.

_____, et al. 1977. *Ecoscience: Population, Resources, Environment.* San Francisco: Freeman.

_____, and **Anne Ehrlich.** 1979. "What happened to the population bomb?" *Human Nature.* 2:1, 88–92.

_____. 1981. *Extinction.* New York: Random House.

Elder, Glen. 1974. *Children of the Great Depression.* Chicago: University of Chicago Press.

Elkins, Stanley M. 1963. *Slavery: A Problem in American Institutional and Intellectual Life.* New York: Grosset & Dunlap.

Elling, Ray H. 1980. *Cross-National Study of Health Systems.* New Brunswick, N.J.: Transaction Books.

Ellwood, David T. 1988. *Poor Support: Poverty in the American Family.* New York: Basic Books.

Elshtain, Jean Bethke. 1988. *Women and War.* New York: Basic Books.

Emery, Robert E., et al. 1984. "Divorce, children, and social policy," in Harold W. Stevenson and Alberta E. Siegal (eds.), *Child Development Research and Social Policy.* Chicago: University of Chicago Press.

England, Paula. 1988. *Comparable Worth.* Hawthorne, N.Y.: Aldine de Gruyter.

Epstein, Cynthia Fuchs. 1988. *Deceptive Distinctions: Sex, Gender, and the Social Order.* New Haven: Yale University Press.

Ermann, M. David, and **Richard J. Lundman** (eds.). 1987. *Corporate and Governmental Deviance.* 3rd ed. New York: Oxford University Press.

Estrich, Susan. 1987. *Real Rape.* Cambridge, Mass.: Harvard University Press.

Ettmore, E. M. 1980. *Lesbians, Women, and Society.* London: Routledge & Kegan Paul.

Etzioni-Halevy, Eva. 1981. *Social Change.* London: Routledge & Kegan Paul.

Evans, P. B. 1981. "Recent research on multinational corporations." *Annual Review of Sociology,* 7, pp. 199–223.

Falk, Richard A., and **Samuel S. Kim** (eds.). 1980. *The War System: An Interdisciplinary Approach.* Boulder, Col.: Westview Press.

Fallows, James. 1985. "The case against credentialism." *Atlantic Monthly* (December), pp. 49–67.

Farley, Reynolds. 1984. *Blacks and Whites: Narrowing the Gap?* Cambridge, Mass.: Harvard University Press.

_____. 1988. *Majority-Minority Relations.* 2nd ed. Englewood Cliffs, N.J.: Prentice-Hall.

Feagin, Joe R. 1975. *Subordinating the Poor: Welfare and American Beliefs.* Englewood Cliffs, N.J.: Prentice-Hall.

_____. 1983. *The Urban Real Estate Game: Playing Monopoly with Real Money.* Englewood Cliffs, N.J.: Prentice-Hall.

Finch, Stuart C. 1979. "The study of atomic bomb survivors in Japan." *American Journal of Medicine,* 66, pp. 899–901.

Finkelhor, David. 1984. *Child Sexual Abuse: New Theory and Research.* New York: Free Press.

_____, et al. 1979. *Who Gets Ahead? The Determinants of Economic Success in America.* New York: Basic Books.

Johnstone, Ronald L. 1988. *Religion and Society in Interaction: The Sociology of Religion.* 3rd ed. Englewood Cliffs, N.J.: Prentice-Hall.

Jones, Elsie F., et al. 1986. *Teenage Pregnancy in Industrialized Countries.* New Haven: Yale University Press.

Josephy, Alvin M. 1982. *Now that the Buffalo's Gone: A Study of Today's American Indians.* New York: Knopf.

Kagan, Jerome, et al. (eds.). 1984. *Emotions, Cognition, and Behavior.* New York: Cambridge University Press.

Kanter, Rosabeth Moss. 1977. *Work and Family in the United States.* New York: Russell Sage Foundation.

Kaplan, H. Roy. 1985. "Lottery winners and work commitment." *Journal of the Institute for Socioeconomic Studies,* 10:2, 82–94.

Kart, Gary S. 1985. *The Social Realities of Aging.* 2nd ed. Boston: Allyn and Bacon.

Katz, Arthur M. 1982. *Life After Nuclear War.* Cambridge, Mass.: Ballinger.

Katz, Jay. 1986. *The Silent World of Doctor and Patient.* New York: Free Press.

Kelly, Raymond C. 1977. *Etoro Social Structure: A Study in Cultural Contradiction.* Ann Arbor: University of Michigan Press.

Kemper, Theodore. 1976. "Toward a sociology of emotions." *American Sociologist,* 13, pp. 30–41.

Kennan, George. 1982. *The Nuclear Delusion.* New York: Pantheon.

Kerbo, Harold R. 1983. *Social Stratification and Inequality: Class Conflict in the United States.* New York: McGraw-Hill.

Kimmel, Michael S. (ed.). 1987. *Changing Men: New Directions and Research in Masculinity.* Newbury Park, Calif.: Sage.

_____, and Michael A. Messner. 1988. *Men's Lives.* New York: Macmillan.

Kitano, Harry L. 1976. *Japanese Americans: The Evolution of a Subculture.* 2nd ed. Englewood Cliffs, N.J.: Prentice-Hall.

_____, and Roger Daniels. *Asian-Americans: The Emerging Minority.* Englewood Cliffs, N.J.: Prentice-Hall.

Kittrie, Nicholas N. 1974. *The Right to Be Different: Deviance and Enforced Therapy.* Baltimore: Penguin.

Kitzinger, Celia. 1988. *The Social Construction of Lesbianism.* Newbury Park, Calif.: Sage.

Kleinman, Arthur. 1979. *Patients and Healers in the Context of Culture.* Berkeley, Calif.: University of California Press.

Klemesrud, Judy. 1981. "Voice of authority: Still male." *New York Times,* February 2, p. 16.

Kluckhohn, Clyde. 1948. "As an anthropologist views it," in Albert Deutch (ed.), *Sex Habits of American Men.* New York: Prentice-Hall.

Knapp, Jacquelyn J., and Robert N. Whitehurst. 1978. "Sexually open marriages and relationships: Issues and prospects," in Bernard I. Murstein (ed.), *Exploring Intimate Life Styles.* New York: Springer.

Kochen, Manfred, and Karl W. Deutch. 1980. *Decentralization.* Cambridge, Mass.: Oelgeschlager, Gunn, and Haine.

Kohlberg, Lawrence. 1966. "A cognitive-developmental analysis of children's sex-role concepts and attitudes," in Eleanor E. Maccoby (ed.), *The Development of Sex Differences.* Palo Alto, Calif.: Stanford University Press.

Kohn, Melvin L. 1963. "Social class and parent-child relationships: An interpretation." *American Journal of Sociology,* 68, pp. 471–480.

_____. 1976. "Occupational structure and alienation." *American Journal of Sociology,* 82, pp. 111–130.

_____. 1977. *Class and Conformity.* 2nd ed. Homewood, Ill.: Dorsey.

Kollock, Peter, Philip Blumstein, and Pepper Schwartz. 1985. "Sex and power in interaction: Conversational privileges and duties." *American Sociological Review,* 50:1, 34–46.

Kramarae, Cheris. 1980. *The Voices and Words of Men and Women.* Oxford: Pergamon Press.

Krause, Elliot A. 1977. *Power and Illness: The Political Sociology of Health and Medical Care.* New York: Elsevier.

Kübler-Ross, Elisabeth. 1969. *On Death and Dying.* New York: Macmillan.

_____. 1975. *Death: The Final Stage of Growth.* Englewood Cliffs, N.J.: Prentice-Hall.

Kuper, Leo. (ed.). 1975. *Race, Science, and Society.* New York: Columbia University Press.

Kwitny, Jonathan. 1984. *Endless Enemies: The Making of an Unfriendly World.* New York: Congdon and Weed.

La Barre, Weston. 1954. *The Human Animal.* Chicago: University of Chicago Press.

Lacy, W. B., J. L. Bokemeier, and J. M. Shepard. 1983. "Job attribute preference and work commitment in the United States." *Personnel Psychology,* 36, pp. 315–319.

Landry, Bart. 1987. *The New Black Middle Class.* Berkeley, Calif.: University of California Press.

Laner, Mary Riege. 1974. "Prostitution as an illegal vocation: A sociological overview," in Clifton D. Bryant (ed.), *Deviant Behavior.* Chicago: Rand McNally.

LaPiere, Richard T. 1934. "Attitudes versus action." *Social Forces,* 13, pp. 230–237.

Larson, Margali Sarfatti. 1977. *The Rise of Professionalism: A Sociological Analysis.* Berkeley: University of California Press.

Lasch, Christopher. 1977. *Haven in a Heartless World: The Family Besieged.* New York: Basic Books.

Laslett, Peter. 1971. *The World We Have Lost.* 2nd ed. New York: Scribner's.

_____. 1977. "Characteristics of the Western family considered over time." *Journal of Family History,* 2:2, 89–115.

_____, and Richard Wall (eds.). 1972. *Household and Family in Past Time.* Cambridge, Eng.: Cambridge University Press.

Lasswell, Harold D. 1936. *Politics: Who Gets What, When, and How.* New York: McGraw-Hill.

Lauer, Robert H. 1982. *Perspectives on Social Change.* 3rd ed. Boston: Allyn and Bacon.

Lehman, Edward W., and Amitai Etzioni (eds.). 1980. *Sociology of Complex Organizations.* 3rd ed. New York: Holt, Rinehart and Winston.

Lemert, Edwin M. 1951. *Social Pathology.* New York: McGraw-Hill.

_____. 1967. *Human Deviance, Social Problems, and Social Control.* Englewood Cliffs, N.J.: Prentice-Hall.

Lengerman, Patricia M., and Ruth A. Wallace. 1985. *Gender in America.* Englewood Cliffs, N.J.: Prentice-Hall.

Lenski, Gerhard. 1966. *Power and Privilege: A Theory of Social Stratification.* New York: McGraw-Hill.

_____, and Jean Lenski. 1987. *Human Societies.* 5th ed. New York: McGraw-Hill.

Leonard, Karen Isaksen. 1978. *Social History of an Indian Caste.* Berkeley, Calif.: University of California Press.

Lerner, Daniel. 1958. *The Passing of Traditional Society.* New York: Free Press.

Levin, Jack, and William C. Levin. 1980. *Prejudice and Discrimination against the Elderly.* Belmont, Calif.: Wadsworth.

_____. 1982. *The Functions of Prejudice.* 2nd ed. New York: Harper & Row.

Levinson, Daniel. 1978. *Seasons of a Man's Life.* New York: Knopf.

Levitan, Sar A., and **Richard S. Belous.** 1981. *What's Happening to the American Family?* Baltimore: Johns Hopkins University Press.

Lewis, Kevin N. 1979. "The prompt and delayed effects of nuclear war." *Scientific American,* 241 (July), pp. 35–47.

Li, Wen Lang. 1982. "Chinese Americans: Exclusion from the melting pot," in Anthony G. Dworkin and Rosalind J. Dworkin (eds.), *The Minority Report* (2nd ed.). New York: Holt, Rinehart and Winston.

Libby, Roger W. 1978. "Creative singlehood as a life style: Beyond marriage as a rite of passage," in Bernard I. Murstein (ed.), *Exploring Intimate Life Styles.* New York: Springer.

Lieberson, Stanley. 1980. *A Piece of the Pie.* Berkeley: University of California Press.

Lifton, Robert J. 1967. *Death in Life: Survivors of Hiroshima.* New York: Random House.

_____, and **Kai Erikson.** 1982. "Survivors of nuclear war: Psychological and communal breakdown," in Eric Chivian et al. (eds), *Last Aid: The Medical Dimensions of Nuclear War.* San Francisco: Freeman.

Light, Ivan. 1983. *Cities in World Perspective.* New York: Macmillan.

Lightfoot, Sarah Lawrence. 1983. *The Good High School.* New York: Basic Books.

Lin, Nam, Walter M. Ensler, and **John C. Vaughn.** 1981. "Social resources and strength of ties: Structural factors in occupational status attainment." *American Sociological Review,* 46, pp. 393–405.

Lincoln, Eric C. 1974. *The Black Church since Frazier.* New York: Schocken.

Linton, Ralph. 1936. *The Study of Man.* New York: Appleton-Century-Crofts.

_____. 1945. *The Cultural Background of Personality.* New York: Free Press.

Lipkowitz, Martin H., and **Sudharam Idupaganti.** 1983. "Diagnosing schizophrenia in 1980: A survey of U.S. psychiatrists." *American Journal of Psychiatry,* 140, pp. 52–55.

Lipset, Seymour Martin (ed.). 1979. *The Third Century: America as a Postindustrial Society.* Chicago: University of Chicago Press.

_____, et al. 1956. *Union Democracy: The Inside Politics of the International Typographical Union.* Glencoe, Ill.: Free Press.

_____, and **Reinhard Bendix.** 1959. *Social Mobility in Industrial Society.* Berkeley, Calif.: University of California Press.

Litwack, Leon F. 1979. *Been in the Storm So Long: The Aftermath of Slavery.* New York: Knopf.

Lockwood, Daniel. 1979. *Prison Sexual Violence.* New York: Elsevier.

Lockwood, David. 1956. "Some notes on 'The Social System'." *British Journal of Sociology,* 7, p. 2.

Logan, John R., and **Harvey L. Motlotch.** 1987. *The Political Economy of Place.* Berkeley, Calif.: University of California Press.

Lorenz, Konrad. 1966. On Aggression. New York: Harcourt Brace Jovanovich.

Lowie, Robert H. 1940. *Introduction to Cultural Anthropology.* New York: Holt, Rinehart and Winston.

Lown, Bernard. 1982. "Physicians and nuclear war," in Eric Chivian et al. (eds.), *Last Aid: The Medical Dimensions of Nuclear War.* San Francisco: Freeman.

Lyons, Albert S., and **R. Joseph Petrucelli.** 1978. *Medicine: An Illustrated History.* St. Louis: Mosby/Times Mirror.

Maccoby, Eleanor. 1980. *Social Development.* New York: Harcourt Brace Jovanovich.

MacCracken, Michael C., and **Frederick M. Luther** (eds.). 1985. *The Potential Climatic Effects of Increasing Carbon Dioxide.* Washington, D.C.: U.S. Department of Energy.

Malamuth, Neil M. 1981. "Rape proclivity among men." *Journal of Social Issues,* 37, p. 4.

_____. and **Edward Donnerstein.** 1984. *Pornography and Sexual Aggression.* Orlando: Academic Press.

Malcolm, Andrew H. 1985. "New generation of poor youths emerges in U.S." *New York Times,* October 20, pp. 1, 56.

Maranto, Gina. 1985. "The creeping poison underground." *Discover,* February, pp. 74–78.

Marmor, Judd. 1980. *Homosexual Behavior: A Modern Reappraisal.* New York: Basic Books.

McClelland, David C. 1961. *The Achieving Society.* New York: Van Nostrand.

McGee, Reece. 1975. *Points of Departure.* Hinsdale, Ill.: Dryden Press.

McGrath, Joseph E. (ed.). 1988. *The Social Psychology of Time.* Newbury Park, Calif.: Sage.

McKeown, Thomas. 1978. "Determinants of health." *Human Nature,* 1, pp. 64–71.

_____. 1988. *The Origins of Human Disease.* Oxford: Basil Blackwell.

McKinlay, John B., and **Sonia M. McKinlay.** 1977. "The questionable contribution of medical measures to the decline of mortality in the United States in the twentieth century." *Health and Society,* 53:3.

McPherson, J. Miller, and **Lynn Smith-Lovin.** 1982. "Women and weak ties: Differences by sex in the size of voluntary organizations." *American Journal of Sociology,* 87, pp. 883–904.

Mead, George Herbert. 1934. *Mind, Self, and Society: From the Standpoint of a Social Behaviorist.* Charles W. Morris (ed.). Chicago: University of Chicago Press.

Mead, Margaret. 1935. *Sex and Temperament in Three Primitive Societies.* New York: Dell.

Melbin, Murray. 1987. *Night as Frontier: Colonizing the World after Dark.* Chicago: Free Press.

Merton, Robert K. 1938. "Social structure and anomie." *American Sociological Review,* 3, pp. 672–682.

_____. 1968. *Social Theory and Social Structure.* 2nd ed. New York: Free Press.

Meyer, Stephen M. 1984. *The Dynamics of Nuclear Proliferation.* Chicago: University of Chicago Press.

Middleton, Russell. 1962. "Brother-sister and father-daughter marriage in ancient Egypt." *American Sociological Review,* 27, pp. 103–111.

Milgram, Stanley. 1967. "The small world problem." *Psychology Today,* 1, pp. 61–67.

Mills, C. Wright. 1956. *The Power Elite.* New York: Oxford University Press.

_____. 1959. *The Sociological Imagination.* New York: Oxford University Press.

Mintz, Beth A., and **Michael Schwartz.** 1981. "Interlocking directorates and interest group formation." *American Sociological Review,* 46, pp. 857–869.

_____. 1985. *The Power Structure of American Business.* Chicago: University of Chicago Press.

Mintz, Steven, and **Susan Kellog.** 1988. *Domestic Revolutions: A Social History of American Family Life.* New York: Free Press.

Mischler, Eliot G., et al. 1981. *Social Contexts of Health, Illness, and Patient Care.* Cambridge, Eng.: Cambridge University Press.

Modelski, George (ed.). 1979. *Transnational Corporations and the World Order.* San Francisco: Freeman.

Money, John, and **Anke A. Ehrhardt.** 1973. *Man and Woman, Boy and Girl.* Baltimore: Johns Hopkins University Press.

Schuman, Howard. 1988. *Racial Attitudes in America: Trends and Interpretations.* Cambridge, Mass.: Harvard University Press.

Schur, Edwin M. 1965. *Crimes Without Victims—Deviant Behavior and Public Policy.* Englewood Cliffs, N.J.: Prentice-Hall.

_____. 1980. *The Politics of Deviance.* Englewood Cliffs, N.J.: Prentice-Hall.

Scully, Diana, and Joseph Marolla. 1983. "Incarcerated rapists: Exploring a sociological model." *Final Report for the Department of Health and Human Services.* Washington, D.C.: National Institutes of Mental Health.

Seligman, Jean, et al. 1984. "The date who rapes." *Newsweek,* April 9, p. 91.

_____. 1980. *The Penalty of Death.* Beverly Hills, Calif.: Sage.

Service, Elman R. 1971. *Primitive Social Organization: An Evolutionary Perspective.* New York: Random House.

Sewell, William H. 1971. "Inequality of opportunity for higher education." *American Sociological Review,* 36, pp. 793–808.

Shaffer, Kay T. 1981. *Sex Roles and Human Behavior.* Cambridge, Mass.: Winthrop.

Shapiro, Arthur K. 1982. "The placebo effect," in W. G. Clark and J. del Guidice, *Principles of Pharmacology.* 2nd ed. New York: Academic Press.

Shattuck, Roger. 1980. *The Forbidden Experiment.* New York: Farrar, Straus and Giroux.

Sherif, Muzafer. 1956. "Experiments in group conflict." *Scientific American,* 195, pp. 54–58.

Sherman, Arnold K., and Aliza Kolker. 1987. *The Social Bases of Politics.* Belmont, Calif.: Wadsworth.

Sherman, Julia. 1978. *Sex-Related Cognitive Differences.* Springfield, Ill.: Charles C Thomas.

Shields, Pete. 1981. *Guns Don't Die—People Do.* New York: Arbor House.

Shilts, Randy. 1988. *And the Band Played On: Politics, People, and the Aids Epidemic.* New York: St. Martin's Press.

Shipler, David K. 1982. *Russia: Broken Idols, Solemn Dreams.* New York: Times Books.

_____. 1985. "The view from America." *New York Times Magazine,* November 10, pp. 33–48, 72–89.

Shorter, Edward. 1975. *The Making of the Modern Family.* New York: Basic Books.

Shott, Susan. 1979. "Emotion and social life: A symbolic interactionist analysis." *American Journal of Sociology,* 84:6, 1317–1334.

Shrag, Peter. 1978. *Mind Control.* New York: Random House.

Sidel, Ruth. 1986. *Women and Children Last: The Plight of Poor Women in Affluent America.* New York: Viking.

Silberman, Charles E. 1971. *Crisis in the Classroom: The Remaking of American Education.* New York: Random House.

Simenauer, Jacqueline, and David Carroll. 1986. *Singles: The New Americans.* New York: Simon and Schuster.

Simon, David R., and Stanley D. Eitzen. 1982. *Elite Deviance.* Boston: Allyn and Bacon.

Simon, Julian L. 1981. *The Ultimate Resource.* Princeton: Princeton University Press.

Simpson, George E., and J. Milton Yinger. 1985. *Racial and Cultural Minorities: An Analysis of Prejudice and Discrimination.* 5th ed. New York: Plenum.

Sitkoff, Harvard. 1982. *The Struggle for Black Equality, 1954–1980.* New York: Hill and Wang.

Sivard, Ruth Leger. 1986. *World Military and Social Expenditures, 1986.* Washington, D.C.: World Priorities.

_____. 1987. *World Military and Social Expenditures, 1987.* Washington, D.C.: World Priorities.

Sklare, Marshall. 1971. *America's Jews.* New York: Random House.

_____ (ed.). 1974. *The Jew in American Society.* New York: Behrman House.

Skocpol, Theda. 1979. *States and Social Revolutions.* New York: Cambridge University Press.

Slater, Philip E. 1955. "Role differentiation in small groups," in A. Paul Hare et al. (eds.), *Small Groups: Studies in Social Interaction.* New York: Knopf.

_____. 1970. *The Pursuit of Loneliness: American Culture at the Breaking Point.* Boston: Beacon.

Smelser, Neil J. 1962. *Theory of Collective Behavior.* New York: Free Press.

Solomon, Lewis C., et al. 1977. *College as a Training Ground for Jobs.* New York: Praeger.

Sommer, Robert. 1979. *Personal Space.* Englewood Cliffs, N.J.: Prentice-Hall.

Sowell, Thomas. 1981. *Ethnic America: A History.* New York: Basic Books.

_____. 1983. *The Economics and Politics of Race.* New York: Morrow.

Spicer, Edward H. 1980. "American Indians," in Stephan Thernstrom, *Harvard Encyclopedia of American Ethnic Groups.* Cambridge, Mass.: Harvard University Press.

Spitz, René A. 1945. "Hospitalism: An inquiry into the genesis of psychiatric conditions in early childhood," in Anna Freud et al. (eds.), *The Psychoanalytic Study of the Child.* New York: International Universities Press.

Squires, Gregory D. 1979. *Education, Jobs, and the U.S. Class Structure.* New Brunswick, N.J.: Transaction Books.

Srole, Leo, et al. 1977. *Mental Health in the Metropolis.* Rev. ed. New York: Harper & Row.

Staples, Robert. 1986. *The Urban Plantation: Racism and Colonialism in the Post Civil Rights Era.* San Francisco: Black Scholar Press.

Stark, Rodney, and William Sims Bainbridge. 1985. *The Future of Religion: Secularization, Revival, and Cult Formation.* Berkeley, Calif.: University of California Press.

Starr, Paul. 1982. *The Social Transformation of American Medicine.* New York: Basic Books.

Stein, Peter J. (ed.). 1981. *Single Life: Unmarried Adults in Social Context.* New York: St. Martin's Press.

Steinberg, Stephen. 1981. *The Ethnic Myth: Race, Ethnicity, and Class in America.* New York: Atheneum.

Stinnet, Nick, and Craig Wayne Birdsong. 1978. *The Family and Alternate Life Styles.* Chicago: Nelson Hall.

Stockton, William. 1978. "Going home: The Puerto Ricans' new migration." *New York Times,* May 12, pp. 20–22, 88–93.

Stone, Lawrence. 1977. *The Family, Sex, and Marriage in England, 1500–1800.* New York: Harper & Row.

Straus, Murray A., and Gerald T. Hotaling. 1980. *The Social Causes of Husband-Wife Violence.* Minneapolis: University of Minneapolis Press.

Strong, P. M. 1979. "Sociological imperialism and the profession of medicine: A critical examination of the thesis of medical imperialism." *Social Science and Medicine,* 13A: 2, pp. 199–215.

Stubbing, Richard A., and Richard Mendel. 1986. *The Defense Game.* New York: Harper & Row.

Sutherland, Edwin H. 1939. *Principles of Criminology.* Philadelphia: Lippincott.

Suttles, Gerald. 1970. *The Social Order of the Slum.* Chicago: University of Chicago Press.

Sweet, Ellen. 1985. "Date rape." *Ms.,* October, pp. 56–59.

Symanski, Richard. 1981. *The Immoral Landscape: Female Prostitution in the Western World.* Toronto: Butterworth.

Szasz, Thomas. 1961. *The Myth of Mental Illness.* New York: Harper & Row.

——————. 1970. *The Manufacture of Madness.* New York: Dell.

——————. 1970. *Ideology and Insanity.* New York: Anchor.

——————. 1974. *The Myth of Mental Illness.* Rev. ed. New York: Harper & Row.

——————. 1986. *Insanity: The Idea and Its Consequences.* New York: Wiley.

Takooshian, Harold, and **Herzel Bodinger.** 1979. "Street crime in 18 American cities: A national field experiment." Paper presented at the annual meeting of the American Sociological Association, Boston, August.

Tanner, Donna M. 1978. *The Lesbian Couple.* Lexington, Mass.: D. C. Heath.

Tavris, Carol, and **Carole Wade.** 1984. *The Longest War: Sex Differences in Perspective.* 2nd ed. New York: Harcourt Brace Jovanovich.

Teitelbaum, Michael (ed.). 1976. *Sex Differences.* New York: Doubleday.

Thomas, Evan. 1986. "Peddling influence." *Time,* March 3, pp. 26–36.

Thomas, Lewis. 1983. *The Youngest Science: Notes of a Medicine Watcher.* New York: Viking.

Tien, H. Yuan. 1983. "China: Demographic billionaire." *Population Bulletin,* 38:2, pp. 1–42.

Tilly, Charles. 1978. *From Mobilization to Revolution.* Reading, Mass.: Addison-Wesley.

Tittle, Charles R., et al. 1978. "The myth of social class and criminality: An empirical assessment of the empirical evidence." *American Sociological Review,* 43, pp. 643–656.

Tobias, Sheila, and **Carol Weissbrod.** 1980. "Anxiety and Mathematics: An Update." *Harvard Educational Review,* 50, pp. 63–70.

Toffler, Alvin. 1970. *Future Shock.* New York: Random House.

——————. 1980. *The New Wave.* New York: Morrow.

Tolchin, Martin. 1988. "Minority poverty on the rise but white poor decline," *New York Times,* September 1, p. B9.

Torrey, E. F. 1974. *The Death of Psychiatry.* New York: Penguin.

——————. 1988. *Nowhere to Go: The Tragic Odyssey of the Homeless Mentally Ill.* New York: Harper and Row.

Touraine, Alan. 1971. *The Post-Industrial Society.* New York: Random House.

Treiman, Donald J. 1977. *Occupational Prestige in Comparative Perspective.* New York: Academic Press.

Troeltsch, Ernst. 1931. *The Social Teachings of the Christian Churches.* New York: Macmillan.

Troll, Lillian E., and **Vern Bengston.** 1982. "Intergenerational development through the life span," in B. B. Wolman (ed.), *Handbook of Developmental Psychology.* Englewood Cliffs, N.J.: Prentice-Hall.

Tsipis, Kosta. 1982. "The physical effects of a nuclear explosion," in Eric Chivian, et al. (eds.). *Last Aid: The Medical Dimensions of Nuclear War.* San Francisco: W. H. Freeman.

Tuchman, Gaye, Arlene Kaplan Daniels, and **James Benet** (eds.). 1978. *Hearth and Home: Images of Women in the Mass Media.* New York: Oxford University Press.

Tucker, Anthony, and **John Gleisner.** 1982. *Crucible of Despair: The Effects of Nuclear War.* London: Menard Press.

Turk, Austin T. 1982. *Political Crime: The Defiance and Defense of Authority.* Beverley Hills, Calif.: Sage.

Twaddle, Andrew. 1973. "Illness and deviance." *Social Science and Medicine,* 7, pp. 751–762.

——————. 1979. *Sickness Behavior and the Sick Role.* Cambridge, Mass.: Schenkman.

——————, and **Richard Hessler.** 1986. *A Sociology of Health.* 2nd ed. New York: Macmillan.

Unger, Rhoda K. 1979. *Female and Male: Sex and Gender.* New York: Harper & Row.

Useem, Michael. 1978. "The inner group of the American capitalist class." *Social Problems,* 25, pp. 225–240.

——————. 1979. "The social organization of the American business elite and participation of corporation directors in the governance of American institutions." *American Sociological Review,* 44, pp. 553–572.

——————. 1980. "Corporations and the corporate elite." *Annual Review of Sociology,* 6. Palo Alto, Calif.: Annual Reviews.

——————. 1986. *The Inner Circle.* New York: Oxford University Press.

Van Baal, J. 1966. *Dema: Description and Analysis of Manindanim Culture (South New Guinea).* The Hague: M. Nijhoff.

Van den Berghe, Pierre. 1978. *Race and Racism: A Comparative Perspective.* 2nd ed. New York: Wiley.

Van Dijk, Teun. 1987. *Communicating Racism: Ethnic Prejudice in Thought and Talk.* Newbury Park, Calif.: Sage.

Vander Zanden, James W. 1983. *American Minority Relations.* 4th ed. New York: Knopf.

Vanfossen, Beth E. 1979. *The Structure of Social Inequality.* Boston: Little, Brown.

Vernon, Raymond. 1977. *Storm over the Multinationals.* Cambridge, Mass.: Harvard University Press.

Vidal, Frederico S. 1976. "Mutayr: A tribe of Saudi Arabian pastoral nomads," in David E. Hunter and Phillip Whitten (eds.), *The Study of Anthropology.* New York: Harper & Row.

Vogel, Ezra F. 1980. *Japan as Number One: Lessons for America.* New York: Harper Colophon.

Volti, Rudi. 1988. *Society and Technological Change.* New York: St. Martin's.

Voslensky, Michael. 1984. *Nomenklatura: The Soviet Ruling Class.* New York: Doubleday.

Wagenheim, Kall. 1975. *Puerto Rico: A Profile.* 2nd ed. New York: Praeger.

Wagley, Charles, and **Marvin Harris.** 1964. *Minorities in the New World.* New York: Columbia University Press.

Waitzkin, Howard. 1986. *The Second Sickness: Contradictions of Capitalist Health Care.* Chicago: University of Chicago Press.

Wallace, Michael D. 1979. "The role of arms races in the escalation of disputes into war: Some new evidence." *Journal of Conflict Resolution,* 32:1, pp. 3–16.

Wallerstein, Immanuel. 1979. *The Capitalist World-Economy.* New York: Cambridge University Press.

Warren, Carol A. B. 1974. *Identity and Community in the Gay World.* New York: Wiley.

Weber, Max. 1946. *From Max Weber: Essays in Sociology.* H. H. Gerth and C. Wright Mills (trans./eds.). New York: Oxford University Press.

——————. 1963. *The Sociology of Religion.* Boston: Beacon Press.

Weinberg, Alvin M. 1966. "Can technology replace social engineering?" *University of Chicago Magazine,* 59 (October), pp. 6–10.

Weiss, Carol H., and **Allen H. Barton.** 1979. *Making Bureaucracies Work.* Beverly Hills, Calif.: Sage.

Weiss, Robert S. 1975. *Marital Separation.* New York: Basic Books.

Weitz, Shirley. 1977. *Sex Roles: Biological, Psychological, and Social Foundations.* New York: Oxford University Press.

Weitzman, Lenore. 1979. *Sex Role Socialization.* Palo Alto, Calif.: Mayfield.

_____. 1985. *Divorce Revolution: The Unexpected Social and Economic Consequences for Women and Children in America.* New York: Free Press.

Westley, Francis. 1978. "'The cult of man': Durkheim's predictions and the new religious movements." *Sociological Analysis,* 39:2, pp. 135–145.

White, Ralph K., and **Ronald O. Lippitt.** 1960. *Autocracy and Democracy.* New York: Harper & Row.

Wicker, Tom. 1982. "War by accident." *New York Times,* November 21, p. 32.

Wilkinson, Rupert. 1984. *American Tough.* New York: Harper & Row.

Williams, Lena. 1985. "To blacks, the surburbs prove both pleasant and troubling." *New York Times,* May 20, pp. A1, B4.

Williams, Robin M., Jr. 1970. *American Society: A Sociological Interpretation.* 3rd ed. New York: Knopf.

Wilson, Robert A., and **Bill Hosokawa.** 1980. *East to America: A History of the Japanese in the United States.* New York: Morrow.

Wilson, William J. 1980. *The Declining Significance of Race: Blacks and Changing American Institutions.* 2nd ed. Chicago: University of Chicago Press.

_____. 1987. *The Truly Disadvantaged: The Inner City, the Underclass, and Public Policy.* Chicago: University of Chicago Press.

Wirth, Louis. 1938. "Urbanism as a way of life." *American Journal of Sociology,* 44, pp. 8–20.

_____. 1945. "The problem of minority groups," in Ralph Linton (ed.), *The Science of Man in the World Crisis.* New York: Columbia University Press.

Wohl, Stanley. 1984. *The Medical Industrial Complex.* New York: Harmony Books.

Wolf, Deborah Goleman. 1979. *The Lesbian Community.* Berkeley, Calif.: University of California Press.

Wolinsky, Frederic C. 1988. *The Sociology of Health: Principles, Practitioners, and Issues.* 2nd ed. Belmont, Calif.: Wadsworth.

Wong, Bernard P. 1982. *Chinatown: Economic Adaptation and Ethnic Identity of the Chinese.* New York: Holt, Rinehart, and Winston.

Woodrum, Eric. 1981. "An assessment of Japanese-American assimilation, pluralism, and subordination." *American Journal of Sociology,* 87, pp. 157–169.

Wright, Charles. 1986. *Mass Communication: A Sociological Perspective.* 3rd ed. New York: Random House.

Wright, James D. 1988. "The worthy and the unworthy homeless." *Society,* July/August, 64–69.

Wrong, Dennis H. 1961. "The oversocialized conception of man in modern society." *American Sociological Review,* 26, pp. 183–193.

Wuthnow, Robert. 1978. *Experimentation in American Religion: The New Mysticisms and Their Implications for the Churches.* Berkeley: University of California Press.

Wynne, Edward A. 1986. "Will the young support the old?" in Alan Pifer and Lydia Bronte (eds.). *Our Aging Society: Paradox and Promise.* New York: Norton.

Yorburg, Betty. 1983. *Families and Societies: Survival or Extinction?* New York: Columbia University Press.

Yulsman, Tom. 1984. "Greenhouse earth." *Science Digest,* February, pp. 41–45, 98–101.

Zald, Mayer N., and **John D. McCarthy** (eds.). 1979. *The Dynamics of Social Movements.* Cambridge, Mass.: Winthrop.

_____, and **Michael A. Berger.** 1978. "Social movements in organizations: Coups d'etat, insurgency, and mass movements." *American Journal of Sociology,* 83, pp. 823–861.

Zborowski, Mark. 1952. "Cultural components in responses to pain." *Journal of Social Issues,* 8:14, 16–30.

_____. 1969. *People in Pain.* San Francisco: Jossey-Bass.

Zelnick, Melvin, and **John F. Kanter.** 1980. "Sexual activity, contraceptive use and pregnancy among metropolitan area teenagers: 1971–1979." *Family Planning Perspectives,* 12, pp. 230–231, 233–237.

Zola, Irving K. 1972. "Medicine as an institution of social control." *Sociological Review,* 20, pp. 480–504.

_____. 1975. "In the name of health and illness: On the socio-political consequences of medical influence." *Social Science and Medicine,* 9, pp. 83–87.

Acknowledgements

CHAPTER 1

1.0 © Kim Newton/Woodfin Camp & Associates
1.1 left, © Luis Villota/The Stock Market; right, © Michael Freeman/Bruce Coleman, Inc.
1.2–1.5 The Bettmann Archive
1.6 The Granger Collection
1.7 The Bettmann Archive
1.8 The Granger Collection
1.9 American Sociological Association
1.10 Courtesy Columbia University, Office of Public Information
1.11 Fritz Goro, LIFE magazine © 1954 Time, Inc.
1.12 © John Launois/Black Star
1.13 © Dennis Brack 1979/Black Star
1.14 © Bob O'Shaughnessy/The Stock Market
1.15 and 1.17 left, The Bettmann Archive
1.17 right, AP/Wide World Photos

CHAPTER 2

2.0 © Spence McConnell 1983/Bruce Coleman, Inc.
2.1 © Bob Abraham/The Stock Market
2.2 © Bob Riha/Gamma-Liaison
2.3 Courtesy of the Norman Rockwell Museum at the Old Corner House, Stockbridge, Mass.
2.4 top, The Bettmann Archive; bottom, © Photri
2.5 left, © Nicholas de Vore III/Bruce Coleman, Inc.; right, © Michael Freeman/Bruce Coleman, Inc.
2.6 © Charles Henneghien/Bruce Coleman, Inc.
2.7 © George Haling Productions/Photo Researchers
2.9 left, © Emil Muench/Photo Researchers; right, © Claus Meyer/Black Star
2.10 © Cathy Bauknight/Gamma-Liaison
2.11 Oil on canvas, 1960. 80 × 70 inches. Collection of Whitney Museum of American Art. Purchase, with funds from the Friends of the Whitney Museum of American Art. 60.63

CHAPTER 3

3.0 © Chuck Fishman 1983/Woodfin Camp & Associates
3.1 © P. Frillet/Sipa Press
3.4 © Norman Myers/Bruce Coleman, Inc.
3.5 © Louis Villota 1986/The Stock Market
3.6 © Brian J. Coates/Bruce Coleman, Inc.
3.7 © Robert & Linda Mitchell
3.8 © John Launois/Black Star
3.9 © Craig Hammell/The Stock Market

CHAPTER 4

4.0 © Nancy J. Pierce/Photo Researchers
4.1 © Bernard Wolf/Omni-Photo Communications
4.2 © Harry F. Harlow, University of Wisconsin Primate Laboratory
4.3 © Ellen Pines Sheffield/Woodfin Camp & Associates
4.4 © Jan Lukas/Photo Researchers
4.5 © Hazel Hankin 1988
4.6 © Victor Engelbert/Photo Researchers
4.7 © Frances M. Cox 1988/Omni-Photo Communications
4.8 © Leif Skoogfors/Woodfin Camp & Associates
4.10 The Granger Collection
4.11 Fritz Goro, LIFE magazine © 1955 Time, Inc.
4.12 © Francois Bota/Gamma-Liaison

CHAPTER 5

5.0 © Randy O'Rourke 1983/The Stock Market
5.1 © David Robert Austen/Stock Boston
5.2 © Jasmin/Gamma-Liaison
5.4 © Charles Gatewood/The Image Works
5.5 © Thomas Hopker 1985/Woodfin Camp & Associates
5.7 The Metropolitan Museum of Art, George A. Hearn Fund, 1956
5.8 AP/Wide World Photos
5.9 © Alon Reininger/Woodfin Camp & Associates

CHAPTER 6

6.0   © Alan Carey/The Image Works
6.1   left, The Granger Collection; right, NYT Pictures
6.2   © Bob Combs/Photo Researchers
6.4   © Joel Gordon 1980
6.5   © Peter Garfield/Washington, D.C.
6.6   © Bersuder/Sipa Press
6.8   AP/Wide World Photos
6.9   The Bettmann Archive
6.10   left, Culver Pictures; right, UPI/Bettmann Newsphotos

CHAPTER 7

7.0   © Peter Miller/Photo Researchers
7.1   left, © Nik Wheeler/Black Star; right, © Bruce Coleman, Inc.
7.2   © Robert Frerck 1982/Woodfin Camp & Associates
7.3   Carmine Church, Florence, photograph Scala/Art Resource
7.5   left, © Bill Pierce/Rainbow; right, © Joel Gordon 1980
7.6   © Frank Fournier/Contact Press Images/Woodfin Camp & Associates
7.7   © Andrew Lawson
7.8   © Jan Lukas 1979/Photo Researchers
7.9   © Joel Gordon 1988
7.10   © Jim Anderson 1981/Woodfin Camp & Associates

CHAPTER 8

8.0   © Ethan Hoffmann/Archive Pictures
8.1   © Paolo Koch/Photo Researchers
8.2   © Luis Villota/The Stock Market
8.3   © George Holton/Photo Researchers
8.4   The Bettman Archive
8.6   Biblioteca Marciana, Venice, photograph Scala/Art Resource
8.8   © Joey Tranchina 1977/Photo Researchers
8.9   top, The Bettmann Archive; bottom, © Diana Walker/Gamma-Liaison
8.11   © Mike Mazzaschi/Stock Boston

CHAPTER 9

9.0   © Alan Carey 1986/The Image Works
9.1   © Bill Anderson/Monkmeyer Press Photo Service
9.2   © Richard Tomkins 1982/Gamma-Liaison
9.3   UPI/Bettmann Newsphotos
9.4   Woolarac Museum, Bartlesville, Oklahoma
9.5   © Stephen Ferry/Gamma-Liaison
9.6 and 9.7 left, The Bettmann Archive
9.7   right, © Daemmrich/Stock Boston
9.8   The Bettmann Archive
9.9   left, AP/Wide World Photos; right, UPI/Bettmann Newsphotos
9.10   © Lester Sloan 1981/Woodfin Camp & Associates

9.11   © Paul Conklin
9.12   Hansel Mieth LIFE magazine © Time, Inc.
9.13   Culver Pictures

CHAPTER 10

10.0   © Jim Olive 1982/Peter Arnold, Inc.
10.1   left, © William Meyer/Click/Chicago Ltd.; right, © Victor Englebert/Photo Researchers
10.3   Oil on masonite, 19½″ × 97½″ (sight), 1934. The Fine Arts Museums of San Francisco, Gift of Mr. and Mrs. John D. Rockefeller 3rd
10.5   top, The Granger Collection; bottom, both The Bettmann Archive
10.6   *Popular Mechanics,* 1950, courtesy of Library of Congress
10.7   both, © June Lundborg Whitworth 1986
10.8   left, © Burk Uzzle 1984/Archive Pictures
10.8   right, and 10.10 © Beryl Goldberg
10.11 The Bettmann Archive
10.13 © Arthur Tress/Photo Researchers

CHAPTER 11

11.0   © Sepp Seitz/Woodfin Camp & Associates
11.1   left, © Bry/Monkmeyer Press Photo Service; right, © Brent Bear/Click/Chicago Ltd.
11.2   © Beryl Goldberg
11.3   left, The Metropolitan Museum of Art, Gift of Frederic H. Hatch, 1926; right, originally published by *New England Monthly*
11.4   The Metropolitan Museum of Art, Bequest of Catherine Lorillard Wolfe, 1887. Catherine Lorillard Wolfe Collection
11.6   top, left © Kevin Bubriski/Archive Pictures; top, right © Roland & Sabrina Michaud/Woodfin Camp & Associates; bottom, © Ira Kirschenbaum/Stock Boston
11.7   The Granger Collection
11.8   Reuters/Bettmann Newsphotos
11.9   The Bettmann Archive
11.11 © Paul Conklin
11.12 UPI/Bettmann Newsphotos
11.14 © Joel Gordon 1987

CHAPTER 12

12.0   © F. Carter Smith/Gamma-Liaison
12.1   © Diane M. Lowe/Stock Boston
12.2   left, © Nat & Yanna Brandt 1985/Photo Researchers; right, © Susan Johns/Photo Researchers
12.4   © Paul Conklin
12.5   © Frank Siteman/Stock Boston
12.7   *Medicine Man Curing a Patient,* color lithograph by Christian Schuessele (after

Seth Eastman), 1851. Philadelphia Museum of Art, Smith Kline Beckman Corporation Fund

12.8–12.10 The Bettmann Archive

12.11 © Eric Kroll/Taurus Photos

12.12 left, © Burk Uzzle/Archive Pictures; right, © George S. Zimbel/Monkmeyer Press Photo Service

12.13 © Frank Morgan/Rainbow

12.14 The Bettmann Archive

CHAPTER *13*

13.0 Shelly Katz/Black Star

13.1 from left to right, © Tim McCabe 1983/Taurus Photos; © Mark Antman/The Image Works; © George Goodwin/Monkmeyer Press Photo Service

13.2 left, © M.P. Kahl/Bruce Coleman, Inc.; right, © Raimondo Borea

13.3 © Rick Kopstein 1988/Mokmeyer Press Photo Service

13.4 © Lebeck, *Stern*/Black Star

13.5 Cast vinyl polychromed in oil, lifesize, 1976. Courtesy O.K. Harris Gallery, New York

13.6 from left to right, The Granger Collection; © Jasmin/Gamma-Liaison; © Gamma Liaison 1984

13.7 © Topham/The Image Works

13.8 left, The Bettmann Archive; right, © Ilkka Ranta/Woodfin Camp & Associates

13.9 AP/Wide World Photos

13.10 left, reprinted by permission of National Rifle Association of America; right, reprinted by permission of Handgun Control, Inc.

CHAPTER *14*

14.0 © Eddie Adams 1981/Gamma-Liaison

14.1 Brown Brothers

14.4 © Arnaud Borrel/Gamma-Liaison

14.6 © Alon Reininger/Contact Press Images/Woodfin Camp & Associates

14.7 © Charles Gupton 1985/Stock Boston

14.8 © Ken Heyman/Archive Pictures

14.9 top, Staatliche Gemäldegalerie, Kassel, photograph Giraudon/Art Resource; bottom, Egg tempera on composition board. 18⅛ × 36⅛ inches. Collection of Whitney Museum of American Art. Purchase, with funds from the Juliana Force Purchase Award. 50.23.

14.10 © Jim Balog 1983/Black Star

14.11 © Ethan Hoffmann/Archive Pictures

14.12 left, The Bettmann Archive; right, © Christopher Morris 1983/Black Star

14.13 © photo courtesy Smithsonian Institution Traveling Exhibition Service. From SITES exhibition *Yesterday's Tomorrows: Past Visions of the American Future*, photographer Joe A. Goulait

14.14 both, © Jacques Jangoux/Peter Arnold, Inc.

CHAPTER *15*

15.0 © Charles Henneghien/Bruce Coleman, Inc.

15.1 The Granger Collection

15.2 left, The Bettmann Archive; right, NASA

15.3 © P. Pearson/Click/Chicago, Ltd.

15.4 from left to right, © Patsy Davidson 1986/The Image Works; © Bob Daemmrich/The Image Works; © Mark Antman/The Image Works

15.5 The Granger Collection

15.6 © Marc & Evelyne Bernheim 1984/Woodfin Camp & Associates

15.7 © Daniel Brody/Stock Boston

15.8 Ducco on wood, 48″ × 36″. Collection, The Museum of Modern Art, New York. Gift of Edward M.M. Warburg.

15.9 © Lester Sloan/Woodfin Camp & Associates

15.10 left, The Bettmann Archive; right, © P. Chauvel/Sygma

15.11 left, The Bettmann Archive; right, © Photri

15.15 © Archive Pictures

15.16 Larry Burrows, LIFE magazine © 1971 Time, Inc.

15 End © John Giannicchi/Science Source/Photo Researchers

TEXT PERMISSIONS

Page 73 From *Genie* by Susan Curtiss, Academic Press, 1977. Reprinted by permission of Academic Press.

Page 87 From "Our Forebears Made Childhood a Nightmare" by Lloyd DeMause. Copyright © 1975 American Psychological Association. Reprinted with permission of *Psychology Today* magazine.

Page 300 "The State of the Art," by Dr. Alvan R. Feinstein, *Journal of the American Medical Association*, 255, March 21, 1986, p. 1488. Reprinted with permission.

Index